LOIRE VALLEY

DUMONT GUIDE
LOIRE VALLEY

by
WILFRIED HANSMANN
translated by
RUSSELL STOCKMAN

STEWART, TABORI & CHANG
PUBLISHERS, NEW YORK

FRONT COVER:
Le Plessis-Bourré (Bob and Ira Spring)
BACK COVER:
Amboise (Allan A. Philiba)
FRONTISPIECE:
Donjon at Beaugency

Library of Congress Cataloging-in-Publication Data
Hansmann, Wilfried.
The Loire Valley. (DuMont guide)
Translation of: Das Tal der Loire.
Bibliography: p. 249
Includes indexes.
1. Loire River Valley (France)—Description and
travel—Guide-books. I. Title.
DC611.L81H3613 1986 914.4'504838 85-2857
ISBN 0-941434-62-1

Published in 1986 by Stewart, Tabori & Chang, Inc.
740 Broadway, New York, N.Y. 10003
under exclusive world-wide English language license
from DuMont Buchverlag GmbH & Co.
All rights for all countries are held by DuMont
Buchverlag GmbH & Co., Limited, Cologne, West Germany.
The title of the original German edition is
*Das Tal der Loire: Schlösser, Kirchen und Städte im
'Garten Frankreichs.'*

The Practical Travel Suggestions were prepared by John Sturman.

Distributed in the United States by
Workman Publishing Co., Inc., 1 West 39th Street,
New York, N.Y. 10018

Printed in Spain.

C O N T E N T S

INTRODUCTION

THROUGH THE ORLEANAIS

THROUGH BLESOIS

THROUGH TOURAINE

THROUGH ANJOU

PRACTICAL TRAVEL SUGGESTIONS

INTRODUCTION

THE RIVER

Stream of light, and sweet, joyous life!
— A U G U S T E   R O D I N

MEASURING 634 MILES, THE LOIRE IS THE LONGEST river in France. It rises on Mont-Gerbier-de-Jonc, a volcanic knoll in the southeastern Massif Central. After being joined by the Allier, it flows in a northwesterly direction into the Paris Basin, only to veer away near Orléans in a broad turn toward the southwest. The Loire then proceeds toward the Atlantic Ocean, into which it empties just west of the city of Nantes.

Below Gien, the valley of the Loire widens considerably, the stream itself frequently dividing into channels in the alluvium of the valley floor. Its upper and middle courses are of moderate size at low water during the summer, with a flow of only 194 cubic feet per second. But the river can swell mightily when the snow is melting in the Massif Central, after sudden storms, or as autumn rains sweep north from the Mediterranean. Within but a few hours, its flow can increase to as much as 85,000 to 95,000 cubic feet per second. When it does, the channels are altered. Dikes protect the adjacent countryside from flooding.

Because of its sandbanks, the Loire is not suited for navigation. Until the nineteenth century, it was used only by small vessels, and since the advent of the railways it has almost completely lost any commercial importance as a thoroughfare. Today, ships ply it only below Angers. Thus to the astonishment of travelers accustomed to heavily trafficked, industrialized rivers, the Loire appears to be a stream of unspoiled beauty and calm. Bordered by grass, reeds, and low shrubbery, overgrown islands or tongues of dry sand interrupt its flow. In places, it resembles an inland lake, and seems to have lost all traces of human activity. In its valley, strung with monuments to a high civilization, the Loire reverts to its primeval state.

THE LANDSCAPES

THE LOIRE OF THE CHÂTEAUX, CHURCHES, AND cities flows for roughly 185 miles between Gien to the east and Angers—lying on a tributary—to the west. The historic provinces through which this stretch of river travels are the Orléanais, Touraine, and Anjou.

In the vicinity of Orléans, a city steeped in history, people refer to the broad valley of the Loire simply as *le Val*. To the north lies the fertile Beauce; to the south the densely wooded Sologne, a favorite hunting reserve of the kings of France. In the wet valley lowlands between Gien and Orléans, pastures and vegetable farms dominate the landscape. But these comprise only part of the lush fertility of the Orléanais. The mild climate of the Loire Valley is also ideal for nurserymen, rose growers, orchardists, and winemakers.

The region around the royal city of Blois serves as a transition landscape between the lowlands of the Orléanais and the elegant parkland of Touraine, with its fields stretching north to the horizon where they merge with those of the Beauce. To the south are the forests of the Touraine and the famous châteaux of Chambord, Cheverny, Villesavin, Beauregard, Fougères-sur-Bièvre, and Chaumont.

Touraine was the homeland of Honoré de Balzac, who was born in Tours. In *Catherine de Médicis*, Balzac quotes his friend the writer Léon Gozlan:

There is one province in France which is never sufficiently admired. Fragrant as Italy, flowery as the banks of the Guadalquivir, beautiful especially in its own characteristics, wholly French, having always been French.... Auvergne is Auvergne, Languedoc is only Languedoc; but Touraine is France; the most national river for Frenchmen is the Loire, which waters Touraine. For this reason we ought not to be surprised at the great number of historically noble buildings possessed by these *départements*, which have taken the name or derivations of the name of the Loire. At every step we take in this land of enchantment we discover a new picture, bordered it may be by a river, or a tranquil lake reflecting in its liquid depths a castle with towers and woods and sparkling waterfalls. It is quite natural that in a region chosen by royalty for its sojourn, where the court was long established, great families and fortunes, and distinguished men should have settled and built palaces as grand as themselves.[1]

Touraine is a landscape of ease and pleasure. Its light is soft, its climate gentle. Here, the Loire and its tributaries cut into a moderately high chalk plateau whose slopes of soft tufa are excellent for vineyards and orchards. Since the local stone is extremely easy to work, it can be seen in all the buildings of the region. In addition, its softness has enabled the natives to carve out whole networks of underground caverns, in which the famous wines of the area are stored at constant temperatures. In many places, people also use such caverns for their own dwellings, taking advantage of their warmth in winter and coolness in summer. These are not temporary shelters hollowed out of the rock, but residences of distinct charm, capable of being enlarged as needed with minimum effort. Often they are concealed behind imposing façades. And just as often the tourist is startled by the smoke rising from the fireplace of one of these underground houses.

The transition to Anjou, beginning near Candes, is imperceptible in the landscape itself. Vineyards and farmland continue to dominate. Here, too, precious wines are stored in rock caverns. But the moderating effect of the Atlantic now makes itself felt, and in Anjou grow palm trees, pomegranates, figs, and mulberry trees. The Loire Valley becomes even wider, and the river itself assumes imposing dimensions and a more constant flow. Countless tributaries link Anjou to the surrounding country.

*T*HE LOIRE VALLEY IN HISTORY

EACH OF THE THREE PROVINCES HAS HAD ITS great moments in history. The earliest to do so was the Orléanais. Its largest city, Orléans, was the capital of the western Frankish kingdom. Carolingian kings also favored the city, and during the succeeding centuries, the Orléanais remained the most important bastion of the French kings.

Anjou's heyday came in the twelfth century, when Henri Plantagenet, the comte d'Anjou, became king of England in 1154. From his mother (Matilda, daughter of England's Henry I), he had inherited Normandy as well as feudal sovereignty over Brittany, and from his father (Geoffrey Plantagenet), Anjou, Maine, and Touraine. Moreover, though marriage with Eleanor of Aquitaine, the divorced wife of Louis VII of France, he acquired Poitou and Guienne along with Gascogne as a French Crown fief. Henri's French holdings, combined with England, made up the Angevin empire, which stretched from England to the Pyrenees and encompassed half the territory of France. It survived for only fifty years, but this was enough time to bring a new building style of extreme boldness and elegance to western France, the so-called Angevin style. Numerous structures along the Loire were built in this style. At the beginning of the thirteenth century, the Angevin empire was destroyed by Philippe-Auguste when the greater part of England's continental holdings were reconquered by the French.

The claim of the House of Valois to the throne of France was disputed by the English king Edward III, who invaded France and triggered the Hundred Years' War, in the course of which first the southwestern and later the northern part of the country fell entirely beneath the rule of England. The Loire, however, remained French, and the last resistance against the English was concentrated in this region. The struggle's turning point was effected by a peasant girl from Lorraine, Joan of Arc, the Maid of Orléans, whose heroic deeds still give rise to nationalist feeling in the valley of the Loire. She liberated Orléans, which had been under siege, and convinced an indecisive dauphin to allow himself to be crowned king of France at Reims.

Touraine came into its own only in the late fifteenth century, as the favorite province of the Valois kings. It was here that the most famous and most grand châteaux were constructed and that the French Renaissance, with its brilliant cultural life, first took root. During the turmoil of the Religious Wars in the second half of the sixteenth century, the kings felt more secure along the Loire than in Paris. It was only under Henri IV that the Loire Valley began to lose prominence as a royal residence in favor of the Ile de France.

CHATEAUX, CHURCHES, AND CITIES: AN OVERVIEW

MORE THAN 300 CASTLES AND CHÂTEAUX LINE the banks of the Loire and stand guard over its adjacent lands. Of these, roughly 100 are open to visitors. Nowhere is it possible to get a better sense of the variety of French aristocratic culture, its love of display, and its changes through history than in the Loire Valley.

Surviving from the tenth to twelfth centuries, a period in which the various counts in the Loire region wrangled with one another over their respective holdings, are the remains of several donjons, or keeps—massive square towers indebted to the stern fortress architecture of the Normans. These were designed solely for defense. The oldest surviving remains of the donjons, dating to roughly 990, are found in Langeais. Those at Beaugency, Montrichard, and especially Loches are in a better state of preservation; from them, one can best visualize living conditions in such fortifications.

Beginning in the twelfth century, these simple fortresses were surrounded by massive ring walls, which were strengthened in turn by round or polygonal towers. The castles at Chinon, Loches, Montreuil-Bellay, and Angers are impressive examples of these newer defense works.

The "classical" Loire château, from the High and late Middle Ages, is a complex guarded by numerous round towers. Often it encloses an inner courtyard and is generally surrounded by a system of moats. The goal of defense was paramount in defining its architecture. Wall-walks with machicolation either run beneath the outer eaves or circle the towers, one of which doubtless served the function of the earlier donjon, providing an ultimate defensible refuge in case of attack. Good examples of this type are the châteaux of Sully-sur-Loire, Chaumont, Langeais, Ussé, Fougères-sur-Bièvre, and Plessis-Bourré.

In the Gothic period, a number of these châteaux were fitted out with a wealth of roof ornament heretofore unknown, consisting of all manner of dormers, turrets, and chimneys. The Château de Saumur is a fine example. The concept giving rise to such ornamentation—that a castle served not merely as a fortification, but as a symbol of a luxurious, princely style of living—

became most prevalent in the Renaissance, when the problems of defense no longer dictated style as they had in the Middle Ages. Charles VIII, Louis XII, and François I undertook campaigns into Italy in an attempt to force their inherited claims to the kingdom of Naples and to Milan. Their political successes were short-lived, but the cultural gain for France was incalculable. The princes of Italy surrounded themselves with luxurious courts marked by elegant deportment and ceremony and they lived in superb Renaissance structures set in the midst of lavish gardens. Naturally, the French rulers wished to enjoy such splendors at home, and so they invited Italian artists and craftsmen to France. Beginning around 1500, the French nobility set about building various châteaux that exceeded in opulence anything previously constructed.

Italian forms were adopted only hesitantly at first. Among the châteaux representing what is, in effect, a prelude to French Renaissance architecture are Amboise, the Louis XII Wing at Blois, and Chaumont. These were built in the traditional Gothic style; the new sense of form is apparent only in certain Italianate ornamental motifs or in the tendency toward overall uniformity.

A Renaissance architecture of truly regal scope only began to flourish along the Loire under François I, its pattern established by the François I wings of the châteaux of Blois and Chambord. These were the first structures to exhibit features found in all Renaissance buildings along

Machicolation along wall-walks is a striking feature of the château at Ussé.

Winding stairway at Chambord.

the Loire—notably, regular layouts and a clear arrangement of façades by means of pilasters and cornices. At the same time, a magnificent style of decorative art developed, as the formal expression of a society that actively cultivated a luxurious style of life. Sometimes lavish and heavy, but more often light and airy, this ornamentation demonstrated once again—following the ornate inventiveness of its Romanesque era and the plant-motif capitals of its Gothic cathedrals—the decorative genius of France. All in all, though, native tradition was more influential than imported innovation. Rarely were Italian models slavishly copied. The French still loved their medieval stone mullions, winding stairs, and steep, dormered roofs, with their thickets of richly ornamented turrets, gables, and chimneys.

Obvious successors of these royal structures are the châteaux of Azay-le-Rideau, Beauregard, Ussé, Villandry, Villesavin, Valençay, and Serrant. By exception, one that explicitly reflects Venetian precedents is Chenonceau.

As a rule, the interiors of these Renaissance châteaux followed traditional design concepts. A salon, for example, will have a band of wood paneling around the base of the walls, large-figured wall tapestries, and a beamed ceiling that has been carved and painted. Its chief fixture is generally a splendidly decorated mantelpiece extending to the ceiling. Furnishings also continue to be essentially Gothic in form. Their ornamentation, however, has become Italian, with ample use of medallions decorated with faces, pilasters, columns, arabesques, grotesques, *putti*, and dolphins.

Two genuinely new achievements of the French Renaissance are the gallery and the garden. Both reflect quite clearly a desire for comfort and luxury: the gallery as a setting for court festivities and the garden as a colorful carpet of plants including all of the delicacies of an earthly paradise.

The kings were not the only builders. Influential officials of the court soon followed suit. It is perhaps not surprising that the most beautiful châteaux—such as Azay-le-Rideau, Chenonceau, and the now almost demolished Bury—were built by courtiers in charge of the royal finances.

The great age of château-building on the Loire ended with the reign of François I. The seventeenth and eighteenth centuries managed to produce only a few more architectural splendors—Cheverny, the Gaston d'Orléans Wing at Blois, Ménars, and Montgeoffroy—as magnificent testimony to the culture of the aristocracy on the eve of its collapse during the French Revolution.

But châteaux are not the only cultural wealth of the Loire Valley. There are also its churches and monasteries, particularly those from the Middle Ages. The oldest church structure still standing in France, Germigny-des-Prés, dates from the time of Charlemagne. Surviving from the Romanesque period are a number of splendid abbey churches, including St-Benoît-sur-Loire, with its relics of St. Benedict; St-Aignan-sur-Cher, and Cunault. The most powerful religious house for women in France was Fontevrault, which has preserved not only its church, but also its unique, twelfth-century octagonal kitchen. A number of pilgrimage shrines stand as magnificent examples of sacred architecture from the High and late Middle Ages:

Le Puy-Notre-Dame, Candes, and Notre-Dame-de-Cléry. Other notable churches are to be found in the cities.

A special branch of sacred art, wall painting, is represented in the Loire region—especially in Liget, St-Aignan-sur-Cher, and Tavant—by important Romanesque examples. The variety of their forms and subjects tends to correct the rigid view of Romanesque art. The frescoes display a sacred calm, of course, but often a sense of immediacy and movement as well; they not only carry forward a venerable tradition, but also experiment with new subjects.

The richest cities in tems of art and architectural monuments are Orléans, Blois, Amboise, Tours, Loches, Chinon, Saumur, and Angers. Even their street arrangement gives some indication of their long history. Loches and Chinon are among the best preserved small medieval towns in France, both dominated by massive castle and fortification complexes on ridges that overlook the charming houses and alleyways crowded below. Blois, Angers, Orléans, and Tours boast cathedrals. Of these, the ones in Orléans and Tours are by far the most important. Blois, Amboise, Saumur, and Angers are known chiefly for their châteaux; Angers, in addition, for its Apocalypse Tapestries, possibly the most extensive series of pictorial tapestries woven in the Middle Ages.

François I, Catherine de Médicis, Diane de Poitiers

IN THE HISTORY OF THE RENAISSANCE CHÂTEAUX of the Loire, three figures stand out. With his love of warfare and the life of the soldier, his even more passionate devotion to women—who seem to have found him irresistible—and to art, François I is the vir-

Henry II's monogram united his initial with that of Catherine de Médicis and Diane de Poitiers.

tual embodiment of the French Renaissance. He spent huge sums on his building projects, and it was he who summoned the aging genius Leonardo da Vinci to France. As his heraldic emblem he chose the salamander, which was believed to be incombustible—a fitting device for a man who spent of himself so lavishly.

François I created the French court, which in turn became the model for all European courts. To this day, it defines our sense of etiquette and breeding. The king transformed women into ladies and men into cavaliers; to the rude delights of the hunt, he added the more refined ones of fêtes and balls, and brought spirit and learning to the ruling class. The importance of the court as a magnetic force field was never more apparent than when François I changed residences. One eyewitness to such a move was the sculptor Benvenuto Cellini, who, in *The Life of Benvenuto Cellini*, reports that "the train of the King drags itself along with never less than 12,000 horse behind it." The royal patron surrounded by cultivated friends—this is how François I wished to be remembered by posterity.

Catherine de Médicis, the vengeful wife, and Diane de Poitiers, the seductive mistress: no story of the Loire châteaux has enticed the popular imagination as has the tale of enmity between these two women, which could not flare up as long as Henri II stood between them. For political and financial reasons, François I married his son Henri to Catherine, a daughter of the Medici family. But Henri preferred to dally with Diane, who had previously enjoyed the caresses of François I. She was thirty-five when the seventeen-year-old Henri fell in love with her, and their relationship endured for more than twenty years. She functioned as the uncrowned queen to whom Henri II never denied a single request, while Catherine, his legal wife, led an underground existence. Diane participated in political affairs, awarded sinecures and dismissed public servants at whim. She even contrived a new source of taxation for the king, who was growing poorer and poorer because of her own extravagance. Every time a bell was rung in the kingdom, a bell tax was to be paid! With this affront to the Church, Diane de Poitiers was able to make herself even more unpopular than she already was. It was only after the death of Henri II, who was killed by a lance wound inflicted in a tournament, that Catherine de Médicis was able to take her delighted revenge. The châteaux of Chaumont and Chenonceau betray her work.

This book offers a tour of the art monuments of the Loire and follows the course of the river, although it also entails a number of side trips into the valleys of its tributaries and at times even farther afield. The starting point is Gien; the end is Angers, in the heart of Anjou.

St-Gatien cathedral at Tours.

THROUGH THE ORLEANAIS

GIEN

WELL KNOWN FOR ITS MANUFACTURE OF FA-
ïence, Gien is the easternmost castle town
in the valley of the Loire. Its handsome
townscape is indebted to Anne de Beaujeu,
the older daughter of Louis XI. Upon
Louis's death, Anne became regent for her
thirteen-year-old brother, Charles VIII.
After he assumed power, she withdrew
with her husband to her country estates,
taking with her the admiration of all who
had dealt with her. In Gien, which had
been Louis XI's gift to her, Anne built the
present château on the site of a fortress
constructed by Charlemagne. She commissioned the arched bridge across the Loire,
and founded various religious houses.
From the bridge is a splendid view of the
town: a row of three-story houses on the riverbank; and above it, the long and less varied complex of the château and the former
collegiate church with its massive bell
tower. This balanced ensemble belies the
fact that Gien was heavily damaged during
the Second World War. In rebuilding it, its
inhabitants were careful to preserve its
late-medieval scale while incorporating all

Anne de Beaujeu

the facilities of a modern commercial and residential town.

The *château*, built between 1484 and 1500, is a two-story, asymmetrical structure with a three-story side wing. A rectangular tower projects from the main wing on the town side, and a round one marks the junction of the two tracts. The polygonal stair towers on the courtyard side become rectangular on the second floor. Compared with other royal castles along the Loire, its architecture is modest; only in conjunction with the buildings of the town does it take on a certain grandeur. Diamond shapes in black brick have been worked into the red-brick walls, and freestone blocks enliven its windows and corners. This diamond pattern became one of Gien's decorative motifs; the neighboring church uses it, and it recurs on the walls of many of the town's structures.

As Gien is situated in the midst of some of France's loveliest hunting grounds, it is only logical that the *Musée International de la Chasse* should have been established here. Its collections of historic hunting weapons are unlike any other in the world. Powder flasks, crossbows, harquebuses, guns richly decorated with engraved designs or damascene work are relics of a time when hunting and falconry were not merely royal sports, but courtly arts. The museum also exhibits a fine collection of local faïence and numerous woven tapestries. In the great hall on the second floor,

famous for its open timberwork in chestnut, there are numerous canvases by François Desportes, a painter of animals during the reign of Louis XIV. His complex and lively scenes of combat between hunting dogs and wild game were inspired by hunts organized by the king. Many of the artist's absorbing studies of dogs (of which the museum owns several examples) were executed in front of the cages of the royal hounds. Another *animalier*, the early-twentieth-century sculptor and engraver Florentin Brigaud, is represented in the museum by fine examples of his art.

The former collegiate chuch of *St-Etienne*, next to the château, was dedicated in 1514. Of the structure built in the Flamboyant style by Anne de Beaujeu, only the tower survives. The nave was destroyed during the Revolution, and a nineteenth-century reconstruction was leveled during the Second World War. From 1950 to 1954, the church was rebuilt as a brick structure designed by André Gélis, chief architect for the Monuments Historiques. Its exterior contrasts and harmonizes with the château, while its three-aisle interior is a kind of Romanesque translated into a modern idiom. Joan of Arc was chosen as the new church's patron, for she stayed in Gien on several occasions and it was from here that she led Charles VII to his coronation at Reims in 1429. The capitals along the central aisle are of Gien earthenware pottery and depict scenes from her life.

SULLY-SUR-LOIRE

SULLY-SUR-LOIRE IS THE FIRST OF THE "CLASSICAL" Loire châteaux downstream from Gien. It is a limestone structure fortified with mas-

sive round towers and surrounded by water.

A Roman castle and stone bridge that

Sully-sur-Loire

spanned the Loire for more than 1,300 feet were demolished during heavy flooding after a storm in 1363. Stones from that bridge were used to rebuild the castle, which rests on original Roman piles. The lords of Sully had owned the fortress since the ninth century; in 1408, it passed into the hands of the counts of La Tremoille. Between 1602 and 1962, it belonged to the dukes of Sully and counts of Béthune-Sully. Today, it is owned by the *département* of the Loiret.

The castle's most famous owner was Maximilien de Béthune, seigneur and marquis de Rosny, chamberlain, privy and state councilor, minister plenipotentiary of France, grand master of artillery, superintendent of fortifications and finances—to name but a few of his titles. He purchased the castle and its lands in 1602. Henri IV elevated the domain to a duchy in 1606 as a reward for the many services that Béthune—or Sully, as he is known in French history—had rendered to the Crown. After Henri IV's assassination in 1610, Sully was removed from office. He lived on his estates like a grand seigneur, keeping a company of a hundred bodyguards and surrounding himself with a small court governed by the strictest etiquette. Tallemant des Réaux reports that this court consisted of fifteen or twenty ancient peacocks and seven or eight old retainers of rank who would line up when a bell rang to pay their respects whenever Sully chose to go out for a walk. They would then fall in behind him. The writer adds: "I believe even the peacocks followed after him."

Sully delighted in carrying his pedantry to extremes. He did not permit a tree to be planted, a piece of furniture to be crafted, or a castle moat to be cleaned without a notarized contract. His industry knew no bounds. With four secretaries, he tirelessly wrote his *Mémoires des sages et royales œconomies d'Estat domestiques, politiques et militaires de Henry le Grand.* The most famous passage in the work deals with a plan for the organization of Europe and the establishment of perpetual peace. An unusual feature of these multivolume memoirs is that they were written in the second person, as though by an editorial board addressing the duke and telling him of all his endeavors, accomplishments, hopes, and perceptions. For fear of prying eyes, Sully had his work published under his personal supervision in a newly constructed tower of the castle, but the title pages were impressed with the notice "Published in Amsterdam."

The oldest portion of the castle is the tall keep facing the Loire and dating from 1363. It is constructed on a rectangular ground plan and strengthened by thick round towers at the corners; two of the towers have lost their machicolation and their pepper-pot roofs. Half towers, also roofless, flank the entrance on the courtyard side, which originally was secured by a drawbridge. The guard room, kitchen, and chapel are on the ground floor. A reproduction of Sully's funeral monument—he died in 1641—from Nogent-le-Rotrou stands in the small oratory next to the second-floor hall; it contains the ashes of Sully and his second wife, Rachel de Cochefilet. The hall on the attic floor, surrounded by wall-walks, resembles the interior of a church, thanks to its massive roof trusses of chestnut in the form of an inverted ship's keel. This timberwork is considered to be the most artful and beautiful to have survived from the Middle Ages. The squared beams were not sawed but hewn from the log with axes, carefully detached from the

sapwood, and placed so that air can circulate around them, which explains why the wood has remained sound for more than 600 years. The bill for this masterpiece of joinery and the timberwork for the four towers still survives, bearing the date of 1363. It tells us that the castle's paymaster granted a certain master joiner Tévenon Foucher five casks of wine valued at eight *écus* plus twenty-four *écus* in coin, but not the *muid* (roughly sixty bushels) of grain that would have been customarily expected.

Old pictures of the castle show the inner courtyard next to the keep surrounded by buildings, some of which have disappeared. The east wing comprises two dwellings from the sixteenth century. They are of different heights and tied together by means of a rectangular tower. The lower structure was rebuilt after being destroyed by fire in 1918. The taller is known as the Petit-Château, and was remodeled by Sully. On the ground floor is his office, where he wrote his memoirs, and on the second floor is his bedroom; both rooms have fireplaces, restored wall tapestries, and heavily restored wooden ceilings.

The Loire originally flowed right by the castle. For protection against high water, Sully built the dike that now serves as an entryway into the complex. A smaller stream, La Sange, was diverted to supply the moats with water.

The outer court, which is also protected by moats, was once surrounded by towers, walls, and buildings. These have disappeared, except for a few foundations. The extensive park, dating back to Sully's time, preserves only traces of its former design. A white marble statue of the castle's most famous owner serves as a fitting accent in the outer court. It was created for another of his properties, the Château de Villebon.

ST-BENOIT-SUR-LOIRE

ON THE OPPOSITE BANK OF THE LOIRE, AND reached from Sully by way of a causeway with a splendid view of the river and the broad, fertile countryside, lies the abbey of St-Benoît-sur-Loire. It is one of France's most famous Romanesque monastery churches and, during the Middle Ages, it was a highly important center of monastic culture. It was founded as Fleury in 651 by the abbot Léodobod from St-Aignan in Orléans. He established here the Rule of St. Benedict. St. Benedict is known as the spiritual father of western Christendom; his relics and those of his sister, St. Scholastica, were brought here by the second abbot, Mummolus, a few years later from Monte Cassino in Italy, where they were in danger of desecration by pillaging Lombards. These extremely precious relics, which had been stolen from the Italian monastery

by a small party of raiders under the leadership of the monk Aigulf, for centuries attracted pilgrims to the abbey—renamed St-Benoît—and brought the monastery into high repute. During the time of Charlemagne, the abbot Theodulf founded the monastery schools of Fleury, and soon their influence was felt throughout the entire Christian world. Their curriculum consisted of theology and the seven liberal arts: grammar, rhetoric, logic, arithmetic, geometry, music, and astronomy. In addition, there was instruction in agriculture, crafts, medicine, and the fine arts. The illuminated manuscripts from the monastery's scriptorium are still sources of wonder.

St-Benoît was repeatedly plagued by fire, but each time its fabric was rebuilt. All that survives of the medieval complex is the abbey church. The monastic buildings disap-

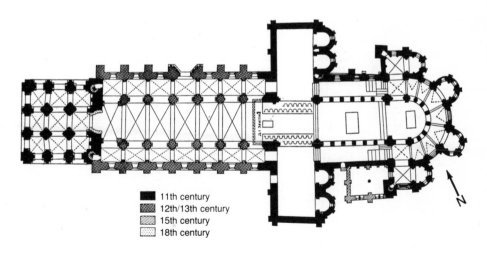

11th century
12th/13th century
15th century
18th century

Floor plan of the abbey church of St-Benoît-sur-Loire.

21

peared after the dissolution of the convent during the Revolution. In 1944, a new community of Benedictines settled here; and in 1959, St-Benoît was again accorded the status of an abbey.

The best view of the low and massive church is from the river. Disregarding countless renovations, it is possible to distinguish the following building phases: the unusual narthex dates from the first half of the eleventh century; the transept with crossing tower and choir with crypt were built between 1067 and 1108; the basilica-like nave dates from 1150 to 1218.

The narthex is the creation of Gauzlin, one of the monastery's most illustrious abbots and an illegitimate son of Hugues Capet. It is assumed that this portion of the church was not completely finished by the

The porch at St-Benoît-sur-Loire.

time of his death in 1030, especially since the whole monastery had been devastated by fire in 1026. In the chronicle of Gauzlin's life, we read that his architect asked him just what sort of a structure he wanted. "One that will be a model for all of Gaul," was his reply. The result was an architectural achievement unlike anything in Romanesque building, but one that did indeed serve as a model for others. The blocklike structure has two stories on an almost square ground plan. Its original third floor was destroyed in 1527 by François I, who sought to punish the monks for their refusal to receive Cardinal Duprat as abbot of St-Benoît. In the seventeenth century, the narthex was provided with its present tentlike roof with belfry and lantern. Its ground floor is open on three sides, each one boasting three arcades with inset arches on half columns. Four massive pillars, also faced with half columns, divide the space into nine bays roofed with groin vaults. Scholars still cannot explain why the two western pillars are slightly out of line. The considerably taller second floor, a place of worship with three altar niches in the east wall, is like the ground floor in layout, but its arcades and pillars are more fully articulated.

The beauty of this masonry of carefully worked stone blocks has been admired since its creation. According to the chronicle of Gauzlin's life, the abbot had the stones brought down the Loire on barges from quarries in the Nivernais.

The splendid capitals serve as the chief interior ornament of the porch. On the ground floor, for example, lush acanthus forms alternate with fantastic beasts and figural scenes. It is possible to make out the Flight into Egypt, the Last Judgment, the Four Horsemen of the Apocalypse, and St. Martin sharing his cloak and being taken up into the glory of heaven by angels. Such scenes were intended to instruct pilgrims and confront them with important concepts of the Salvation. The figures were carved to conform to the shapes of the capitals, and thus they seem archaic and stiff. However, the inner modeling demonstrates the sculptors' feeling for ornament, as exemplified in the rhythmic flow of draperies. We know the name of at least one of these masters, for chiseled into one of the capitals on the front façade are the words *Vnbertvs me Fecit* (Umbertus made me).

The same attention to detail is evident in the church's interior. This large space, typical of Benedictine churches, is characterized by its white stone of a slightly reddish cast and the uniform rhythm of its wall arrangement. In terms of architecture, the choir is most interesting. The side aisles of the nave lead past the choir, which is consecrated to the Virgin, and into an ambulatory around its high, semicircular apse. The ambulatory, consecrated to St. Benedict, is set back by one bay from the choir. Such ambulatories are characteristic of pilgrimage churches, proving especially useful for processions. On either side of the main axis, a three-quarter-round chapel extends beyond the main apse. Two additional chapels with semicircular apses are placed to the side, one next to each of the bridging bays in front of the main apse. The beauty of this choir derives from its divisions based on the motif of the round arch. First come the majestic arcades above tall columns, through which light filters from across the ambulatory; above the arcades is a small blind triforium serving as a band of three-dimensional ornament; then, just below the base of the barrel vault at the back of the choir, is a wreath of large round-arch windows. The strikingly barren wall sur-

faces between the arcades and the triforia in the nave and vaults were once covered by paintings.

A special treasure is the richly patterned mosaic floor surrounding the high altar in the main choir. Recently restored, it has been placed in the present choir, although excavations carried out in 1958 and 1959 revealed that it had been part of a previous structure. For a long time, it was believed that the floor had come from Italy and had been presented to the church by Cardinal Duprat around 1535. In truth, the cardinal added only a few ornamental pieces to it.

The transept dates from the same period as the choir, whose altars were consecrated in 1108. To the east of each arm are two semicircular chapels; those of the south arm have been reconstructed.

A great number of capitals carved with striking narrative scenes are preserved in the choir and the transept. They provide a lively picture of the Romanesque imagination. Compared with those of the narthex, many of these capitals seem more advanced in style and are reminiscent of the famous contemporary capital sculptures in churches of neighboring Burgundy. In addition to events from the Old and New Testaments are incidents from the life of St. Benedict. Some of the capitals carry inscriptions in which the name of one monk, Hugo, constantly recurs. He is portrayed kneeling before the Virgin Mary in the company of St. Benedict and commending himself and his family to Christ. Once he gives his full name, Hugo de Sancta Maria, and it is assumed that he created this capital and a number of others.

The nave dates from the late twelfth and early thirteenth centuries, and with its pointed-arch arcades and ribbed vaulting reveals the transition to the Gothic style. The north portal, with its important cycle of Early Gothic sculptures, was built around 1200. The six jamb figures are poorly preserved and scarcely identifiable (the inside one on the right is Abraham). In 1562, during the Religious Wars, the soldiers of the prince de Condé, leader of the Huguenots, vented their rage on these figures. The figures in the arch area are in good condition, however. God the Father sits in majesty in the tympanum. He is holding an open book and is surrounded by the Evangelists, each inspired by his symbol. This type of Majestas Domini, familiar from manuscript illustrations, is rarely used as a tympanum ornament. The inside of the archivolts in decorated with angels bearing candlesticks, incense containers, and censers; the outside, with apostles. On the lintel, which has been supported by a basket-handle arch since the Renaissance, the transportation of the relics of St. Benedict and St. Scholastica is depicted in three successive scenes: on the left, a party of monks places the bones from an open sarcophagus into a basket; in the center, the relics (St. Benedict's in a casket, St. Scholastica's in a reliquary) bring the dead back to life; and on the right, the monks of Fleury await the arrival of their brethren, who bear the treasure on their shoulders.

The relics of St. Benedict rest in the crypt beneath the choir. Squat round pillars arranged in a semicircle outline two ambulatories around the massive central pillar, which is hollowed out and contains the casket with the saint's bones. The casket itself was redesigned in 1964.

Dating from the tenth century, a small two-aisle chapel just off the crypt is considered to be the oldest part of the church. Few of its original appointments have survived. The only objects worthy of special mention are the choir stalls from 1413 and the tomb of Philippe I, which was remodeled in the thirteenth century. One famous item is the tiny Mumma Casket, made of wood and covered with chased and gilded copper plates. It was found beneath the high altar in 1642. Named after its donor, the abbot Mummolus, the Mumma Casket is one of the few surviving examples of Merovingian art, and dates from the time of the monastery's founding in the second half of the seventh century. Twelve figures, presumably representing apostles, stand as though transfixed on the roof slabs.

GERMIGNY-DES-PRES

GERMIGNY-DES-PRÉS IS AS UNIMPOSING A TOWN as its neighbor St-Benoît-sur-Loire; it contains a simple church of modest dimensions that lacks exterior ornament. At first glance, the church appears to be merely the village's idyllic focal point, set on an overgrown square and next to the parish garden. But in the larger context of European architecture, the church is of extraordinary importance. It was built as the oratory of his private villa by Abbot Theodulf of Fleury of St-Benoît-sur-Loire. Theodulf, in addition to being abbot, was bishop of Orléans and chancellor and adviser to Charlemagne. He was a poet and an active patron of the arts. It is thought that he consecrated his private chapel on January 3, 806. The abbot fell victim to palace intrigue in 818, and soon the building began to fall into decay. The villa was put to the torch in the second half of the ninth century, presumably during a raid by Normans or Vikings. The church continued to stand, although badly damaged, and its significance was quickly forgotten. In the fifteenth century, it was enlarged by the addition of a nave and some smaller extensions. Not until the nineteenth century did scholars recognize its uniqueness and attempt to restore it to its original condition, though. In substance, of course, little of the original structure survives, but the restoration has recovered its essential architectural concept.

Theodulf's building was in the form of a Greek cross on a ground plan 34 feet square. Originally, a slightly horseshoe-shaped apse projected from each side; the eastern, or choir, apse was flanked by smaller apses, which have not been restored. The existence of these apses was suspected in the nineteenth century, but it was not until 1930 that excavation brought their foundations to light. The west apse and its adjacent walls were razed to accommodate the fifteenth-century nave.

Inside, four pillars set off the central space, which is roofed by a restored cupola resting on high walls pierced by arcades. Directly above rises the tower. The arms of the cross have barrel vaults, while the lower corner rooms have cupolas and groin vaults. The spaces are defined by the clear lines of the pillars and arches. One has the feeling of being in separate chambers or cells varying in shape from the low, bulging apse to vertical shafts of various heights. The church is small but not confining, since the walls and the pillars are not massive. It presents an endless variety of views; and its symmetrical ground plan is only perceived sequentially, as the identical treatment of each of the side walls becomes apparent in turn.

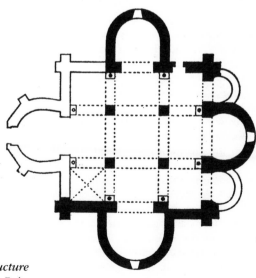

Floor plan of the original structure of the church at Germigny-des-Prés.

The small size and intricacy of the church are emphasized by details. The dividing arches are supported by columns that are scarcely as tall as a person and that show distinct entasis; they are on high pedestals in front of slender wall panels. The columns in the main apse support not the wall, but a seemingly independent series of arches; only waist-high, these columns appear to be nonstructural embellishments. The four slender pillars that set off the central space are decorated with different moldings on their various sides, and thus were not conceived, in this respect at least, as integral elements.

In the ninth-century annals of Fleury, the chapel is described as so marvelously executed that nothing equaled it in all of Neustria (the western Frankish kingdom, corresponding roughly to northern and northwestern France). Formal precedents for it may have been Byzantine cruciform cupola churches, possibly as reinterpreted by the Visigoths in Spain, Theodulf's homeland. The Fleury annals note that the church was considered an imitation of Charlemagne's palatine chapel in Aachen, but that the only thing it had in common with that structure was its central symmetry. This contemporary interpretation is instructive, for it reveals something of the builder's high claims: he was making visible his close tie to the imperial court by imitating the emperor's architecture and seeking to share in the dignity it made manifest. Further, the annals tell us that in his attempt to outdo even the chapel in Aachen, Theodulf had the interior of his oratory decorated with flowers, stucco, mosaics, and a marble floor—all at great expense. It dazzled all who saw it. But little of this splendor survives. For example, all that remains of the stucco work are symmetrical shrubs with broad-leaf clusters—a motif prevalent in Islamic art—in the niches; cocoonlike, fine-spun rosettes in the window embrasures of the main apse; and a lovely band of rosettes above the upper arcade of the main apse.

Around 1840, children coming from the church were observed playing with little mosaic stones. An investigation followed, and beneath a number of layers of whitewash was found a portion of the mosaics from Theodulf's time. Today, the only piece of mosaic suggesting the splendor of Theodulf's conception is the one in the semidome of the main apse. It is the only mosaic surviving from the Carolingian period, and although heavily restored, comes close to its original state in terms of composition and style. The Ark of the Covenant from the Old Testament is depicted, with two golden angels standing on top of it. Two other angels of monumental size stand on either side of the Ark and point to it. Between them is suspended the right hand of God. The main colors are deep blue and gold, with traces of purple and green. The Latin inscription reads: "Behold here the sacred oracle and the cherubim and the radiance of the Ark of God's Covenant. And if in contemplating it you seek to make contact with the Lord of the Thunder, then include the name of Theodulf in your prayers." Stylistically, the mosaic is closest to Roman mosaics from the eighth and ninth centuries, but it is also related to contemporary miniature painting from the school of Fleury.

The remaining mosaics, with the exception of a few small remnants in the blind arcades of the main apse, were destroyed in the nineteenth century. Fortunately, the lost mosaics were reproduced in watercolor before they were demolished. A foliage pattern decorated the wall above the arch leading to the main apse, and the barrel vault in front of it and the cupola were decorated with cherubim. In the cupola was an inscription in silver letters: "I, Theodulf, have consecrated this temple to the Glory of God; may all who come here remember me."

The iconographic program also points to Theodulf himself. He is held to have been the author of the *Libri Carolini*, which were directed against the Byzantine cult of icons and rejected all depictions of Christ and the saints. Images of the Ark of the Covenant were acceptable inasmuch as the ark was inspired by God and the Holy Ghost.

The apse mosaic of Germigny-des-Prés is an image of this ark. The flanking angels, the foliage in both mosaic and stucco, and the two cherubim in the barrel vault follow the description in 1 Kings 8: 6–8 of the holy of holies in the Temple of Solomon.

Rarely are we able to see as unmistakably as here the individual intent and theological conviction of the builder of a medieval structure, although, of course, we must remember that Germigny-des-Prés was not a public church; it was a private oratory in whose appointments a personal vision was deliberately expressed.

CHATEAUNEUF-SUR-LOIRE

IN THE SEVENTEENTH CENTURY, A SECRETARY OF state to Louis XIV, Louis Phélypeaux de la Vrillière, expanded a tenth-century castle in Châteauneuf-sur-Loire. The moats and defense walls of the tenth-century structure still survive, but La Vrillière's "Petit Versailles" disappeared in 1803, except for some outbuildings, the orangery, the pavilions flanking the forecourt, and an octagonal structure with a cupola. The last named remnant is now part of the Hôtel de Ville and houses the *Musée de la Marine de la Loire*. A broad stepped terrace complete with canal, staircase, and bridge leads from the former courtyard of the château to the bank of the Loire and a park. It is especially pleasant to visit this park in early summer, when the rhododendron are in bloom.

The splendid marble tomb of La Vrillière, who died in 1681, stands in one of the arcades of the nave of the church of *St-Mar-*

tial, built around 1600. It was commissioned in Rome by his son Balthasar, the inscription records, "as an eternal testament to his love and gratitude." The sculptor was probably Domenico Guidi, a pupil of Bernini. It arrived in Châteauneuf by ship in 1686. The life-size grand seigneur is depicted kneeling on a sarcophagus and draped in the cloak of the Order of the Holy Ghost. An angel beside him shows him the splendors of heaven. This work is remarkable for the virtuoso execution of its draperies and the minute depiction of details like laces and borders, all of it exemplifying the exuberance and theatricality of the Roman Baroque. Caryatids as figures of death in the arch embrasure flank the main grouping. Thanks to a brilliant restoration, it is nearly impossible to tell that this monument, like the church itself, was heavily damaged during the Second World War.

ORLEANS

THERE IS A SAYING THAT EXPRESSES PERFECTLY this city's stature in the history of France: "Paris is the head of France; Orléans, its heart." In ancient Gaul, the settlement was known as Genabum, but the Romans gave it the name Aurelianis—whence Orléans. It became a royal city at the beginning of the seventh century under the Merovingians, and served as the capital of the western Frankish empire. It was also favored by the Carolingians. Under the bishop Theodulf (ca. 800), builder of Germigny-des-Prés, Orléans became an intellectual center as well—long before its famous university was founded by Philippe IV le Bel (the Fair) in 1305.

Orléans was as famous for its commerce as for its scholarship. Thanks to its excellent location at the northernmost arc of the Loire—where it comes closest to Paris—and on the threshold of Burgundy and Berry, it teemed constantly with merchants from all over the country. In the eighteenth century, large factories were built, and some of them still stand. Since the Second World War, Orléans has industrialized progressively and has expanded into the larger suburban area of Paris.

For more than 500 years, Orléans has celebrated on May 7 and 8 a festival commemorating the most glorious event in its history, its liberation during the Hundred

ORLEANS

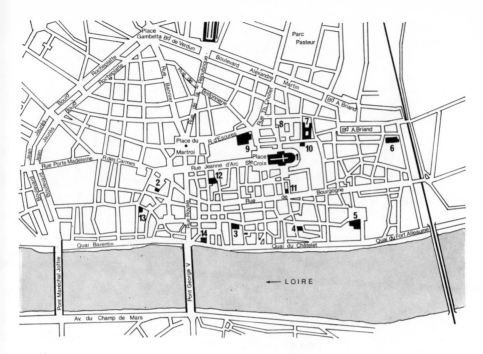

Orléans
1. cathedral of Ste-Croix. 2 St. Paul's tower. 3. St-Donatus. 4. St-Pierre-le-Puellier. 5. St-Aignan. 6. St-Euvert. 7. Lycée Jeanne d'Arc, with the crypt of St-Avit. 8. old cemetery. 9. Hôtel de Ville. 10. Former bishop's palace, now the Bibliothèque Municipale. 11. Salle des Thèses (old university library). 12. Musée des Beaux-Arts. 13. Hôtel Toutin. 14. Maison de la Coquille.

Years' War by Joan of Arc, the Maid of Orléans. Paris and three-quarters of the country were in English hands, but not Orléans. Thus the enemy troops laid siege to it in the autumn of 1428. True to her divine mission to free Orléans and have her king crowned at Reims, Joan entered the city at the head of a small army on April 29, 1429. One enemy stronghold after another fell. Joan was struck by an arrow in the shoulder, but the saints appeared to her and helped her to conquer the pain. When she threw herself back into the battle and took up her banner, the English went into a panic. They capitulated on May 8.

ORLÉANS IS BUILT ON THE NORTH BANK OF THE Loire. Boulevards now follow the circular course of the city walls, which were constructed when Orléans was expanded in the sixteenth century. The focal points of the urban complex are the Place du Martroi, which was a cemetery outside the settlement in Gallo-Roman times, and the cathedral of Ste-Croix.

The Place du Martroi is linked to the riv-

*In this nineteenth-century rendering, Joan of Arc herself
draws out the arrow that wounded her.*

er by the Rue Royale, which leads directly from the Pont George V, named after the English king to commemorate the Anglo-French alliance during the First World War but actually built between 1751 and 1761. The square attests to the city's connection to Joan of Arc, for in its center stands an equestrian statue of her executed in 1855 by the sculptor Denis Foyatier. Raising her eyes to God in gratitude for her victory, she holds a lowered sword in her right hand. Reliefs with scenes from her life by Vital Dubray circle the monument's base.

The monumental proportions of both monument and square create a successful whole. The buildings on the west side were destroyed by bombs in 1940, but have been replaced by new ones that do not detract from the historic integrity of the square. In 1759, the duc d'Orléans erected the *Chancellerie* on the corner where the Rue Royale runs into it. The structure houses the city archives and boasts a gabled façade that was heavily damaged in 1940. A matching structure, the *Chambre de Commerce*, was built to its east in 1865.

The Rue Royale was laid out at the same time as the Pont George V. It was lined with uniform buildings with arcades. Although destroyed for the most part in 1940, these structures were reconstructed in the original style.

A nineteenth-century addition to the city was the Rue Jeanne d'Arc, which runs from the Rue Royale toward the west front of the cathedral of Ste-Croix. Orléans always has been proud of this historic structure, and it was felt that it was not adequately highlighted in the design of the city center. Thus in 1840 it was decided to create this street, with its rigid uniformity, as nothing but a perspective setting for the cathedral. Even then, however, people decried the street's coldness and pomposity.

Few cathedrals are considered to be such monuments to French history as the cathedral of *Ste-Croix*, the origins of which date back to the fourth century. It is necessary to bear in mind the unusual fate of the structure before dismissing it, as did Marcel Proust, who judged this the ugliest cathedral in France.

As bishop of Orléans, St. Euvert constructed the first church for the new Christian community circa 375. The foundations of this building, a three-aisle basilica with a transept and apse, were excavated in 1937. They are visible beneath the present choir. Legend has it that as Euvert was consecrating his church, the hand of God appeared above him and blessed the building, the assembled crowd, and the celebrant himself. The bishop immediately interrupted his ceremony, for God had completed it. Thus all the succeeding structures, being "temples consecrated by the hand of God," have never been dedicated by mortals. Even in the present church, visitors look in vain for any consecration cross on the walls. To commemorate the miracle, the hand of God has been painted on the keystone of the choir arch.

In Bishop Theodulf's time, around 800, a round structure whose floor was decorated with mosaics was added to the fourth-century basilica. Various remnants of it may still be seen. It was here that Charles le Chauve (the Bald), a grandson of Charlemagne, was crowned king of the West Franks in 848.

Fire destroyed the town and its church in 989. Robert le Pieux (the Pious) and Bishop Arnoul I and their successors worked until the twelfth century on the construction of a huge new building in the form of a pilgrimage church, with an ambulatory, choir chapels, a nave with two aisles, and twin towers above the west front. In its time, this structure was one of the largest churches in France. But its foundations were weak. First cracks appeared, and in 1278 and 1286 major portions collapsed such that it seemed futile to restore them.

Soon afterward, on September 11, 1287, the cornerstone of the present cathedral was laid; this time, all the newest techniques for construction and vaulting were applied. Work was begun on the choir and its chapels, while the old church to the west of the new choir continued to be used. The Gothic choir was completed in 1329.

Work was then interrupted by the Hundred Years' War. When Joan of Arc entered the city, she passed through the Romanesque nave in order to pray in the Gothic choir. Once the war ended, work began on the transept, which was completed, together with the crossing tower, by 1511. Then came four bays of the nave, extending as far as the west façade of the Romanesque structure.

In 1568, during the Religious Wars, Huguenots destroyed the still unfinished cathedral except for the choir, some of the side chapels, and two bays of the nave. For thirty years, the building stood as a tempo-

rarily repaired ruin, until Henri IV visited in 1599. The king was convinced that he could offer no better proof of the sincerity of his conversion to Catholicism than by seeing to the rebuilding of this cathedral in the heart of his kingdom. Thus he vowed that he and his successors would "restore the church of Ste-Croix to its former splendor."

In 1601, he laid the cornerstone of the reconstruction, which was to incorporate those portions still standing. Of the choir, for example, which was completed in 1632, the thirteenth- and fourteenth-century chapels had survived. The main choir was completely rebuilt in the Flamboyant style, following the pattern of the surviving sixteenth-century bays of the nave.

From 1627 to 1690, work proceeded on the transept, which by order of Louis XIV was to be built "in the Gothic order." The designs for it were drawn by the Jesuit architect Martellange. In classical fashion, he provided the transept façades with portals surrounded by columns and pediments. Above them, he placed rose windows in the form of the sun, in the center of which, as the sun god, was the head of Louis XIV surrounded by his motto, *Nec Pluribus Impar* (No one compares with him). The pediments were fitted out with tracery windows, and the flat surfaces were adorned with tracery arcades and quatrefoils, with polygonal towers accenting the corners so that the façades, according to a contemporary comment, seemed "sufficiently Gothic."

For the west front, with its three-bay vestibule and two towers, begun in 1767, the king's architects studied the designs of other Gothic cathedrals in France and combined them to produce a new, enlightened, and classical effect. By 1793, the west front was finished, but the Revolution brought renewed destruction and prevented the completion of the entire structure. The western portions of the nave were linked to the tower façade in 1829. In 1858, Emile Boeswillwald rebuilt the crossing flèche, patterning it after the one in Amiens cathedral. The tops of the towers, destroyed by bombs in 1944, have been restored to their original form.

What is unique about this cathedral is that even during the age of the Baroque, when architects were basing their ideas on antiquity, the Gothic tradition was never wholly severed but merely reinterpreted. Having been born in France and having attained in France its highest perfection, the Gothic style of the cathedral of Ste-Croix offers a symbol of national continuity.

Thanks to its clean, clear lines, the interior of this five-aisle basilica appears to have been created at one cast, and it is difficult to believe its construction extended over some 700 years. Few of the original appointments have survived.

On the altar of the axial choir chapel, the Chapelle de Notre-Dame-de-la-Compassion, there is a marble Pietà by Michel Bourdin from 1623.

Also preserved are the unusually ornate choir stalls, which are among the best examples of French court carving. They were executed between 1702 and 1706 by Jules Degoullons after designs by Jacques V. Gabriel. Medallions with scenes from the life of Christ alternate with festoons containing symbols of Judeo-Christian worship. They were commissioned by the art-loving Cardinal Pierre du Cambout de Coislin, who was bishop of Orléans from 1666 to 1706 and whose portrait hangs in the ambulatory. This painting is attributed to Hyacinthe Rigaud.

Among the major events celebrated in the cathedral were the beatification of Joan of Arc in 1909 and her canonization in 1920. A chapel on the north side of the choir was consecrated to her. A marble statue of the Maid on the altar was executed by André César Vermare in 1912. It depicts her in triumph and supported by leopards, symbols of conquered England. Vermare's marble tomb of Cardinal Touchet, bishop of Orléans from 1894 to 1926, stands to the side of the altar; it depicts the cardinal kneeling in eternal supplication before the saint. It was he who fervently pressed for her canonization, and it was his wish that he be buried before her altar. The sacristy houses a small but exquisite collection of treasures: eleventh-century Byzantine enamels, examples of thirteenth-century goldsmiths' work, as well as decorated crooks from bishops' croziers, rings, altar utensils, and fragments of vestments found in tombs within the cathedral. A group of seventeenth-century paintings includes a depiction of Christ bearing the Cross by the Spanish master Francisco de Zurbarán.

NONE OF THE OTHER CHURCHES IN THE CITY CAN remotely compare with the cathedral of Ste-Croix in importance. All that survived of the Late Gothic church of *St-Paul* after

The cathedral of Ste-Croix in Orléans.

the bombings in 1940 were its Italianate tower and the chapel of Notre-Dame-des-Miracles, both from 1627. The latter shelters a sixteenth-century Black Madonna. An older portrait of the Madonna, which was held to be miraculous as early as the fifth century and to which Joan of Arc commended herself, was burned by Huguenots in 1562. The Black Madonna is credited with the chapel's miraculous survival; though German bombs struck all around it, the chapel remained undamaged.

St-Donatus, the parish church for the ancient quartier du Châtelet, and *St-Euvert*, on the eastern edge of the old city, were medieval foundations. Both were destroyed during the wars of the fifteenth and sixteenth centuries and were rebuilt in different forms.

St-Pierre-le-Puellier, which essentially dates from the twelfth century, has been secularized. *St-Aignan*, a former monastery church, commemorates the bishop of Or-léans who saved the city from Attila and the Huns in 451. Robert le Pieux built a church above the saint's tomb in 1029, and the crypt of that structure, most of which dates from the ninth century, has survived. Excavations have brought to light some remarkable capitals. The present church is a creation in the Flamboyant style from the period right after the liberation of Orléans by Joan of Arc in 1429. Its Romanesque predecessor had been destroyed during the Hundred Years' War because it stood outside the city walls and could have served the English as a siege tower. In 1567, Calvinists tore down the nave of the newer church, so that only its transept and choir—with wreath of chapels—were left standing.

The collegiate church of *St-Avit* was destroyed in 1428, but its crypt from the period around 1000 survives beneath the Lycée Jeanne-d'Arc on the Rue Dupanloup.

The number of notable secular buildings

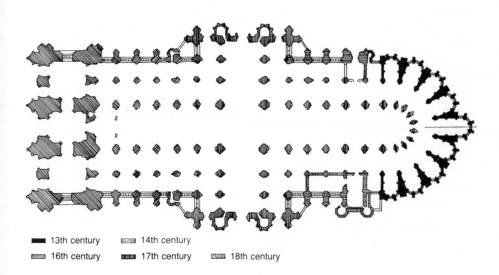

| ■■■ 13th century | ▦ 14th century | |
| ▨ 16th century | ▦ 17th century | ▧ 18th century |

Floor plan of the cathedral in Orléans.

CATHEDRAL · ❖ · of Ste CROIX · ❖ · ORLEANS

likewise is no longer large. The *Hôtel de Ville*, near the cathedral, was originally the palace of the bailiff of Orléans, Jacques Groslot. Built in 1530, it still displays Late Gothic building conventions in its lively alternation of brick and stone and in its stone mullions. A grand flight of steps leads to lovely Renaissance portals. The building was remodeled considerably in the nineteenth century, when the side wings were added. At that time, the staircase was also changed to accommodate a statue of Joan of Arc, a bronze copy of a marble sculpture at Versailles created by Princess Marie d'Orléans. Her father, Louis-Philippe, presented this replica to the city. In the garden behind the Hôtel de Ville the remains of the Chapelle St-Jacques have been set up. They date from the end of the fifteenth century.

The *Musée des Beaux-Arts* is one of the finest provincial museums in France, with important collections of French and foreign paintings, sculptures, and works on paper. It is housed in a recently constructed building near the cathedral and the Hôtel de Ville, and its architecture combines functional interior exhibition spaces with a traditional Orléanais exterior. Many of the works in the collection were acquired from châteaux, churches, and religious communities in the province, among them the famous Château de Richelieu. Masterpieces from Richelieu include eight canvases from the late sixteenth century by Martin Freminet depicting the four Evangelists and the four Fathers of the Church. A cycle of paintings, *The Four Elements*, executed by Claude Deruet, is also from Richelieu. Other important works are Philippe de Champaigne's seventeenth-century portrait, *St. Charles Borromeo*, and, from the eighteenth century, François Boucher's *Dovecote*, Claude Vignon's *Triumph of St. Ignatius*, and Hubert Robert's *Landscape with Ruined Tower*. A magnificent portrait of Madame de Pompadour from 1763 is by François Hubert Drouais. Works by Louis LeNain, Frans Pourbus the Younger, and others are also exhibited.

From the nineteenth century are important neoclassical works by Gérard, Girodet, and Gros, and romantic paintings by Chassériau, Dehordencq, and Eugène Devéria. Early nineteenth-century landscapes by Charles Daubigny and Gustave Courbet are in the collection, as are symbolist compositions from the latter part of the century. Paul Gauguin, native of Orléans, is represented by two canvases, *The Edge of the Forest* (1873) and *A Festival* (1888). The museum also includes a good collection of twentieth-century works by Maurice Denis, Marcel Gromaire, Chaim Soutine, Franz Kupka, and a group of sculptures by Max Jacob.

The collection features canvases by Italian masters Tintoretto, Correggio, the Carracci, and others, as well as paintings by Dutch artists Willem van de Velde and Jan van Goyen. A masterpiece by Velázquez, one of the collection's treasures, represents St. Thomas.

French sculptures from the eighteenth and nineteenth centuries include works by Jean-Antoine Houdon, Jean-Baptiste Pigalle, Claude-Michel Clodion, David d'Angers, Jean-Baptiste Carpeaux, and Antoine-Louis Barye. Twentieth-century works by Auguste Rodin, Antoine Bourdelle, and Aristide Maillol are also exhibited. In addition, the museum has an excellent collection of drawings, prints, and pastels, among them over 1,000 drawings by the early twentieth-century sculptor Gaudier-Brzeska.

A long-unused cemetery to the north of the cathedral was surrounded by a pointed-arch gallery (ca. 1500).

The former seventeenth-century bishop's palace on the Rue Dupanloup is now the *Bibliothèque Municipale*. From its garden, which is still bounded by a portion of the Gallo-Roman city wall, there is a splendid view of the nearby choir of the cathedral.

The once-famous university did not survive the Revolution. The only part of it still standing is the fifteenth-century *Salle des Thèses* (library), with a two-aisle, vaulted hall on the Rue de Bourgogne. The Préfecture across from it is housed in a former Benedictine monastery from the seventeenth century.

Two important Renaissance buildings are notable. The *Hôtel des Créneaux* consists of a fifteenth-century portion with bell tower, on the Place de la République, and an early sixteenth-century wing with a uniform façade, facing the Rue Ste-Catherine. The *Hôtel Cabu*, dating from around 1550, stands on the opposite side of the Rue Ste-Catherine. With the exception of its elegant façade, the entire structure was destroyed during the war. It has been rebuilt as the *Musée Historique*.

One of the loveliest Renaissance structures in the Orléanais is the *Hôtel Toutin* on the Rue Notre-Dame-de-Recouvrance. It was completed in 1540, and the arcaded gallery around its inner courtyard deserves a visit. Also worthy of mention are the Renaissance structures on the Place du Châtelet, near the river, and the sixteenth-century *Maison de la Coquille*, on nearby Rue de Pierre-Percée, so named for the large shell in the decor of its façade.

CLÉRY-ST-ANDRE

THE COLLEGIATE CHURCH OF NOTRE-DAME-DE-*Cléry*, one of France's most important sacred buildings in the Flamboyant style, towers like a cathedral above the low houses of the village of Cléry-St-André. A thirteenth-century pilgrimage church consecrated to the Virgin was destroyed by the English in 1428. Charles VII and Jean, comte de Dunois (known as the Bastard of Orléans) and comrade-in-arms of Joan of Arc, began rebuilding it in 1449. Louis XI, a great votary of the Madonna, continued the construction; as dauphin, in 1443, he had vowed to do so if he prevailed against the English—as he did—at the siege of Dieppe.

As king, he showed his favor to the church and its canons. Each time he was faced with a difficult decision, he would come to Notre-Dame-de-Cléry to pray to the Madonna. To design his tomb for the church, he commissioned the greatest painter and the most important sculptor in the realm: Jean Fouquet and Michel Colombe. He was buried here in 1483.

The church is a basilica with seven bays, a nonprojecting transept, and a two-bay choir with a slightly more than semicircular apse and ambulatory. A tower from the earlier church on the north side of the present structure dates from the early four-

The tomb of Louis XI.

teenth century, having been spared from destruction by the English. Beginning in 1449, the church's architects were Pierre Chauvin, who was in the service of the duc d'Orléans, and Pierre Le Paige, who took over in around 1460 and brought the structure to completion in 1485.

The interior is almost 260 feet long and 89 feet high. It is imposing because of the weightlessness of its elevation and the harmony of its pointed-arch arcades, moldings, and half columns, which fan out into the ribs of its vaulting. The pointed windows, with their Flamboyant tracery, all of which have lost their original stained glass except for the central window of the choir, admit an excess of light into the space. The wall surfaces above the arcades of the nave probably were decorated with wall tapestries.

AN IMPORTANT FIXTURE IS THE TOMB OF LOUIS XI, beneath the easternmost arcade on the north side of the nave. It was placed on a diagonal so that the life-size figure of the king faces the altar of the Virgin, with its miracle-working image, in front of a choir screen. Surrounded by four *putti* with cartouches, the king kneels on a marble slab and prays to the Madonna. "I felt that he has the appearance of a knave," La Fontaine, author of the *Fables*, wrote, "and in fact that is probably what he was."[2] It is the work of the sculptor Bourdin and was executed in 1622. It replaces the original bronze statue commissioned by the king, which was destroyed by Huguenots in 1562.

The remains of Louis XI and his wife, Charlotte de Savoie, which were also desecrated by Huguenots, lie in a vault near the tomb. Tanguy de Châtel is buried in an adjacent tomb. He was hit by a cannonball during the siege of Bouchain in 1477,

while trying to watch the artillery fire with Louis XI, who was leaning on him for support. His dying wish was to be buried before an image of the Virgin. The king rewarded Tanguy's loyalty by choosing as his resting place a spot next to his own. A slab on the south side of the nave protects the heart of Charles VIII, who completed the rebuilding of the church.

An oak statue of the Madonna enthroned with the Christ Child on her lap stands on the nineteenth-century high altar. Its age is a matter of debate. Some argue that it is a twelfth-century sculpture discovered, according to tradition, by a farmer working his fields in 1280. Others maintain it is a reproduction created after the devastation of the Religious Wars. In any event, all of France's kings from Philippe IV le Bel to Louis XIV paid homage to this miracle-working image and prayed before it.

The richly carved choir stalls were a gift from Henri II and are decorated with grotesques and with the initials of Henri and his mistress, Diane de Poitiers. The central choir window dates from the reign of Henri III; the upper part depicts the miracle of the Pentecost, while below is Henri III, surrounded by the Evangelists, establishing the Order of the Holy Ghost.

The church originally had ten chapels, but only a few survive. The three-bay Chapelle du Dunois, on the south side of the nave, has splendid tracery windows; it contains the tomb of Dunois (died 1468) and various members of his family. Dunois had commissioned Simon du Val to build the chapel in 1463. The buttress supporting the nave, which had to be accommodated in the new space, forced the architect to run the peak of the vaulting in a zigzag line.

Even more elaborate is the two-bay Chapelle St-Jacques, which was built between

1515 and 1518 by the dean of the church, Gilles de Pontbriand, and his brother François, chief steward to François I. The two are buried here. They had the room roofed with lavish vaulting that outlines panels adorned with stucco reliefs. Pilgrims' staves with beggars' sacks and flagella in combination with ermine spots, the heraldic device of Anne de Bretagne, appear in alternate fields. The staffs recall that the chapel was the first station for pilgrims from Orléans on their way to the shrine of Santiago de Compostela in Spain. The keystones display the alliance coat of arms of France and Brittany and that of the Pontbriand family. Motifs from these coats of arms, including the bridge as the key symbol of the Pontbriands, adorn the walls and carry the decorative variety of the vaulting into the lower portion of the room. Additional ornament is provided by the sculptured canopies above the tomb niches. Several of the sculptures in the chapel are worthy of notice: St. James, the patron saint of pilgrims (wood, sixteenth century); St. Sebastian (wood, seventeenth century); and the Virgin Mary (stone, sixteenth century).

The loveliest portal in the church is the one leading into the sacristy, which was also at one time a tomb chapel. The vegetal forms ornamenting this doorway are the type of richly stylized decorations that inspired Art Nouveau in the late nineteenth century. A window opening above the portal discloses the oratory of Louis XI, where he could take part in the Mass without being seen by the congregation.

BEAUGENCY

BEAUGENCY IS A CHARMING, QUIET LITTLE TOWN. Little time is required for a tour of its architectural monuments. Most of them line the Place de St-Firmin, which preserves the name of a sixteenth-century church destroyed during the Revolution. Only the tower of that structure survives, and it dominates the square. A statue of Joan of Arc commemorates her liberation of the city in 1429. The blocklike keep built in the late eleventh century by the barons of Landry towers above the town's low houses; known as the *Tour de César*, it is one of the most beautiful examples of medieval fortress architecture in France. Slender vertical shafts of projecting masonry break up its tall expanse of wall. Its top and interior have been destroyed.

The neighboring *château*, with portions dating from the fourteenth and fifteenth centuries, was acquired in 1442 by Jean, comte de Dunois. He added the three-story wing that now houses the *Musée Dunois*. Collections of local costumes, headdresses, waistcoats, and numerous examples of Orléanais furniture are presented in the château's many rooms, which have been set up as period rooms. Its sole decorative touch is the polygonal stair tower that was constructed by one of Dunois's descendants, Jean II de Longueville.

The church of *Notre-Dame*, across from the château, dates from the first half of the twelfth century. It was formerly part of an Augustinian abbey. Its interior is one of the most impressive of its kind in the Orléan-

Beaugency

ais, although wooden vaulting installed in the seventeenth century is much too low and compromises its effect. Short, massive columns mark off the five-bay basilica nave, which opens into a nonprojecting transept and two-bay choir with semicircular apse, ambulatory, and three chapels. The rounded wall of the choir is supported by more slender columns with lancet arches, above which is a band of paired blind arcades that continues as an open triforium along the choir bays.

Notre-Dame was the setting for the Council of Beaugency of 1152, which annulled the marriage of Louis VII and Eleanor of Aquitaine. Forty bishops were assembled in the newly built structure, with the archbishop of Bordeaux presiding as the pope's representative. Eleanor then married Henri Plantagenet, comte d'Anjou and later Henry II of England. To that marriage she brought great portions of the Crown fiefs of France, and thus sowed the seeds for the Hundred Years' War.

One twelfth-century house still stands on the Rue du Points-de-l'Ange. Known as the *Maison des Templiers*, it has on its second story arcaded windows in the Romanesque style. The most ornate secular structure in the town is the *Hôtel de Ville*, built by Charles Viart in 1526. Its façade, restored in the nineteenth century, includes a whole repertory of Renaissance decoration. Its council chamber boasts lovely seventeenth-century embroidered panels, four of which depict pagan sacrifices, and four others the continents, which once were in the abbey of Notre-Dame. The thirteenth-century *Tour de l'Horloge* and gateway near the Hôtel de Ville is a remnant of the town's medieval fortifications.

THROUGH BLESOIS

TALCY

IN *LE CHÂTEAU DE TALCY*, JACQUES HOULET RE-marks that Talcy is the least imposing châ-teau of the Loire, but the most affecting.[3] Whether standing in its courtyard or pok-ing about in its rooms and outbuildings, one has the impression that its inhabitants have just left, so completely has everything been preserved. No restorer has covered over the signs of wear. None of the pieces of furniture seems merely arranged as though in a museum, as in most of the oth-er unoccupied Loire châteaux. Nowhere else is it possible to form a clearer picture of manorial life in earlier centuries.

The château, which stands at quite a dis-tance from the river in the fertile Beauce, and is situated on the village's main street with the rest of the houses, was given its present form by a Florentine financier, Ber-nardo Salviati. A cousin of Catherine de Mé-dicis, he had settled in France and was in the service of François I. In 1517, he bought the property, which has a history traceable to the thirteenth century, and re-ceived permission to provide the château with the "walls, towers, battlements, em-brasures, drawbridges, outworks, ramparts, and other defensive features" of a fortified residence. But he exercised his rights to only a modest degree. Except for the five embrasures of a wall-walk and a row of decorative machicolation, the "defensive features" of the façade are not noticeable.

Salviati's oldest daughter, Cassandre, has assumed a place in the history of French lit-erature thanks to her romance with the poet Ronsard. The two met at a ball in the Château de Blois, and Ronsard proceeded to praise her beauty in countless poems.

Over the centuries, the château had many owners, all of whom endeavored to preserve the character of the structure as stamped by Salviati. Well into advanced age its last owner, Mademoiselle Valentine Stapfer, guarded its store of furnishings, carpets, and household effects like a na-tional treasure. After her death her heirs sold the entire estate to the government, making it clear in the contract that the in-ventoried furnishings were never to be removed.

It is astonishing that Salviati, although

Italian, modeled a totally French country château in the traditional style; it does not display the slightest traces of the architectural forms of the Italian Renaissance, which in the early sixteenth century represented to the French nobility the very height of elegance.

THE COURTYARD OF THE CHÂTEAU IS ENTERED through a massive fifteenth-century keep with polygonal corner turrets and a wall-walk that was added by Salviati after 1520. This battlement was left unfinished on the stair tower facing the courtyard. The south and east wings of the château—both from the sixteenth century—form two sides of the courtyard, which resembles that of a large estate. The flat-arch arcades of a gallery open the ground floor of the south wing, next to the keep, and the gables above visually bracket the arcades in pairs. The east wing is comparatively plain. But the round well in the courtyard, with its charming slate cupola resting on three columns, and Cassandre's rosebush, a carefully tended symbol of her relationship with Ronsard, draw one's gaze away from the sober wall surface. A round basin next to the well served as a reservoir. The west side of the courtyard originally was closed off by another wing, which burned down (along with a corner tower of the keep) in the sixteenth century.

The rooms of the château are more stately than luxurious. The first of special interest is the garden salon, a rustic room with a beamed ceiling and a mantelpiece on which traces of old painting have been found. Completely preserved from the time of the Salviatis is the vaulted kitchen, with a flat-arch fireplace and bake oven complete with mechanized spit for roasting joints of meat. It also boasts a meat cooler.

Among the various bedrooms furnished with canopy beds are the chambers in which, according to tradition, Charles IX and his mother, Catherine de Médicis, once slept. These rooms, however, are furnished in part with pieces that date from the seventeenth and eighteenth centuries. It is true that Catherine de Médicis and her son visited Talcy, probably on many occasions. At least one visit was political: Jean Salviati, Catherine's cousin and friend, arranged a diplomatic meeting at the château in 1562 between them (Charles IX being at that time only a nine-year-old boy) and the prince de Condé, the Calvinist leader.

A door near the head of the bed in Catherine de Médicis's room leads directly into the chapel of the château, which now serves as parish church for the village. Structurally, the church is integrated into the château's east wing.

Two exceptional rooms are the dining room and the Grand Salon, both furnished in the eighteenth century. The dining-room floor is composed of white octagonal tiles and smaller black square ones. The room's woodwork, beamed ceiling, and furnishings—all original—are also white. In striking contrast is the linen wallcovering, with a painted pattern of red, blue, and white Indian liana blossoms against a turquoise background. A copper lavabo still hangs on the wall, and there is a cooling vessel that can be filled with ice. One could scarcely hope for a more impressive glimpse into the cultivated dining quarters of eighteenth-century château life.

The Grand Salon occupies the entire second floor of the keep. The customary beamed ceiling lends a rustic character to the room, while the elegance of the space derives from its furnishings. The tile floor is covered with a huge Savonnerie carpet, the wall panels between wooden moldings are hung with Aubusson tapestries depicting scenes from mythology—the death of Eurydice, Venus and Adonis, Zephyr and Flora, the birth of Bacchus—and a black and gold lacquer commode serves as a special focal point. But most astonishing is the number of exquisite chairs and sofas, all of which are covered in red satin, grouped around three gaming tables. Almost all of the popular eighteenth-century seating types are represented: two *canapés* (sofas), a *bergère* (easy chair), eight *fauteuils à la Reine* (armchairs), four cabriole-leg chairs, and two side chairs, all bearing the signature of the leading Parisian furniture maker, Jean-Baptiste Lebas. The gaming tables—one triangular, one square, one expandable—betray the salon's function.

Behind the wall next to the gate of the kitchen courtyard, with its stand of nut trees, is a horse pond through which the animals were driven to clean the mud from their hooves. In one of the barns is a fully functional seventeenth-century wine press. The courtyard's most striking structure is a cylindrical sixteenth-century dovecote. Very few structures of this type still exist. Symbols of the aristocracy, most were destroyed during the Revolution, for since the Middle Ages only feudal lords had been privileged to maintain dovecotes of this kind. From the outside, it appears almost completely closed, but inside its thick wall are well over 1,000 nesting places; it is possible to reach the tasty birds by means of ladders attached to a turning device.

The entire complex of the Château de Talcy is aligned along a single axis. It approaches the keep from the south as an *allée*, crosses the courtyards as a cobbled carriageway and, after leaving the kitchen courtyard, bisects a stately park and garden area. A wrought-iron gate opens into a wood planted with regular rows of trees. Beyond this, a semicircular staircase leads to the garden. (This is a vegetable garden and orchard as well as a pleasure garden.) To the north, the garden is bounded by a forest with cleared lanes that radiate into the Beauce.

MÉNARS

THE BEST VIEW OF THE CHÂTEAU DE MÉNARS, ONE of the few Baroque châteaux along the Loire, is from the opposite bank of the river. The château is excellently suited to its site. It is a play of horizontals: the river, the stepped terraces of the garden, the double flight of steps, the two rows of windows, and the expansive slate roofs. Equally delightful is the view from the château's terrace, across the upper garden parterre and the Loire toward the forest park of the Château de Chambord in the distance.

The most famous owner of the château was the marquise de Pompadour, mistress of Louis XV. Although of middle-class origin, she managed to become, thanks to her twin merits of beauty and intellect, a powerful force at Versailles. The king referred to her as the most enchanting woman in France. For almost twenty years, she proved indispensable to him, for no one at court was as clever as she at inventing delights with which to stave off his boredom. In her passion for the fine arts and architecture, she exerted a marked influence on the entire *style Louis XV*. She bought châteaux, beautified them, and sold them a short time later. In 1760, she acquired the estate and château at Ménars, which had been built after 1637 by Guillaume Charron and later enlarged and surrounded with splendid gardens by his nephew Jean-Jacques. Madame de Pompadour hoped to find in it a peaceful setting for her retirement, for although she was only thirty-nine, her health was failing and she could see that the king's loyalty to her was waning.

She commissioned Jacques-Ange Gabriel, the king's foremost architect, to redesign the château and furnish it with all the latest comforts. Gabriel, creator of the Place de la Concorde in Paris and the Petit Trianon at Versailles, tore down the château's two unequal outer wings and replaced them with ones better suited to the proportions of the central structure. He also created the single-story buildings along the main courtyard; they visually set off the two-story main building and screen small housekeeping courtyards on either side. The building along the east side was the *conciergerie*; the one to the west still houses the kitchens, which are connected to the château by an underground passage. The corners and windows of the original château had been set off with cut stone in contrast to the stucco wall surfaces. Gabriel used the same picturesque style for the new buildings.

Madame de Pompadour was the envy of the court for her elegant taste in decorating apartments. At Ménars she took great care in her planning. Today, the woodwork, the lintels above the doors, the mirror frames, and the marble fireplaces in some of the rooms—all exquisitely reserved in their ornamentation as an anti-

dote to the playfulness of the Rococo—suggest the marquise's unerring sense of form.

The rooms on the ground floor are entered from the vestibule in the center of the main wing. The vestibule also served as a dining room and originally opened onto both the garden and the courtyard. The walls of the adjacent Grand Salon were covered with tapestries embroidered with garlands of flowers against a red background. Among the floor's other rooms decorated by Madame de Pompadour were a reception room, a bedroom with a bed *en impérial*, a dressing room, a boudoir, and a study. In the boudoir, she kept her lovely collection of porcelain: five Chinese vases mounted on gilded copper stands and eighty-eight smaller pieces of Chinese porcelain. None of her collection is preserved in the room today.

Madame de Pompadour was granted only four years in which to enjoy her peaceful place in the country. A contemporary of hers, Dufort de Cheverny, remarks in his memoirs that every three months she made a great display of journeying to Ménars, where she spent huge sums of money. Although despised in Paris, here she was beloved by her subjects because of her generosity. In February 1764, the marquise contracted an inflammation of the lungs, and she died at Versailles on April 15.

She left Ménars to her brother Abel Poisson, marquis de Marigny who, thanks to his sister's influence, had risen to the post of superintendent of Louis XV's palaces. He continued the work on the château that had been interrupted by his sister's death, completing it and adding a few more improvements. He widened the main wing by erecting a one-story, flat-roofed pavilion on the courtyard side and replaced the already decaying flat roofs *à l'italienne* on the outer wings with the present ones *à la française.*

The new architect was the builder of the Panthéon in Paris, Jacques-Germain Soufflot, with whom the marquis was closely acquainted. Soufflot built the Orangerie and the adjacent Temple d'Amour, a round structure crowned by a cupola, with short extensions on either side, embossed columns, and pilasters. In its rotunda, Marigny placed a statue of Abundantia, for which Madame de Pompadour is supposed to have served as a model. The original statue gave way to one of Louis XV, which was in turn replaced by the present one of Venus. A copy of the Abundantia adorns the center of the garden parterre, one of Marigny's additions. Contemporary engravings show that Madame de Pompadour's ornamental garden lay somewhat lower than the present-day one. Simple stepped hedges led down to the Loire. Marigny designed a more imposing descent to the river by means of symmetrical ramps. The marquis also provided a large number of garden sculptures, but the busts of Roman emperors along the garden façade of the château are practically all that remain at Ménars. Two sphinxes on the ramp walls next to the river are amusing in that they pay homage to current feminine fashion. They are also said to bear the facial features of Madame de Pompadour and her rival, Madame du Barry.

One of the park's most private areas is the elongated pond surrounded by trees near the riverbank, commonly known as the *Bain de Madame de Pompadour.* On its uphill side, Soufflot created a masterful little piece of architecture in 1771: a vaulted grotto for a spring, with a round arch and two rectangular passages opening onto the pool. In his design of the façade, with its severe geometric lines, Soufflot was clearly influenced by the Italian architect Andrea Palladio.

Marigny redesigned another part of the park, the *bois bas,* in the *chinois* style just then becoming fashionable.

Nowhere along the Loire is there a more splendid tree-lined *allée* than the so-called stepped *allée* leading from the château's east side. Madame de Pompadour planned it as a drive lined with linden trees in place of an earlier one planted with elms, and she oversaw the beginning of its construction. (It was completed by her brother.) The row of lindens runs along the bank of the Loire for more than half a mile, interrupted in the middle by the belvedere. All along the *allée* are views over the river as far as Chambord.

The marquis de Marigny lived at Ménars chiefly in the summer and spent the winter in his palace in Paris. He estimated that he and his sister had spent a total of 5.3 million livres on the château, and he boasted of owning "one of the loveliest estates in the kingdom." A contemporary visitor confirmed that

it would fill an entire volume if one wished to describe all the riches of this enchanting residence. Everything that art and nature have to offer is combined in this one paradisiacal spot. It took us four hours just to tour its unique apartments. Paintings by the greatest masters, sculptures of marble and bronze, antique vases, rare books, agate, porphyry, porcelain—all of this has been assembled here.[4]

After the marquis's death in 1781, the splendor of Ménars rapidly paled. His heirs quarreled, and furnishings and art treasures had to be sold to pay the pensions established by Madame de Pompadour in her will. Most of the sculptures that Marigny had placed in the gardens were not sold until the late nineteenth century; the most valuable were bought by members of the Rothschild family. Since 1939, the château has belonged to the Manufacture des Glaces et Produits chimiques de St-Gobain, Chauny et Cirey, better known as the Compagnie de St-Gobain, which uses it as a conference center and pays for its upkeep. This corporation is the successor to the Manufacture des Glaces, from which Gabriel ordered the mirrors and windowpanes for the château on behalf of Madame de Pompadour.

The park at Ménars is surrounded by a wall almost 10 miles long, and is bisected by highway N152. This road also originates with Madame de Pompadour, who had it constructed so that she could reach the estate more conveniently from Orléans. The marquis de Marigny extended the road as far as Blois.

BLOIS

BLOIS IS A ROYAL CITY, AND ITS HISTORY IS CLOSE-ly linked to that of its *château*. The changes in French architecture from the time of Louis IX (St. Louis) to that of Louis XIII are apparent in this structure. Built on a rise between the valleys of the Loire and the Arrou, the château dominates the city. It surrounds an irregular quadrilateral courtyard and fronts the Place du Château, once the castle's fortified forecourt.

Facing this square is the brick Louis XII Wing, with its ornate decoration in stone, and the Salle des Etats abutting it on the northwest side. The outwardly unimposing Salle des Etats is the oldest part of the château, built in the thirteenth century by the counts of Blois. After the last of that line, Guy de Châtillon, was predeceased by his sole son and heir in 1391, he sold the powerful countship to Louis d'Orléans, the brother of Charles VI. This prince's older son, Charles d'Orléans, became—at the age of seventy-one—the father of a son who was crowned king as Louis XII in 1498; he chose Blois, the town in which he had been born, as his residence.

Louis XII immediately set about remodeling the old château. In around 1500, he built the L-shaped two-story wing that bears his name. Nothing could better attest to his good taste than this architecture, with its balanced proportions, its wealth of ornamental details in Late Gothic forms, and its lively contrast of materials. All the splendor of its decoration is concentrated on the round-arch portal leading into the courtyards, above which in a Flamboyant niche is a life-size statue of the king on horseback. Unfortunately, the original of this statue was destroyed during the Revolution. It was replaced in 1856 by the present one, which does not altogether resemble the original as seen in old engravings. Also new is the crowned porcupine, the symbol of the king, between the initials—*L* for Louis and *A* for Anne de Bretagne, whom he married in 1499—below the niche. The royal initials and coats of

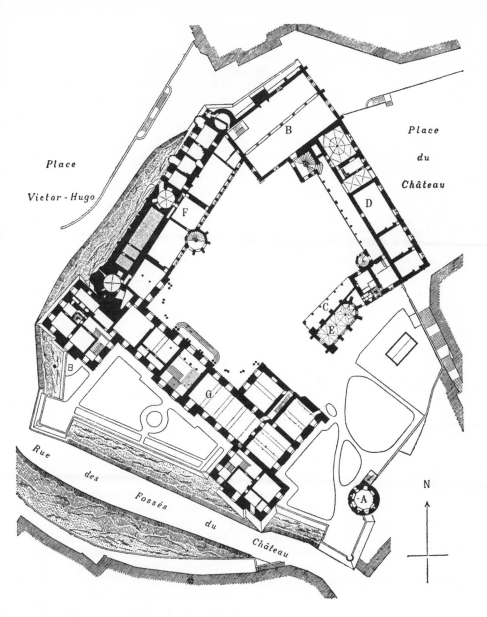

Floor plan of the château at Blois (after Lesueur)
A Tour du Foix. B Salle des Etats. C Gallery. D Louis XII wing. E Chapelle de St-Calais.
F François I wing. G Gaston d'Orléans wing.

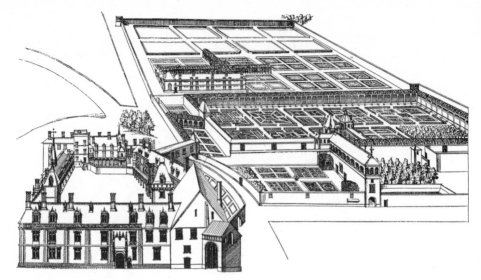

View of the château and gardens at Blois, after Du Cerceau.

arms may also be seen in the gables of the dormers, and the porcupine crowns the pedestrian passage next to the carriageway.

Two dissimilar stair towers flank the courtyard façade of the Louis XII Wing. This side is open on the ground floor, with an arcade of flat arches that continues as a gallery on the southeast side, also built by Louis XII, along the Chapelle de St-Calais. While the outer façade seems forbiddingly imposing in its refinement, the courtyard side has a homey look. It, too, was executed in the Late Gothic style, yet it conveys traces of the Italian *grandezza* that Louis XII had become acquainted with on his campaigns in Italy. Unmistakable borrowings from Italy are the arabesques on the panels of the arcade pillars and the *putti*, dolphins, eagles, masks, cornucopias, and plant forms that decorate the capitals.

Almost nothing survives in the interior of this wing from the time of Louis XII. Contemporary sources relate that the dominant furnishings were wall tapestries. The second floor of the Louis XII Wing houses the *Musée des Beaux-Arts*, a collection notable for its sixteenth- and seventeenth-century French paintings and for an admirable group of portraits. A work by the Flemish master Peter Paul Rubens represents Marie de Médicis as France. Eighteenth-century portraits by Pierre Mignard include elegant depictions of Gaston d'Orléans and Anne of Austria, and an imposing representation of Louis XIV. The château also houses the small *Musée Archéologique* (ground floor of the François I Wing), with objects from the Gallo-Roman period that have recently been excavated at Blois.

The Chapelle de St-Calais also dates to the reign of Louis XII. It was consecrated in 1508. It originally had a nave and an only slightly shorter, narrower choir. The choir, heavily restored in the nineteenth century, is all that survives. The nave was torn down in the seventeenth century to make room for the Gaston d'Orléans Wing of the château.

One could scarcely imagine a richer contrast than that between the Louis XII Wing and the wing built by his successor, François I, to the northwest. Yet the interval between their building was a mere fifteen years. While the former holds to traditional forms and experiments with new elements only hesitantly, the latter is a full-blown Renaissance structure. Inspired by Italian models, to be sure, it shows an independent development in its ornamental forms.

François I acceded to the throne as a twenty-one-year old in 1515. He was married to Claude de France, a daughter of Louis XII (the Reine Claude, a variety of plum, was named after her). She had inherited Blois, and immediately after his father-in-law's death, François began the construction of the northwest wing, for he wished to make Blois into a commanding residence to be used in alternation with the Château d'Amboise. Some of the invoices through 1518 are extant, and they document the rapid progress of his undertaking. The work must have been completed at the latest by 1525, for in that year François I set off for Italy and was captured near Pavia, leaving no more money for building in the royal coffers. The sculptures on the building's pilasters were left unfinished, and the niches were left empty of statues.

The king's architect may have been the Italian Domenico da Cortona, who had worked for Charles VIII and is known to have been living in Blois at the time the wing was built. But this attribution is a matter of debate. The documents do tell us that the master mason was Jacques Sourdeau, who also worked at Amboise and Chambord.

The three-story François I Wing is not a wholly new creation, but incorporates pieces of earlier buildings. A thick wall extending to the roof divides the wide suites of rooms on the courtyard side from the narrower ones facing the city. This wall was originally the medieval ring wall guarding the castle of the counts of Blois, and was strengthened with semicircular defense towers that are still visible in the ground plan. Two suites had been built up against the inner side of the ring wall, and

Louis XII

Blois

François I merely had them joined and unified by means of a new courtyard façade and his famous octagonal stair tower. Even before the work was completed, it became obvious that with its width of only one room, the structure would be unimposing; thus it was decided to place a second line of rooms with a new façade outside the ring wall. With this second suite, the château no longer had the look of a fortress. The many loggias of the exterior façade provided a view of the garden terraces laid out during the reign of Louis XII.

This outer façade is surprisingly asymmetrical, with no apparent logic to either the arrangement of the loggias or the rhythm of the single or paired pilasters. With its bays of different width, clearly determined by the disposition of the interior, the façade extends outward from a medieval round tower sheathed in galleries, and then abruptly breaks off. The loggias are simply deep window embrasures, and do not connect with one another. Here and there, as accents lending vitality to the overall design, a corbeled balcony or the apse of a chapel juts out. There also is a wealth of sculptural embellishment, including the royal emblems. In *Journey*, La Fontaine described his impression of the façade: "The part François I built, if looked at from the outside, pleased me better than all the rest; there I saw numbers of little galleries, little windows, little balconies, little ornamentations: without order or regularity, and they made up a grand whole which I liked."

With its clear division by pilasters, the courtyard façade appears at first glance to be more uniform than the exterior façade. But the windows were placed, not according to a strict exterior design, but to conform with the room arrangement. They are sometimes close together, sometimes farther apart, producing an uneven visual rhythm. The façade is also broken by the magnificent pierced stair tower. For Balzac in *Catherine de Médicis* it is

a moorish caprice, designed by giants, made by dwarfs, which gives to this wonderful façade the effect of a dream. The baluster of this staircase forms a spiral connecting itself by a square landing to five of the six sides of the tower, requiring at each landing transversal corbels which are decorated with arabesque carvings within and without; this bewildering creation of ingenious and delicate details, of marvels which give speech to stones, can be compared only to the deeply worked and crowded carving of the chinese ivories. Stone is made to look like lace-work. The flowers, the figures of the men and animals clinging to the structure of the stairway, are multiplied step by step. On the keystone the chisels of the artists of the 16th century have contended against the naive cutters of images who fifty years earlier had carved the keystones of Louis XII's two stair-ways.

However dazzled we may be by thus viewing forms of indefatigable labor, we cannot fail to see that money was lacking to François I for Blois, as it was to Louis XIV for Versailles. For more than one figure lifts its delicate head from a block of rough stone behind it, more than one fantastic flower is merely indicated by chiseled touches on the abandoned stone, though dampness has since laid its blossoms of mouldy greenery upon it....

The richness of seigneurial garments, the luxury of female adornment, must have harmonised wonderfully with the lace-work of these stones so delightfully manipulated. From floor to floor as the king of France went up the marvelous stairs of his château of Blois, he could see the broad expanse of the beautiful Loire, which brought him news of all his kingdom. If instead of building Chambord in a barren lonely plain two leagues away François had built it where seventy years later Gaston built his palace, Versailles would never have existed, and Blois would have been necessarily the capital of France.[5]

Many portions of the façades and the staircase have been destroyed either wantonly or through weathering over the centuries. And much more was lost because of restoration attempts in the nineteenth century. The same can be said of the Louis XII Wing. Yet had it not been for these restorations, the architecture would have lost all its original radiance.

The ground floor, which preserves portions of the medieval complex, was doubtless given over to housekeeping and servants' quarters. The luxurious king's chambers were on the second and third stories.

It would be a mistake to expect to find here the movable furnishings originally adorning these rooms, for in the sixteenth century they were constantly packed up and taken along whenever the king changed his residence. All that survives is something of the fixed appointments. Moreover, Duban, the nineteenth-century restorer of the château, covered the walls and ceilings with colorful decorations of his own invention; they dress up the rooms magnificently, but have nothing to do with historical precedent. As a document of that era's concept of monument preservation,

Duban's style has undeniable value; but it did, to some extent, change the original disposition of the rooms.

The Grand Salon, on the second floor behind the stair tower, preserves two original ornate mantelpieces and the doorframes from the time of François I; they display splendid arabesques and the royal animal symbols. On the second floor, the best preserved room from that period is Catherine de Médicis's study. Its walls are completely covered with woodwork divided into 237 vertical panels, most of which contain arabesques of one kind or another. Portions were renovated in the nineteenth century, as were the coffered ceiling and the mantelpiece. Four panels cleverly hide secret cupboards, which could be opened by means of a pedal hidden in the baseboard. The idea that these are the cupboards in which Catherine de Médicis kept her poisons is only a popular fantasy. In a dramatic scene in Balzac's *Catherine de Médicis*, she hides secret papers in the cupboard, only to be caught in the act by her daughter-in-law, Mary Stuart, because she is unable to close the opened panel quickly enough. Next to the study is Catherine's oratory and the bedroom in which she died in 1589. She had thought herself safe at Blois, for her astrologer, Cosmo Ruggieri, had predicted that she would die at St-Germain.

The third floor was the apartment of Henri III, Catherine's third son. It was here that he had the powerful duc de Guise murdered in 1588. The château guides insist on painting this most sensational event in lurid colors, directing tourists to the actual spots where each dramatic scene occurred. But don't be fooled! The spaces have been altered since the sixteenth century, and historical sources tell us only that the duke was pitilessly cut down in the king's own chamber.

The most impressive room in the entire château is the Salle des Etats in the oldest part of the complex. It was here that the counts of Blois were accustomed to hold their audiences, give parties, receive honors, and administer justice. It was here that Henri III convoked the Estates General in 1576 and 1588, from which the room takes its name. Columns and pointed-arch arcades divide it into two aisles, each with wooden vaulting. The room was constructed in the early thirteenth century and restored in the nineteenth, at which time the much too theatrical wall painting was executed. Monumental seventeenth-century Gobelin tapestries, including various scenes from the life of Constantine the Great after cartoons by Rubens, hang on the walls.

The newest portion of the château is the wing on the southwest side of the courtyard. It was begun in 1635 by François Mansart, the architect to Louis XIII, on commission from the king's brother, Gaston d'Orléans. Gaston had been awarded the countship of Blois as an appanage and was heir presumptive to the throne. Mansart's design called for razing all the existing parts of the château and replacing them with a four-sided structure that would have been one of the most magnificent château complexes of French classicism. But when a successor—the later Louis XIV—was born to the king in 1638 and Gaston's chances of attaining the throne became remote, his building funds were withdrawn. Thus only those portions of the old château standing in the way of his new main wing were destroyed, among them a part of the François I Wing and the nave of the Chapelle de St-Calais.

The Gaston d'Orléans Wing has three floors, a central pavilion with short side wings facing the courtyard, and corner pavilions projecting from the exterior side. Its mansard roof helps to define its separate elements. Mansart was forced to adopt an asymmetrical design because of the terrain—clearly apparent in the ground plan—but he did succeed in creating symmetrical façades by utilizing the staircase in the central pavilion to mask the offset between the courtyard and exterior fronts. Both façades are delineated by pilasters, most of them in pairs and rising on each floor to increasing splendor through the classical Doric, Ionic, and Corinthian orders. This return to strictly classical forms distinguishes Mansart's style from that of the François I Wing, where such forms were imaginatively redefined. Moreover, Mansart was extremely sparing in his use of sculptural ornament. Curved colonnades with double columns, restored in the nineteenth century, fill the corners of the courtyard in an elegant manner. They also provide a third dimension to this side and tend to lead the eye to the main pavilion's central bay. The bay is highlighted by double columns, a triangular pediment, figures, a coat of arms, and trophies, and is crowned by a partially restored bust of Gaston d'Orléans.

The interior remained unfinished and unoccupied until the nineteenth century; it now houses the Bibliothèque Municipale. Gaston d'Orléans managed to see only the nearly completed stucco work in the stairwell of the central pavilion before he died in 1660 in the François I Wing. The staircase was not constructed until 1932, following Mansart's plans.

FROM THE TOUR DU FOIX, A REMNANT OF THE château's medieval fortifications, is a lovely view of the church of *St-Nicolas*, the former Benedictine abbey church of St-Laumer, which looms above the

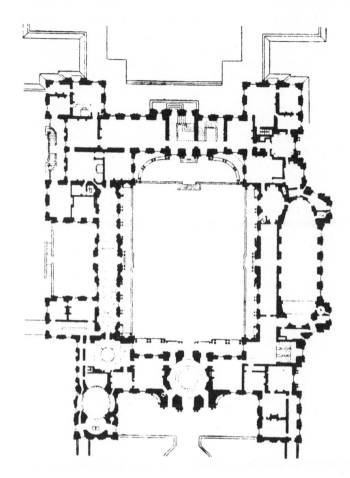

François Mansart's floor plan for the Gaston D'Orleans Wing.

surrounding houses. This is a four-bay basilica with twin towers on its façade, a transept, and a two-aisle ambulatory choir complete with chapels. The monks erected the choir, transept, and first bay of the nave between 1138 and 1186. The adjoining western sections were built at the beginning of the thirteenth century; the central chapel off the choir, in the fourteenth century. The massive pillars and half-columns in the nave already reveal Chartres's influence. In the choir, beautifully carved historiated capitals decorate the columns. An altarpiece by an anonymous fifteenth-century painter hangs in the church. The monastery buildings, from the seventeenth and

73

eighteenth centuries (the originals were destroyed by Huguenots), have served as a hospital since the Revolution.

A showy entrance façade with pilasters and volutes—as though deliberately balancing the François I Wing across from it—adorns the church of *St-Vincent-de-Paul* on the Place Victor-Hugo, erected by the Jesuits in the mid-seventeenth century.

The gardens of Louis XII, created by the Neapolitan priest Pacello da Mercogliano, once extended up the slope to the south of the church as far as the present-day train station. They were laid out on three terraces and divided into rectangular beds with richly ornamental designs. Beds of this type can be seen today only at the Château de Villandry. The *Pavillon d'Anne de Bretagne* is one of the structures in the garden that has survived. According to the engraving by Du Cerceau this summerhouse connected the lower Jardin de Bretonnerie and the main ornamental garden, the Jardin de la Reine. To construct the vine-covered wooden gallery that surrounds it the king summoned the best joiners in the realm. The pavilion itself, one of the queen's favorite structures, was built of brick and stone like the Louis XII Wing of the château and may well date from the same period, around 1500. Short terrace wings extend like the arms of a cross on either side of the octagonal central part, with its steep slate roof. One of the wings was expanded into a chapel, where Louis XII was accustomed to pray. The pavilion now serves as the city's tourist office. The gardens fell into ruin at the end of the seventeenth century.

Not many extant secular buildings show how people close to the king lived. Florimond Robertet, baron d'Alluye, was minister of finance under Charles VIII, Louis XII, and François I, as well as builder of the now

destroyed Château de Bury, to the west of Blois. His early sixteenth-century town house, the *Hôtel d'Alluye*, still stands at 8, Rue Saint-Honoré. Its street front of brick and stone seems to compete in its wealth of ornament with the Louis XII Wing of the château, which clearly inspired it. A two-story loggia with flat-arch arcades opens onto an inner courtyard. Medallions decorated with the heads of Roman emperors adorn the loggia balustrade in the best Italian manner.

A few other sixteenth-century buildings are worthy of notice: the *Hôtel de Guise*, also boasting a frieze with medallions on its courtyard side (18, Rue Chemonton); the *Hôtel de Jassaud* (5, Rue Fontaine-des-Elus); the *Hôtel Sardini*, with an oratory adorned with frescoes (7, Rue du Puits-Châtel); and the *Hôtel de Condé* (3, Rue des Juifs).

Despite heavy damage inflicted by the Second World War, the town's flavor, with its narrow streets climbing up and down the slopes, has been preserved. Aside from the château, the dominant structure on its skyline is the elevated cathedral of *St-Louis*. A sixteenth-century structure was leveled by a hurricane in 1678. All that remained was its prominent tower, which rises above a Romanesque ground floor. Slender pairs of columns divide its upper stories, and a double lantern crowns its elegant form. The money required to rebuild the nave—a wide, vaulted basilica in the Late Gothic style—was provided by the daughter of the bailiff of Blois and lord of Ménars, Marie Charron; she had been married in St-Louis to Colbert, Louis XIV's minister of finance. Beneath the choir is an interesting crypt dating from the tenth and eleventh centuries.

Behind the choir of the cathedral stands the former bishop's palace, now the *Hôtel de Ville*, which was built in 1725. Both the building itself and its splendid terraced garden leading down the slope are creations of Jacques Gabriel. The same architect received a life pension of 2,000 livres for his design for the elegant Pont Gabriel spanning the Loire; it was constructed around 1720 by the engineer Robert Pitrou. Destroyed by German troops during the Second World War, it has been rebuilt in its original form. The road to Chambord leads across it.

CHAMBORD

IN 1539, WHEN EMPEROR CHARLES V WAS GIVEN an extravagant reception by François I in the still uncompleted Château de Chambord, the emperor called it "the epitome of all that human artifice can create." Almost four decades after this event, Jacques Androuet Du Cerceau published engravings of the château in his compendium of the most famous architectural monuments in France (*La seconde volume des plus excellents Bastiments de France*), praising the beauty of its masses, the splendor of its elevation, and the convenience of its interior. Even today, if one glances through Du Cerceau's book of engravings, it is obvious that Chambord's massiveness and innovation surpass everything else constructed at the time.

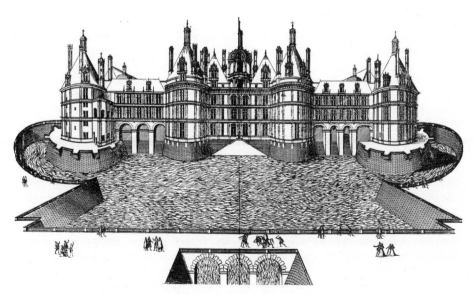

Chambord, northwest façade (after Du Cerceau, 1576).

The history of its building is by no means as clear as one might expect. Why did the king build it in the first place? The châteaux of Amboise and Blois were residences that came to him with the Crown. But Blois did not belong to him; it was his wife's, and François I wanted a structure that would serve as his personal symbol of majesty. As a site, he selected a plain in the densely wooded Sologne, a favorite hunting reserve, where a medieval château already stood. This château, some 3 miles from the river and 10 miles east of Blois, belonged to the Crown, as did the whole of the region; the king promptly had the château razed. The forest itself covered an area of 13,500 acres, and was soon enclosed by order of the king by a wall that is 20 miles in length. The park is now a national game preserve, abounding in wild boar and deer.

On September 6, 1519, the king entrusted the supervision of the entire château project to François de Pontbriant. The architect's identity remains unknown. Possibly, it was Domenico da Cortona, who lived in Blois and stood in the king's service. However, we do know the identities of the leading master masons who executed the plans: Jacques Sourdeau, his son Denis Sourdeau, Pierre Trinqueau (a bondsman given his freedom during his employment on the project), and Jacques Coqueau.

Work began in 1519, but because of the swampy terrain, the laying of the foundations was difficult and costly, and progress was slow. Construction stopped altogether five years later when the king embarked on his Italian campaign. Not until 1526 was a new superintendent appointed and construction resumed. Over the next 12 years, as many as 1,800 workers were continually employed on the site. The central portion, the keep, was completed in 1533. Its towers and the pavilions on the corners of the roof terrace were erected in 1537. This keep was all that Emperor Charles V saw when he visited in 1539.

Only spotty information has come down to us concerning construction over the next few years. The king's own apartments were not finished until 1547, the year of his death. Traditional belief has it that he spent a total of only forty days at Chambord.

His son Henri II continued his work, but because of the Religious War, the king's own death in 1559, and a constant shortage of money, this far too ambitious project would remain unfinished. Even so, it achieved the effect that François I originally intended, and added to his posthumous fame. "I have seen a great deal of splendid architecture in my life," wrote the Venetian ambassador Geronimo Lippomano in 1577, "but never anything more beautiful and lavish than this."[6]

Chambord's use and upkeep have been troublesome from the start. The most important of François I's successors to hunt and to stage brilliant festivities here was Louis XIV. Here, too, Molière gave the premiere of *Le Bourgeois Gentilhomme* before the king in 1670. It so delighted its audience that four repeat performances were demanded. Louis XV assigned Chambord to his father-in-law, Stanislas Leczinski, the exiled king of Poland. Later, as the residence of the maréchal Maurice de Saxe, it became the setting for a lavish court life under the protection of the maréchal's private army, which was made up of Germans, Poles, Hungarians, Tartars, Turks, and blacks; the last, composing the Première Brigade, were mounted on white horses.

Activity at Chambord died out after the death of the marshal in 1750. During the

Revolution, there were numerous demands that its "huge mass of useless stones" be cleared away. All that prevented this was the immense cost of such an undertaking. The revolutionaries had to be content with stripping the château of its furnishings and auctioning them off. Napoleon, wishing to preserve the château by making it useful, turned it over to the Quinzième Cohorte of the Légion d'Honneur. He later presented it to the maréchal Berthier, but by 1820, after the marshal's death, it was up for sale. Thanks to the initiation of Count Adrien de Calonne, a national collection was taken up with the aim of acquiring Chambord and offering it to the duc de Bordeaux, a grandson of Charles X and the last descendant of the older line of the House of Bourbon. This plan proved successful. After long hesitation, Charles X accepted the donation in the name of his grandson and pretender to the throne, the comte de Chambord, who lived for the most part abroad. Extensive restorations were carried out that saved the château from ruin. The count, who never did accede to the throne, became acquainted with his possession only in 1871, when he stayed here for a total of two nights. In 1914, the state confiscated it from his heir Elie de Bourbon because he was serving as an officer in the Austrian army.

FOR ALL THE UNACCUSTOMED SPLENDOR OF ITS details, Chambord is firmly rooted in French architectural tradition. The château consists of two quadrilinear buildings: a low structure—most of it unfinished—measuring 512 by 384 feet and provided with round corner towers; and the colossal keep, likewise fortified with round corner towers, which projects into the Cour d'Honneur from one of the long sides of the low structure. It is clear that this overall design was borrowed from the Château de Vincennes, but here its effect is no longer medieval. The basic design principles of this architecture are symmetry, a strict division of wall surfaces by means of pilasters and cornices, and a leisurely succession of arcades and rows of windows. Many have called it excessive, but its only excess is its vast size. Each elevation is held in check by a sense of proportion and pleasing relationships. Du Cerceau points out that the château's great beauty was further enhanced by a moat, in which it was reflected. But since the standing water tended to create an unbearable stench in the summertime, Stanislas Leczinski had the moat filled in and covered its site with broad parterres.

The real architectural marvel at Chambord is its three-story keep. Rising above a square ground plan, it houses in the center an open staircase made up of two intertwined spiral stairways that begin at differ-

Molière

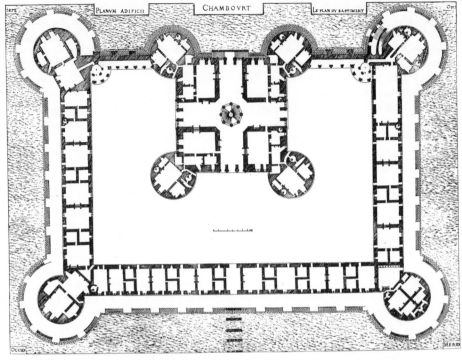

Floor plan of the château at Chambord (after Du Cerceau, 1576).

ent levels and never meet. On each floor, huge salons extend from the staircase in four directions, leaving room for four corner apartments incorporating the adjacent round towers. The critical architectural idea of Chambord is this Greek cross arrangement with the staircase in the center. There is reason to believe the idea is Leonardo da Vinci's. François I had summoned the Italian artist to his court at Amboise, where he died in 1519, the year in which the construction of Chambord was begun. We know the king had had a number of proposals drawn up, and it is unthinkable that he would not have asked Leonardo's advice. The form of the staircase is Italian in origin, and Leonardo had drawn such stairways.

Because of the monumentality of the architecture, it is easy to overlook the delightfully varied sculpture on the pilaster capitals: cupids frolicking, delicate acanthus leaves unfolding, little lizards scurrying around the corners.

Outside, the staircase culminates in a splendid lantern—the present one is a copy installed in 1891—the focal point in the profusion of unusual ornamental superstructures that enliven not only the main roof, but also the roofs of the four corner pavilions and the outer towers. As though in a miniature city, one walks among its streets, alleyways, intersections, and squares. What seem to be richly carved and ornamented miniature buildings are in fact towers, turrets, chimneys, dormers, and niches.

We do not know whether François I planned to use the roof terrace as a setting for his courtly festivities, but it seems unlikely that it was meant to be only a pleasant spot from which to survey the surrounding forest. The idea of providing the roof area with a wealth of ornament and of dazzling the eye with a variety of chimneys and dormers was certainly not new. Louis I, duc d'Anjou, had furnished the Château de Saumur with a similar display a century and a half earlier. But Chambord was no longer a mere play of ornamental forms. The lilies—singly and in bunches—the crowns above the windows, the letter *F* in varying sizes, the salamander device, the F.R.F. (François, Roi de France) in slate on the top of a chimney—all make a political statement.

The château's rooms—there are 440 of them—constitute a labyrinth:

thirty feet of gallery, then...two doors, across a room, again ten feet of corridor, up a staircase, into an anteroom, down some steps, now two rooms in sequence, a little side room into which opens a twisting passage that is scarcely wider than a person's body, a bend, two steps, a door, and suddenly the dim light of an empty, unidentifiable space with square windows and cross-shaped mullions; behind this, still another door, another corridor, a passageway, other steps.[7]

This is not a palace meant for permanent living. To leave it at that, however, would be to overlook the essence of its architecture. Du Cerceau stresses the uniqueness of its carefully planned disposition of space around the central staircase and its adjacent salons. He uses the word *commodité*. By this he does not mean simple domestic comfort, but a rational architectural scale and its effect apart from any particular residential function. It is in this core area where we can appreciate the architectural principles of Chambord; it is ideal architecture, an image of the ideal sovereignty of the king.

For years, the state authorities have attempted to at least partially refurnish Chambord's almost completely ransacked rooms, if possible by gathering museum pieces evocative of the personalities important in its history.

In a salon on the ground floor its builder's passion for hunting is recalled by a series of six tapestries, the Histoire des chasses du Roi François. Based on cartoons by Laurent Guyot, they were executed in Paris in the latter half of the seventeenth century. The king's study was located on the second floor of the northeast tower (Tour Robert de Parme). It was on a windowpane here that he scratched with the diamond in his ring the words *Souvent femme varie, Bien fol est qui s'y fie* (Woman is often fickle; great fool he who trusts her). Visitors now look in vain for the king's disenchanted inscription, for—as the legend goes—when Louis XIV discovered it 130 years later in the presence of Marie Mancini (Mazarin's niece whom he loved but could not marry), he gallantly smashed the pane. The walls of this room and its canopy bed flaunt sixteenth-century Italian red-velvet hangings with wide gold borders. These are not the authentic furnishings, but serve as a lovely substitute. The original wooden door, complete with François I's monogram and salamander, leads into the king's sitting room, which preserves a barrel-vaulted ceiling with sculptured coffers.

The queen's suite, located between the apartments of François I and the seventeenth-century royal bedchamber, features a series of magnificent tapestries after cartoons by Rubens. They depict scenes from the life of the Emperor Constantine.

A royal apartment was outfitted on the second floor of the keep for Louis XIV, and it was later used by Stanislas Leczinski and the maréchal de Saxe. Its most splendid room is the parade room, with a lavish bed in an alcove reconstructed after contemporary examples. The delicately carved wall paneling is original. It came from Versailles, and was a gift to the marshal from Louis XV. These apartments are hung with tapestries and paintings. A portrait by the French Renaissance painter Jean Clouet represents Henri III; by Pierre Mignard is a study of Anne of Austria from the seventeenth century. This suite also houses mementos of the comte de Chambord. In Louis XIV's time, theatrical performances were given in the adjacent Salle des Gardes to the

southwest. It was here that Molière premiered *Le Bourgeois Gentilhomme.*

On the upper floor are objects of the hunt. Various arms and trophies as well as animal paintings by seventeenth-century Flemish masters (including Frans Snyders) are exhibited. A series of tapestries show hunting scenes from classical mythology, including the Story of Meleager (who led the Calydonian boar hunt) and the Story of Diana, the huntress. These exquisite tapestries were executed after cartoons by Toussaint Dubreuil.

The chapel in the northwest tower, planned as a counterpart to François I's room in the northeast one, was begun under Henri II. In its present form, it goes back to the Baroque.

The terrace of the keep offers magnificent views. It overlooks the vast gardens of the château and at one time provided nooks for rendezvous and conversation. From the terrace, the court traditionally watched the return of the hunts. Chambord's terrace is designed in an Italianate manner, with richly sculpted gables, capitals, chimneys, spires, turrets, and a lantern.

VILLESAVIN

ANYONE INTERESTED IN SEEING WHAT SORT OF house a member of the royal court would build for himself after directing and keeping the books for the work on Chambord should make a visit to Villesavin. The château is only 5 miles south of Chambord's park. It was built in 1537 by Jean Le Breton, adviser and secretary of state to François I, administrator of the countship of Blois, and chief supervisor of the accounting office.

After his death, his role as administrator passed to his widow, Anne Gédouin, and then to their daughter, Léonore Breton—proof of the king's special esteem for this family. He also entrusted Anne Gédouin with the administrative, building, and financial concerns of Chambord, and Léonore Breton later served as one of its custodians.

Le Breton was a man of refined artistic

sensibilities, and it is not surprising that he built a château that was far in advance of its time. Thanks to its livable layout and elegant proportions, it appears to be a kind of protest against the forbidding and confused luxuriousness of Chambord. The four-bay, one-story central structure with a tall hip roof is flanked by two square pavilions. Between the inner bays is a two-story ornamental area with a curved roof and an open lantern, which boasts a bust of François I in an arched niche on the ground floor and a statue of Diana the Huntress in a square niche above. A perpendicular wing on one side and a wall on the other enclose a generous courtyard, with two additional pavilions providing strong accents toward the front. Richly ornamented dormers cut into the slope of the roofs. The models for the pavilions, which dominate the loose arrangement of the complex, are easily discovered on the terrace of the keep at Chambord. It is clear that Le Breton must have taken his masons, stonecutters, and even materials from that larger project.

The jewel of Villesavin, executed by Italian artists, is a marble fountain on a tall base in the middle of the courtyard. With its rich carving, it gives testimony to Le Breton's refined taste and heightens the atmosphere of elegance that envelops the visitor.

Villesavin has suffered greatly over the centuries. The moats in which the complex was once mirrored have been filled in. The present owner is endeavoring to complete the château's restoration, which will necessitate much new work, especially needed because of its badly weathered stone.

The kitchen is the best preserved of the rooms. The left front pavilion houses the chapel, with fragments of original sixteenth-century frescoes attributed to Niccolo dell'Abbate. For a long time, this structure served as a kennel.

Other interesting items at the château are a splendid devecote, similar to the one at Talcy, and a collection of antique carriages in the barns.

*B*EAUREGARD

AROUND THE MIDDLE OF THE SIXTEENTH CENTURY, the Château de Beauregard belonged to Jean du Thiers, humanist and secretary of state to Henri II, whose love of books and the fine arts were lauded in one of Ronsard's eclogues:

Such sums in golden sequins [gold coin] paid for these proud volumes passed down through the ages; such great names greet us from their title pages, men of the likes of Pindar and Simonides. A fit adornment to fair Beauregard, your home: the flower of Greece, the pride of ancient Rome.[8]

Situated at the southern edge of the Forêt de Russy above the valley of the Beuvron, the Beauregard we see today is only a remnant of the château that belonged to Jean du Thiers. Jacques Androuet Du Cerceau celebrated the earlier complex as one of the most magnificent château in France. According to him, the structure was laid

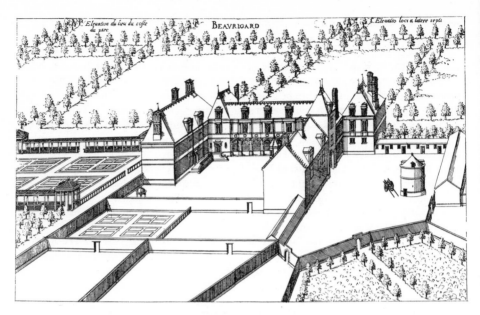

View of Beauregard (after Du Cerceau, 1607).

out as a manor house with an eye to functional convenience, but artistic considerations had in no way been neglected. Du Cerceau's engraving shows an asymmetry in the disposition of the separate structures, doubtless as a result of the incorporation of an older hunting lodge that occupied the site. The main buildings were disposed around a courtyard that was closed off by walls. Additional courtyards, including a large housekeeping area with a dovecote, extended to the north and east, each clearly marked off by further walls. To the south and west of the château lay the ornamental gardens, orchards, and vineyards, whose regular layout counterbalanced the irregularity of the courtyards and the discrete wings of the château.

The two-story core structure from du Thiers's time survives, although various changes have been made to it, especially in the nineteenth century. The central section has an arcaded gallery on the ground floor, and even in Du Cerceau's time, this appears to have been Beauregard's dominating architectural motif. It is flanked by single-bay wings from which dissimilar side wings extend back. The plainness of the surface arrangement of the façades gives them a balanced calm. By comparison, the nineteenth-century dormers seem too lavish. The original dormers, as seen in Du Cerceau's engraving, were much simpler. The back side, which faces the sloping terrain of the former vineyards, was drastically altered in the seventeenth century but is now restored to Du Cerceau's original plan.

To decorate the interiors, du Thiers employed Italian artists from the court of the king. Niccolo dell'Abbate painted frescoes for the chapel after drawings by Primaticcio. The chapel was demolished in the nineteenth century, but a fragment of the frescoes is preserved in the Musée des Beaux-Arts in Blois. The Cabinet des Grelots, du Thiers's small study next to the library, is completely paneled in carved oak highlighted with gold. One of the coffers in the ceiling displays the du Thiers coat of arms, three gold hawk's bells in blue. The bell motif is repeated in the room's decoration. The combination of delicacy and vigor in these panels is delightful and the room seems like an oversize jewel box. The upper panels are decorated with paintings, each of which has a theme. Executed by Francesco Scibec di Carpi, they depict manuscripts, gold objects, weapons, musical instruments, toys, piles of apples, and a wine press—symbols of scholarship and of country pleasures.

On the second floor of the main wing is the château's famous portrait gallery. It was created in the early seventeenth century by a later owner of Beauregard, Paul Ardier, treasurer of the exchequer under Louis XIII, and by his son. Above a series of arcades are 363 portraits of historical figures. The works are arranged in rows, each row dedicated to the reign of a king of France, from Philippe VI to Louis XIII. The French queens and courtiers are depicted, as are famous personages from throughout Europe. Isabella of Castile is represented, as is the explorer Amerigo Vespucci. These elegant portraits present for the visitor a magnificent "history lesson." The delicate decorative painting on the lower part of the walls and on the beamed ceiling is by Jean Mosnier (who also worked at Cheverny) and features the emblems and coats of arms of several French kings. The floor of this gallery is also priceless, for it is made entirely of Delft tiles. Blue against a white background, the tiles depict an early sixteenth-century army on the march.

Other rooms in the château display collections of seventeenth- and eighteenth-century furniture. As at many of the Loire châteaux, Beauregard's kitchen is open to visitors. This one boasts a vast collection of copper pots and baking molds, and contains two large fireplaces.

CHEVERNY

THE HISTORY OF THE PRESENT CHÂTEAU DE CHEVERNY, which was built to replace a sixteenth-century structure, begins with a crime of passion. In 1589, the heir to Cheverny, Count Henri Hurault, married Françoise Chabot, the eleven-year-old daughter of France's chief equerry. An ardent soldier, Hurault was absent for long periods in the service of his king. Not overly fond of him to begin with, his young wife soon made him a cuckold by disporting with her page. In time, Hurault caught them in the act and promptly dispatched his rival with his sword; he then forced his unfaithful wife to choose between the dagger and poison. She took the poison. According to an entry in the church records, the doctors discovered a five-month fetus in her womb.

Cheverny

The king, who had awakened Hurault's suspicions with a joke and felt not altogether innocent in the whole affair, meted out an extremely mild sentence on the count, banishing him to Cheverny. Soon afterward, Hurault married Marguerite Gaillard, the beautiful daughter of the provincial governor and a woman of considerable artistic taste. It was her dislike of the antiquated château, with its fortification towers and memory of tragedy, that moved the count to undertake the construction of a more comfortable residence.

The plans were provided by an architect from Blois, Jacques Boyer, who presumably began work on the new structure in 1626. Since he died only six years later, he failed to see it completed in 1634.

Massive and symmetrical, Cheverny is a monument to the *grand siècle*—designed for comfort and the display of refinement. The design is simple and unprecedented. There is only one two-story wing with a narrow staircase in the center and massive pavilions as outer accents. On the north side, the pavilions extend past the line of the building by one bay and thus form a shallow courtyard.

It is above all the château's roofs that give it its shape. Each component has its own roof: domelike roofs on the pavilions and hip roofs of different heights and widths on the three divisions of the central wing. The arrangement of their façades is also varied. The dominating motif of the entrance façade, which is exquisitely structured by horizontal lines, is a row of busts of emperors, which underscores the architecture's aristocratic pretensions. On the back and the end façades, the horizontal lines have been reduced to simple squared stones on the corners and around the windows, producing a more rustic effect.

Cheverny's original interiors remain almost intact. During the Revolution, the château's owner, the comte de Saint-Leu, stayed at Cheverny and saved it from being sacked and confiscated. The rooms are of considerable artistic interest, and, though decorated with rare furnishings and objets d'art of the seventeenth and eighteenth centuries, they preserve a comfortable appearance. Cheverny's treasures are lovingly maintained by the present owner, the marquis de Vibraye, a descendant of the Huraults.

The vestibule and stairwell in the center provide access to the apartments. Following Chenonceau's example, the staircase is a double one; the vaulting above its parallel flights rests on the columns that divide the two sets of steps. These supporting elements are adorned with carefully carved festoons of flowers, weapons, and symbols of the arts, referring to the special interests of the Hurault family. The unknown sculptor of this beautiful staircase left us only his initials and date—"F.L. 1634"—on the first-floor balustrade.

Along with the staircase, the rooms that have been preserved virtually in their original state are the Salle des Gardes and the Appartement du Roi, both on the second floor. The Salle des Gardes, the largest room in the château, serves as an anteroom to the Appartement du Roi and is therefore somewhat reserved in its furnishings. The focal point of the room is a splendid mantelpiece with figures of Mercury and Venus that flank a painting, *The Death of Adonis*, by Jean Mosnier; additional paintings on either side illustrate the Adonis legend. A Gobelin tapestry across from it depicts the rape of Helen; it was woven after a painting by François Franck from 1621, which is now in the Musée des Beaux-Arts in Tours. A priceless collection of weapons and armor adorns the remaining walls. The ceiling beams are decorated with arabesques, flowers, and the Hurault coats of arms. More interesting, however, are Mosnier's delicate paintings in the lower wall panels, in which the main motifs are flower emblems. Each type of flower is accompanied by a Latin epigram that either refers to its nature or suggests a metaphorical significance. For example, the motto with the blue Canterbury bell reads: "Although I am small, I wear the color of the sky." The climbing begonia, native to the remote Americas and only recently introduced to Europe, serves to symbolize the esteem accorded to the cherished guest housed in the Appartement du Roi. Deciphering such visual puzzles and discussing their often obscure allusions in learned conversation was a favorite pastime. Thus it is not surprising that written attempts to elucidate this cycle date from as early as the eighteenth century. The figures painted in grisaille alongside the flowers—Muses, arts, and gods as personifications of specific concepts—help to explain the emblems or call to mind interesting associations. The Canterbury bell, for example, is associated with music, which the ancients held to be of divine origin. Next to the climbing begonia stands Mercury, the god of commerce.

The Appartement du Roi was held in readiness for a visit from the king or another illustrious guest. Blue, gold, and red, the heraldic colors of the host, dominate the room's decor. Sculpted and painted figures from classical mythology adorn the ceilings and walls. There is hardly a space that has not been embellished with color or carving, organized by the clear lines of the woodwork framing. The ceiling, the mantelpiece, and the panel above the entry (its counterpart on the opposite door has been lost) relate the legend of Perseus in paintings by Mosnier. Even more remarkable are Mosnier's paintings in the lower wall panels, depicting scenes from the third-century Greek romance *Ethiopica* by Heliodorus of Emesa. This work, which tells of the love affair between Theagenes and Chariclea, circulated in numerous translations in the sixteenth century and strongly influenced the Baroque novel of love. The tale was not a frequent subject for painters, and its use at Cheverny indicates the literary refinement of the lord of the house. The wall tapestries, after cartoons by Simon Vouet, depict scenes from the *Odyssey*, and presumably were created in a Paris workshop in around 1640. These tapestries, more than the other decorative elements, give the room its sense of splendor, which is heightened by the gilded Renaissance mantelpiece and a bed of state with a canopy of Persian silk embroidered in colorful flowers and figures. This is not the original bed, but it is an appropriate substitute for the overall ensemble of this magnificent room.

The gallery and dining room on the ground floor were refurbished in the nineteenth century. The painted wood paneling depicts scenes from *Don Quixote*, some of which were painted by Mosnier in the seventeenth century, and some in the nineteenth. On the other side of the vestibule, the Grand Salon has paneled walls with grisaille paintings from the seventeenth century and some noteworthy canvases, including Pierre Mignard's lovely portrait of Marie Johanne de la Carre Saumery, Elisabeth Hurault's daughter-in-law.

There is also a magnificent portrait of Cosimo de' Medici by Titian. This masterpiece had been lost for centuries and was discovered at Montereau, where it was used to cover a well. Another fine portrait at Cheverny is of Jeanne d'Aragon; it was painted by a member of the school of Raphael. Both the Grand Salon and the Petit Salon are furnished with rare Louis XIV and Louis XV pieces. A Chinese lacquered commode and a clock embellished with bronzes by Caffiéri, both from the Louis XV period, are especially notable. The Petit Salon is hung with tapestries of genre scenes designed after cartoons by the Flemish painter David Teniers. Other rooms on the ground floor are sumptuously decorated. Paintings in these apartments include a sixteenth-century portrait of the comtesse de Cheverny by Jean Clouet and a fascinating eighteenth-century self-portrait by Hyacinthe Rigaud.

The exquisitely kept grounds of the château, which are not open to the public, are considerably simpler in design than they were originally, and numerous outbuildings have disappeared. The elegant little Orangerie, standing on the central axis of the château to the north, dates from the eighteenth century.

The marquis de Vibraye is a well-known huntsman. His pack of about 80 hunting dogs in the kennel in one of the outbuildings and a small hunting museum—housing some 2,000 pairs of stag's antlers—are among the attractions of Cheverny.

*F*OUGERES-SUR-BIEVRE

FOUGÈRES-SUR-BIÈVRE IS A COUNTRY CHÂTEAU IN the middle of a village; it is more imposing for the austerity and ponderousness of its fabric than for any artistic merits. Its history reaches back to the eleventh century. In the fourteenth century, all but its square keep was razed by Edward, the Black Prince, a son of the English king Edward III.

The estate came by marriage to Jean de Refuge, whose son, Pierre de Refuge, an adviser to Charles d'Orlèans and the treasurer to Louis XI, was granted the right in 1470 to rebuild Fougères as a fortress. Although its moats were filled in during the Renaissance and its windows were enlarged, its fortresslike character remains unchanged.

The central courtyard is surrounded by four asymmetrical wings. The medieval keep and a thick round tower comprise the exterior accents of the high and forbidding entrance façade. The portal leading to the courtyard is flanked by additional round towers incorporated into the connecting wing. This wing and the round corner tower are furnished with wall-walks. The housekeeping courtyard is in front of the portal, and it was necessary to pass through it to reach a long-vanished drawbridge at the entrance to the castle.

Only in the inner courtyard does one begin to sense that the castle was truly livable. The wing next to the residential tower is only one story high and opens onto the courtyard through the flat arches of a gallery. It would be difficult to conceive of a greater contrast than that existing between these arches and the otherwise closed and restrained wall surfaces. The only other ornamental touches are the dormers, with finials and coats of arms; the portals, with ogee arches; and a few bits of sculpture.

The castle changed hands frequently. After the Revolution, it served for a time as a spinning mill, and then as housing for field workers. It was finally bought by the state in 1932. Little that is noteworthy has survived inside except for some lovely mantelpieces and roof timbers shaped like an inverted keel. The people of the surrounding area appreciate the atmosphere of the castle and celebrate weddings and other family occasions within its walls.

CHAUMONT

CHAUMONT IS ONE OF THE FEW LOIRE CHÂTEAUX to relate directly to the river. In the tenth century, Eudes I, comte de Blois, erected a castle on top of a steep cliff above its banks as a defense against his rival for possession of Touraine, Foulques Nerra, comte d'Anjou. The complex passed into the hands of the lords of Amboise in the eleventh century, and in the twelfth century, it was razed and rebuilt. When Pierre d'Amboise allied himself with other feudal lords against Louis XI in the fifteenth century, the king confiscated the castle and demolished it. But Pierre d'Amboise succeeded in regaining royal favor and was permitted to reconstruct the fortress. His oldest son, Charles I d'Amboise, began this undertaking in 1465, building the northwest wing—which was directly above the river and which no longer stands—and the Tour d'Amboise. His son Charles II, who served Louis XII as Marshal of France, admiral, lieutenant general in Italy, and royal steward, completed the castle before his death in 1511. Living as he did for many years in Milan, he must have commissioned Cardinal Georges d'Amboise, his uncle and Louis XII's minister, to oversee its construction.

Charles II　　　　　　　　　　　*Cardinal D'Amboise*

Catherine de Médicis purchased Chaumont in 1560. She then forced Diane de Poitiers, the mistress of her deceased husband, Henri II, to take it in exchange for Chenonceau, which she wished for herself. Diane found the atmosphere of Chaumont too gloomy, however, and spent the rest of her life at the Château d'Anet.

In the eighteenth century, Jacques-Donatien Le Ray turned Chaumont into a center of the art industry. In addition to various other workshops, he set up a small factory in the château to produce ceramic medallions, to which he was able to attract the Italian sculptor Giovanni Battista Nini. Nini's terra-cotta portrait medallions of famous persons were much sought after for the fineness of their execution, and they brought him considerable wealth.

Thanks to the workshops that Le Ray had installed, Chaumont was considered a useful structure and so was spared from destruction during the Revolution. In 1810, Le Ray's son, who went to America to seek his fortune, turned over the château for the duration of his absence to Madame de Staël. Banished from Paris by Napoleon, she wrote *On Germany* here and gathered about her a circle of intellectuals, including the German poets August Wilhelm von Schlegel and Adelbert von Chamisso. Chamisso described the château in a delightful letter:

Chaumont—on the southern or left bank of the Loire—stands on a commanding bluff. Across the esplanade of its inner courtyard and from the battlements of its lovely, old, solid, Gothic towers, one has the most splendid view over the broad, beautiful, and majestic river and the highway running along the opposite shore into a lush, green, and seemingly endless plain dotted with vineyards, villages, fields, and forests. My window, at which I am writing, looks out at this charming landscape from the wing at the back of the courtyard, elegantly framed between the château's chapel and the opposite wing.[9]

The last private owner of Chaumont was Prince Amédée de Broglie, who acquired the château through marriage and had it completely restored. He sold it to the state in 1938.

The château, with its three surviving wings, opens out toward the river. The fourth wing was demolished in the eighteenth century because it blocked the owners' view of the Loire Valley. From the park side, the château's massive round towers give it the character of a fortress. The oldest sections are the northwest wing and the smooth, forbidding round Tour d'Amboise at the west corner, with its 12-foot-thick walls. This tower could serve as a last refuge for the castle's inhabitants, for although it is adjacent to the living wings, it is independent of them; a narrow spiral staircase embedded in its wall connects its various floors.

The courtyard is reached by way of the drawbridge at the southeast corner, which is flanked by closely set round towers. Coats of arms and other sculptural ornaments enliven the smooth white walls of cut stone. On the left-hand tower is the coat of arms of Cardinal Georges d'Amboise; on the right-hand tower, the device of Charles II d'Amboise supported by "savages." The coat of arms of France and the initials of Louis XII and Anne de Bretagne—surrounded by the lilies of France and the ermine dots of Brittany—appear above the round-arch passage. Below these is a niche containing a statuette of the Madonna. A frieze runs around the towers and the adjacent wings of the building: two intertwined C's (for Charles and Catherine d'Amboise) alternating with flaming hills. The latter is an attempt to illustrate the origin of the name Chaumont as *chauds monts* (hot mountains), but etymologists insist that this is a mistaken derivation. Instead, they trace it back to the Latin *calvus mons* (bald mountain). The intertwined D's alternating with hunting symbols above the machicolation of the wall-walk refer to Diane de Poitiers.

Next to the chapel, which stands at the north end of the east wing, looms the Tour St-Nicolas. Popular legend has it that this is the tower in which Catherine de Médicis locked herself with her astrologer, Cosmo Ruggieri, to question the stars about the fate of her sons.

The view from the terrace opposite the entry is more likely to captivate than are the heavily restored façades of the courtyard. The top floor of the southeast wing was provided in the nineteenth century with a long balcony with a tracery balustrade. The gallery in front of the southwest wing dates from the same period. The polygonal stair tower next to the carriageway preserves its imaginative decorations in the lower portions. These are Late Gothic ornamental forms hesitantly blended with Italian Renaissance motifs. The coat of arms of Cardinal d'Amboise appears once more

Chaumont

above the door. The upper portions of this tower have been restored. Another stair tower in front of the northwest wing preserves a portal that is purely Late Gothic in form.

Few of the château's original interior appointments have survived. Today, its rooms are set up like museum galleries, with mainly wall tapestries and furnishings from the sixteenth to eighteenth centuries. In the Salle des Fêtes is a noteworthy seventeenth-century Italian floor of Majolica tiles that depicts hunting scenes. Prince Amédée brought it to Chaumont from a palace in Salerno. It was he who laid out the park at Chaumont, and in 1877, he turned Le Ray's workshops into carriage houses and stables, true palaces for horses and ponies with all the imaginable luxuries. The stables enclose a former dovecote in which the sculptor Nini set up his kilns in the eighteenth century. The prince had it remodeled as a manège for his children's ponies.

THROUGH TOURAINE

AMBOISE

IN HIS FAMOUS BOOK OF ENGRAVINGS, *LE SE-conde volume des plus excellents Basti-ments de France*, Jacques Androuet Du Cerceau describes the Château d'Amboise:

> Because the kings have so often re-sided here, this palace has long been famous as one of the first-rank struc-tures in France. It lies on an elevation above the Loire, with the town spread-ing at its feet. Nearby, there is a mar-velous forest. From this castle, you can look upstream or down; I cannot re-call that I have ever enjoyed such an overpowering view down the river. From the incomparable terraces sur-rounding it, you can easily see the city of Tours and the abbey of Marmoutier, even though they are seven miles away. But in fact, you can see much farther, your gaze losing itself in the distance. The structure not only is built up on the river side, but also pre-sents one side to the city, which it dominates. It is heavily fortified on all sides. Two massive towers some ten or eleven spans in diameter rise above a rock foundation at the foot of the ring wall and are incorporated into it. Inside these towers, it is possible to drive horse carriages up from below to the higher level of the castle's courtyard. And there are numerous separate buildings. Those next to the ring walls are well built ... but there are also some built simply of half-tim-bers.... The garden is a bit too narrow for its length; it is entirely enclosed by walls. In the center of the main court-yard is a church built in the latest style, and projecting from the ring wall toward the city is a small chapel.[10]

The overall arrangement of the château has changed little since the early seventeenth

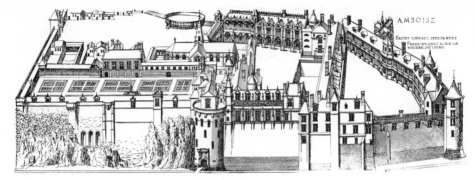

View of Amboise from the Loire side (after Du Cerceau, 1607).

century, but only a few of the buildings that Du Cerceau depicts have survived. To appreciate fully the grandeur of this royal residence, it is necessary to recall his engraving.

Amboise became a royal possession in 1434, when Charles VII confiscated the castle of the lords of Amboise. But the castle plateau was transformed into a huge building site only under Louis XI and especially his son, Charles VIII, who had spent his childhood here. More than 170 masons and 70 hodcarriers were employed full time. Charles VIII was impatient to see the work completed, and he pushed it forward mercilessly. Even in winter there was no interruption; torches were used to illuminate the site at night and to warm the frozen stone to the working point. The vast project was financed in part out of income from the salt tax.

In 1494, Charles VIII undertook a campaign into Italy, where he came to appreciate the wealth of that country's patrician palaces and the splendor of its court life. "My brother," he wrote from Naples in 1495 to the duc de Bourbon, "you cannot imagine what beautiful gardens I have in this city. Truly. It is as though all that was

lacking was Adam and Eve to make them into an earthly paradise, they are so very lovely and full of delightful and unusual things." He went on to say that he was bringing back with him painters who could create the most beautiful beamed ceilings, more beautiful and splendid than anything to be met with in France.[11]

The campaign was not successful politically, but it marked the birth of the French Renaissance. In his train, Charles VIII did indeed bring to Amboise a host of Italian artists, including—as the sources assure us—a clever inventor who could hatch chickens artificially. A shipment of carpets, books, paintings, sculptures, and furniture was sent to France from Naples, with which Charles set about furnishing his new castle. "One could say nothing at all about it or one could fill twenty pages," an eyewitness reports, "for what the decorator Nicolas Fagot brought from remotest Italy into the heart of France was nothing more or less than the entirety of Italian art, that art which would cause countless marvels to blossom in Amboise, in Gaillon, and in the whole of the kingdom."[12]

Even before work on the castle was completed, Charles VIII suffered a fatal accident on his way to watch a game in the moat. He struck his head quite hard on a low door lintel; at first, he thought nothing of it, but he soon lost consciousness. He was placed on a bag of straw, and he never got up again.

Louis XII, Charles VIII's cousin and successor, chose Blois as his residence, but he had the work at Amboise brought to completion. The castle became the residence of Louise de Savoie, comtesse d'Angoulême and mother of François I. Here the future king spent his youth, watching the masons and gardeners and becoming fluent in Italian. When he was crowned, he selected Amboise as his residence and undertook further expansion of the complex. He also summoned to his court the great genius Leonardo da Vinci. Brilliant festivities were held here, and it was here that François I began to create the French court. All the artistic and intellectual life and society of the country now was to be found near the person of the king. The seventeenth- and eighteenth-century kings only expanded into gigantic proportions what François I had established.

The heyday of Amboise as a royal residence ended in 1560, during the reign of François II. Spurred on by the prince de Condé, a group of Huguenots planned to seize the fifteen-year-old king in Blois, and to remove him from the influence of the Guise family, the power behind the throne. Hearing of the plot, the court fled to Amboise, followed by the conspirators. Easily put down, 1,200 of them were hideously executed. Although it was she who had urged her son to command the executions, Catherine de Médicis three years later

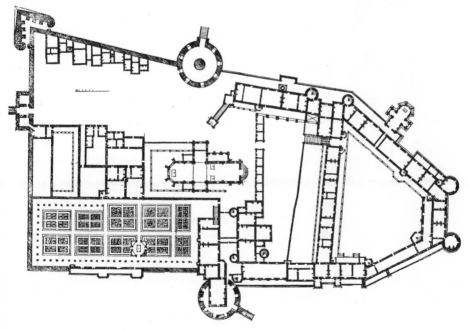

Floor plan of Amboise (after Du Cerceau, 1607).

signed the Edict of Amboise, which permitted the free practice of the Protestant faith. It was the last royal act in the palace, for a king never lived at Amboise again.

In the seventeenth century, the château served as a state prison. In the following century, the château and the barony of Amboise belonged to the duc de Choiseul, but he was more interested in the pleasure palace he had built at nearby Chanteloup. A great number of its buildings were torn down at the beginning of the nineteenth century. It is now the residence of the comte de Paris, who preserves the château, through his Foundation St-Louis, as a heritage of France.

THE TOUR OF THE CASTLE MOUNT, NOW BEAUTIFully landscaped, begins at the Chapelle St-Hubert, finished in 1493 and gracefully situated atop a projection of the defense wall. The chapel formed an adjunct to the queen's apartments, which stretched in front of its entrance, and served as her oratory. It consists of a single nave bay, a transept, and a choir with beveled corners, all in the Flamboyant style. The filigree Gothic ornamentation on its roof and its flèche were restored in the nineteenth century. However, the exterior's real jewel is the double portal, with its lintel displaying an exquisitely carved relief, which on one side depicts St. Christopher carrying the Infant Christ, and on the other St. Hubert encountering a stag with a crucifix between its antlers. The sculptures in the tympanum are not original and are a bit too heavy for the overall design. They represent Charles VIII and Anne de Bretagne kneeling before the Madonna.

The interior is resplendent with embellishment in the Flamboyant style. It presumably was created by Flemish stonecutters, as was the relief of St. Christopher and St. Hubert above the entrance. Since 1874, a collection of bones has been interred in the left transept, among which are some believed to be those of Leonardo da Vinci. He was buried in 1519 in the church of St-Florentin, which used to stand in the center of the castle mount. The church was razed in the early nineteenth century, and it was not until 1869 that excavation was undertaken in a search for Leonardo's remains. Countless graves were uncovered, and finally just what the searchers had hoped for in their enthusiasm came

Charles VIII

94

AMBOISE

to light: a skull and the fragments of a tombstone with the letters *Leon—* and *—inc—*.

The only one surviving of the numerous wings of the château seen in Du Cerceau's engraving is the Logis du Roi, and even it has been heavily restored. The part of it facing the Loire, flanked by a rectangular pavilion (the remains of the medieval keep) and the round Tour des Chevaliers (or des Minimes), was constructed under Charles VIII. Louis XII and François I added the perpendicular wing adjoining it.

The ground floor of the older section consists of two vaulted galleries, the one on the Loire side opening out into an arcade. On the second floor is the Salle des Etats, the ribbed ogive vaulting of which rests on slender columns adorned with the lilies of France and the ermine dots of Brittany. All of this was restored in the nineteenth century. In 1560, hundreds of

Protestant conspirators were collected in this room before being hanged from the railings of the Logis balcony; since then it has been called the Balcon des Conjurés (conspirators).

The remaining rooms of the castle are set up like a museum. After Langeais, Amboise has the richest collection of Late Gothic and Renaissance furnishings to be found in any of the Loire châteaux.

Also surviving, although in part restored, are the towers—the Tour Hurtault, on the south side, and Tour des Minimes, facing the Loire—in which it was possible to drive up to the castle mount with a horse and carriage. When Emperor Charles V visited Amboise in 1539, François I wished to stage his guest's nighttime arrival with special pomp. He had the interior walls of one of these towers (presumably the Tour Hurtault) hung with tapestries and the spiral ramp inside it brightly illuminated with torches. Just as the emperor was halfway up the tower, the tapestries caught fire from one of the torches. Panic ensued, and it was a miracle that the emperor escaped without suffocating. The king accused several guardsmen of responsibility for the accident and wanted to have them hanged; however, the emperor magnanimously pardoned them.

AFTER THE CASTLE, THE CITY'S MOST IMPORTANT structure is the former priory church of *St-Denis*, which was built in the twelfth century as a three-bay basilica with transept, crossing tower, and choir. The choir vaulting and the side chapel were renovated in the fifteenth century, and the south side aisle was enlarged in the sixteenth. Facing the city, a richly ornamented but heavily restored round-arch portal leads into the interior.

The large altar retable in the choir, the work of Antoine Charpentier, dates from the seventeenth century. The painting of the Holy Family is attributed to Claude Vignon. Other important works of art in the church include a life-size sculptural group of the Entombment and a reclining Mary Magdalene, both from the sixteenth century. Also noteworthy is *La Femme noyée*, a marble figure of what is said to be a drowned woman, also from the sixteenth century and attributed to Francesco Prima-

97: At Chambord (Fred Mayer/Woodfin Camp).

98–99: A view of Chambord (Harvey Lloyd/The Stock Market).

100: Brissac-Quincé (Gea Koenig).

101: At Saumur (Allan A. Philiba).

102–103: Saumur and the river as seen from the château (Aileen Ah-Tye).

104–105: Interior at Beauregard (Fred Mayer/Woodfin Camp).

106: The Cher river at Chenonceau (John F. Mason/The Stock Market).

107: Chenonceau (Mark Segal).

108: In the garden at Chenonceau (Aileen Ah-Tye).

109: View of Chenonceau (Allan A. Philiba).

110–111: Loire vineyards (Allan A. Philiba).

112: Drawbridge leading to courtyard at Chaumont (Adam Woolfitt/Woodfin Camp).

SVITE DV REIGNE DV ROY LOVIS XIII DV NON DEPVIS 1610 IVSQVES A LANNEE 1643

ticcio. In the baptismal chapel is a seventeenth-century painting of St. Francis of Paola being received at Amboise in 1482 by the future Charles VIII.

The church of Notre-Dame-de-Grève, which assumed the name *St-Florentin* from the castle church after it was destroyed, was built around 1480 by order of Louis XI, who had forbidden the townspeople to enter the church on the castle mount. Opposite the church stands the early sixteenth-century house of the treasurer of France, Pierre Morin. Since 1855, it has served as the *Hôtel de Ville*. The *Porte de l'Amasse* is a surviving fragment of the town fortifications, above which the Tour de l'Horloge was erected between 1495 and 1500. The area around this gateway is one of the most charming sections of Amboise.

The promenade along the riverbank boasts a fountain created by Max Ernst from 1966 to 1968. It consists of a number of figures—large toads, frog-faced creatures, and what appears to be a cat—on bases of different shapes. The whole grouping is playful and almost facetious. The fountain was a gift to the city from the artist.

OUTSIDE OF TOWN IN THE VALLEY OF THE AMASSE, by way of the Rue Victor-Hugo from the foot of the castle, is the small manor house of *Clos-Lucé*, with its memory of Leonardo da Vinci. Clos-Lucé, earlier known as Cloux, was built at the end of the fifteenth century by Etienne Le Loup, chief steward to Louis XI. Later it belonged—virtually as a dependency of the castle—to Charles VIII and to Louise de Savoie. François I assigned it to Leonardo as a place to live in 1516.

Louis XII had endeavored to talk the artist into coming to France. But it was finally his successor, François I, who succeeded in doing so, largely thanks to the intercession of the French painter Jean Perréal. The arrival of Leonardo was testimony to the intellectual importance of François I's reign. Understandably, the king treated Leonardo with extreme generosity, asking nothing but the pleasure of his conversation.

In Leonardo's time, Clos-Lucé consisted of only two wings in brick and stone, with a polygonal stair tower at the corner between them and an adjacent chapel. The north wing was added in the nineteenth century. Visitors are shown the very room in which, according to Giorgio Vasari, the master is supposed to have died in the arms of François I on May 2, 1519. But the king was not even in Amboise at the time. The supposed deathbed is just as doubtful as Vasari's description. A famous drawing of the Château d'Amboise attributed to Leonardo, a reproduction of which is in this room, depicts it as it appeared from Clos-

Weathercock showing royal arms.

113

Lucé. For a long time, it was thought that Leonardo was the creator of the frescoes in the little chapel; now spoiled by attempts to restore them, they may have been done by one of his pupils.

Although none of Leonardo's art is exhibited at Clos-Lucé, a special tribute to the artist's genius is housed in the museum's basement: working models of some of Leonardo's extraordinary inventions built from his own plans. The cardinal of Aragon may even have seen the drawings of a flying machine, a turbine, a parachute, and a gear-driven automobile—a few of this farsighted genius's ideas now brought to life.

FROM HIGHWAY D31, WHICH LEADS SOUTH OUT of town through the Forêt d'Amboise, a drive branches off to the *Pagode de Chanteloup*. This unusual structure and several small pavilions are all that remain of one of the most splendid palace complexes of eighteenth-century France. Built in 1713 by Robert de Cotte, the Château de Chanteloup was acquired in 1761 by the minister to Louis XV and governor of Touraine, Etienne-François, duc de Choiseul. He commissioned the architect Louis Denis le Camus to enlarge the palace and enrich its appearance. He dreamed of creating a palace and gardens that could compete with Versailles in this superb landscape at the edge of the Forêt d'Amboise. In the early nineteenth century, the palace was sold for demolition. Even so, surviving pictures and documents permit us to form some idea of

St-Denis

Tower of the Amboise château.

the duke's highly cultivated style of life. Some of the priceless furnishings from the palace and some magical paintings by Boucher may be seen in the Musée des Beaux-Arts in Tours.

The duke had the land around the palace, which was completely embedded with gardens, marked off by a nearly symmetrical network of *allées* and wooded lanes, all of which converged on the palace axis near a large pond that still exists. The focus of the entire layout of the palace and its park was the pagoda. A surviving drawing in the Cabinet des Estampes in Paris shows what a commanding focal point it was when viewed from the south courtyard of the palace.

It should come as no surprise to discover a structure in the Chinese style from a period when the China craze was at its height in all the princely courts of Europe. What is remarkable about the building is the motive behind its construction. Choiseul had liked Madame de Pompadour; but after her death, the prime minister refused to acknowledge the king's new mistress, Madame du Barry. She demanded revenge, and Louis XV satisfied her by banishing Choiseul to Chanteloup. But the duke had many friends who remained true to him even after he had been removed from office. They visited him at Chanteloup, where he staged a constant succession of parties and hunts, enjoying more delightful times with them than ever before. In order to create a lasting testament to these friendships, he commissioned Le Camus to design this pagoda, which was built between 1775 and 1778.

It consists of seven tiers. The open, round salon at its base is surrounded by columns. A stairway leads up to the succes-sively smaller spaces. Balconies at every second level provide wonderful views of Amboise, the pond below, and the surrounding forest. A slight depression in the ground reveals the position of the parterres of the palace gardens. In the salon on the second level, which is completely faced with marble, the duke had a plaque installed with the following inscription: "Etienne-François, duc de Choiseul—touched by the demonstrations of friendship, kindness, and respect accorded him during his exile by so many people who troubled to visit him here—erected this monument as an eternal manifestation of his gratitude."

CHENONCEAU

GUSTAVE FLAUBERT WROTE:

I can scarcely describe the unique calm and aristocratic serenity of the Château de Chenonceau. . . . Standing at the end of a grand *allée*, somewhat apart from the village, which seems to hold back out of respect, surrounded by forest in the middle of a large park with lovely stretches of lawn, and built right on top of the water, it extends its turrets and its square chimneys up into the sky. The Cher gurgles beneath the high arches, whose sharp edges cut through its waters. Its sinuous motion is robust and at the same time calm, and its quiet melancholy is without ennui or grieving.[13]

Throughout its history, women have played the major role in the fortunes of this château. Beginning in the thirteenth century, the land around the present village of Chenonceaux belonged to the de Marques family, who built a castle beside the Cher. This structure was razed in 1411 by order of Charles VI because the lord of the castle had taken up arms against him. But soon a new castle was built, the donjon and moats of which survive. Belonging to it was a mill, which had been built on massive pillars above the Cher.

Pierre de Marques, who inherited the place in 1460, had no sense of how to manage it, and debt forced him to sell successive portions of the holding. The buyer in each case was Thomas Bohier, the chief tax collector for Charles VIII, Louis XII, and François I. With relish and perseverance, he waited for the utter ruin of the de Marques family; after twenty years the entire property was finally his. Bohier also

Chenonceau

managed to acquire large tracts of land around Chenonceaux, and the king granted him all the rights and privileges of an estate lord.

In 1513, Bohier began to tear down the old castle, with the exception of its round keep, and to build the present château above the foundation of the mill in the river. He was forced by matters of state to spend some years in Italy, but his wife, Katherine Briçonnet, supervised the construction.

After eight years, the château was finished; but the Bohiers were able to enjoy it only briefly: Thomas died in 1524; Katherine, in 1526. When an audit disclosed that Bohier owed a huge sum of money to the state treasury, his son and heir proposed an arrangement with François I, deeding him Chenonceau and various other properties.

In 1547, Henri II acceded to the throne, and his mistress, Diane de Poitiers, begged him to give her the château. Since he never refused her anything, the wish was granted.

Diane had Philibert de l'Orme design a bridge across the Cher and lay out a large garden parterre to the northeast of the châ-teau. This was to be a pleasure garden, as well as one for growing fruits and vegetables. She asked the owners of the loveliest gardens in Touraine to donate cuttings. The archbishop of Tours dutifully contributed grafts from his most precious fruit trees, rosebushes, lily bulbs, and—as particular rarities—melons and artichokes. In addition, Diane planted grapevines, mulberry trees (to raise silkworms), strawberries, and violets. Jacques Androuet Du Cerceau praised a nearly 20-foot fountain in the center of the garden as an especially successful addition.

Diane enjoyed the beauties of Chenonceau in deep draughts. It is said that she dived naked into the current of the Cher at sunrise, then surfaced and rode off on a white horse.

Her idyll ended with the death of Henri II in 1559. Henri's widow, Catherine de Médicis, forced her hated and now defenseless rival to exchange Chenonceau for the much less inviting Chaumont. Like Diane, she admired Chenonceau, and she immediately set about planning an expansion that would have made the château the most ambitious sixteenth-century structure in France. Du Cerceau published the design for it, presumably developed by Jean Bullant, in his famous book of engravings. All that was completed from these plans was the two-story gallery above the bridge.

The festivities arranged by Catherine at Chenonceau are famous. Descriptions of some of them have come down to us; for example, a fête for her son Charles IX in 1563 began with a triumphal procession:

Everyone approached Chenonceau by way of a long *allée* bordered by canals. Singing sirens emerged from these waterways and were greeted by nymphs stepping out of the woods. At the sound of the singing, satyrs appeared, stirred by it to run off with the sirens. Mounted knights then leaped forward to defend the women, and after endless swordplay, all proceeded to pay homage to the king. At this point, there was a barrage of cannon fire from the galleries and the château itself, and fireworks were set off above the river. . . .

The nymphs [were] swathed in silver fabrics and rose and blue veils, with numerous gemstones at their necks and waists and priceless bracelets on their arms. The knights were completely outfitted in silver and red with capes of blue velvet, while the satyrs wore hairy costumes of gold and silk.

That evening, there was a party for the king, his lords and princes, and the entire court. After dinner, the king initiated the dancing with Madame, his sister, and he also danced with the costumed players who had earlier served as nymphs and knights. Now they were dressed like natives of Poitou, and appeared with a bagpiper to perform the dances of that region. The women wore silver brocade, blue, and pink, their hair all covered with gems, and the men were costumed in silk and velvet in blue, white, and pink with silver braid.

As soon as he had risen the next morning, the king went for a walk in the gardens, where he discovered his pages attacking a boar. After the animal had been killed, the king went in to breakfast, then joined the ladies and numerous courtiers in costume for an excursion down the river.

After dinner, there was a concert, at which the king, Monsieur [the future Henri III], and Madame, his sister, the prince of Navarre, the marquis Conty, Lord de Guise, the little Ozances, Bordeille, Curtin, and Luze all appeared dressed as shepherds in gold brocade set with gems and white satin.

The next day, the king took part in a *battue*. A huge wild boar was killed with long lances by the prince and the lords with him, all of whom were on horseback and masked. It was a splendid hunt, and numerous other boars were taken while the king watched from the stands with the queen mother, Monsieur and Madame, Princess Condé, Lord le Grand, Lord Bourbon, and Lord de Guise, the prince de la Roche-sur-Yon, Lord d'Estampes, and countless others.

After supper that evening, there was a huge display of fireworks on the river put on by Cornelio de Fiesco.

The next morning, the queen mother accompanied the king to breakfast in the park, and into the aviary containing numerous birds from exotic lands. They were served by all the queen's daughters and by Madame. These women were dressed in the costume of Picardy, with dark red skirts of velvet and satin and bonnets of woven linen. In their hair, they wore countless jewels. Their aprons and sleeves were made of silver brocade, and their cloaks, of purple. It was a lovely breakfast consisting of sweets and all manner of fruits.

During dessert, fifty-four barques draped with garlands staged a sea battle on the river.[14]

Catherine de Médicis willed Chenonceau to Louise de Vaudémont, duchesse de

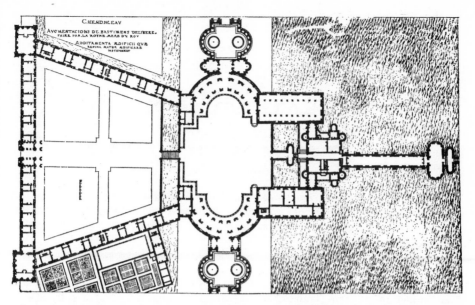

Catherine de Médicis' plan for the expansion of Chenonceau (after Du Cerceau, 1607).

Lorraine and wife of Henry III. After the king's assassination in 1589, Louise spent the rest of her life in mourning at the château, wearing only white and insisting that her rooms be furnished in black.

In the château is a portrait of the charming Madame Dupin by Jean-Marc Nattier. She and her husband, the farmer-general Claude Dupin, acquired Chenonceau in 1733. They furnished it lavishly and re-planted the gardens, which had gone to ruin. Madame Dupin was a lover of the arts and sciences, and the intelligentsia of France converged on her salon. Jean-Jacques Rousseau served as tutor to the Dupin children, and in his *Confessions*, he writes of the time he spent at the château: "Life was absolutely delightful in that lovely place; I ate very well and grew fat as a monk." Both Madame Dupin and the château survived the Revolution because of the respect in which she was held by the townspeople.

In the nineteenth century, Madame Pelouze tried to preserve the old splendor of the château and spent her fortune on its faithful restoration. Since 1913, Chenonceau has belonged to the Menier family.

THE CHÂTEAU IS STILL APPROACHED ALONG THE park *allée*, which Charles IX used for his entrance. Tall plane trees line the roadway. On either side are the canals from which sirens emerged during that brilliant fête in honor of the king.

Two sphinxes at the end of the *allée* guard the entrance to the gardens, which are laid out between the park and the château and are almost surrounded by water. The larger parterre framed by a terrace and lying to the east is the garden of Diane de Poitiers, while the smaller one on the op-

119

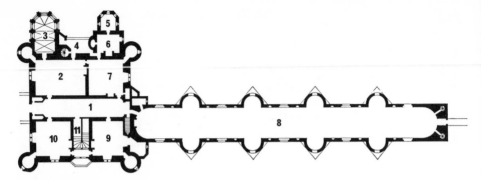

Floor plan of Chenonceau château (ground floor) 1. vestibule. 2. Salle des Gardes. 3. chapel. 4. terrasse. 5. library of Catherine de Médicis. 6. Cabinet Vert. 7. chambre de Diane de Poitiers. 8. gallery. 9. chambre de François I. 10. chambre de Louis XIII (Salon de Louis XIV). 11. stairway.

posite site was laid out by Catherine de Médicis. In their present state, both parterres are nineteenth-century creations. The idea of embellishing the lawn surfaces with delicate scrollwork is Italian.

The central lawn area, which is bisected by the main axis leading to the château, is bounded on the west side by an elongated structure known as the Bâtiment des Dômes, so called because of its strangely wavelike curving roof, which was reconstructed in the nineteenth century. Catherine de Médicis had it built—possibly by de l'Orme—to house her servants, aristocratic guests, and officers. It now houses a wax museum, with scenes from Chenonceau's history.

The approach to the château leads across a moated terrace, the site of the fifteenth-century castle belonging to the de Marques family. All that remains of that complex are a well with a playful wrought-iron top and the round Tour de Marques, with staircase turret. Bohier had the keep modernized and its entrance furnished with a Renaissance doorframe.

The château is unique among French Renaissance structures, both for its placement in the landscape and for its ground plan. The bridge over the Cher and its two-story gallery were later additions, and they obscure the original artistic form of the structure. In contrast to the earlier building on the site, Chenonceau is built out above the river. Defense considerations had nothing to do with such an unusual placement; Bohier merely wished to be able to enjoy the river landscape from all four sides of his château. For that reason, each of its façades—originally including the southern one, later hidden by the bridge—was provided with balconies or terraces.

The château was built above a square ground plan. Four round towers at its corners accentuate the two-story block, but they were not built as fortifications. The north and west fronts, including the dormers cutting through the roof, are rigidly symmetrical. The original south front should be thought of as having been similar to these. Chenonceau is one of the earliest

French buildings to have been designed, according to the precepts of the Italian Renaissance, with perfectly balanced proportions. The east front reveals a traditional taste for picturesque asymmetry. The chapel and a pavilionlike two-story extension jut out from the façade; both have beveled corners and rest on projecting foundations surviving from the earlier mill. The dormers and chimneys enliven the severity of the elevations without upstaging the clarity of their arrangement.

Catherine de Médicis must have felt that the entry façade was not imposing enough. She had the side windows doubled and pilasters with caryatids set up between them. This change was reversed in the nineteenth century, and the caryatids now stand in the park to the east of the *allée*.

On both floors, the interior is divided in half by a gallerylike vestibule, its width precisely half that of the adjoining rooms. The staircase is located next to the vestibule in the exact center of the west side. A similar arrangement is found in Venetian palaces, and it is possible that Bohier deliberately imitated a bit of Venice above the Cher. Like the exteriors, the disposition of the interior rooms reveals a newly awakened need for regularity and ideal proportions. At the same time, there are still a number of traditional architectural forms. For example, the ground-floor vestibule, once flooded with light from a window on the south end before the bridge gallery was built, contains old-fashioned zigzag ribbed vaulting resting on delicately sculptured consoles. In its floor tiles, which unfortunately have been nearly worn away, you can still read the motto of Bohier, *S'il vient à point, me souviendra* (When it is completed, it will call me to mind), an obvious indication that Bohier wished to secure posthumous fame with his château.

On both floors, two large rooms open from the vestibule on either side. A carved oak door whose decorative panels contain likenesses of St. Thomas and St. Catherine, the patron saints of Bohier and his wife, leads into the Salle des Gardes. This door also carries Bohier's motto. This room once was adorned with an Italian (or Italian-inspired) majolica floor in blue, gold, bistre, and green, which is now almost totally destroyed. It is only around the edges that a few surviving tiles still give an idea of the ornamental richness with which the château's first inhabitants wished to surround themselves. Also surviving is the original fireplace, with the coat of arms of Bohier. The lovely sixteenth-century Flemish wall tapestries are not part of the original furnishings, however.

The adjacent chapel, from 1521, reveals transitional forms between the Gothic and the Renaissance. It consists of two bays and a five-sided choir. It was consecrated by Cardinal Antoine Bohier, Thomas's brother and the archbishop of Bourges. One is struck by the obvious graffiti on its walls from the sixteenth and eighteenth centuries. The older ones—dated "1543" and "1546"—were left behind by Scottish soldiers in the service of Mary Stuart. The owners of the château once followed the Mass from the balcony above the entrance. The chapel is adorned with a sixteenth-century marble bas-relief of the Madonna and Child.

The so-called Chambre de Diane de Poitiers contains a sixteenth-century fireplace by the noted sculptor Jean Goujon. The portrait of Catherine de Médicis on its mantelpiece was painted by Henri Sauvage in 1901. The Flemish wall tapestries depict the Triumph of Charity and the Triumph of Authority. A painting of the Madonna and Child, from the seventeenth

Chenonceau

century, is attributed to Bartolomé Esteban Murillo.

The two neighboring rooms in the extension are the Cabinet Vert and the library of Catherine de Médicis. The cabinet still has its beamed ceiling painted in green; its walls were formerly covered in green velvet. It is richly furnished with a painting of the Holy Family by Andrea del Sarto and one of a martyr by Correggio, as well as an Oudenaarde tapestry. The tiny library preserves a remarkable fine coffered and carved wooden ceiling from 1521.

The two remaining ground-floor rooms are named after François I and Louis XIII. The Chambre de François contains the château's most magnificent fireplace. The walls are covered in painted canvas from the nineteenth century in imitation of leather paneling from the sixteenth. Two paintings are worthy of notice: *Diane de Poitiers as the Huntress Diana*, a full-length portrait probably painted at Chenonceau and attributed to Francesco Primaticcio; and *The Three Graces* by Carle van Loo, in reality the full-length portraits of three sisters who were mistresses of Louis XV. Furnishings include a magnificent fifteenth-century Italian cabinet inlaid with ivory and mother of pearl.

In the Chambre de Louis XIII (Salon de Louis XIV) hangs a portrait of Louis XIV by Hyacinthe Rigaud in a lavishly carved gilded frame, typical of the rich style developed under the Sun King. This was a bread-and-butter present from the king after a visit to Chenonceau. A dramatic painting of Christ with St. John is thought to be Rubens's work, and in this room is Nattier's portrait of Madame Dupin. The large fireplace, with its emblems of François I and Claude de France, was restored in the nineteenth century.

The staircase leading to the second floor consists of two parallel flights in the Italian style. It is roofed with ribbed vaults and coffers. A loggia with windows on the first landing above a corridor connecting the adjacent rooms provides a view of the river.

The arrangement of the second-floor rooms is identical to that of those on the ground floor. The four rooms connected by the vestibule are museum re-creations in the sixteenth-century style. Exquisite Gobelin tapestries hang in these rooms. The vestibule is decorated with Oudenaarde tapestries of hunting scenes and with sculptures of Roman emperors in Carrara marble brought from Florence by Catherine de Médicis.

The attics at one time housed a small convent of Capuchin nuns. The rooms were separated from the rest of the château by a drawbridge that could be raised at night.

The kitchen and housekeeping rooms are located in the massive substructure of the old mill, on which the château was erected. Thanks to the clever use of this space, all portions of the floors above could be given over to living and entertaining.

The gallery was an architectural idea with which the new Renaissance style became associated. Extensive galleries became the favored setting for court society. The two-story gallery on top of Diane de Poitiers's bridge was built by Catherine de Médicis—possibly after a design by Bullant—in 1580. The 197-foot-long structure abruptly breaks off before it reaches the opposite bank of the river. According to Du Cerceau's engraving, it was to terminate in a small perpendicular structure rounded on its narrow ends.

The new structure's exterior architecture seems somewhat cool compared with that of the older château. Semicircular projections rise from the pillars of the bridge on the lower, unornamented story and serve as balconies off the more elaborate floor above. Dormers provide decorative accents to the roof surface.

Today the gallery interiors seem quite plain. Their most important ornaments are the large fireplaces at either end. The lower one has a floor of black and white tiles and a wooden beamed ceiling, to which a portion of the mourning decor ordered by Louise de Vaudémont was attached in the nineteenth century. The niches in the walls presumably were filled with sculptures.

The exterior projections serve inside as intimate alcove windows, to which it must have been pleasant to withdraw from the festivities. One gets a sense of how lovely such parties suspended above the river must have been.

During the First World War, the owner of the château, Gaston Menier, set up a military hospital in the gallery. During the Second World War, it served as a safe means of flight: the entrance to the château lay in German-occupied France, but the opposite bank of the Cher was part of unoccupied Vichy France.

MONTRICHARD

THE TOWN OF MONTRICHARD DESERVES A BRIEF visit. It consists of ancient houses and charming streets, above which towers one of the most famous donjons in France. At the end of the tenth century, Foulques Nerra, comte d'Anjou, was in possession of the Touraine cities of Amboise, Loches, and La Haye. Threatened by the lords of St-Aignan and of Pontlevoy, he was determined to enlarge his holdings. In order to gain control of the valley of the Cher, in 1010 he took possession of the promontory of Montrichard, right next to the river, and built a wooden keep on top of it. The site was strategically favorable, for at the foot of this elevation was the intersection of the roads between Tours and Bourges and between Blois and Poitiers. Between 1110 and 1130, one of Foulques's descendants, Hugues, replaced the wooden structure with the present stone donjon, which was patterned after the one at Loches. Until well into the fifteenth century it belonged to the lords of Amboise. In 1461, it was acquired by Louis XI, who often stayed here in order to worship the miraculous painting of the Madonna in the church in neighboring Nanteuil. In 1476, Louis's daughter Jeanne de France married Louis, duc d'Orléans (the future Louis XII), in the chapel attached to the castle at the foot of the hill, now the parish church of Ste-Croix. This marriage was contracted only to please the king. After he assumed the Crown, Louis XII divorced Jeanne in order to marry Anne de Bretagne. Jeanne loved living at Montrichard, and the townspeople adored her for her kindness and simplicity. She was canonized as Ste. Jeanne de Valois in 1950 by Pope Pius XII.

The Crown sold the castle in the late sixteenth century, and it subsequently passed through numerous hands. During the following century the structure was allowed to deteriorate severely.

The core of the fortress is a square

Montrichard (drawing by B. Ebhardt).

twelfth-century *keep* of three stories, strengthened by buttresses. The ground floor served as a storehouse and had a beamed ceiling. The only floor suited for living was the second one, which was lighted by pointed-arch windows. A door on the south side led directly into this level. The top story had a flat roof and boasted a battlemented wall-walk. Henri IV had the top 13 feet of the walls removed in order to weaken the structure's defensibility in the event that it fell into enemy hands. A staircase built into the wall connected the three floors within. It is still possible to climb these stairs; from the top of the keep is a magnificent view of the town; the sub-urb of Nanteuil, with its pilgrimage church from the twelfth, thirteenth, and fifteenth centuries; and the bridge across the Cher.

As the castle chapel, the church of *Ste-Croix* dates to the twelfth century. However, the only portions of it actually surviving from that time are the pillars and arcades along the south side of the nave. The north aisle dates from the sixteenth century; the choir and chapels, from the eighteenth; and the south aisle and tower, from the nineteenth. The façade of Ste-Croix, an excellent Romanesque example, combines geometric solidity with fine detailing. Note the elegant arcades and the beautifully carved moldings on the portal.

ST-AIGNAN-SUR-CHER

ST-AIGNAN-SUR-CHER, LYING ON AN ELEVATION above the Cher Valley, has two massive structures that dominate its skyline: a Romanesque church with famous wall paintings in its crypt, and a Renaissance château.

At the end of the ninth century, monks

from the monastery of St-Martin in Tours built a chapel here in honor of the Virgin. After it had received relics of the sainted Bishop Aignan of Orléans, the church became a favorite pilgrimage goal, and at the beginning of the eleventh century, it was replaced by a new structure. The present church was erected on the site between the end of the eleventh century and the beginning of the thirteenth, and a seminary originally was attached to it.

It is a four-bay basilica with a transept that does not project beyond the line of the side aisles and an ambulatory choir with three chapels. A massive narthex tower to the west and an equally massive crossing tower mark its exterior.

Despite radical renovation in the nineteenth century, it is one of the most impressive Romanesque ecclesiastical interiors in the Loire. Its architectural elements are strongly delineated, with a rich wall elevation, round arches in the choir, and slender shapes in the choir, transept, and nave. The vaulting reveals that construction was begun in the eastern end and moved west. The choir and the transept have barrel vaulting, while the nave boasts domelike cross-ribbed vaults between pointed transverse arches, already revealing something of the Early Gothic style.

The two-bay chapel of Notre-Dame-des-Miracles off the south aisle dates from the sixteenth century, and houses notable paintings in its vaults, including depictions of the archangel Michael as dragon-slayer and weigher of souls. Remains of painting from the same period may be seen also in the chapel of the river boatmen, which is above the Lady Chapel.

A number of wall paintings in an extraordinary state of preservation are in the crypt beneath the choir. They escaped restoration in the nineteenth century only because the space had been leased as a wine cellar. Corresponding to the layout of the choir, the crypt consists of a main apse with a single vaulted bay in front of it, an ambulatory, and three chapels.

The oldest paintings are in the main apse and in the central and south chapels. The main apse contains a Christ in Majesty with St. Peter and St. James, their elongated forms depicted in motion. Peter, who is handing the keys to Christ, is healing cripples, while James listens to confessions and gives absolution. The inscription reads *Confitemini Alterutrum Peccata*, and the scene illustrates the connection between the forgiveness of sin and the healing of the sick, as set out in Matthew 9:5 and James 5:13–16.

The theme of healing also dominates the rest of the surviving paintings. In the south chapel, whose vaulting is crowned by a medallion depicting the Lamb of God supported by angels, is a series of scenes from the legend of St. Giles: Giles giving his cloak to a half-naked invalid; healing a man who has been bitten by a snake; and praying for the salvation of an endangered ship at sea. A fourth scene has been destroyed.

In the central chapel, off the ambulatory, is a fragment of a painting of the raising of Lazarus.

The figures in the St. Giles scenes help to date the paintings to the late twelfth century. The bodies are in the style of the High Romanesque, and the folds in the drapery are indicated by parallel or radiating lines; but their movements now are rhythmic.

In addition to these paintings, there are some examples from the fifteenth century. On either side of the Christ in Majesty of the main apse, for example, appears the donor, Louis II de Chalon. On one side, he is commending himself and his two wives to John the Baptist, St. Anne, and the Virgin and Child; on the other, to the Mater Dolorosa at the foot of the Cross. The Chalon coat of arms appears above the Christ in Majesty. The Last Judgment is depicted on the vaulting in front of the apse, and the Crucifixion adorns the west wall.

An imposing flight of 144 stone steps leads to the sixteenth-century *château*. Its interior is closed to visitors, but it is possible to stroll around its courtyard and enjoy the splendid view it offers of the valley of the Cher.

Before the lords of Husson built this château, they lived in the adjoining medieval fortress, which they abandoned following completion of the new structure. All that remains of it are a few ruins. The new castle, in the Renaissance style, opens onto the courtyard from two wings. A polygonal stair tower was added in the nineteenth century.

VALENÇAY

VALENÇAY, WHICH LIES ON THE BORDER BETWEEN Touraine and Berry, belonged to one of the most intriguing personalities in the history of France: Charles Maurice de Talleyrand-Périgord, grand seigneur of the Age of Enlightenment, supreme diplomat, cynic, and master of the bon mot.

Born in Paris in 1754, Talleyrand was afflicted from childhood with a limp. At the age of twenty-five, he was ordained, and at thirty-four was named bishop of Autun. In 1789, the first year of the Revolution, he gained a seat in the Estates General and became a member of the Constituent Assembly. His career from then on, the result of the coldest calculation, was marked by incredible reversals: in 1790, he was named president of the National Assembly; in 1791, he resigned as bishop and was excommunicated; in 1797, after having been forced into exile in the United States, he became foreign minister under the Directory; in 1799, he resigned to accept the same office under the Consulate of Napoleon Bonaparte; in 1802, he was readmitted to the Church as a layman by the pope and married; in 1804, he was made grand chamberlain by Napoleon; in 1807, he resigned as foreign minister and became a secret opponent of Napoleon, who dismissed him as grand chamberlain in 1809; in 1814, after Napoleon's abdication, he became president of the provisional government and, once again, foreign minister, serving as France's representative at the Congress of Vienna (1814–15); he was forced to resign in 1815 and was again named grand chamberlain; as ambassador in London he took part in the Revolution of 1830; and in 1838, he made his peace with the Church and died.

Napoleon wanted his minister well housed, so that he could entertain diplomats in splendid style. Talleyrand could hardly have found a more imposing château in which to entertain than Valençay; it stands in the middle of a large park high above the valley of the Nahon and enjoys a sweeping view of the whole region. Valençay was one of the two or three largest feudal domains in France, with twenty-three towns included in it. Fittingly, this impres-

128

sive relic from the *ancien régime* fell into the hands of the most splendid and tenacious survivor from that earlier society.

Jacques d'Estampes, whose family had acquired the seigniory in the fifteenth century, began building himself a château on the site of an earlier country castle in 1540. Estampes had come into money through his marriage with Jeanne Bernard d'Estiau, the daughter of the treasurer of Anjou, and he felt he could aim high: nothing less than an amalgam of Chambord and Chenonceau would be appropriate to his situation. Thus he had his architect design four wings around an inner courtyard, with massive round towers at the corners, as at Chambord, while the north wing was to be highlighted in the center by a keeplike entrance pavilion like the one Thomas Bohier had created at Chenonceau.

Of this plan, the only portions actually built were the northwest tower (Vieille Tour), with its domelike roof; the adjacent half of the two-story north wing, with arcades facing the courtyard; and the entrance pavilion. The other half of the north wing remained one story, and was closed off with a round tower that is much too small in relation to the rest of the château. Estampes certainly envisioned a palace far

Valençay

too grandiose for his purse, but it is unmistakably clear that, in its execution, he demanded distinct quality. The façades were adorned with an elegant arrangement of pilasters, and the three-story entrance pavilion, with its round turrets on the outer corners, was furnished with a wall-walk whose consoles are heavy with sculptured embellishment.

It was only in the middle of the seventeenth century that Dominique d'Estampes, a descendant of the first builder, added an east wing—which no longer exists—and the surviving park wing in the style of the original portions. The southwest tower (Tour Neuve) was finally built in the second half of the eighteenth century by the enormously wealthy farmer-general Legendre Villemorien-Luçay. He also provided the park wing with a new façade on the courtyard side—an open gallery on the ground floor and Colossal pilasters—and he ordered the mansard roof.

Such was the building acquired by Talleyrand in 1803. He informed Napoleon that the purchase price was beyond his modest means; but Napoleon had commanded him to buy such a place and agreed to come up with the difference.

Talleyrand had the open gallery on the park wing closed in with windows and its interior completely redesigned in the Empire style as a place to house his guests. The most prominent "guests" were the Spanish king Ferdinand VII and his family, whom Napoleon banished to Valençay between 1808 and 1814. His choice of Valençay was intended to humble Talleyrand, who had fallen out of favor. The emperor also wished to remind the statesman that it was he who had helped to pay for the estate. He even made his former minister responsible for keeping track of the royal family and seeing that they were entertained. Talleyrand obliged with a degree of equanimity that baffled the rest of the world.

For six years, then, Valençay was the scene of parties and perpetual intrigue. On lovely summer evenings, the château terrace was transformed into an outdoor ballroom, with guitarists hidden in the shrubbery to delight the noble Spaniards with boleros. For their further entertainment, their host had a little theater built near the entrance to the park; it survives to this day.

After Talleyrand's fall from grace as minister to Louis XVIII, he retired to Valençay for good. In 1829, he made over the domain to his grandnephew, Napoleon-Louis de Talleyrand, on whom Charles X bestowed the title comte de Valençay. The property still belongs to Talleyrand's descendants, who do their best to keep alive something of the atmosphere from the time when their illustrious ancestor lived here.

Only a few rooms in the park wing are open to visitors, but they provide a good idea of the comforts of life in the early nineteenth century. The tour begins in the lower gallery, which is furnished with busts and portraits. From here, one enters the Grand Salon with its Empire-style furnishings, including a mahogany table that is said to have been brought back from the Congress of Vienna. Among the portraits is a handsome likeness of Talleyrand by Pierre-Paul Proudhon. Portraits are also the main appointments in the adjacent Salon Bleu. One of the most elegant rooms in the château is the Chambre de la Comtesse on the ground floor of the Tour Neuve, which is completely decorated in pale green, gray, and white. One of its occupants was the enchanting Duchess Dorothée de Dino, a niece of Talleyrand and his lover in his old age. Displayed in the room is a collection of

Sèvres porcelain plates, the remnants of a service presented to the owner of the châ teau by Napoleon. The adjacent anteroom houses a collection of portrait engravings.

The château's most lavish room is the Chambre du Roi on the second floor; it was occupied by Ferdinand VII. The highlights of the room are its splendid canopy bed, the wallcoverings painted with the legend of Psyche in grisaille, and the Italian gouaches on the panels below. The ante-chamber is again given over to engravings. A brief glimpse of the upstairs gallery is sufficient. Talleyrand had it filled with undistinguished Italian landscapes.

The landscaped courtyard in front of the entrance pavilion is a virtual paradise for birds. Swans and ducks swim in its pools, and peacocks perch on the pillars of the fence enclosing it.

A museum containing mementoes of the famous statesman has been set up in one of the late eighteenth-century outbuildings near the entrance gate. It displays his countless medals, some articles of his clothing, and a delightful collection of English and French caricatures of him.

Talleyrand founded a free school for girls in the town, and designated the crypt beneath its chapel as his final resting place.

NOUANS-LES-FONTAINES

NOUANS-LES-FONTAINES HAS A THIRTEENTH-CEN-tury church that is worth visiting if only for its altarpiece, *The Lamentation of Christ*, a major example of Late Gothic painting in France. It is still not known where the painting came from; it cannot have been commissioned for this quite modest village church. The work went unnoticed for centuries, almost totally obscured with grime. Then in 1931, the critic Paul Vitry recognized it as a work by Jean Fouquet and his atelier, and promptly published it as such.

Fouquet was born in Tours, the son of a priest, in around 1420, and died there around 1480. Contemporaries considered him the greatest painter of the century. He was especially noted for his portraits and miniatures, but is also recorded as a master at monumental church paintings. His sole surviving work in the genre is the altarpiece at Nouans, a true masterpiece.

The work is painted on wood and clearly has been cut down somewhat. Even so, it still measures almost 8 feet wide by almost 5 feet high, unusually large dimensions for that time. Two old men are lifting Christ's body and placing it in Mary's lap as John looks on from behind. This carefully composed main grouping is counterbalanced by the figure of the picture's donor, a cleric in flowing robes kneeling near the right edge. He is thought to be the prior of Autainville, Jacques Maussabré. St. James appears behind him. In the background, three grieving women provide a somber contrast to the main figures, which stand out in their lighter-colored garments.

The large size and the cool ceremoniousness of Fouquet's composition is counterbalanced by its wealth of detail. But the artist's sympathetic rendering of the grieved figures makes *The Lamentation of Christ* an intensely moving and evocative altarpiece.

MONTRESOR

THE BELLICOSE FOULQUES NERRA BUILT ONE OF his numerous fortresses designed to control Touraine on the rocky promontory above the valley of the Indre in around 1000. Some remains of its square keep survive, surrounded by a twelfth-century ring wall.

In the late fourteenth century, the castle belonged to Jean de Bueil, the chief crossbowman of France, who was killed at the Battle of Agincourt in 1415. He fortified the complex, adding its outer ring wall, round towers, and gatehouse (now in ruins), closely flanked by two particularly massive towers. Additional artillery towers were provided in the fifteenth century.

Imbert de Bastarnay—heir to Montrésor, councilor to Louis XI, and grandfather of Diane de Poitiers—abandoned the medieval fortress at the beginning of the sixteenth century, preferring to build himself a more comfortable residence without such defenses. This is a rather modest, square, two-story *château* with round towers facing the Indrois Valley. It has little round turrets on projecting buttresses, a polygonal stair tower on the courtyard side, and tall dormers. In its structure, the whole layout still appears to be Late Gothic, yet the newly awakened sense for regularity that was characteristic of the Renaissance is unmistakable.

In the nineteenth century, the château belonged to the Polish Barnicki family, which had it completely restored and newly furnished. The rooms preserve the form given them at that time. They contain a notable collection of paintings by French, Italian, and Polish masters as well as a small but exquisite store of gold- and silverwork.

Imbert de Bastarnay also began construction of the neighboring collegiate *church* (now the parish church), which is one of the most important sacred structures fom the Renaissance in France. It was consecrated in 1532 and completed in 1541.

The building has an aisleless nave and a cruciform ground plan. Architecturally, like the château, it is still Late Gothic in form, with a five-sided choir, ribbed vaulting, and tracery windows in the Flamboyant style. Its Renaissance character comes from its ornamentation. The entrance façade, with its austere arrangement and its decorative elements—sadly for the most part destroyed—is certainly equal to the greatest creations of the French Renaissance. Auguste Rodin made a drawing of this front.

Bastarnay (died 1523) had an eye toward his posthumous fame, for he insisted that his tomb be placed in the very center of the church. Destroyed during the Revolution, it was crudely restored in 1875 and set up in its present position in the nave. Its base is decorated with sculptures of the apostles beneath arcades. On the lid, surrounded by angels, Bastarnay and his wife and son are portrayed life size, laying side by side with folded hands. Numerous portions of the work have been reconstructed in plaster, but the surviving marble sections still give an idea of the original quality of this tomb, which is often attributed to one of the greatest sculptors of the French Renaissance, Jean Goujon.

Other sixteenth-century works are the choir stalls, with their medallions carved with faces, and two stained-glass windows.

In the chapel to the left of the choir is a particularly noteworthy painting of the Annunciation. It glows with a bright, silken light, and is the work of the seventeenth-century painter Philippe de Champaigne. It comes from the collection of Cardinal Fesch, Napoleon's uncle, and was donated to this church by Count Barnicki.

*L*IGET

THE CARTHUSIAN MONASTERY OF LIGET, SITUATed between Montrésor and Loches, was founded by Henry II of England in 1177. According to an inscription once placed above the entrance to the Charterhouse, he did so in penance for the murder in 1170 of his former friend and chancellor, Thomas à Becket, the archbishop of Canterbury. The church built at the time of the monastery's founding now stands in ruins. Most of the other buildings in the extensive complex, now a private estate, date from the eighteenth century.

The jewel of Liget is the *Chapelle St-Jean*, which stands in a field near the edge of the woods several hundred yards north of the Charterhouse. Apply at the gatehouse for the key to it, then follow a dirt track that branches off from the road toward Loches.

Erected in the second half of the twelfth century, the structure presumably was the monastery's first chapel. It is a rotunda of white cut stone with rounded windows, a delicate cornice that bends to accommodate them, a frieze of small arches, and a low conical roof. The exterior has been heavily restored and seems somewhat artless. The monks enlarged it by adding a nave on the west side around 1200; but with the exception of a small fragment, it has disappeared.

The interior is decorated with some of the loveliest frescoes from the period in all of France. It is likely that they were executed at about the time the nave was built.

Seven windows divide the wall area into as many panels. The cycle of paintings, which survives only in fragments, begins at the window level to the right of the low south door. Its first subject is the Tree of Jesse. The patriarch sits holding in his right hand a branch symbolizing the lineage linking him to Jesus. To his left, the Virgin is depicted as a stalk rising from the root of Jesse; like a flower, the Christ Child emerges from her head. The seven doves of the Holy Ghost hover about him. Other major panels illustrate the Nativity, the Presentation in the Temple, the Descent from the Cross, the Women at the Tomb, and the Death of Mary. This last scene, placed above the south door, is the most splendid of all, marvelously composed and imbued with a rich solemnity. Apostles with bowed heads surround the lifeless Madonna, while in their midst, Christ lifts his mother's soul in the form of a child and hovering angels reach down to take it into heaven.

The window embrasures are embellished with figures of saints, and a meander frieze runs above the six large panels. The paintings in the cupola have been lost, for it had to be rebuilt in the nineteenth century. A seventeenth-century document notes that in the cupola, Christ was depicted in majesty with the seven angels of the Apocalypse, thus serving as an eternal reference point for the entire cycle.

The iconography and the style of the frescoes are from two traditions. The artist, who probably was important in his time, based his compositions on Italian and Byzantine models; the depiction of the Death of Mary was a uniquely Byzantine tradition. Yet stylistically, he was rooted in the tradition of west-central France; there is not a trace of Byzantine inspiration in either his figures or their modeling. The colors—white, ocher, red, green, a little blue, and numerous harmonious shades of gray—are thoroughly Western. The artist probably made use of a pattern book based on Italo-Byzantine images that was far removed from the originals; because of its having been repeatedly copied by Western artists, none of the stylistic elements of Byzantine art remained. The painter of Liget re-created these compositions in ascetic, linear, and flat forms that are a distillation of the grand style of the Early Romanesque.

The lower part of the wall, now completely bare, once was adorned with a painted white drape hanging down in rich folds. Remnants of it could still be seen a century ago.

*L*OCHES

ONE OF THE BEST-PRESERVED SMALL TOWNS IN France, Loches still bears the imprint of its long and varied history. It owes its founding to the strategic virtues of the rocky promontory on which its fortress complex was built. This entire hill is circled with walls and towers. The keep, which serves as the town's landmark, rises above the southwest corner of the fortress, and the Logis du Roi stands at the northeast end above the steepest cliffs. Between these two structures are the former collegiate church of St-Ours and what remains of the medieval city. The castle mount was thus a complete town in itself, set apart from the one spread at its feet. Its defense walls were once surrounded by moats, which have been transformed into gardens and promenades. There were also walls around the lower town, and inside these, below the church and the Logis du Roi, was a separate, smaller walled area known as the Fort St-Ours. Today only portions of it remain.

IT IS BEST TO BEGIN A TOUR OF THE TOWN WITH the architectural monuments inside the fortress. The only access to the complex from the lower town is by way of the *Porte Royale*, a tall, closed structure erected in the fifteenth century between two thirteenth-century round towers. The entire gatehouse is ringed with machicolations, and you can still see slits in the walls that once accommodated the timbers of a drawbridge. The building is now the *Musée du Folklore*, a collection of local antiquities and costumes. Behind the gatehouse is the *Musée Lansyer*, dedicated to the nineteenth-century landscape painter Emmanuel Lansyer. In this, his house, are displayed his own works and pages from the sketchbooks of his friend Eugène Delacroix.

A castle crowned this rocky promontory

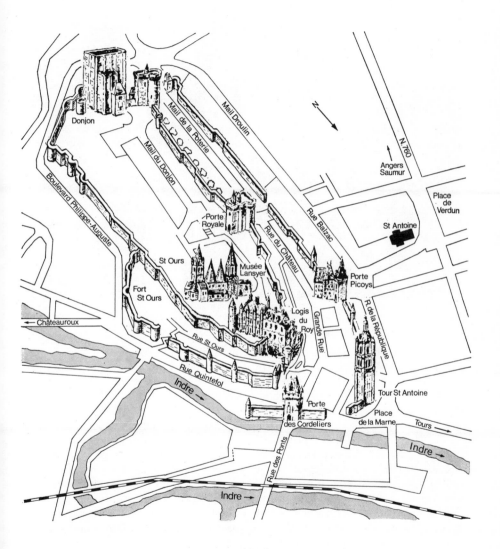

Map of Loches

135

Loches

as early as the sixth century, but it was razed in 741 and replaced by a new one. In 840, Charles le Chauve (the Bald) presented the fortress to one of his vassals, whose daughter then married Foulques le Roux, comte d'Anjou—an ancestor of Henri Plantagenet. The castle thus fell to the English Crown when Henri became Henry II of England in 1154. For years, it was fought over by England and France before Philippe-Auguste recaptured it for France in 1205. It was linked to the French Crown once and for all by Louis IX in 1249.

The most striking part of the complex is its *keep,* one of the oldest and best preserved of its type in France. It is Norman in style, and was erected on the south and most vulnerable side of the city at the end of the eleventh century, presumably by Geoffroy Martel. Portions of its west wall are even older.

It is a massive square tower 121 feet tall. It is pierced by only a few small windows, and in case of siege, it offered sure protection to the inhabitants of the fortress. Three of its faces are structured and strengthened by semicircular buttresses set against slender strips of projecting wall. These ornamental vertical elements may have been taken over from wooden structures with the same function. The walls are more than 9 feet thick, and are made of filling stones embedded in coarse, hard mortar, which were then faced with smooth stone blocks. A low portal and staircase juts out from the north side. The sole access to the main tower was by way of the staircase, which runs around the inner face of the walls of this extension. At the top of the staircase is a room with a fireplace—doubtless functioning as an anteroom to the hall on the second floor of the tower—and on the top floor, a chapel boasting a semicircular apse.

The tower itself was divided into three living floors, which are readily identifiable from the three fireplaces in the west wall, one above the other, and by the set-backs in the walls on which their floor joists once rested. The ground floor, divided in two by a partition supporting the floor of the hall above, presumably served as a storeroom, and had no door to the outside. The stairs in the extension led to the tower's second floor, from which a staircase built into the east wall provided access to the floor above it. In addition to this staircase were various corridors leading through the masonry of the walls and ending in culs-de-sac. They probably were meant to confuse attackers who might force their way into the structure and could thus be captured by its defenders. The keep served as a prison for a long time, which helps to explain its good state of preservation.

The keep was strengthened with further fortifications between the twelfth and fifteenth centuries. The Tour Ronde—also known as the Tour Neuve—to the west, was erected in the fifteenth century by Louis XI. Designed as a watchtower at the junction of the walls of the keep precinct with those of the fortress ring and the town below, it was fitted out with the most up-to-date defensive features of its time. The Tour Ronde also was used by Louis XI to hold his most important prisoners in iron cages. Suspended from the ceiling of the cell, and many not big enough for a man to stand in, the cage would rock each time the prisoner moved. Cardinal Balue, one of Louis XI's ministers and a strong advocate of the use of the cages, eventually found himself in one after being arrested for having conspired with the enemy during the wars with the duc de Bourgogne. He remained suspended for eleven years.

The Martelet, from the same century, consists mainly of underground dungeons. Visitors are shown the cell in which Louis XII kept Ludovico Sforza, the duke of Milan and patron of Leonardo da Vinci; he languished for eight long years, only to collapse and die on the day of his release. To pass the time, he covered the walls of his cell with paintings of mostly military subjects, and with inscriptions. Lower down is the cell that held the bishops of Autun and Le Puy after their arrest for having conspired against François I. During their stay, they sculpted an altar and the Stations of the Cross in the cell's stone walls.

The *Logis du Roi*, the castle at the fortress's northern tip, contrasts radically with the older donjon. It was begun in the mid-fourteenth century, and was intended to provide somewhat more comfortable quarters than those available within the keep's massive walls. From its terraces is a spectacular view of the roofs of the lower town and of the Indre threading through the lush pastureland of Touraine.

The castle consists of two wings, one placed behind the other. The older, higher section, built for Charles VII, still has all the attributes of a fortified castle. Semicircular towers project from the side facing the city and are connected by a wall-walk. A short passageway links this wing to a round tower known since the sixteenth century as the Tour la belle Agnès. The tower's semicircular stair turret rests on a sculpted

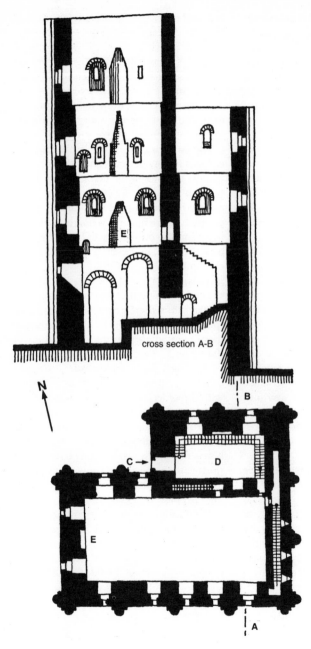

cross section A-B

N

Cross section and floor plan of the keep at Loches
A-B Cross section
C Entrance
D Stairways
E Fireplace

console depicting a pair of lovers. The great hall in this wing, the Salle de Jeanne d'Arc, was the setting for one momentous confrontation: it was here that Joan of Arc met with the apprehensive dauphin after her victory at Orléans and begged him to permit himself to be crowned at Reims as Charles VII. The newer wing dates from the time of Charles VIII and Louis XII, and boasts the richer decoration typical of the transition from the Late Gothic to the Renaissance.

The rooms in the castle are almost devoid of art. The exceptions are the tiny, jewellike Oratoire d'Anne de Bretagne and another room in the newer wing. The walls and architectural members of the oratory are covered with carved ermine dots—the heraldic emblem of Brittany—and knotted cords. Anne chose this latter device, associated with St. Francis of Assisi, as her own personal symbol in homage to the gentle Italian saint. The cords and ermine dots are even worked into the altar supports. In a nearby room is a triptych of the Carrying of the Cross, the Crucifixion, and the Deposition from the school of Jean Fouquet, dated 1485 (originally in the church of St-Antoine), and paintings of Charles VII's mistress, Agnès Sorel.

Agnès Sorel was the first mistress of a French king to be openly acknowledged and installed in a royal residence; she lived in the tower of the old wing that now bears her name. Her family recognized her great beauty at an early age. The king's cousin Isabella d'Anjou took her as a companion and presented her at court. One charitable source relates that Agnès resisted the king's advances at first, but before long she was appearing in jewels of great splendor. The future Louis XI hated her, and she moved to Loches to keep out of his way. One legend has it that Agnès communicated with her lover by means of torch signals flashed at night from the towers of her castle. But this probably was a fiction invented by a romantic chronicler, for Agnès and Charles VII had no qualms about being seen together in public.

Agnès spent her last years at Loches, and before she died at the age of twenty-eight—perhaps by poison at the instigation of Louis—she made a number of generous donations to its collegiate church to guarantee her burial there. But after her death in 1450, its priests appealed to the king, asking that he bury his mistress in the castle rather than in the church. The king cheerfully consented, provided that they return the money she had given them. Horrified, the priests promptly overcame their scruples.

The tomb of Agnès Sorel thus stood in the church until 1793, when it suffered heavy damage during the Revolution. It was thoroughly restored in 1809, at which time it was set up in the Tour la belle Agnès. The monument is attributed to Jacques Morel, and depicts the king's lovely mistress in life size lying atop a black marble sarcophagus and flanked by mourning angels. Even in this limestone image, it is possible to see something of her vaunted beauty; it is believed that the face was taken from Agnès's death mask. Two lambs lie at her feet. These are both symbolic of gentleness and an allusion to her given name (the Latin *agnus* means "lamb"). Her folded hands are an invention of the nineteenth-century restorer; originally they held a book.

The silhouette of the former collegiate church of Notre-Dame, known since the nineteenth century as *St-Ours* (after the town's only parish church, destroyed during the Revolution), is at first glance utterly confusing. Between its two tall towers are two pyramid-shaped structures seemingly quite out of place. Only after one has explored the interior does one recognize that these lower towers are only the pointed, octagonal vaults above the two bays of the nave.

The church is a blend of various period styles. It was founded near the end of the tenth century by Geoffroi Grisegonelle, comte d'Anjou. However, the oldest portions of the present structure—the bell tower, with its massive buttresses, through which one enters the church, and sections of the side walls of the nave and north transept—date back to the eleventh century. The three-apse choir, the greater part of the transept, the crossing tower, the octagonal portion of the bell tower, and the narthex were all built in the twelfth century. The pyramids above the nave and the south side aisle also date back to the same period, although in their present form, they are nineteenth-century reconstructions. A similar pyramid may be seen on the famous convent church at Fontevrault.

The church's architectural sculpture is particularly noteworthy, especially that of the portal in the narthex. Its archivolts are carved with fantastic beasts and monsters, creatures from the Romanesque bestiary. The monumental sculptures surrounding this portal have been severely damaged, but it is still possible to identify an Adoration of the Magi as the central grouping and, to the right of it, the three kings asleep beneath one blanket as an angel appears to

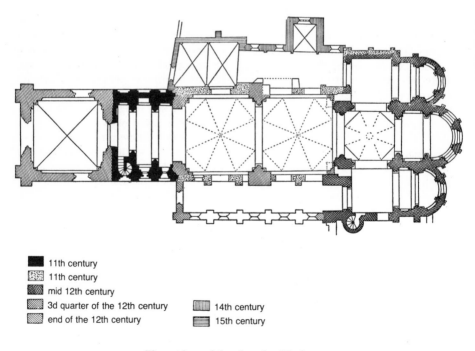

11th century
11th century
mid 12th century
3d quarter of the 12th century
end of the 12th century
14th century
15th century

Floor plan of the church of St-Ours.

them in a dream and warns them of Herod. Two saints flank the portal, but only one of them—Peter with his key—can be identified.

Be sure to notice the stone font next to the portal. It has been fashioned from a fragment of a Gallo-Roman altar. The church's narrow crypt preserves a fresco from the second half of the eleventh century with a likeness of St. Brice, who succeeded St. Martin as bishop of Tours.

THE LOWER TOWN OFFERS A NUMBER OF DE-lightful narrow streets and charming structures. Two gatehouses are special landmarks. The more impressive of the two is the late fifteenth-century *Porte des Cordeliers* (Franciscans), with round corner towers and a wall-walk. This was once the town's main entrance. It stands right next to the River Indre and is, with the adjacent buildings, beautifully mirrored on the river's surface. Pilgrims on their way to the shrine of St. James of Santiago de Compostela used to pass through this gate.

Less imposing is the *Porte Picois*, which probably dates from the second third of the fifteenth century. Its charm actually derives from the gracious *Hôtel de Ville*, which is attached to it. François I authorized the building of this structure in 1519,

but disputes over the expropriation of properties on which it was to stand delayed its construction for years. It was not until 1535 that its architect, Jean Beaudouin, could actually begin work on it, skillfully utilizing the extremely limited site between the gatehouse and the town wall. He erected a building with high windows in the best Renaissance style, perpendicular to the wall and tied to the gatehouse by means of a towerlike structure containing a staircase.

Two more Renaissance structures have survived in the nearby Rue du Château. The *Maison du Centaure* takes its name from a sculptural ornament depicting Hercules—in the form of François I—slaying the centaur Nessus. The neighboring building, adorned with pilasters, is the *Chancellerie*; it bears the date 1551 along with the motto *Prudentia Nutrisco, Justitia Regno* (I instruct with prudence and rule with justice).

The most striking Renaissance structure in the lower town is the slender *Tour St-Antoine* (1529–75), which is the bell tower from a chapel no longer standing. It is possible that it also served as a watchtower. Its splendid two-story crown was inspired by those of the façade towers of the cathedral of St-Gatien in Tours.

AZAY-LE-RIDEAU

MANY PEOPLE CONSIDER AZAY-LE-RIDEAU TO BE the loveliest of the Renaissance châteaux of the Loire, even the quintessential example of that architecture. In *The Lily of the Val-*

ley, Balzac aptly describes it as a "diamond cut in facets," with the Indre as its setting.

In the twelfth century, the estate belonged to Ridel (Rideau) d'Azay, from whom it takes its name. A ruined medieval castle on the site was razed and the present château begun in around 1518 by Gilles Berthelot, treasurer of France and mayor of Tours. Inasmuch as state business kept him away for extended periods, it was left to his wife, Philippe Lesbahy, to oversee the château's construction in much the same way as Catherine Briçonnet supervised the building of Chenonceau. The master mason Etienne Rousseau was summoned from Tours, and it is assumed that he served as building foreman. Denis Guillourt laid the foundations in 1518.

Berthelot did not live to see his château completed. One of his relatives, Jacques de Beaune de Semblançay, the superintendent of the royal finances and a man to whom Berthelot owed his job, was accused of having mismanaged public moneys and was summarily hanged. Berthelot's own conscience was none too clean. He took to his heels, and died a short time later. François I confiscated the château in 1528 and bestowed it on Antoine Raffin, the captain of his guard, in gratitude for his loyal service during the Italian campaign. The estate was acquired by the state in 1905.

Azay-le-Rideau

142

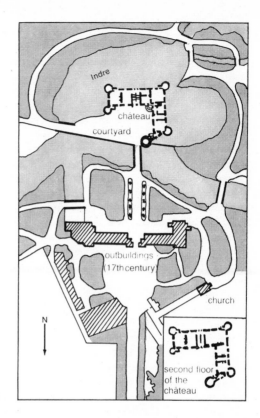

Map of the grounds at Azay-le-Rideau.

The situation of Azay-le-Rideau is enchanting. Built on a foundation of pilings, it seems to float on the Indre; a lovely park with broad lawns extends right to the edge of the water. The château comprises one main wing and a shorter perpendicular side wing. Presumably, the original plan called for two additional wings enclosing an inner courtyard. Round corner towers with conical roofs serve as accents, and since they are supported by consoles, they lend an air of weightlessness to the whole. Machicolation extends around the walls facing the river. This is clearly only a decorative element, however, for rising above it are a number of richly ornamented dormers, which carry the lines of the lower window bays up into the steep roof area. Older engravings show that there was once a low, thick tower next to the shorter wing on the courtyard side, doubtless a surviving portion of the medieval castle. A taller round tower replaced it in 1845. The corner tower on the courtyard side of the main wing dates from 1856. Both were carefully matched to those on the outer corners.

Balzac's image of a faceted diamond was well chosen. The entire structure exhibits clear proportions: a perfect harmony exists between the smooth walls of cut white stone, the sculptural ornaments placed on them, and the beautifully carved cornices

143

and pilasters. Everything is in balance, thanks to skillful use of repetition and variation. The flawlessness of this architecture may owe something to the refined taste of Philippe Lesbahy, the actual builder of the château.

An ornate double portal and stair tower interrupts the rhythmic symmetry of the courtyard side, its gable rising well into the roof area. Prominent among its embellishments are the salamander of François I and the ermine of Claude de France beneath the double windows and the royal initials on the gable. But Azay was never a royal residence. It was built by a courtier who was eager to defer to his sovereigns and bent on flattering them. Berthelot and his wife were not completely self-effacing, for their initials—G, B, and P—appear in monumental size and florid style on the dormer gables.

Inside, only the staircase and kitchen retain their original form. The staircase was something of an innovation in sixteenth-century architecture, for instead of being constructed as a spiral, it consists of straight flights and landings similar to those at Chenonceau. Panels and pendants adorn its ceilings, the panels embellished with either rosettes or profile heads of French kings and queens from Louis XI through Henri IV.

The spacious kitchen has shallow cross-ribbed vaulting. Its floor level was raised in the nineteenth century, for in high water it was frequently flooded. The original level is preserved only around an imposing fireplace and a pump well reaching down directly into the Indre.

The remaining rooms at Azay-le-Rideau have been appointed with priceless furniture, paintings, and wall tapestries from the sixteenth and seventeenth centuries. Notable among them are a secretary embellished with six ivory panels of scenes from Callot's engravings *Misères de la Guerre*, and a painting after Clouet of Gabrielle d'Estrées, mistress of Henri IV.

ON THE RIGHT SIDE OF THE ROAD LEADING TO the château stands the church of *St-Symphorien*. It combines a south aisle from the eleventh century with a north one from the twelfth and sixteenth centuries. The west front of the older aisle survives as only a much older—ninth-century—fragment; a pointed-arch window was cut through at a later date. Originally, it was graced by two rows of arcades containing archaic figures. These early sculptures are highly expressive, but the only one that can be positively identified is the Christ in the center of the upper arcade. From what we know of the history of the church, the figures likely date to the mid-eleventh century.

SACHE

THE MANOR HOUSE OF SACHÉ IS A SHRINE FOR ALL admirers of Honoré de Balzac, who spent much of his life here in the heart of his beloved Touraine. In his novel *The Lily of the Valley*, which was written at Saché and takes place in its immediate environs, Balzac describes the house as a melancholy place

full of harmonies too solemn for superficial people but dear to the aching souls of poets. For that reason, I too came to treasure its silence later on, its huge leafless trees, and the vague shroud of mystery that enveloped the whole lonely valley. And every time I caught sight of this trim château that had so captivated me at first glance from the slope of the next hillside, I would again let my eyes rest on it with contentment.

The asymmetrical late sixteenth-century structure rests on foundations that date to the Middle Ages, but architecturally it is rather unimposing. Its romantic charm derives from its location on a gentle slope overlooking meadows; on one side is the village, and on the other, a splendid stand of sturdy oaks at which Balzac never ceased to marvel.

The story of Balzac's connection to Saché might well have been lifted from one of his own novels. The estate's owner at the beginning of the nineteenth century was Jean de Margonne, the lover of Balzac's mother, Laure Sallambier. She was an enchanting Parisienne some thirty-two years younger than her husband. It is likely that Jean de Margonne was the father of Laure Sallambier's younger son, Henri, a boy on whom she lavished her affection to the virtual exclusion of the eight years older Honoré. As though to make up for his mother's neglect of him, Jean de Margonne took Honoré under his own wing, offering the use of his place in the country whenever he wished. Balzac came here only occasionally as a boy, but after 1830, having embarked on his career as one of France's most popular writers, he stayed here with increasing regularity. In Paris, he was continually plagued by his publishers and creditors; at Saché, he could be ensured the peace and solitude he needed for his writing.

Honoré de Balzac

The château is now a Balzac museum, preserved as much as possible in the manner the writer knew. A straight flight of steps leads to the de Margonne family apartments. They include a handsome dining room and a grand salon remarkable for its original trompe l'oeil wall hangings. It was in this room that Balzac read aloud to his host and his guests from his work in progress.

Balzac's own modest room, his "monk's cell" as he called it, is on the top floor and looks out on his beloved oak trees. It served as bedroom, study, and sitting room all in one. Some years ago, restorers brought to light a few fragments of wallpaper from the period around 1820, a dotted pattern against a bright yellow background and edged with a frieze of laurel leaves. It was decided to re-create the paper, so that now the room appears exactly as it did when Balzac used it. The bed in the alcove, the rustic writing table, and the writing instruments themselves all belonged to the novelist.

Balzac would start writing at 5:00 A.M., first in bed and later at his writing table. He always kept the curtains drawn, preferring to work by lamplight. He worked until late afternoon, stopping only to eat a bit of bread and drink coffee that he brewed himself over a spirit flame. Many of his chief works were created here in an industrious frenzy. "The days are not long enough for me," he often complained. "It is not inspiration or dedication that I lack, but time."

The rest of the rooms on this floor are set up like a museum. The room next door to Balzac's own contains caricatures of him and his contemporaries as well as mementoes of the novelist's stay in Russia with Countess Hanska, with whom he kept up a famous correspondence and whom he finally married shortly before his death.

Among the numerous portrait studies of Balzac is one by the sculptor Auguste Rodin, done in preparation for his famous bust of the novelist. When Rodin began work on this commemorative sculpture, Balzac had been dead for some forty years. Rodin therefore took as his model a corpulent drayman from Azay-le-Rideau who was said to resemble the writer.

From the manuscripts and galleys on display, it is possible to form some idea of Balzac's manner of working. Typesetters refused to work on any given page of his for more than two hours, and one can only sympathize with them. After he was finished correcting them, the galleys looked like hopelessly tangled cobwebs.

The view over the valley from the main upstairs room is one of the loveliest sights at Saché. To the left is the little village church and the cemetery in which the young countess in *The Lily of the Valley* is finally laid to rest after a life filled with renunciation.

*T*OURS

TOURS, THE HEART OF TOURAINE, WAS ORIGINALLY a Roman settlement. It was first mentioned by the geographer Ptolemy in the second century A.D. He called it Caesardonum (Caesar's Hill), but since the fourth century, it has been known as some form of Urbs Turonum, or City of the Turones (a tribe of Gauls). It stood at the junction of several important roads linking it with neighboring cities. Trading flourished accordingly, and in the fifth century, the city already numbered some 20,000 inhabitants. Remnants of Roman Tours are still found in the vicinity of the cathedral.

Tours is unusual in that it incorporates two old centers that developed independently of each other. This came about thanks to the fame of its third bishop, St. Martin. While Martin was still a soldier in one of the Roman legions—so the legend goes—he shared his cloak with a beggar, and once he had become bishop, he firmly established Christianity in Touraine. He died at Candes in 397, and was buried in accordance with Roman custom in public ceremony outside the city of Tours, to the west. St. Brice, Martin's successor as bishop, erected a small chapel over his grave; a

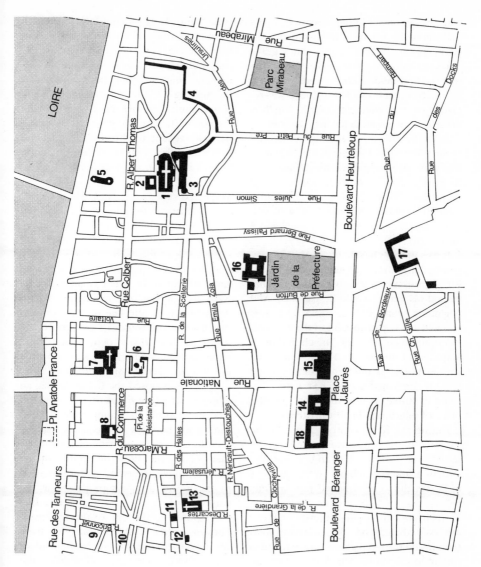

Map of Tours
1. *Cathedral of St-Gatien.* 2. *La Psalette, cloître de St-Gatien.* 3. *Musée des Beaux-Arts.* 4.
Roman walls. 5. *Tour de Guise.* 6. *Fontaine de Beaune.* 7. *Abbey church of St-Julien.* 8.
Hôtel Gouin. 9. *Musée du Gemmail.* 10. *Place Plumereau.* 11. *Tour Charlemagne.* 12.
Tour de l'Horloge. 13. *St-Martin.* 14. *Palais de Justice.* 15. *Hôtel de Ville.* 16. *Préfecture.*
17. *Train station.* 18. *Post office.*

place of pilgrimage and a monastery eventually grew up around it. Reports of repeated miracles wrought at the saint's grave attracted increasing streams of pilgrims, so that the first modest chapel came to seem unworthy of such a sacred shrine. It was replaced by a magnificent church, which is described in great detail by Gregory of Tours in his *History of the Franks*, written around 580: "It is 160 feet in length and 60 feet wide; its height up to the ceiling is 45 feet; in the chancel, it has 32 windows, and in the nave, 20, with 41 columns; the entire structure contains 52 windows, 120 columns, and 8 doors, 3 in the chancel and 5 in the nave."[15]

It was in this church, on St. Martin's day in 498, that Clovis, the founder of the Frankish empire, had solemnly announced that he and his family would be baptized. And beginning with Clovis, St. Martin was adopted as the patron saint of the Frankish rulers and their subjects. The church of St-Martin in Tours was a Frankish national shrine. As late as the tenth century, Pope Leo VII confirmed that after St. Peter's Basilica in Rome, it was the most popular place of pilgrimage in all Christendom.

During the ninth century and into the early tenth, the Normans repeatedly penetrated as far as Tours with an eye to its destruction, and on each occasion, the relics of St. Martin were removed just in time. During one of their attacks, in 903, the church and adjacent monastery were burned to the ground. The shrine was soon rebuilt, and the monks surrounded it with a ring of fortifications. This fortress became known as Châteauneuf to distinguish it from the older walled city to the east. In the eleventh century, Tours fell to Foulques Nerra; through his descendant Henry II of England, Touraine became a fief of the English Crown, and was not regained by

France until 1242. Not until the fourteenth century, during the Hundred Years' War, were the two centers enclosed in a single ring wall that also served to secure the settlements since grown up between them. A second ring wall built in the sixteenth and seventeenth centuries more than doubled the size of the city, and gave it the shape it basically retains to this day. The second wall was replaced in the nineteenth century by a ring of broad boulevards.

THE FOLLOWING VISIT TO HISTORIC TOURS BEgins in what was the ancient city; it is now dominated by the cathedral of *St-Gatien*. The Roman settlement was built on the south bank of the Loire and was roughly trapezoidal in shape. It was 1,150 feet long and 740 feet wide. Major remnants of its walls are still standing, including a round corner tower in the Rue du Petit-Cupido that marked the southeast corner. To the south, the Roman wall bent outward in a wide curve, along the inner side of which the Rue du Général-Meusnier now runs. This curve enclosed the Roman arena, an elliptical structure measuring 470 by 406 feet and capable of seating some 12,000 spectators. Remains of the arena may be seen in the cellars of many of the houses that occupy the site. The section of the wall continuing westward is now obscured by the former archbishop's palace, at the west end of which is a round tower that corresponds to the one to the southeast. Portions of the wall that extended from this tower in a straight line to the bank of the Loire were used as foundations for the cathedral towers.

Litorius, the second bishop of Tours, built a church on this site around 338. In the sixth century at the latest, it was leveled by fire. Gregory of Tours then erected a splendid new structure, which was con-

The cathedral of St-Gatien in Tours.

secrated in 590. A third bishop's church, built early in the twelfth century, burned down a short time later, in 1167. It was immediately restored, but by the beginning of the thirteenth century it was already dangerously weakened, for it had been built of extremely soft stone. Portions of that structure were incorporated into the towers

and south transept of the present cathedral.

The choir we see today was begun around 1239 and completed around 1280. The relics of St. Martin and of his companions were installed in this new structure with great ceremony in 1267. In the fourteenth century, the cathedral was placed under the patronage of St. Gatien, the first

149

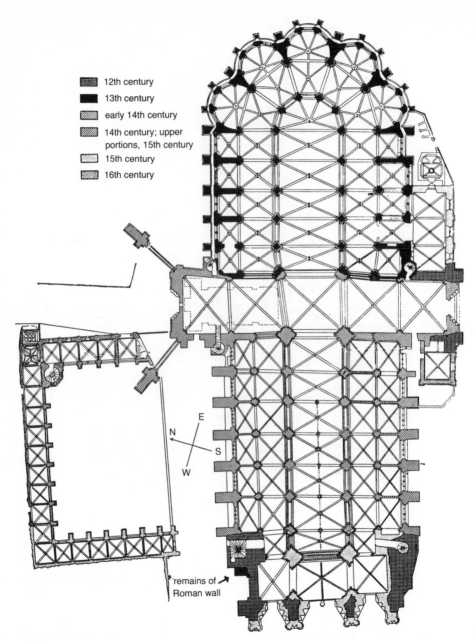

12th century

13th century

early 14th century

14th century; upper portions, 15th century

15th century

16th century

remains of Roman wall

Floor plan of the cathedral in Tours.

bishop of Tours, who had brought Christianity to Touraine in the third century.

At the beginning of the fourteenth century, the cathedral chapter determined to proceed with construction, incorporating those portions of the transept of the twelfth-century Romanesque church still considered sound. The work was entrusted to Simon du Mans, who also created the two eastern bays of the nave. The remaining bays were also begun in the fourteenth century, but were completed a century later by the architect Jean de Dammartin. Dammartin also worked on the tower façade, which then occupied Jean Papin and Jean Durand until the end of the fifteenth century. The fantastic cupolas of these towers are thus Renaissance creations: the north one was installed in 1507, and the south one followed in 1547. With them, the cathedral was finally complete after over three centuries of building.

Huguenots soon ravaged the newly completed structure, however, and destroyed its portal statues, which have never been replaced.

The tower façade displays a wealth of ornamental forms in the Flamboyant style. It would be difficult to imagine a more ornate architecture, yet the Renaissance cupolas fit in with it perfectly well. The south tower, which houses the bells, is open to visitors. It is well worth the climb to see up close the inexhaustible ingenuity that went into the decoration of these cupolas.

The most splendid architecture in the church after its western façade is the choir, which towers above the Place Grégoire-de-Tours. François Salet writes:

Though it does not approach the dimensions of the choirs at Amiens or Paris [Notre-Dame], the one at Tours appears in the context of this splendid old square . . . as a model of serene and harmonious design. With the carefully controlled play of lines in its double buttresses, one above the other, the simple and elegant detailing of its upper windows, and the clear, unbroken symmetry of its chevet, this ensemble constitutes the purest, if not the most magnificent, example of architecture in the age of St. Louis.[16]

The interior appears to be vast, but it is completely without heaviness. It is as though all the experience from cathedral building in France had here been brought into play. The two eastern bays of the nave are laid out with five aisles like those of the long choir, while the western ones have side chapels instead. The nave is completely separated from the side aisles by massive pillars, while the paired side aisles are treated as single spaces. The choir, with its tall, three-story elevation, served as the pattern for later construction. The upper wall is completely given over to the lighted triforium and the windows above it. Yet compared with the choir there is a tendency toward greater verticality in the nave, into which tracery was introduced. This tendency attests to the change in stylistic sensibility that occurred between the middle of the thirteenth and beginning of the fourteenth century. Nevertheless, the overall impression is still close to that of the High Gothic, thanks to the form of the vaulting. Its panels slope toward the sides, and its abutments are set well down between the windows, such that the windows and their arcades are largely obscured from the side. The same impression is preserved in the western bays, which date from the fifteenth century. Irregularities in the ground plan are most obvious in the transept. They are the result of the architect's obligation to incorporate foundations and even some of the wall masonry from the Romanesque structure. This also explains the discrepancy in the widths of the nave and the choir.

The high choir and the three central choir chapels have their original stained glass from the second half of the thirteenth century. With their brilliant blues, reds, greens, and yellows, these windows are the most splendid of the interior ornaments. They illustrate, for the most part, the legends of the saints and familiar scenes from the Bible.

The cathedral's other appointments are not particularly noteworthy, with one exception—the marble tomb in the first south choir of two of the children of Charles VIII and Anne de Bretagne. The work was originally placed in the basilica

of St-Martin in 1506. Having survived the Revolution, the monument was rescued from that church before it was demolished and was set up in its present location in the cathedral. The tomb base is the work of an Italian master, Jérôme de Fiesole. It immortalizes two small boys, Crown Prince Charles-Orland (wearing a crown, died 1495) and Prince Charles (died 1496). The figures of the boys, accompanied by angels smoothing pillows under their heads and bearing coats of arms, are thought to have been executed by French sculptors; possibly they were pupils of Michel Colombe, Tours's most important Renaïssance sculptor. With their open eyes and plump cheeks, the faces of the dead princes seem full of the warmth of life. A contemporary has recorded that Charles-Orland was a handsome child, precocious and fearless.

He fell victim to an epidemic of smallpox at the Château d'Amboise. The other two children of the royal couple, born after Charles-Orland and Charles, also died at tender ages.

The three wings of the Cloître de la Psallette extend from the cathedral to the north. *Psallette* means "choir school," and it was here that young boys were trained for their roles in church services. The oldest section is the western gallery, from the mid-fifteenth century, which houses a library on its second floor. In the small archives room that serves as an antechamber to the library, thirteenth- and fourteenth-century frescoes from the church at Beaumont-Village are exhibited. The room, which dates from 1520, is vaulted with slender ogives. The remaining two wings, joined by a decorative pierced stair tower, were built between 1508 and 1524.

The former archbishop's palace has occupied its present site in the southwest corner of the Roman wall since the time of Gregory of Tours. The present structure is composed of two sections: the wing next to the Roman tower, built in the seventeenth century, and the larger palace adjoining it, which dates from the second half of the eighteenth. The portal leading into its courtyard was set up in 1778, utilizing portions of a demolished triumphal arch commemorating Louis XIV.

The building has not served its original function as bishop's residence since the Revolution, and the *Musée des Beaux-Arts*, which was founded at that time, has been housed here since 1910. The core of its collection is made up of works from the ruined châteaux of Richelieu and Chanteloup and from the great abbeys of Marmoutier and Bourgueil. It has been supplemented through the years by works on permanent loan, generous gifts from private collections, and purchases by the state. As a result, it is now one of the most important provincial museums in France.

The museum's collection includes outstanding paintings from various periods. Medieval and Renaissance art (exhibited on the ground floor) features Jean Fouquet's *Portrait of a Monk*. Two particular treasures of the museum are Andrea Mantegna's *Christ in the Garden of Gethsemene* and *Resurrection*. These panels were originally part of the high altar at San Zeno in Verona and were painted between 1456 and 1459. The central panel of the group, a *Crucifixion*, is now in the Louvre.

A magnificent group of eighteenth-century French paintings offers examples by major masters. A suite of rooms in the palace facing the garden, furnished with fine period pieces and *objets d'art*, provides the perfect setting for many of these works. A salon in the style of Louis XV brings together pictures from the Château de Chanteloup, including several works by Boucher. Paintings by Coypel, Lancret, Rigaud, Lemoyne, and Nattier are also exhibited. An elegant portrait of the duc de Richelieu is by Louis Tocqué.

Italian paintings of the seventeenth and eighteenth centuries include works by Giovanni Battista Pittoni, Giovanni Piazetta Battista, Sebastiano Conca, and Francesco Fontebasso, as well as two dramatic landscapes by the north Italian master Alessandro Magnasco. Canvases by Rubens highlight the museum's Flemish painting collection and include his *Ex-Voto* and a mythological scene, *Mars Crowned by Victory*. Among the Dutch pictures is Rembrandt's small panel, *Flight into Egypt*. This work from 1627 is an early example of the artist's celebrated chiaroscuro style. Works of the German, Austrian, and Swiss schools include Franz-Anton Maulbertsch's grisaille

Apotheosis of the Order of the Trinity, a flamboyant example of the Viennese Baroque.

Nineteenth-century French paintings (on the museum's third floor) include examples of Delacroix, Degas, and other masters. A fine collection of sculptures includes Houdon's bronze *Diana the Huntress*, as well as works by Jean-Baptiste Lemoyne. The nineteenth-century sculptor François Sicard, who worked in Tours, is represented by a poignant, large-scale statue of George Sand. Models for Sicard's civic sculpture include caryatids for the Hôtel de Ville in Tours.

The Musée des Beaux-Arts exhibits fine French furniture, and noteworthy pieces include a late-eighteenth-century carved wood cupboard, an early-eighteenth-century Chinese lacquered commode with bronze ornaments, and a carved and gilded wood console from the Louis XVI period. Tapestries and fabrics from the seventeenth and eighteenth centuries, French and Italian faïence, Limoges enamels, eighteenth-century clocks, and examples of fine porcelain complete this fascinating collection.

After visiting the museum, one should not neglect a climb to the terrace above the garden. From it, one can scan 1,500 years of Western architectural history, beginning with the ancient wall surrounding the Roman city, and moving to the Gothic cathedral, with Renaissance cupolas on its towers, and the archbishop's palace, with its seventeenth- and eighteenth-century façades.

Tours also had an impressive donjon, which was built in the twelfth century by Henry II of England to defend the Loire bridge in the northwest corner of the city. It was further strengthened in the thirteenth century with walls and towers, of which two are still to be seen. In the northeast one, the *Tour de Guise*, the son of Henri, duc de Guise, was imprisoned for three years following his father's assassination at Blois.

TWO PARALLEL MEDIEVAL STREETS, THE RUE Colbert/Rue du Commerce and the Rue de la Scellerie/Rue des Halles, link the city with the former town of Châteauneuf, which grew up around the basilica of St-Martin. They are narrow commercial lanes full of life and color. If one chooses to take the Rue Colbert—the through street leading from Chinon to Amboise in Roman times—one passes through the sixteenth-century aristocratic quarter. The lovely little *Place Foire-le-Roi*—a free market square provided by Jean II le Bon (the Good) (1355) and François I (1545)—is ringed with gabled town houses. The house at No. 8 was formerly the charming mansion of Philibert Babou de la Bourdaisière, superintendent of finances under François I. It was built in 1524.

After bombings in 1940, a façade and a gallery with a Renaissance chapel above it are all that survive of the sumptuous mansion of another superintendent of finances under Louis XII and François I. This one belonged to Jacques de Beaune de Semblançay, who ended on the gallows because of his suspected misuse of tax moneys. In front of it stands the lavish *Fontaine de Beaune*, from 1511—restored—which the superintendent commissioned from Bastien François and Martin François, the nephews of Michel Colombe.

The former abbey church of *St-Julien*, at the intersection of the Rue Colbert and the Rue Nationale, goes back to a fifth-century Merovingian foundation. A storm in 1225 destroyed all but the tower of a tenth- or eleventh-century structure. The present

View of Tours in 1561.

church, built between 1225 and 1259, is a five-aisle basilica with transept and a flat-ended, three-bay choir flanked on either side by two low aisles. Its lovely interior is distinguished by slender columns with high ribbed vaults and tracery triforia.

All that survives from the buildings on the former monastery is the vaulted twelfth-century chapter house to the north of the church. The *Musée du Compagnonnage* is on the floor above it. *Compagnonnage* refers to what in effect were early trade unions, organized beginning in the late fifteenth century against the monopolistic medieval guilds. Through the *compagnonnage* system, a journeyman perfected his skill, and the local lodges fought for better pay and working conditions. *Compagnons* thus were persecuted, and membership in the unions was secret.

The museum displays the best works of all crafts—blacksmith, stonecutter, wheelwright, cabinetmaker—which journeymen had to submit to be accepted into the union. In the monastery's wine cellars is the *Musée des Vins de Touraine*. It has exhibits not only on wine itself and on the tools of winemaking, but also on the relationship of wine to religion, social customs, and history.

The city's most splendid secular building is the *Hôtel Gouin*, on the Rue du Commerce, which was built by a wealthy merchant and judicial family, the Gardettes, in the sixteenth century. In substance, the house dates from the late fifteenth century, and its back with a stair tower remains unchanged since that time. The front façade was expanded impressively in the sixteenth century, with the addition of an ornamented entry and a short loggia wing to the left, which was later balanced by a matching one on the opposite side. The wall and pediment surfaces are covered with lavish Renaissance ornamentation. Repeatedly restored and then gutted by fire in 1940, the Hôtel Gouin now has more or less its original appearance and serves as the *Musée d'Art Médiéval et de la Résistance.* Sculpture and decorative arts from both the medieval and Renaissance periods are exhibited, along with documents and mementoes of the French Resistance during the Second World War.

The core structure in the section of Tours that had developed as Châteauneuf was the basilica of *St-Martin,* of which only two towers survive. It was built in the eleventh century, and served as the prototype of the great pilgrimage churches of that period, among them Santiago de Compostela in Spain. St-Martin in Tours was one of the way stations for pilgrims heading for Compostela. After several fires, the church was expanded in the thirteenth century until it was the largest in all Western Christendom. With a length of 360 feet, it exceeded that of the cathedral by almost 43 feet. It had a

The Hôtel Gouin on the Rue du Commerce.

156

nave with four side aisles and twin towers on the west front. Two additional towers marked the ends of the transept. The choir, with the tomb of St. Martin in its center, had a double ambulatory and a wreath of chapels.

During the Revolution, the church was transformed into a military stable. Robbed of its lead roofs, the structure partially collapsed in 1797; in 1802, the prefect of Tours ordered that it be demolished. All that remains are the north transept tower (Tour Charlemagne), the south façade tower (Tour de l'Horloge), and the east walk of the cloister of the monastery, from the early sixteenth century. The Rue des Halles was put through where the choir and nave once stood, supposedly as an indication that the cult of St. Martin had been forever extinguished.

But interest in the tomb of St. Martin was by no means dead. When excavations brought it to light in 1860, France was swept by a wave of enthusiasm. A number of prominent persons demanded that the old church of St-Martin be rebuilt. However, the state and city of Tours refused to give up the Rue des Halles. Finally, a compromise was reached. Between 1887 and 1902, a considerably smaller church in the Romanesque-Byzantine style was erected above St. Martin's tomb in a north-south direction. Its architect was Laloux, and his structure is worthy of one of the holiest of Christian shrines in the West. The church is a cruciform basilica with crossing tower, beneath which the saint's tomb is sheltered in the crypt. A bronze statue of the saint crowns the cupola, and one of St. Martin's actual relics was fitted into the right hand, which is raised in benediction.

The nave is lined with granite columns and is extraordinarily effective. The likenesses of bishops, kings, and saints who helped to build the basilica or honored it with a visit appear as ornaments on the capitals.

A few wall towers survive from the ring of fortifications that once surrounded the precinct of Châteauneuf. The town's merchants, attracted by the flow of pilgrims, settled to the north, between the monastery and the bank of the Loire. Thus a picturesque, bustling quarter grew up around the Place Plumereau. During the nineteenth century, the town's commercial activity migrated to the area of the boulevards to the south, where the new, modern Tours was developing. The old merchant town lost its attraction, and its buildings fell into decay. The area suffered further damage in the bombings of 1940. For these reasons, a thorough renovation of the area has been under way for the past few years, one that has become a model project for modernization attempts all over Europe. The first phase of the project concentrated on the *Place Plumereau* and the block of buildings immediately to the north of it. The old architecture consists in part of half-timbering and in part of masonry construction. The buildings were renovated from inside out, and in each case, it was decided either to preserve their traditional interiors or to replace them with modern living spaces. However, all of the buildings' exteriors were restored to their original state. The entire inner core of the block was demolished, making room for communal courtyards. This renovation area has become a desirable address again, with a wealth of refurbished indigenous architecture and a distinct quality of life.

The center of modern Tours surrounds the Place Jean-Jaurès, at the intersection of the Rue Nationale and the boulevards Béranger and Heurteloup. Here the traffic surges and the sidewalk cafés and restaurants have mushroomed. Two unharmonious buildings dominate the square where the Rue Nationale runs into it: the *Palais de Justice*, constructed between 1840 and 1843, with its façade of Doric columns, and the splendid *Hôtel de Ville*, built by Laloux between 1896 and 1904.

THE CHÂTEAU OF LE PLESSIS-LÉS-TOURS, IN THE southwestern part of the city, was built after 1463 by Louis XI, and it became his favorite residence. He died here in 1483. The original complex was considerably more extensive than it is now. All that survives is a two-story wing, built of brick and embellished with cut stone, and a polygonal stair tower.

From Le Plessis-lés-Tours, we head back toward the Loire to the former priory of *St-Cosme*, which in the Middle Ages stood on an island in the river. A number of canons from the abbey of St-Martin in Tours joined together to form a new monastic community here in 1092. Its most famous prior was the poet Pierre de Ronsard, who died at St-Cosme in 1585. His tomb was rediscovered in 1933 in the monastery church, which had stood in ruins since the Revolution. It was carefully reinterred in the same spot. In addition to the twelfth-century

The château of Le Plessis-lés-Tours

The abbey of Marmoutier.

church choir, the monks' refectory, from the same century, is also preserved. Ronsard lived in the prior's house, dating from the fifteenth century and remodeled in the seventeenth. The house now includes a small lapidary museum and works that evoke the poet's life.

THE ABBEY OF *MARMOUTIER*, TO THE NORTHEAST of the city and on the north side of the Loire, was once one of the richest and most powerful monasteries in Christendom. It also dates back to St. Martin, who loved solitude and established a community of monks here in 372, after he had become bishop of Tours. At first they lived in the chalk caves above the river, but their monastery, destroyed by the Normans in 853, had become famous by the early ninth century under the abbot Alcuin of Northumbria, who established here a monastic school and a renowned scriptorium. Benedictines from Cluny settled here in 982, and a long period of prosperity began. As late as the seventeenth century, Marmoutier controlled over 200 priories and domains in France and England. Sold as a national property, the abbey was dissolved in 1818. Since 1847, the domain has belonged to the Sisters of the Sacred Heart.

Little remains of its once extensive complex of buildings. Still surviving are the thirteenth-century gatehouse, the Portail de la Crosse, with its tower and defense wall. Visitors may see the bell tower consecrated by Urban III, who here called for the First Crusade; the Repos de St-Martin, a primitive chapel used by the saint with the remains of a Romanesque extension; a cruciform dug-out chapel in which St. Gatien celebrated Mass during times of persecution; and the cells of St. Gatien, St. Patrick, and St. Brice. All the cells were dug out of the hillside caves by the hermits who dwelt in them; that of St. Patrick has the remains of a medieval stained-glass window showing the shamrock as the symbol of the Trinity.

LUYNES

THE CHÂTEAU DE LUYNES, SITUATED HIGH ABOVE the village in a side valley to the north of the Loire, is an imposing example of medieval fortress architecture. Although closed to visitors, it nonetheless deserves a glimpse. The best view of it is from the village cemetery on the hillside across from it.

The castle was the seat of the barony, later the county, of Maillé, which was highly respected in Touraine. The first fortress on this strategically important site above the valley was destroyed by the counts of Anjou in 1096. The lord of Maillé rebuilt it at the beginning of the twelfth century. The basic form of the present structure presumably dates back to that time. An essential part of the complex, its keep, disappeared in the seventeenth century.

The castle consists of a rectangular cur-

Luynes

tain of wall secured with massive towers on three sides. Those to the north and east are now only stumps. The west side, with its four round towers, looks just as it did in the Middle Ages. Both of the middle towers, with their large bosses, date from the fifteenth century; the two outer ones were built two centuries earlier.

In 1465, Hardouin de Maillé cut large windows into the towers and ring walls and built an elegant residential wing of brick and stone with an octagonal stair tower against the inside of the west wall. This building was heavily restored in the nineteenth century.

The estate was acquired in 1619 by Charles d'Albert, lord of Luynes in Provence and future minister and keeper of the seal to Louis XIII. The new owner managed to get the king to elevate the countship to a peer duchy with the name Luynes.

In 1650, the Late Gothic structure was extended to the south by a wing from which short side wings extended toward the courtyard. These side wings are all that remain of the expansion.

Outside the castle stands the single-aisle *church* of a college of canonesses. It was founded—as a male institution—by the lord of Maillé in 1486.

Many of the houses in the town are hollowed from the rock, while others are sixteenth-century wooden structures. The beautifully constructed wooden roof of the fifteenth-century *market* is still supported by its 500-year-old oak pillars.

Not far from the present castle, there was a fortress in Roman times. Presumably it was linked to an *aqueduct*, of which several arches survive a little less than 1 mile north of Luynes; they date from the fourth century at the latest.

One mile north of Luynes are the ruins of a Roman aqueduct.

LANGEAIS

THE LITTLE TOWN OF LANGEAIS, ON THE NORTH bank of the Loire, is documented as early as the fifth century, when it was called Alangavia. Foulques Nerra, comte d'Anjou, in his drive to conquer the territories possessed by the counts of Blois and Tours, built a fortress here in the late tenth century. The ruins of that square keep still stand. It is thought to be the oldest keep in existence, and one of the first to have been built of stone. The castle fell to the English in 1427, during the Hundred Years' War. They released it in exchange for a ransom payment under the condition that all but its keep be demolished.

The new castle below Foulques's fortress was built, between 1465 and 1469, by order of Louis XI, who hoped to secure the Crown domains. Its actual builder was his treasurer and privy councilor, Jean Bourré. Until 1631, it remained a Crown possession, given in usufruct by the king to a succession of nobles. It was ultimately purchased in 1886 by Jacques Siegfried, who wished passionately to restore it to its original state and who spent his time refurbishing its interior in the style of the fifteenth and sixteenth centuries. In 1904, he willed it, complete with its furnishings and art treasures, to the Institut de France.

Langeais

One of the most significant and brilliant events in the history of Langeais was the marriage of Charles VIII to Anne de Bretagne here in 1491. The marriage had a lasting influence on French and European history. By it the union of Brittany and France was established, preventing the fall of the former to the Hapsburgs. A marriage contract had already been drawn up between Anne, the heiress to Brittany, and Maximilian of Austria, the later emperor. Charles VIII was engaged to Maximilian's daughter, Margarete of Austria. Anne was, however, convinced to dissolve the marriage contract and to marry the young king of France. To secure the union of Brittany and France, it was stipulated in the marriage contract that if Charles were to die before Anne without leaving an heir, she would marry his successor. This is precisely what happened. Charles suffered a freak accident and died at Amboise, and in 1499 Anne remarried, becoming the wife of Louis XII.

Contemporary expense books document the lavishness with which the bride arrived at the castle of Langeais for the marriage ceremony in 1491. In her luggage she had two camp beds. The more modest of the two was made of black, white, and violet damask, of which 51 yards had been used for the curtains and canopy and 19 yards for the coverlets; in addition, more than 12 yards of red taffeta had been used to line the canopy. The second, more lavish bed consisted of a canopy, drapery, and curtains of dark red and gold brocade. The canopy valance and drapes of violet and gold brocade were edged with a heavy black silk fringe. All of this was lined in red taffeta. The tent fittings and the inner furnishings of the carriages used up more than 12 yards of black and 3 yards of dark red velvet.

While journeying Anne wore a padded petticoat of black satin, for which 6 yards of black velvet were required for the bottom hem alone. Over the petticoat, she wore a dress of black velvet lined with the finest sable; 9 yards of velvet and 139 sable pelts were used in its making.

But most elaborate of all was her wedding gown, of gold brocade covered with elegantly worked appliqué, for which this fabric came to be called *drap-d'or-trait-en-levé*. This gown had first a lining of fine black lamb, but when this was judged insufficiently lavish, it was replaced by one requiring 1,160 sable pelts.

The king saw to it that the castle was furnished as richly as possible. The accounts describe gold-embroidered and silken draperies as well as tapestries covering the bare walls.

IT IS UNUSUAL TO COME ACROSS A LOIRE CHÂTEAU in the middle of a town, as is this one. Foulques Nerra's keep and the royal castle below it, still equipped for defense but equally suited for courtly living, represent the beginning and the end of the Middle Ages. Three massive round towers, with typically set-back top stories and conical roofs, lend three-dimensionality to the exterior façade of the main wing. Two closely placed towers, one of them an especially thick corner tower on the north side, the new keep, flank the entrance, in front of which is the drawbridge restored by Siegfried. The section to the left of the drawbridge was a residential wing, with a second one angling off from it. A covered wall-walk over 425 feet long runs around the entire exterior façade. The moat that originally surrounded the castle has disappeared. With its polygonal stair tower and its slender dormers above the window axes, the courtyard side seems less severe and militant than does the exterior façade. Despite the asymmetries in its ground plan and elevations, the structure displays remarkable stylistic unity, considering that it was built within a period of only four years. It has also been spared any major changes since that time.

Siegfried exercised astonishing sensitivity in refurnishing the interior as it might have looked at the time it was finished and in the decades immediately following. In purchasing objects for it, he sought the advice of artists and scholars. The majority of the furnishings—richly ornamented cupboards, chests, benches—are original, many of them of Italian provenance. However, the collector did not shrink from using copies in order to be able to present as complete and accurate a picture of the period as possible. He had beds, wall paneling, and floor tiles copied after contemporary examples. Along with its paintings and sculptures, the most valuable pieces in the collection are the more than thirty fifteenth- and sixteenth-century wall hangings, many of them from Flanders and some from the Aubusson works.

The most impressive of the immovable furnishings are the fireplaces. One in the Salle des Gardes was built in the form of a castle with heads looking out from behind its battlements. The Salle des Gardes has the only original tiled floor in the castle. Local tradition has it that the wedding of Charles VIII and Anne de Bretagne took place in the Grand Salon on the second floor of the south wing. Dominating the furnishings in this room are seven panels from the tapestry cycle of the Nine Heroes, from around 1530. A wedding chest—which actually belonged to Anne—is perhaps the most evocative of the numerous pieces of furniture. A diptych of portraits of the royal couple also recalls the festivities of 1491.

The château's garden, in the style of the fifteenth century, has been reconstructed after contemporary miniatures. Siegfried and his wife are buried farther up the slope, at the foot of the ancient keep.

VILLANDRY

OUR CHIEF SOURCE CONCERNING THE MAGICAL gardens that once graced the Renaissance châteaux of the Loire is the engravings of Jacques Androuet Du Cerceau. Contemporaries spoke of the gardens as images of the earthly paradise, but none have survived. Thus we are fortunate in being able to enjoy the gardens of Villandry, the only re-creations of those earlier splendors in France.

The Château de Villandry dates back in part to the Middle Ages. Until 1639, it was known as Coulombières; and it was here on July 4, 1189, that Henry II of England met with Philippe-Auguste to conclude the Peace of Coulombières. An ill and broken man, Henry returned to Chinon, where he died only two days later.

It was bought in 1532 by François I's adviser and secretary of state, Jean Le Breton, who was also the builder of Villesavin. He had the entire fourteenth-century structure demolished except for a single corner tower and erected a new castle on the foundations of the old one; it was one of the last to be built on the Loire in the Renaissance style. The new structure consisted of three two-story wings around an inner courtyard, the side wings opening onto the court in arcades and ending in matching pavilions. The medieval moats were preserved.

The façades are neatly balanced, with pilasters, double cornices, and high dormers emphasizing the window axes. As at Villesavin, which he built a short time later, Breton's schooled eye for symmetry and elegant proportions is everywhere apparent.

The castle remained in the Breton family until the eighteenth century. Later owners made numerous changes to the building and its surroundings. Its restoration in the style of the sixteenth century was entirely the work of an art-loving Spanish doctor, Joachim de Carvallo. He bought Villandry from a druggist in 1906, and immediately set about removing the Baroque additions from its façade, restoring it to its original condition, and having the trees in its English-style garden cut down. He then laid out the Renaissance gardens, inspired by the engravings of Du Cerceau. Carvallo did not slavishly copy the patterns he found in Du Cerceau's book; he also permitted himself to be influenced by designs from his native Spain.

There are three garden parterres, each on a different level and connected by staircases and ramps. They can best be seen from the eighteenth-century terraces on the slope to the east. On the middle level, perpendicular to each other and separated by a moat, are the two parts of the ornamental garden, with their precisely manicured designs outlined by boxwood and yew hedges and filled with colorful plantings of flowers. Fountains provide an ac-cent. These were based on Spanish and Moorish designs. The most imaginative part of the ornamental garden is that below the viewing terrace. The four square beds closest to the château symbolize four kinds of love: innocent love is represented by hearts, masks, and flames; tragic love by swords and dagger blades; passionate love by a labyrinth of deformed hearts; and fugitive love by fans, horns, and billets-doux. The colors of the flowers in these squares have also been carefully chosen: pinks represent innocent love; reds, tragic; mixed colors, passionate; and yellows, fugitive. The parterre ends on the opposite side of the moat in an area containing three varieties of crosses: the Maltese cross, the cross of Languedoc, and the cross of the Basque country. Figural areas of a similar kind appear in Du Cerceau's engravings.

On the top level—and laid out, unlike the others, in the Baroque style—is the water garden, with a pool in the center flanked by areas of lawn and surrounded by plantings of lime trees. The fountain feeds the garden moat, which runs in turn into the moat surrounding the château. Above the water garden is an orchard, its trees planted in precise rows after the example of Du Cerceau.

The highlight of all these re-creations is the vegetable garden, on the lowest level. The garden is composed of nine large beds, each with a different interior design formed by the outlining hedges within which the vegetables grow. Flowers add a colorful accent to the various greens of the vegetables—which are planted in gradations of greens, so that the symmetry of the designs is emphasized by the symmetry of the colors—and fruit trees mark the corners of the squares. Only vegetables known to have been common in sixteenth-century France are cultivated.

Grape arbors run between the garden's squares; and when the fruit is ripe, its aroma is tempting.

The château is filled with Spanish furniture collected by Carvallo. A fine group of paintings includes examples by the Spanish masters Velázquez, Ribera, Zurbarán, and Goya. Two sixteenth-century Italian works represent St. Paul and St. John. The most fascinating aspect of Villandry's decoration is the thirteenth-century Mudéjar ceiling imported from Toledo. Installed in a room on the second floor, this sumptuous coffered ceiling is gilded and decorated with Islamic designs. It offers a glimmer of Spain in the heart of France.

USSE

SEEN FROM ACROSS THE RIVER, THE CHÂTEAU d'Ussé stands out a brilliant white against a background of dark foliage. It is the quintessential castle. The writer Charles Perrault was inspired by a visit to Ussé to create his fairy tale *Sleeping Beauty*.

The structure was begun before 1480 by the de Bueil family. It incorporates portions of a preceding castle. Ussé was still unfinished when it was sold in 1485 to Jacques d'Espinay, a chamberlain to Louis XI and Charles VIII. He and his son Charles brought the project to completion by 1535.

The château originally had four wings around an inner courtyard. But one of its seventeenth-century owners, Louis de Valentinay, had the north wing torn down to free the view of the Indre valley. In front of the now opened complex, a terraced garden was laid out down the slope, and a flat-roofed extension in the classical style was added to the west wing. After numerous owners, Ussé was acquired late in the nineteenth century by the comte de Blacas, whose descendants still occupy it.

With its thick round towers and interior wall-walks, the château preserves the look of a medieval fortress. Its courtyard entrance was originally situated on the east side, between the two close-set towers whose top floors, like those at Langeais, are smaller than the lower floors above the machicolation. Behind the polygonal projection from the east façade was originally a chapel, and its octagonal flèche rises above the courtyard side. The round keep on the southwest corner stands on the foundation of an earlier fortress.

The courtyard façade of the east wing still reflects the Flamboyant style, although it was slightly altered during restorations in the nineteenth century. The front of the west wing, from the age of François I, was changed somewhat in the seventeenth century. The south connecting wing was built as an open arcade; sometime around 1500, floors were added on top of it, and it gained its present form in the seventeenth century.

Some rooms are set up as a museum. The most notable of them is the Chambre du Roi, which was furnished for Louis XIV but never honored by a visit from him. It still has the original wallcovering of red silk patterned with chinoiserie in white and the royal bed *à la polonaise* with a canopy of the same material and matching chairs. Corinthian columns separate the sleeping area from the rest of the chamber and heighten the ceremonial atmosphere of the room. Fine examples of eighteenth-century furniture also add distinction.

The chapel, built somewhat apart from the château in the park, is a perfect example of French Renaissance church architecture. Jacques d'Espinay ordered in his will that it be built, and his son Charles and Charles's wife, Lucrèce de Pons, carried out his wishes between 1520 and 1538. Both inside and out, the two are commemorated by the appearance of their initials, *C* and *L*. The chapel was consecrated in 1538, and in the same year, a college of six canons was founded to staff it.

It is a four-bay hall with choir and pointed-arch vaults. In structure, then, the chapel is still totally Gothic. But it is embellished with a wealth of Renaissance ornament of incomparable delicacy. The outside buttresses end in candelabra instead of finials. The entrance bay is splendid; the portal and a pointed-arch window above it are surrounded by filigree relief of an extraordinary vitality. Three-dimensional busts in medallions—Christ and his apostles—are, for the period, a new and unusual motif in French art. The Charterhouse of Parma probably served as a model.

A door to the sacristy displays the same wealth of forms as does the entrance. Also preserved are the choir stalls from around 1535, which are ornamented with lovely figures and arabesques. Among the chapel's other noteworthy appointments are a polychrome terra-cotta Madonna, attributed to Luca Della Robbia, and a Tuscan triptych, both from the fifteenth century.

CHINON

Chinon, Chinon
Petite ville, grand renom
Assise sur pierre ancienne
Au haut le bois, au pied
la Vienne.

Chinon, Chinon
A small town, of great renown
Erected on ancient stone
Above it the forest, and below, the Vienne.

WITH THESE VERSES, FRANÇOIS RABELAIS ERECTED in *Gargantua and Pantagruel* a literary monument to his childhood home. It would be impossible to describe the town more briefly or more accurately. The best view of it is from the Quai Danton across the Vienne, where you can see the full length of the town extending along the foot of a ridge. Above it, beyond a ring of trees, rise the remains of the castle.

There was a fortress on this ridge even in Roman times, and the counts of Blois erected one of their many castles here in the tenth century. In 1044, it fell to the counts of Anjou, and after Henri Plantagenet became king of England, he chose Chinon as his primary residence, commanding that it be almost completely rebuilt. He died here in 1189, grieving over his betrayal by his son Richard, Cœur de Lion.

Philippe-Auguste conquered Chinon for the French Crown in 1205, and it continued to serve as a royal residence. The most famous event to take place here was the meeting, in 1429, between Joan of Arc and the indecisive and cowardly dauphin. It

Fortress at Chinon.

was here that she exhorted him to reconquer his territories lost to the English during the Hundred Years' War.

Chinon continued to be the seat of government through the reign of Charles VII, and numerous houses in the town recall this period of bustling court life. Succeeding Kings tended to come here less and less. In the seventeenth century, the castle was acquired by Cardinal Richelieu, whose family kept possession until the Revolution. Poorly maintained, it succumbed increasingly to decay, and its weakest portions were razed. It was only around the middle of the nineteenth century that an effort was made to repair its walls, and then only because they threatened to fall onto the town.

It is difficult to form an accurate picture of the original fortress. It is made up of three distinct strongholds separated by dry moats. On the east end of the ridge are the ruins of the *Fort St-Georges*, with its chapel now completely vanished except for the crypt. Henry II built this section in the twelfth century. He named it after the patron saint of England, to protect the main access to the central fortress, which was especially vulnerable at this end. This outer fortification served to house a large garrison.

A deep trench separates the Fort St-Georges from the central fortress, the largest portion of the complex. A wooden drawbridge once led across to the gateway in the Pavillon de l'Horloge, but now a stone bridge has taken its place. The core of this tower probably dates to the fourteenth century. With a height of 115 feet, it is the only completely preserved structure on the castle mount. It takes its name from an old clock and a bell cast in 1399 mounted in the lantern on its roof; the bell, called Marie Javelle, still rings out the hours.

The almost completely decimated *Château de Milieu*, on the site of the Roman fortress, comprises an area roughly 590 feet long by 260 feet wide; it is now planted with gardens and trees. This is surrounded by a twelfth- and thirteenth-century ring wall with truncated towers. On its northwest corner stands the Tour d'Argenton, which is semicircular on the outside and flat on the inside. It dates from the fifteenth century and served as a prison. The semicircular Tour des Chiens, in the center of the north wall, was built in the thirteenth century and presumably was named after the royal hounds, which were housed in it.

The residential apartments were placed on the more pleasant south side above the town and the river. An attempt at their reconstruction has been made in recent years. Rooms on the ground floor have been restored and include a guard room and the kitchen, in which hangs a seventeenth-century Aubusson tapestry that depicts Joan of Arc recognizing the dauphin. All that remains of the Grand Logis, in which the meeting between Joan and Charles took place, is the west gable wall and its handsome fireplace. This hall was situated, as were all the king's living quarters, on the second floor of the lodge. It was reached by means of a stone staircase, a few steps of which survive. These are hallowed stones to the French people because they were trod by Joan of Arc.

In an earlier building on this site, Henry II died in 1189. He had just concluded a humiliating treaty with Philippe-Auguste at Coulombières (Villandry) and had learned that many of his vassals and even his son Richard had given their allegiance to the French Crown. Losing his will to live, Henry fell silent and soon died. Even his servants proved treacherous, for they stripped

A street in Chinon.

his body of his clothing and jewels; his one remaining ally, Guillaume le Maréchal, had to borrow money to bury Henry in clothes deserving of a king.

A second deep trench separates the western portion of the fortress, known as the *Fort du Coudray*, from the larger central area. The two enclosures are linked by a stone bridge. The ring wall of this western fort, which is also nicely landscaped, is strengthened by massive towers. The one at the southeast corner is the many-sided Tour de Boisy, from the thirteenth century, containing a vaulted chamber that once served as a chapel. From the platform at the top is a spectacular view of the valley and town below. The east side is protected from attack by the round Donjon du Coudray, the thirteenth-century keep. The graffiti visible inside are said to have been the work of Knights Templar imprisoned here in 1308; the mystical nature of some of the drawings—Yin and Yang symbols, swastikas—indicate that the order may have dabbled in magic, as was charged at the trial of those imprisoned here. Before this keep was built, the Tour du Moulin, which is strengthened by outworks and dates from the twelfth century, served the same function. The portion of the west wall next to it goes back in part to the mid-tenth century. It was heightened in the twelfth century and strengthened by the addition of the towers.

Across the road leading to Tours, opposite the north walls of the citadel, a sign points out the Clos de l'Echo, a well-known echo point. French visitors love to stand here and shout in the direction of the castle:

Les femmes de Chinon sont-elles fidèles?

Echo: *Elles?*

Oui, les femmes de Chinon?

Echo: *Non.*

A STROLL THROUGH THE TOWN TAKES YOU BACK to the late Middle Ages. Narrow, winding alleys and countless half-timbered or limestone buildings from mostly the fifteenth and sixteenth centuries create a picturesque townscape. The center of Roman and medieval Chinon was the Grand Carroi, the intersection of the Rue Voltaire, the east-west axis of the Roman town; the Rue du Grand-Carroi, which leads to the bridge across the Vienne; and the Rue Jeanne d'Arc, a narrow street climbing up to the castle. In front of the house on the corner of the Rue Voltaire and the Rue Jeanne d'Arc is a fountain on which the Maid of Orléans is supposed to have stepped when dismounting from her horse on her arrival in 1429. The Rue Voltaire is lined with houses from the fifteenth through eighteenth centuries, and is considered one of the best preserved historic streets in France.

Near the Grand Carroi is the elegant *Hôtel des Etats-Généraux*. This stone structure, from the fifteenth and sixteenth centuries, houses the *Musée du Vieux Chinon*. On the ground floor are examples of local folk art. The second floor offers a series of beautifully furnished rooms, and in the main hall is a portrait of Rabelais by Delacroix. On the third floor are objects dealing with local history, relics of Joan of Arc, and St. Mexme's cope, brought to France during the Crusades. Gothic chests, statues of the Virgin, and other pieces are included.

The oldest church in Chinon, the collegiate church of *St-Mexme*, was turned into a saltpeter plant during the Revolution. Its crossing tower collapsed in 1817, destroying the eastern part of the structure as it fell. The surviving nave, from the tenth century, was later remodeled as a school. The side aisles have disappeared. The

St-Mexme, the oldest church in Chinon.

narthex, to the west, and its flanking tower on the north side date from the eleventh century, while the tower on its south side is a fifteenth-century reconstruction.

In 1964, an unusual fresco was discov-ered in the nearby *Chapelle Ste-Rade-gonde*. This Late Romanesque chapel was built over the site of an earlier one, which had been erected by the Merovingian queen Radegonde to honor John the Recluse, a hermit who had lived in a cave on this spot. The fresco, painted around 1200, depicts a hunt, perhaps one with members of the royal Plantagenet family as participants: King John; his wife, Isabelle d'Angoulême; and his mother, Eleanor of Aquitaine.

St-Etienne, a five-bay hall church with a two-bay choir and polygonal apse, was built between 1477 and 1483. One enters its elegant interior through a splendid double portal in the Flamboyant style.

The church of *St-Maurice* below the castle, where Joan of Arc is said to have prayed, goes back to Henry II. It was originally built with a three-bay nave and with a bell tower on its north side. A choir bay with a north side chapel was added at the end of the twelfth century; a south choir chapel, in the fourteenth; and a south side aisle, in the sixteenth. The tower is crowned by a fifteenth-century stone cupola. The twelfth-century spaces have lovely, high vaulting in the Angevin style; they are richly ornamented with figures, including as keystones in the nave a depiction of Christ and the Lamb of God, each supported by a wreath of angels. An inscription in the pavement near the center of the nave reads *Henricus II Rex Anglorum aedificam.*

The *bridge* across the Vienne was also built originally by Henry II. However, only a few of its twelfth-century arches survived its destruction by the Germans in 1944.

---

*T*AVANT

OUR REASON FOR VISITING THE VILLAGE CHURCH of *St-Nicolas* in Tavant is its frescoes, which were painted in the mid-twelfth century. This unimposing structure of white stone blocks was originally a basilica from around 1120, with nave and side aisles, transept, crossing tower, choir, and chapels off the arms of the transept. It presumably was built by monks from the abbey of Marmoutier, Tavant having been founded as a priory by that house toward the end of the tenth century. The church has lost its side aisles and the southern chapel, while the northern one has been walled up. A triple-arch entrance portal, distinguished by filigree ornamentation, takes up the entire width of the nave; its side portions have been reduced to narrow blind arches.

One has to imagine the whole interior— which is characterized by half-columns with primitive capitals, rounded transverse arches, and barrel vaults—as having been completely embellished with paintings like the ones that survive, although heavily damaged, in the choir. They were discovered beneath the whitewash only in 1945. In the apse vault is a Christ in Glory with the symbols of the Evangelists and angels. The barrel vault over the rest of the choir is divided into two picture areas, in which it is possible to make out familiar scenes from the childhood of Christ: the Annunciation, the Visitation, the Nativity, the Slaughter of the Innocents (?), the Annunciation to the Shepherds, and the Flight into Egypt.

The real surprise is to be found in the crypt of the church. The heavy vaulting is supported by eight stocky pillars, and it is somewhat difficult to move in the tiny space. The walls and vaults were all painted with small figures. These paintings are among the best preserved and most highly individual of French Romanesque frescoes; created by the same artists who worked in the choir of the church, they apparently were never whitewashed. All the scenes and separate figures betray a delight in the play of lines, and seem like mere sketches, rather than monumental paintings against the white plaster. The pictorial program also appears to have been improvised, and it is difficult to make out any logical sequence. There is a blend of everything from biblical scenes (Adam and Eve at work in the Garden, Cain and Abel, Saul [?], David with his harp, Mary, Christ in Limbo, the Descent from the Cross, the crucifixion of Peter) to hagiographic depictions (female saints), ethical allegories (vices, demons), and cosmological subjects (Atlases, Sagittarius [?]). This variety may reflect the wishes of the artists' patron.

CHAMPIGNY-SUR-VEUDE

THE RENAISSANCE *CHAPELLE ST-LOUIS* AT CHAMPIgny-sur-Veude is the loveliest of its type in the Loire and contains a wonderful store of stained glass. Yet it is thanks only to chance that it still survives. In the first half of the sixteenth century, Louis I de Bourbon, duc de Montpensier, and his son Louis II erected a château here on the foundations of a medieval fortress. The chapel was built between 1508 and 1543. Cardinal Richelieu, the all-powerful early-seventeenth-century French statesman, began building a residence in the nearby town of Richelieu in 1625. He looked on the magnificent château at Champigny with displeasure and sensed that it outshone his own creation. Accordingly, he acquired it from Gaston d'Orléans, the brother of Louis XIII, and promptly had it torn down. The chapel was also supposed to have been razed. But Urban VIII refused to give his consent and placed it under the legal protection of the Vatican, for while serving as papal nuncio in France, he had had occasion to celebrate Mass in it and remembered how beautiful it was.

The chapel is a four-bay hall structure, with a choir ending in beveled corners. Its form is unmistakably Gothic, but its elements were completely modified in the Renaissance style, like those of the chapel at Ussé or the church at Montrésor. On the buttresses, for example, are little canopies of round bars around a strong round pillar instead of the expected finials. Along the side walls are vaulted arcades running through the buttresses and open to the outside in segmented arches. These arcades connect the small chapels next to the choir with the narthex, which is cast in the purest of Renaissance forms based on Italian models. The exterior of this narthex is embellished with Corinthian pilasters and half-columns and an entablature. A high, round-arch opening leads inside. Here the walls are broken up into two stories, with Ionic columns below and Corinthian ones above, separated by a continuous entablature and framing niches for sculpture, now completely empty. Above the deep crowning entablature is a barrel vault ornamented with coffers. There is a surfeit of decoration, consisting mainly of symbols and emblems: two wings, the heraldic device of the Bourbon-Montpensier family; the crowned *L* of Louis de Bourbon; the

Cardinal Richelieu

girdle of the Ordre de Notre-Dame-du-Chardon, which was founded in 1360 by one of Louis de Bourbon's ancestors; and much more.

The chapel's interior is totally dissolved in the glowing colors of its stained-glass windows, which constitute a complete cycle unmatched in any other structure along the Loire. They were commissioned around 1550 by Cardinal de Givry, the bishop of Langres. The occasion for this act of generosity probably was the marriage of his niece Jacquette de Longwy to Louis II de Bourbon.

The focus of the cycle is the Crucifixion, which is depicted in the central window of the choir. Below this is St. Louis, one of the most important French kings of the Middle Ages, who reigned as Louis IX from 1226 to 1270 and died while on a Crusade. His wife, Marguerite de Provence, is depicted next to him. The remaining windows contain thirty-four portraits of members of the House of Bourbon-Montpensier, above which are shown events from the life of St. Louis: (left to right) his anointment, his education, his acquisition of holy relics, his penance and charity, his vow to undertake a Crusade, his embarkation, the capture of Damiette, the Battle of Mansura, his return from the Crusade, and his death in Tunis.

The only object in the room is a marble statue of Henri de Bourbon-Montpensier, which dates from the seventeenth century. It originally graced his tomb in the right-hand side chapel, which was desecrated during the Revolution.

A twelve-year legal battle with the duc de Richelieu, the cardinal's heir, resulted in the return of Champigny to the daughter of Gaston d'Orléans, Anne-Marie-Louise, who was known as the Grande Mademoiselle. She proceeded to transform the farm buildings, which had also been spared, into a charming three-wing château in classical proportions; even now, the structure attests to her exquisite taste. The château is privately owned and is not open to visitors.

177: View of Azay-le-Rideau from the Indre River (Aileen Ah-Tye).

178–179: Near the château at Azay-le-Rideau (Luis Villota/The Stock Market).

180: Round corner tower at Azay-le-Rideau (Mark Segal).

181: View of Azay-le-Rideau from the park (Mark Segal).

182: Vouvray vineyard (Adam Woolfitt/Woodfin Camp).

183: Joan of Arc memorial in Orléans (Allan A. Philiba).

184–185: Statue of Joan of Arc in Orléans (Allan A. Philiba).

186–187: Valençay (Fred Mayer/Woodfin Camp).

188: Villandry's vegetable garden (Sonja Bullaty).

189: Villandry (Allan A. Philiba).

190–191: Hearts in the ornamental garden at Villandry (Angelo Lomeo).

192: The bed of the old moat at Loches (Aileen Ah-Tye).

THROUGH ANJOU

CANDES

CANDES, AT THE CONFLUENCE OF THE LOIRE AND the Vienne, is linked to the name of St. Martin of Tours. It was here that he founded a church in honor of St. Maurice, here that he liked to withdraw for monastic retreats, and here that he died in 397. The *Golden Legend* of Jacobus de Voragine relates that

after his demise, the people of Poitiers and of Tours came together, and a great battle broke out between them. The people of Poitiers said: "As a monk he is ours; we want to have him back; he was directed to us." But the people of Tours said: "He was taken from you and given to us by God." At midnight, when the people from Poitiers were all asleep, the corpse was taken out through the window by the others, and carried up the Loire to Tours in a boat.

In the last quarter of the twelfth century, construction of the present pilgrimage church of *St-Martin* was begun on the site where the saint had died. Its choir and tran-

sept were completed during this first phase of building; its three-aisle hall nave was erected around the middle of the thirteenth century. The church looks like a fortress. In the fifteenth century, the strong, towerlike corner structures of the west front and the north portal vestibule were provided with battlements and machicolation. Legend has it that the church was fortified to protect the sacred vial that St. Martin had brought here containing blood from the martyrs of the Theban Legion. A more practical reason was that a refuge was thought desirable after all the plunderings during the Hundred Years' War.

The irregularity of the spaces on the north side of the choir and transept is particularly noticeable when one studies the ground plan. Scholars assume that the architect began with the little Chapelle St-Martin on the north side of the choir bay, which consists of an aisle and a semicircular apse. It is supposed to mark the site of the saint's deathbed. A stained-glass window depicts how the monks from Tours sneaked the corpse of the aged Martin past

Candes

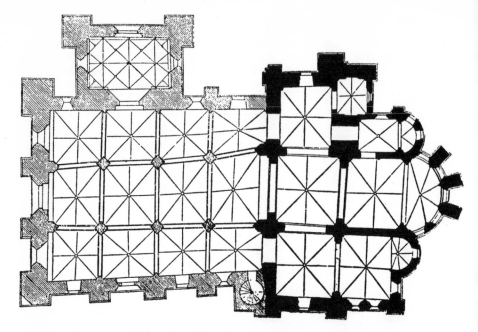

Floor plan of the Chapelle St-Martin at Candes.

the sleeping monks from Poitiers and placed it in a boat on the Loire.

The church then grew up around this chapel, clearly incorporating portions of older structures. This is the only way to explain the thick wall between the north arm of the transept and the chapel. A second chapel fills the corner between the transept and the Chapelle St-Martin. The main choir ends in a large apse, flanked by a smaller one with a single bay to the south as a counterpart to the older chapel.

The four-bay nave is also distorted in its ground plan, since it was necessary to conform to the bays of the transept. However, this does not detract from the interior space, which is dominated by slender and precisely carved clustered columns. As in the older eastern portions, eight-ribbed Angevin vaults spread across each bay. In addition to the richness of the architectural members, there is a variety of figural sculpture, a typical feature in Anjou at this period. Especially marvelous is the care with which the figures were executed; some even retain their original coloring. The architect not only utilized the entire formal repertoire of Angevin and Poitevin art, but also took inspiration from the great churches in Le Mans, Bourges, and Tours.

One of the unusual architectural features of Candes is the narthex, on the north side of the nave, with the Chapelle St-Michel on its second floor. To break up the monotony of the tall wall mass, the architect placed three levels of columns in front of it. The largest row, in the middle, which is cut into by the pointed-arch portal, he left without ornamental figures. Many of the sculptures intended to be set between the columns on the bottom row were never completed, and even the bases supporting the ones ultimately installed—now sadly in great disrepair—were left as simple bosses. The upper row was completely filled with figures of saints; but the portion above the portal was destroyed when battlements were installed in the fifteenth century.

In contrast to the massiveness of its exterior, the inside of the narthex is surprisingly delicate. A quite fragile-looking pillar on a high polygonal base supports palmlike ribbed vaulting. Like the façade, the church portal is richly sculpted with figures. On the tympanum, Christ appears as world judge between the Virgin and St. John. Additional scenes from the Last Judgment were begun on the inner archivolts, while the outer ones remained completely unworked. The portal jambs and the back wall of the narthex are fitted out with figures of saints in arcades consisting of columns and trefoil arches. In addition to the apostles and various female saints, it is possible to identify Abraham and Isaac in front of the sacrificial altar. Even more unusual than these partly fragmentary figures, which are comparable in style to those on the cathedral at Reims, are the delicate sculptures on the base of the jambs. Small heads wearing crowns or turbans are framed by sinuous foliage combined with birds, dragons, monsters, and sirens. They cannot have been created before 1225 to 1230, while the statues above them date from around 1250.

*F*ONTEVRAULT

DESPITE CONSIDERABLE DAMAGE DURING AND after the Revolution, the buildings of the former abbey of Fontevrault still constitute one of the most extensive monastic complexes in France. Robert d'Arbrissel, the son of a priest and a brilliant preacher in support of the Crusades, founded a hermitage in this wooded region in 1099, hoping to lead the life of a recluse with a few of his friends. He was soon joined by hundreds of men and women, harlots and lepers among them. This diversity required a special organization for the monastic community, and Robert d'Arbrissel established it with reference to the words of Christ on the Cross to John: "Son, behold thy Mother." Thus the women's convent (Ste-Marie) was consecrated to Mary; and the community of monks (St-Jean), to John. At the head of the entire complex was the abbess of Ste-Marie. The arrangement was meant to express—true to Christ's words—the spiritual motherhood of Mary. Also with an eye to Christ, who did not turn his back on fallen women and lepers, Robert d'Arbrissel set up two additional monastic communities: St-Lazare for the lepers, and La Madeleine for repentant whores.

Rich donations, especially from the counts of Anjou, sustained the monastery. Established according to the Rule of St. Benedict, the order was confirmed by the bishop of Poitiers as early as 1106, and it rapidly spread through the whole of the realm of the counts of Anjou and later kings of England. These rulers promptly speci-

Fontevrault, layout of the abbey complex.
1. *Gatehouse and stables.*
2. *Passageway to abbey.*
3. *Abbey church.*
4. *Royal tombs.*
5. *Gallery wing.*
6. *Great cloister.*
7. *Chapterhouse.*
8. *Chapel of St-Benoît.*
9. *Small cloister.*
10. *Infirmary of St-Benoît.*
11. *Passageway to the infirmary.*
12. *Renaissance staircase.*
13. *Romanesque refectory.*
14. *Romanesque kitchen.*
15. *Priory of St-Lazarus.*
16. *Abbess's palace.*
17. *Superintendant's office (19th century).*
18. *Residence of Louis XV's daughter (1739).*
19. *Convent of La Madeleine.*

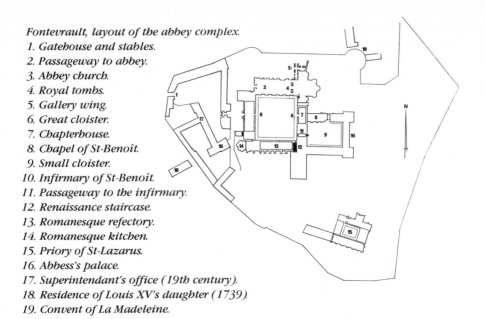

fied the mother house at Fontevrault as their final resting place.

All thirty-six abbesses of Fontevrault were of noble blood, fourteen of them princesses. The nuns, too, came generally from aristocratic circles. Small wonder then that, with an annual income of 80,000 livres, Fontevrault was the wealthiest women's convent in France on the eve of the Revolution. Its members lived as though at a princely court. The abbey was to suffer horribly during the turmoil of the Revolution, and it eventually succumbed altogether. Its buildings were plundered and ravaged, and some of them were burned down. Several of its nuns ended on the guillotine.

In 1804, Napoleon turned what was left of the complex into a prison, a function it served until 1963. Over the past two decades, a thorough restoration of the convent has been under way.

THE HEART OF THE COMPLEX IS THE CONVENT OF Ste-Marie, including the convent church, the great cloister, the chapter house, and the famous kitchen. To the south, somewhat apart from this core area, lies the priory of St-Lazare. The community of St-Jean and the convent of La Madeleine have disappeared, largely destroyed during the Revolution. They stood to the east of the main buildings.

To enter the abbey from the village, one passes through a gatehouse (ca. 1785), to the left of which extend the sumptuous stables of the abbesses. This building had just been completed at the outbreak of the Revolution in 1789, and still attests to the wealth of the convent shortly before its demise. Also dating from the second half of the eighteenth century is the abbess's palace, which lies on the south side of the entry courtyard opposite the Romanesque abbey church. The rest of the buildings surrounding this courtyard were built mostly in the nineteenth century and were part of the prison.

In front of the great cloister is a remarkable example of First Empire architecture: the low entrance portal to the former prison boasts columns in the Egyptian style and projecting pavilions ornamented with faceted stone blocks. It is held to be the work of the architect and engineer Normand, to whom Napoleon entrusted the remodeling of the abbey in 1804.

The *abbey church*, badly mutilated by prison installations in the nineteenth century, has been thoroughly restored, and now looks as it did when it was built in the first half of the twelfth century. It is one of the loveliest Romanesque churches in Anjou. Its basilicalike ambulatory choir, with three chapels and stately, close-set arcade,

was consecrated to the Virgin, along with the transept, by Calixtus II in 1119. Above the aisleless nave (1160) rise four cupolas supported by deeply projecting pillars. Blind arcades break up the wall area and add three-dimensionality to the space, which was patterned after that of the cathedral of Angoulême. The cupolas and wall arcades were renovated in 1906, when the several levels of prisoners' dormitories installed in 1830 were finally removed. The exuberant capital sculptures of the wall arcades are largely restorations, while those of the vaulting pillars are for the most part original.

The church acquired special status as the burial place for members of the English royal House of Plantagenet. Four tomb figures survive, even though they were heavily damaged during the Revolution, when

Fontevrault

199

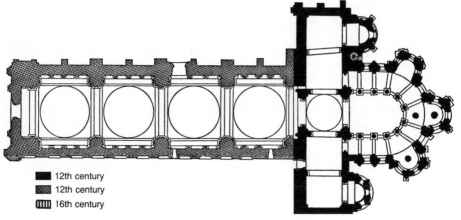

12th century
12th century
16th century

Floor plan for the abbey church at Fontevrault.

the bones of at least eight members of the royal family were dumped along with their stone likenesses on the floor of the crypt (now closed). The statues were subjected to major restoration in the nineteenth century. They are larger than life size and rest on draped catafalques; their garments were carved with great care, resembling those of a body lying in state. This type of tomb monument is unusual, and there are no examples of it outside western France. Three of the figures can be positively identified by inscriptions found on them:

Henri II, duc de Normandie, comte d'Anjou, and king of England from 1154 to 1189. He died at Chinon and specified that he be buried in the abbey church. This is the oldest effigy of any English king.

Eleanor, duchesse d'Aquitaine and comtesse de Poitou, who became the wife of Henry II after her divorce from the French king Louis VII, thus bringing about one-third of France to the English Crown. She died at Fontevrault in 1204 at the age of eighty-one.

Richard, Cœur de Lion, comte de Poitou, duc d'Aquitaine, and king of England from 1189 to 1199. He was mortally wounded at Chalus.

The identification of the fourth figure is disputed. She is thought to be Isabelle d'Angoulême, the second wife of King John, who died as a Fontevrault nun in advanced age in 1246. She was buried in the convent cemetery, and was only later transferred to the church.

The first three tomb figures are carved in limestone, and were executed shortly after 1200. The so-called Isabelle d'Angoulême is in wood and presumably was made in imitation of the earlier ones in the mid-thirteenth century. The polychrome painting on the sculptures dates from the Baroque period and the nineteenth century.

Little remains of the Romanesque convent buildings. Along with a reform in the order of Fontevrault in the second half of the fifteenth century, the buildings were also renovated, especially under the abbesses Renée de Bourbon (1491–1534), Louise de Bourbon (1534–75), and Eléonore de Bourbon (1575–1611).

Next to the north arm of the church's transept there is still a short gallery wing, which was added in the late fifteenth century. In 1515, Renée de Bourbon had the Romanesque *refectory* redesigned and fitted out with a massive, nine-bay ribbed vault, above which cells for forty-seven nuns were created. The two westernmost bays were reserved for the new kitchens. The adjacent (south) walk of the cloister was built at the same time, while the remaining ones were completed in the mid-sixteenth century. Its keystones and consoles are ornamented with motifs from the Passion. They serve as perpetual reminders of the spiritual foundation of the Fontevrault order.

Dating from the time of the abbess Louise de Bourbon is the east walk of the cloister, with its Renaissance staircase and two-aisle *chapter house*, above which is a dormitory. The chapter house contains ribbed vaulting that spreads like a tent between consoles and pillars. One enters it through an exquisitely ornamented Renaissance portal, renovated in the nineteenth century. Wall paintings by Thomas Pot of Angers date from after 1563, and depict scenes from the Passion and the Death and Assumption of Mary. Until the eighteenth century, portraits of abbesses from the Bourbon and Rochechouart families were added to these much-restored paintings. Eléonore de Bourbon had a novitiate wing added off the chapter-house wing sometime after 1575.

Extending to the east of the great cloister are the wings of the *infirmary* of St-Benoît, for old and invalid nuns. Its single-aisle chapel dates to around 1180. The remaining buildings, which are arranged around the smaller cloister of St-Benoît, were erected in the seventeenth century.

Death played a major role in the monastic ritual of Fontevrault, for it called to mind the dying Christ on the Cross, whose words had been cited in the founding of the complex. If a nun appeared close to death, she was brought into the chapel, where she was given Extreme Unction. She then made a confession before the assembled chapter. During the death struggle, she was covered with a hair shirt and placed on a bed strewn with ashes, while the nuns gathered around her and recited the Apostles' Creed. Once she had died, a cross was drawn on her winding sheet with the drippings from a sacred candle.

The priory of *St-Lazare* stands to the south. It also encloses a central cloister. Once leprosy had disappeared in the time of Louis XIV, the priory was turned into a home for convalescent nuns. The aged mothers and sisters of the nuns could also find shelter here if they wished to end their days at Fontevrault. The only portions of the twelfth-century priory still intact are the church, portions of the refectory, and the chapter house. All the rest dates mainly from the seventeenth century.

The most famous structure at the abbey of Fontevrault is its Romanesque *kitchen*, the only surviving one of its kind. Others are known from old engravings. The one at Fontevrault was built between 1144 and 1189 with funds donated by Henry II. For a long time, it was unclear just what had been the function of the octagonal building roofed with a stone pyramid and surrounded by a wreath of apses. Some thought it the hideout of the medieval bandit Evrault, who with his band had made the surrounding forests unsafe and who had given his name to a small spring—Fontaine d'Evrault—and thus to the abbey; indeed, the

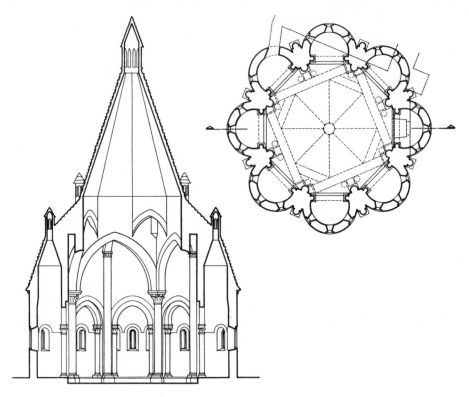

Floor plan and side view of the Romanesque kitchen.

building became known as the Tour d'Evrault. Others assumed that it was the burial chapel of the Plantagenets. It was an English scholar who finally enlightened the French about its actual use. Eugène Viollet-le-Duc later described the kitchen in great detail in his *Dictionnaire raisonné de l'architecture* and was the first to explain the functional significance of its structure. A number of reconstruction suggestions were made before the building was renovated in 1902. Unfortunately, the one that differed most from Viollet-le-Duc's convincing reconstruction was the one selected.

The kitchen is built entirely of stone, and was set apart from the rest of the abbey's buildings so that it would not be an annoyance with its smoke and cooking smells. The apselike structures, which since 1902 have had window slits set into blind arches, were once closed fireplaces. There originally were eight; those on the east side were sacrificed when the new kitchens at the end of the refectory were built in the early sixteenth century. The smoke escaped through pipes rising out of their roofs. These roofs were originally half-cupolas, not the conical ones seen today. Any remaining smoke could escape through smaller chimneys around the edge of the roof pyramid, while hot cooking fumes were funneled out through the huge hollow space of the pyramid itself. Some of the structural elements are borrowed from church architecture; for example, the columns with leafy capitals placed in front of the walls. The window slits cut through in this century are misleading and lend the appearance of a wreath of chapels to the apselike fireplaces.

In the twelfth century, the nuns prepared meals here—chiefly meat and fish—for at least 500 people. Meats were readied for roasting on great tables beneath the central pyramids, while fires crackled in the fireplace niches.

THE PARISH CHURCH OF *ST-MICHEL* STANDS ONLY a short distance outside the abbey precinct. It was built by the abbess Audeburge in around 1170 to serve those merchants, craftsmen, masons, and artists who had settled outside the convent walls and lived by its patronage. The church has a single aisle, a choir with splendid Angevin vaulting, and a wealth of ornamental sculpture. Its western bay dates from the fifteenth century, and an eighteenth-century arcade surrounds its plain exterior.

The interior houses a number of priceless furnishings that were rescued from the abbey church, most notably some of its altars. Among them is part of the high altar, with a richly carved and gilded tabernacle commissioned in 1621 by the abbess Lou-

The Tour d'Evrault, once the abbey's Romanesque kitchen.

ise de Bourbon. A side chapel preserves a number of paintings. The most important of them is a Crucifixion by Etienne Dumonstier, who served as chamberlain at the court of Henri II and Catherine de Médicis. Various figures arranged beneath the Cross were given the features of members of the royal family. The praying Mary Magdalene in the center is Catherine de Médicis, while the Mary wearing a cloak adorned with lilies is Elisabeth of Austria, the wife of Charles IX. Next to her, wearing a crown, is Mary Stuart, accompanied by her husband François II. The cavalryman thrusting his lance into Christ's side is Henri II; this may be an allusion to Henri's own death, for he was mortally wounded by a lance during a tournament in 1559.

An *allée* of lime trees leads away from the main entrance to this church, and to the right of it stands the convent's cemetery chapel of *Ste-Catherine*, built at the beginning of the thirteenth century. Nuns began to be buried within the precinct of the convent after the reforms instituted in the fifteenth and sixteenth centuries. The chapel is perfectly square and rises above a vaulted charnel house. The upper space has vaulting that begins as an octagon but then rises to form a funeral lantern—now a restoration—towering above the roof like one of the kitchen chimneys.

*M*ONTSOREAU

THE CHÂTEAU DE MONTSOREAU IS INTERESTING for its strategic location; it was built to control Loire shipping as well as traffic along the road between Chinon and Saumur. After the Revolution, it was divided among several owners, and the interior was badly cut up. The entire complex fell to ruin in the nineteenth century. It finally was acquired by the state and carefully restored. Alexandre Dumas's novel *La Dame de Montsoreau* had a great deal to do with keeping the name of this château alive despite its derelict condition.

The lords of Montsoreau can be traced back to the eleventh century. On the site of an earlier structure, the present castle was built around the mid-fifteenth century by Jean de Chambes. Confidant of and diplomat to Charles VII, he had been richly rewarded for his service to the king. Since 1820, highway N147 has run between the riverbank and the castle's base. Originally, the waters of the Loire washed up against its foundations, and a moat connected to the river surrounded the complex.

The castle consists of a two-story main wing above a high foundation and flanked by pavilion towers. From the outside, it appears to have been designed completely for defense purposes, even though a fortified castle in the medieval sense was scarcely required in the mid-fifteenth century. From the treatment of its roof area, it is clear that its builder was interested in giving an impression of power and wealth. Two-story dormers embellished with Gothic ornamentation rise from the wallwalk, belying the fortresslike character of the lower part of the structure. The pavilion towers were once topped with tall, concave pointed roofs rising well above the roof of the main wing; they disappeared

View of Montsoreau (Gaignières, 1699).

in the nineteenth century. Short side wings extend from the pavilions on either side of the courtyard. At their corners are polygonal stair towers. The east wing connects with a semicircular tower also lacking its roof and possibly incorporated from an older structure. The stair tower in the east wing, built around 1520, has a richly decorated door and window bay in the Renaissance style, complete with arabesques, medallions, and *putti*. A relief above the third window continues to puzzle architectural historians. In it, monkeys are seen raising a stone block with the help of a chain, and above them an inscription reads IE. LE. FERAY (I will do it).

Some of the rooms still have their original beamed ceilings and fireplaces. Since 1957, the château has served as the Musée des Goums, a memorial to the conquest of Morocco and to the Moroccan cavalry units, the Goums.

From the wall-walk there is a superb view of the river as far west as the silhouette of Saumur. From this height, it is easy to see how the castle was linked to the village, which is now known especially for its white wines.

MONTREUIL-BELLAY

HIGH ABOVE THE VALLEY OF THE THOUET RISES the Château de Montreuil-Bellay, a picturesque complex of buildings inside a massive girdle of walls. The irregular ring wall, with its projecting round towers, dates to the thirteenth century, when the castle belonged to the counts of Melun. The wall encloses four structures: the Château Vieux (or Châtelet), the Château Neuf, the Petit Château, and the kitchen.

The *Château Vieux* was built in the thirteenth century and remodeled in the fourteenth century. It is actually only a heavily fortified entrance structure attached to the ring wall and providing access to the inner precinct of the castle from the town. Its narrow portal, originally secured by a drawbridge, is flanked by massive round towers.

The d'Harcourt family acquired the castle in 1415. Toward the end of the fifteenth century, it was given its present appearance by Guillaume d'Harcourt, who built the *Château Neuf* (ca. 1485–1505), a tall and slender structure looming above the valley. Smooth round towers at its corners underscore the defensive nature of the building on the land side, while the polygonal stair tower on the courtyard side attests to the owner's desire for the new grandeur of the Renaissance.

Several of the château's rooms still have their original fireplaces and beamed ceilings. The only one of particular interest, however, is the two-bay, elegantly vaulted chapel decorated with some heavily damaged fifteenth-century frescoes: a Last Supper, a Crucifixion, various saints, and, in the panels of the vaulting, hovering angels holding musical instruments.

Next to this chapel is the *Petit Château*, which was doubtless built at around the same time as the Château Neuf. It comprises two tiny wings at an angle to each other and with a highly unusual layout of rooms. Four completely separate apart-

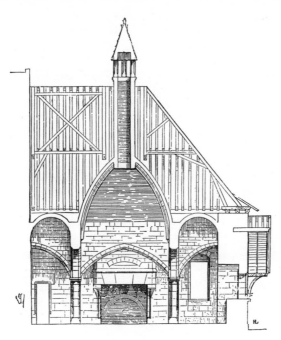

Side view of the Montreuil-Bellay kitchen (after Viollet-le-Duc, 1875).

ments are contained in it, each with its own round stair tower. These presumably were occupied by the four canons of the collegiate church, who also served as keepers of the d'Harcourt archives. Local tradition has it that they spent more time roistering than writing and keeping the files in order.

Another structure dating from the late fifteenth century is the *kitchen*. This square building was placed against the ring wall next to the Petit Château. It is often pointed out that it may have been patterned after the convent kitchen at Fontevrault, and, indeed, they are similar in their placement at a distance from the buildings they served. Their layout is also somewhat the same; but formally, the one at Montreuil-Bellay cannot compare with its more illustrious cousin. Each of the side walls accommodates a fireplace, and a massive pyramid topped by a tall chimney and supported by four round pillars rises above the center of the kitchen. The tall roof was intended to funnel out the smoke and cooking fumes. The large window to the front was used, according to Viollet-le-Duc, for bringing in stores.

The present parish church of *Notre-Dame*, inside the ring wall, is the former collegiate church built between 1472 and 1484 by Yolande de Laval, Guillaume d'Harcourt's wife. It consists of a single aisle and a polygonal choir, and its not too lavish ornamentation adheres completely to the Flamboyant style. A small oratory to the left was reserved for the castle's owners.

WELL WORTH A SIDE TRIP IS LE PUY-NOTRE-DAME, some 5 miles southwest of Montreuil-Bellay, with its twelfth- and thirteenth-century church that dominates the landscape for a considerable distance. It houses a girdle that belonged to the Virgin Mary that was thought to alleviate the pains of childbirth, and thus it became a much frequented pilgrimage church. When Anne of Austria, Louis XIII's wife, was expecting a child, she had the girdle placed around her waist in hopes of a successful delivery. In time, she gave birth to the future Louis XIV.

The stately hall church, with nave and side aisles, is fascinating to architectural historians because it blends typical building forms from Anjou and Poitou. Its entrance façade, for example, which is somewhat forbidding and flanked by corner towers, was patterned after that of the cathedral at Poitiers; the forms of its pillars and vaults were borrowed from the same church. The square choir with its diverse vaulting, however, corresponds to Angevin building customs, as does the rich figural sculpture in the vault area (compare St-Serge in Angers). The fourteenth-century bell tower, on the south side of the nave, contains an unusual stepped and pointed-arch niche, adorned with .little columns and corresponding curved molding on its archivolts. It serves as the ornate setting for a sixteenth-century statue of the Madonna and Child.

SAUMUR

THE SKYLINE OF SAUMUR, ONE OF THE LOVELIEST along the entire length of the Loire, is dominated by three structures: close to the river is the two-part Hôtel de Ville; to the left and somewhat farther back, the powerful crossing tower of the church of St-Pierre; and atop a rocky hill, the fortress-like castle, which has always served as the focus of the town's history.

As a possession of the counts of Anjou and kings of England, Saumur was incorporated into French Crown lands at the beginning of the thirteenth century. Even in the Middle Ages, the town profited greatly from winegrowing and the export of wines.

In the sixteenth century, Saumur was a stronghold of the Reformation. Henri IV installed as governor of the town Philippe Duplessis-Mornay, who was referred to by his contemporaries as "the Huguenot pope." He was a soldier and scholar, and he established a Protestant college attended by students from all over Europe. He fortified the town and raised it to economic prosperity.

Its decline began under Louis XIV with the revocation in 1685 of the Edict of Nantes, which had granted full religious freedom to Protestants. A large number of its inhabitants left the town. Although the establishment of a cavalry school in the late eighteenth century and continuing trade in wine prevented total economic ruin, the revocation of the Edict of Nantes, and its aftereffects, can still be felt. Today, Saumur has 7,000 fewer inhabitants than it did in its heyday in the seventeenth century.

The *castle* is famous for an unusual reason. It was depicted in great detail by the Limbourg brothers as background architecture for the illustration of September in *Les Très Riches Heures du duc de Berry* (ca.

Saumur

1410). As the Limbourgs depicted it, the castle was the creation of Louis I, duc d'Anjou, who had inherited the domain from his father, Jean le Bon, in 1356. Louis was determined to create a residence for himself that would rival in luxuriousness those of his brothers Charles V and Jean, duc de Berry. Using the strong foundations of an earlier castle complex, he built four wings fortified by corner towers around an inner courtyard. Although the existing towers were round, the new ones were polygonal with projecting vertical strips of wall at their corners. The castle was designed totally for defense; but even from without, there was ample indication of the brilliant household maintained within. The roof area above the wall-walks was lavishly decorated with dormers, chimneys, crocketed gables, countless lilies from the duke's coat of arms, and gilded weather vanes. The latter were found to be all too dazzling when the sun was shining—or such, at least, was the objection of one of Louis's successors, René le Bon. The overall appearance was bewildering, and the Limbourg brothers managed to capture it in awesome detail.

To stand at the spot where the miniature was sketched is fascinating. The rich roof embellishment is now gone, but even so, enough details remain as they were almost 600 years ago, when the Limbourgs depicted the castle. The gatehouse has disappeared, as has the kitchen, with its chimneys and its central pyramid like those of Fontevrault. The slope on which the delightful grape harvest appears in the miniature—a portion added to the painting at the end of the fifteenth century by Jean Colombe—is still cultivated. Now, as then, the grapes are picked from carefully pruned vines.

The area immediately next to the castle has been radically changed. When Duplessis-Mornay lived here, he had the Italian architect Bartolomeo build massive fortification walls and bastions around it. After the governor's death in 1621, the castle began to fall into disrepair. The northwest wing collapsed and was never rebuilt. In 1810, Napoleon ordered it turned into a state prison, and, indeed, it had already served as a jail through much of the seventeenth and eighteenth centuries. Between 1830 and 1890, it served as an armory and barracks. The state acquired it in 1906 and restored it for use as a museum.

One enters the courtyard through a turreted gatehouse, which was originally secured by a drawbridge, as seen in the *Très Riches Heures*. The courtyard façade of the northeast wing rests on flat-arch arcades. A

Floor plan of the Saumur chateau.

polygonal tower on the north side contains the Escalier d'Honneur; this opens to the courtyard on each floor in the form of a loggia adorned with tracery.

A small modern structure in the courtyard was built over a shaft almost 200 feet deep, which once lay beneath the lost northwest wing. It may have been a well, but some maintain that it was a supply shaft connected by means of an underground passage to a wall tower next to the Loire. Foodstuffs and munitions could thus be brought in directly from the river and hauled up into the castle with a winch.

In the southeast wing one can descend into the dungeons. A large vaulted space beneath the courtyard apparently served as a cistern. It is also possible to climb the western corner tower, which commands a magnificent view of the town and the river.

Two remarkable museums are housed in the castle's rooms, both of which may be visited only with a guide. The *Musée des Arts Décoratifs* is an important collection of works from the medieval and Renaissance periods. An exquisite group of Limoges enamels is exhibited, as are fine examples of French faïence. Sculptures in various media, paintings, furniture, and ecclesiastical ornaments survey the arts of the thirteenth to sixteenth centuries. From the seventeenth and eighteenth centuries are examples of French porcelain, furniture, and tapestries. One of the château's treasures is a series of tapestries from the fifteenth and sixteenth centuries representing the History of Titus, the Roman emperor. For equestrians, the *Musée du Cheval* is a visual feast. It offers a thorough survey of the natural and cultural history of the horse: skeletons ranging from fossils of prehistoric horses to that of the English Derby champion Flying Fox; Arab, Japanese, American Western, and women's saddles (including one invented by Catherine de Médicis); bits and stirrups from ancient Greece to the present; and English equestrian prints, including one by George Stubbs. Saumur is the traditional center of French equestrianism. The cavalry school founded in 1768 is still in operation, and is especially famous for its Cadre Noire, a riding team that makes its major appearance each July during the Grand Carrousel de Saumur.

The dominant structure in the old town at the foot of the castle is *St-Pierre*, an early-thirteenth-century single-aisle church with transept, powerful crossing tower, and choir from the late twelfth century. The side chapels along the nave date from the fifteenth and sixteenth centuries. Its entrance front was destroyed by fire in 1674, but was rebuilt in the style of the original. Among its appointments are precious sixteenth-century wall tapestries depicting the lives of St. Peter and St. Florent, and fifteenth-century carved choir stalls.

The area around the church contains a number of fifteenth- and sixteenth-century houses, many of which are currently being restored. It served as the setting for Balzac's novel *Eugénie Grandet*.

The abbey church of *Notre-Dame-de-Nantilly* contains a revered twelfth-century wooden sculpture of the Madonna and

The abbey church of Notre-Dame-de-Nantilly.

Child, which is held to work miracles. The original single-aisle structure dates from the first half of the twelfth century; its transept was renovated in the fourteenth. Louis XI, a devoted worshiper of the Madonna, expanded the church between 1470 and 1483 by the addition of a south aisle in the Flamboyant style. The king's lavishly ornamented oratory now serves as a baptismal chapel. Notre-Dame-de-Nantilly owns a great store of tapestries. Rare works from the fifteenth and sixteenth centuries and fine Aubusson tapestries from the seventeenth century decorate the church. Some pieces from the collection are on loan to the Musée des Arts Décoratifs, at the castle.

Another church consecrated to Mary is *Notre-Dame-des-Ardilliers*, a little more than half a mile upstream from the Loire bridge on the Quai Mayaud. It takes its name from a miraculous Pietà discovered by a peasant in a clay field in 1454. It was first set up in a wayside shrine; in 1553, a special chapel was built to house it, and it became a major pilgrimage site. In the seventeenth century, the chapel was entrusted to the Oratorians, for whom the still existing convent buildings were built between 1628 and 1643. The church, a cen-

trally symmetrical structure with cupola—destroyed during the Second World War but since restored—and a long nave, was begun in 1655, but the dome was completed only in 1693, thanks to a generous donation from Louis XIV. The nave, flanked by two chapels, was built in 1673 to take the place of the 1553 chapel. At the same time, the monumental altar retable was created by the sculptors Biardeau and Antoine Charpentier. A central Crucifixion group was added to it in 1856 by the artistic canon Choyer. He also created the altar retable for the Chapelle Richelieu, which was renovated in 1855. The miraculous sculpture, a work presumably dating from the fifteenth century, may be seen here.

The most notable secular building in Saumur is the square, fortresslike *Hôtel de Ville*, with wall-walks, corner turrets, and a tall roof pyramid topped by a lantern. Built in the early sixteenth century, it was originally part of the town wall, which ran directly along the bank of the Loire. The architect Joly-Leterme expanded it in the nineteenth century by adding a new wing in the Renaissance style that provides a lively contrast with the older section of the building.

CUNAULT

THE CHURCH OF *NOTRE-DAME* AT CUNAULT, SET in one of the loveliest riverbank landscapes of the Loire, is one of the most impressive Romanesque churches along the whole length of the river. Its exterior is not particularly striking, and even at first glance, it is evident that it is the product of various building phases. The church's power and grandeur is experienced only inside.

The church was built by Benedictine monks from the abbey of St-Philibert in Tournus, who owned a richly endowed priory in Cunault. One of the reasons it was laid out on such a magnificent scale was that its relics attracted hordes of pilgrims. It boasted the remains of St. Maxenceul, who presumably introduced Christianity to Cunault and is thought to have been a

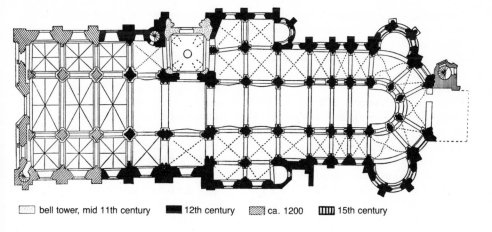

Floor plan of Notre-Dame at Cunault.

pupil of St. Martin of Tours. (The ruins of the parish church consecrated to Maxenceul, which collapsed during a hurricane in 1754, may still be seen in the middle of the village cemetery.) Two additional relics were doubtless even more attractive to pilgrims: a vial of dust from the stable in Bethlehem where Christ was born, proclaimed to be dried mother's milk of the Virgin Mary; and a ring purported to be the one given her at her marriage to Joseph.

The priory was dissolved in 1741 by the bishop of Angers, and its holdings were transferred to the Seminaire St-Charles in that city. A new wall was built, dividing the church in two: its nave served in the stead of the ruined parish church, while its choir was sold to a local farmer who used it as a barn. Badly deteriorated, the church became the property of the state in 1842, and was soon thoroughly restored. For reasons of economy, the roofs were simplified at that time much to the detriment of the church's external appearance.

The oldest part of the structure is the mid-eleventh-century tower, an important example of church architecture in Anjou at the beginning of the Romanesque. As a survivor from an earlier building of which nothing more is known, it was incorporated into the north side of the new nave. The diversity of the round-arch arcades on the upper part of the tower and the wealth of architectural sculpture, rarely matched in the Loire, distinguish it from the building's newer sections. A monumental blind arcade lower down contains two remarkable capitals: the one to the left depicts the Annunciation, with Mary seated on an X-shaped chair and the archangel Gabriel standing in front of her; the right-hand one shows two men, one standing in a boat and reaching for a fish held out by a mermaid or siren, a symbol of worldly temptation.

Work on the church started in the beginning of the twelfth century. It is a hall with nave, side aisles, and pseudotransept whose short arms are graced by chapels to the east. The extended ambulatory choir has a semicircular back wall—a form typical of pilgrimage churches—and two apsidal choir chapels. A third chapel, once on the central axis, has disappeared. The north choir chapel is embellished with sculptures similar in richness to those of the tower.

Towering clustered columns support the relatively short vaulting bays and dominate the spatial perspective with their clean, three-dimensional lines.

Building clearly proceeded from east to west. One notes that the bays become progressively wider in this direction. The eight eastern ones, counting from the triumphal arch, have barrel vaults over the nave, while the ambulatory, side aisles, and arms of the pseudotransept have groin vaults. Only the tower bay is topped by a cupola. The three western bays, erected in the Plantagenet style with eight-part ribbed

vaults, belong to the period around 1200. With the exception of these latter sections, the architecture is strongly influenced by the style of Poitou.

The church's treasures are its exquisitely carved capitals, well over 200 of them. Some, however, especially in the choir, are nineteenth-century re-creations.

On the tympanum above the main portal of the west façade is a seated Virgin with the Christ Child on her lap. Angels, supported by thin bands of cloud on either side of her throne, swing censers in honor of the Queen of Heaven. Additional smaller angels, now completely missing or badly damaged (as is the Madonna), flanked the base of her throne. Traces of pigment still adhere to the sculpture, which was created along with the western portions of the church (ca. 1200).

BRISSAC-QUINCE

DESPITE THE BEAUTY OF ITS DETAILS, THE CHÂteau de Brissac does not enchant at first glance. Its unusually tall proportions are not what one expects of a Loire château, and the seemingly accidental conglomeration of its separate elements is bewildering. What we see, as the twelfth duc de Brissac, Pierre de Cossé, so aptly put it, is "a half-completed new château in a half-destroyed old one."[17]

The main façade is flanked by two massive round towers from the fifteenth century, with set-back top stories like those at Langeais, Ussé, and Le Plessis-Bourré. The towers were part of a castle built by Pierre de Brézé, a minister to Charles VII and Louis XI. Brézé was killed in 1465 at the

Battle of Montlhéry. His son Jacques married a daughter of Charles VII and Agnès Sorel, only to discover her one day in an all too intimate relationship with one of his friends. He promptly killed them both. This event spawned a number of unpleasantnesses for the Brézé family, and may have led to their decision to sell Brissac in 1502 to the chamberlain of Charles VIII, René de Cossé. It belongs to his descendants to this day.

The old Brézé castle had suffered a great deal during the Religious Wars, so in 1606, Charles II de Cossé, marshal of France and first duc de Brissac, decided to build a new one; he entrusted its design to the architect Jacques d'Angluze. Only half of the ambi-

The château de Brissac.

tious new project was completed, however, for the owner died in 1621. His son and heir had no interest in continuing his father's work.

First to be constructed was the slender, five-story entrance pavilion, which was to form the center of the main wing. As such, it was built into the north round tower, in which the family lived during the construction. Later, of course, this tower would have been torn down to make room for the planned north wing. Only the south wing was actually built, it too pressing against one of the earlier towers that was doubtless scheduled for demolition.

All of the building's ornamental sculpture is concentrated on the three-bay entrance pavilion, behind which a staircase

tower is concealed. Before the Revolution this section seemed even narrower, for it was crowned by a bell tower with a statue of Mercury on its tip. The floors are adorned with pilasters of the five classical orders—Tuscan, Doric, Ionic, Corinthian, and Composite—the orders rising with the ascending floors. The large, round-arch openings of the central bay are flanked by smaller arched niches or windows. Squared stones cut across the pilasters and surround the window and door openings, providing additional vitality to the façade. Two additional wings in the same style and also dating to this period of construction enclose, with the main wing, a narrow inner courtyard.

The long north wing, ending in another

215

skyscraper of a five-story pavilion, was added after 1621 by Louis de Cossé, the son of Charles II. This completely destroyed the architectural balance of the structure.

The château is still inhabited by the de Cossé family and is furnished with numerous treasures. A tour starting in the vestibule leads first through the eighteenth-century Grand Salon, with a richly carved and gilded beamed ceiling. In the Petit Salon is a lovely painting by Michel Garnier from 1785; it depicts the seventh duc de Brissac, Jean-Paul-Timoléon de Cossé, surrounded by his family. The dining room opens off to the north, and boasts a musicians' balcony and a tapestry cycle with scenes from the history of Alexander the Great and the rape of Helen of Troy.

On the second floor is the Grande Galerie, containing portraits of the ducal family. Two paintings are particularly notable. One, by Fabien Gautier d'Agoty from the second half of the eighteenth century, is a military portrait of Jean-Paul-Timoléon de Cossé as marshal of France. The other is an amusing full-figure portrait of the matronly Widow Clicquot, the shrewd and industrious champagne queen immortalized in Wilhelm Busch's *The Pious Helene* ("The Widow Clicquot's bubbles pass / so charmingly up through the glass"). Reclining at Madame Clicquot's feet is her granddaughter and last descendant, Anne de Mortemart, the later duchesse d'Uzès and grandmother of the twelfth duc de Brissac. She died at the age of eighty-six while galloping on horseback after a deer during a hunt. The painting was done by Léon Cogniet in 1859.

The last rooms included in the tour are the chapel in the south tower; the Salle de la Chasse, containing Flemish carpets illustrating the varieties of the sixteenth-century hunt; the Salle de Mortemart, with large-figure tapestries and priceless furnishings; the museumlike Salle des Gardes; and the Salle de Judith, in which Louis XIII reconciled with his mother, Marie de Médicis.

SERRANT

THE OVERALL APPEARANCE OF THE CHÂTEAU DE Serrant is that of a princely residence. The château stands in a large park, and its three wings form a formal entry courtyard whose outer side is accented by corner pavilions and an imposing portal. The complex is surrounded by a moat, in which the back of the building is beautifully reflected. Its thick round towers topped by cupolas are reminiscent of those at Valençay.

A castle belonging to the de Brie family stood on this site in the Middle Ages; in the mid-sixteenth century, Charles de Brie began replacing the old structure with the present one. By the time he died in 1593, the costs of construction had completely ruined him. Yet all that was finished was the left half of the main wing (as seen from the courtyard), with its large corner tower, and a central section containing a staircase. The property was first sold in 1596 to Hercule de Rohan, duc de Montbazon, and in 1636, it was acquired by the diplomat and aesthete Guillaume Bautru. Bautru completed the main wing. His son Guillaume added the side wings, accented the outer corners of the courtyard with two-story pavilions where towers had stood in the medieval layout, and erected the heavy entrance portal.

The outer façades of both the main building and the pavilions are enlivened by contrasting building materials: a brown quarry stone predominates, while the openings are framed by carefully cut lighter stone. The lighter stone is used exclusively on the courtyard sides. The placement of pilasters along these façades is a borrowing from architecture of the time of François I, but, especially on the long central wing, it seems strikingly ineffectual. The gateway leading into the courtyard was played up deliberately to conceal from visitors approaching along the central axis the shortcomings of the main façade. A balustrade running along the attic story and circling the towers was added in the nineteenth century.

The chapel dates from the early eighteenth century, and is attributed by some scholars to Jules Hardouin-Mansart. Its most distinguishing feature is the marble tomb of Nicolas Bautru, marquis de Vaubrun, nephew of the château's builder. Vaubrun was wounded in the Battle of Altenheim in 1675, and died soon afterward. His widow commissioned this work in 1677 from Antoine Coysevox, the most illustrious sculptor at the court of Louis XIV, but it was not completed until 1705. In front of a dramatic wall of black marble framed by Corinthian columns, the marquis reclines on his sarcophagus like a victorious general; his wife kneels beside him in mourning. The widow's grief was thought excessive even by her contemporaries. Madame de Sévigné relates that she seemed half crazed as she had her husband's body brought home to Serrant and interred in a ceremony that was even more lavish than that staged for Henri de la Tour d'Auvergne, vicomte de Turenne, Louis

XIV's most decorated general. She goes on to say that the widow kept her husband's heart on a little credenza with lighted candles on either side of it, spending all the time between lunch and supper on her knees before it.[18] A gilded lead relief on the base of the monument depicts the Battle of Altenheim. This relief and the figures on top of the sarcophagus were executed by Coysevox. The Victory holding a hero's wreath over the dying marquis's head is the work of Gaspard Collignon.

The most striking of the château's interior features is its main staircase. It was designed in the Renaissance fashion with parallel flights of stairs separated by partitions and adorned with exquisitely coffered vaults and ceilings.

The château was acquired in 1749 by the Irish shipping magnate Anthony Walsh, who soon contrived to be given the title comte de Serrant. His son and daughter-in-law were taken into Napoleon's court, Madame de Serrant as lady-in-waiting to Empress Josephine. The estate later passed by marriage to the de la Trémoille family, and is now the property of Prince de Ligne La Trémoille.

Visitors are shown a number of rooms furnished in the nineteenth century, including a dining room papered with lovely landscapes and a 20,000-volume library. A painting above the library fireplace shows Anthony Walsh providing ships to the English heir apparent from the House of Stuart, Charles Edward (Bonnie Prince Charlie); attached to the frame are the carved arms of England that adorned one·of the frigates that carried the prince to Scotland in 1745. One of several bedrooms in the Empire style was specially decorated for a visit by Napoleon in 1808. It contains a splendid bust of Empress Marie-Louise by Antonio Canova.

*L*E PLESSIS-BOURRE

THE CHÂTEAU DU PLESSIS-BOURRÉ IS A PERFECT example of a feudal residence from the late Middle Ages that was eminently defensible but capable of offering a gracious style of living. It consists of four wings with round corner towers—the strongest designed as a keep—and is surrounded by a large square moat.

It was built by Jean Bourré, privy councilor and treasurer to Louis XI. Bourré acquired the domain of Plessis-le-Vent in 1462, and henceforth added his name to it. He went on to serve as secretary of finance under Charles VIII and Louis XII. He died in 1506.

The courtier was an experienced builder. It was he who oversaw the building of Langeais for Louis XI. He began the creation of his own residence in 1468, while work at Langeais was still in progress. Thanks to his considerable wealth, he was able to rush its construction, and it was ready for him to move into by 1473. Because of the relatively rapid building, the entire complex seems to be of a piece. Bourré may have been in haste, but he insisted on only the best materials. The stone, for example, came from the Boullay quarries near Saumur. It cost him a fortune, but it was a wise investment, for it still looks as fresh as when it was first cut 500 years ago. The corner keep has the same covered wall-walk and stepped-back top floor as do the towers at Langeais.

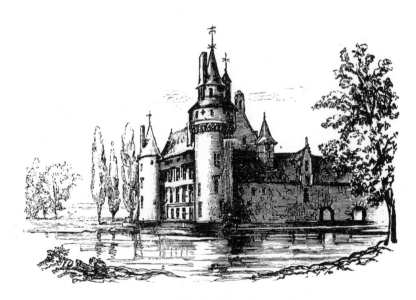

Plessis-Bourré.

A fire in 1974 destroyed some of the outbuildings, which date from the Baroque period. They were grouped around a courtyard from which a stone bridge leads across the moat to the château. A portal structure bristles with machicolation and was secured by a drawbridge. The residential wing is across from the entrance, accented by its greater height of three stories, its dormers, and its corner stair towers. The other wings around the central courtyard, except for the gatehouse and an adjacent chapel, were built lower to allow a maximum amount of light into the main wing. The design of the whole complex was no longer dictated by medieval fortress requirements, yet there were still provisions for defense. A terrace extending along the base of the wings and towers provided positions for cannon in the event that attackers threatened to cross the moat.

A number of furnished rooms are shown to visitors. The most impressive is the Grand Salon, which has delicately carved paneling. The Salle des Etats, dominated by a massive fireplace, preserves some lovely ribbed vaulting and its original floor tiles.

The most important room in the château is the Salle des Gardes on the second floor, with its painted wood ceiling unlike any other in France. The ceiling's twenty-four panels, twelve on either side of the central beam, are embellished with emblematic paintings intended as puzzles for the diversion of guests. Eight of them have figures and moralizing verses, while the remaining sixteen present mainly animals with specific symbolic meanings. The ceiling has been interpreted as an indication of Bourré's fascination with alchemy.

MONTGEOFFROY

RARELY DOES ONE ENTER A LOIRE CHÂTEAU WITHout the feeling that one is in a museum where each table and chair and work of art has been carefully placed in an attempt to approximate the original atmosphere.

The Château de Montgeoffroy is a considerable exception in this regard. The bulk of the furnishings are those collected by the château's builder, and most of them still stand exactly where he intended. In no other château in France can one form as complete a picture of a landed aristocrat of taste on the eve of the Revolution.

The man who built Montgeoffroy was a field marshal and governor of Alsace, Louis-Georges-Erasme de Contades, whose ancestors had acquired this medieval estate in the seventeenth century. Contades began construction of the present château in 1773, after plans by the Paris architect Nicolas Barré. Portions of earlier buildings were incorporated in the new design.

The château stands at the bottom of a gentle slope in the midst of its great acreage, to which it is linked by radiating lanes. Two flat-roofed pavilions and an imposing wrought-iron gateway, joined to the main building by low walls, set off the château precinct from the surrounding fields.

The two-and-a-half-story main wing is majestic in its simple, balanced proportions. Its central bay is topped by a triangular pediment containing the sole sculptural ornament of the entire structure: the Contades coat of arms flanked by trophies. Two shorter side wings project from the main wing, and low pavilions next to the back corners tie the main wing to the stables, carriage houses, and the chapel to the side of the courtyard. The chapel and the two round towers at the end of the farm buildings were incorporated from the preceding, sixteenth-century château. A small pavilion centered behind the main building serves as a charming *point de vue*.

The complex was completed with astonishing speed. It seems to have been completely furnished by 1775, for in that year, an inventory was made of its entire contents—even the kitchen utensils! It is possible to carry this inventory with you as you tour the château, and to discover most of the items right where they were 200 years ago.

It appears that the marshal purchased all the movable furnishings *en bloc* in Paris. They complement the wall paneling and the architecture to perfection. Thanks to his military past and his good connections, the aging marshal survived the first years of the Revolution. When he died, in 1793, the inhabitants of the nearby village of Maze saw to it that nothing was removed from the château.

Although the mansion is still occupied by the Contades family, a number of its ground-floor rooms are open to the public. A billiard room and small sitting room lead to the Grand Salon, with its elegantly restrained and strictly geometric paneling. The fireplace, andirons, wall sconces, gilded bronze chandeliers, chairs and sofas, console tables, table clock, and barometer on the wall—all may be found in the inventory from 1775.

The marshal set aside the suite of ground-floor rooms facing the park as an apartment for a Madame Herault. A carmine Venetian brocade was chosen as the wallcovering in the main room, with matching bed curtains, coverlet, upholstery, and draperies around the bed niche. The original fabric has been preserved, and its effect against the several shades of gray in the woodwork is most striking. The inventory gives us some idea of how comfortably Madame could rest in her sleeping niche: "A bed with a horsehair mattress, two fustian bolsters, a featherbed, two pillows—one of them of horsehair—and two woolen blankets."[19] The adjacent sitting room still has its original chintz wallcovering.

The last room shown is the dining room. Like all the other rooms, it contains nothing particularly showy; it simply reveals the marshal's refined sense of clarity and form. One object that contrasts with the sober paneling is a porcelain stove with a stylized palm tree rising above it, a gift to the governor from the city of Strasbourg. A graceful wrought-iron railing surrounds the body of the stove, further enhancing its decorative effect. In this room as well, the chairs and the chandelier survive from the original inventory.

Montgeoffroy also retains a magnificent collection of eighteenth-century paintings. Portraits and other works by Hyacinthe Rigaud, François-Hubert Drouais, Pourbus the Younger, Carle Van Loo, François Desportes, and others testify to the refined, sophisticated taste of the marshal.

The chapel was built in 1543 by Guillaume de La Grandière and Marie de Soucelles. An original stained-glass window survives; it depicts God the Father, the Nativity, and the chapel's two builders.

The stable buildings across the courtyard from the chapel house a collection of coaches and carriages, and in the round tower is an ornately stuccoed saddle room.

ANGERS

ANGERS, THE CAPITAL OF THE HISTORIC PROVINCE of Anjou and the modern *département* of Maine-et-Loire, is a charming, modest-size city surrounded by lovely parks and boulevards. In terms of art, it is one of the richest towns in France. The areas around the castle and the cathedral of St-Maurice preserve much of their historic character, but apart from these two centers, the bulk of the town's architecture is made up of nine-teenth- and twentieth-century commercial buildings only occasionally interspersed with older structures. The outer boulevards were built along the course of the old fortification walls in the nineteenth century.

The town's history is basically that of its fortress, which has often been compared with a Crusader's castle. The steep promontory above the valley of the Maine was

Fortress at Angers.

221

the site of a fortress even in Roman times, when the city was called Juliomagnus. The counts of Anjou recognized the strategic advantages of the location and chose to build their residences here. The present fortifications were erected by command of Louis IX in 1230, after Anjou had been absorbed by the French Crown following King John's forced surrender of his Angevin lands in 1204. Construction of the massive, five-sided fortress took a full ten years; in 1246, the king conveyed it along with the countship to his brother Charles.

The complex comprises seventeen round towers connected by a curtain wall on four sides, while on the fifth, facing the river, the natural cliffs provided adequate protection. A deep dry moat on two sides of the wall now serves as a landscaped run for a herd of fallow deer. At one time, there were two entrances into the castle precinct, but now there is only the Porte de Ville. The towers originally rose well above the wall and boasted conical roofs, but in 1585, during the Religious Wars, Henri III ordered the demolition of the entire fortress, fearing that the Protestants might gain control of it and take refuge inside. Dismantling the complex proved too difficult, and ultimately only the height of the towers was reduced—with one exception. The resulting platforms proved to be useful as positions for cannon, which were only then coming into use. From the seventeenth century, the fortress served mainly as a prison.

Only the northwest corner tower was left at its original height, since it served as the base for a windmill in the sixteenth century. Visitors are now permitted to climb it, and from the top a spectacular view of the town, the Maine, and the castle mount can be obtained.

The *Chapelle Ste-Geneviève*, once at-tached to the *Logis du Roi*, is one of the few structures still standing inside the fortress. Both were built in the early fifteenth century by Louis II, duc d'Anjou. His son, who is still revered in Anjou as René le Bon, erected the *Petit Château* next to this chapel, ornamenting it with round towers and surrounding it with elegant gardens and enclosures for animals. The *Logis du Gouverneur*, in the southeast corner of the ring wall, dates from the eighteenth century, although much of its fabric is considerably older. The landscaped gardens were designed after the Second World War by Bernard Vitry, who based them on sixteenth-century models. The tour of the walls leads to a special little garden containing rare plants already familiar to the dukes of Anjou and depicted in fifteenth-century tapestries. Next to the garden is a vineyard laid out in the old manner: the vines are secured to slate instead of wooden posts in order to take advantage of the warmth stored in the stone.

The *Musée des Tapisseries*, situated in the castle, is dispersed among three buildings. In the Logis du Roi and the Chapelle Ste-Geneviève are displayed stories from the Life of St. Martin (1460) and the Passion Tapestries (late fifteenth century). The four Passion scenes are notable for their rich colors and as exquisite examples of the *millefleurs* tradition in tapestry design. The Logis du Gouverneur houses tapestries from the sixteenth and seventeenth centuries, including *millefleurs* designs with birds and animals and La Dame à l'Orgue, from the series La Dame à la Licorne (1513–30). But the most important series is exhibited in a building specially designed for it by Vitry in 1953 to 1954.

The Apocalypse Tapestries are to the history of medieval tapestry weaving what the windows of Chartres Cathedral are to that of medieval stained glass. Of all the tapestries ever woven in France, the fourteenth-century Angers Apocalypse is one of the two oldest cycles in existence. Moreover, it is possibly the largest cycle ever loomed.

It was commissioned by Louis I, duc d'Anjou, the art-loving builder of the castle, at Saumur. He first had designs prepared by Hennequin de Bruges, court painter to his brother Charles V, providing him with patterns in the form of miniatures borrowed from his brother's library. These cartoons, preserved in the Bibliothèque Nationale, were then submitted to Nicolas Bataille, Paris's most famous weaver, for transformation into tapestries. The entire cycle was completed by 1380, after only seven years.

The original Apocalypse cycle consisted of at least eighty-four scenes on seven tapestries—the number seven, according to St. John the Evangelist, symbolizing perfection. Each tapestry was roughly 20 feet high, and five of them were almost 80 feet long. We do not know just where in the castle the duke had them hung; possibly they were only displayed outside on festive occasions. It is recorded that the duke's son, Louis II, decorated the archbishop's palace at Arles with them on the occasion of his marriage in 1400. A native of Arles, Bertrand Boysset, was able to admire them at that time, and wrote enthusiastically: "It would be impossible for anyone to capture, either in writing or in spoken words, the splendor, the beauty, and the elegance of these tapestries."[20] René le Bon ultimately inherited the Apocalypse from his father, and he presented them to the cathedral, where they were hung in the nave and transept on high holy days. Only in the Baroque period did people cease to admire them and fail to recognize their value. The cathedral chapter put them up for sale in 1782, but no one was found to buy them.

During the Revolution the tapestries were cut up for use as blankets, bedside runners, and tarpaulins to protect the orange trees from frost during the winter. In 1843, the bishop of Angers succeeded in retrieving a large number of these fragments from the overseers of the cathedral estates, and an extensive search turned up still others. Nonetheless, roughly one-third of the scenes were lost forever.

The first tapestry is almost complete, and the fourth and fifth are preserved in their original dimensions. What remains of the others are only individual scenes and fragments; in many instances, it is impossible to tell to which part of the cycle they belonged.

At the edge of each tapestry is a figure sitting on a throne and holding a book. A damask curtain rises behind him until it is gathered into a stone baldachin above. On top of this baldachin stand two angels, each holding a flag. One flag is adorned with the lilies of the Angevin coat of arms; the other, with the brown cross with double arms adopted by Louis d'Anjou as his personal emblem. The seated figure surveys a huge space in which the various visions described by St. John are depicted in separate panels. The scenes are arranged in two horizontal rows, each containing seven pictures. Their backgrounds are alternately red and blue, forming a kind of checkerboard pattern. Below each picture, there originally was a short text, doubtless a somewhat abbreviated passage from Revelation; traces of them were still visible in the nineteenth century, but they have since disappeared. Along the top edge of each tapestry was a strip of sky dotted with either stars or clouds, in the center of which were clusters of angels either playing musical instruments or singing in choirs. The position of the jubilant angels high above the terrible scenes of the Apocalypse was a deliberate reminder that the faithful must maintain their courage and faith even under the heaviest of trials. The strip along the bottom edge represented the earth as a meadow strewn with flowers. There probably were also depictions of numerous little animals, but two rabbits are all that survive. Very little of the upper and lower sections are left: the upper suffered the greatest wear each time the tapestries were hung up and taken down; the lower dragged on the floor.

An attempt to make the work even more splendid is evident as the weaving progressed. The earliest scenes have simple monochromatic backgrounds, and this very simplicity makes some of them especially powerful. Those in which Christ holds a sword in his mouth as a symbol of the force of his teachings are among the most successful of the entire cycle. In other scenes, it makes for a certain monotony. To confront this weakness, the background space between the figures was filled with ornament—large flowers, grapevines, and

occasionally butterflies whose wings are patterned with the duke's lily device or the ermine dots of his duchess, Marie de Bretagne.

Even more remarkable than the variety of the backgrounds is the skill with which the artists varied the image of St. John. He is present in each scene, at times participating in the action and at times merely watching or listening to it. In one, he bends forward intently, while in the next, he gazes toward heaven; now he folds his arms, now he holds them outstretched; here he wrings his hands, while there he extends an admonishing finger. He expresses a vast range of responses: resignation, puzzlement, perplexity, terror, dismay, fear, pity, disdain, revulsion, joy, happiness, and finally sheer ecstasy as he beholds the New Jerusalem.

Although it is no longer possible to interpret each scene without a knowledge of the text it was intended to illustrate, our

delight in the tapestries is by no means deterred: a delight at the wealth of forms, the splendor of the garments and the backgrounds, the eloquence of figures and their gestures, and, especially, the seemingly inexhaustible inventiveness that enlivens the entire narrative.

During excavation for the new exhibition hall, workmen uncovered portions of the Chapelle Ste-Geneviève-St-Laud, an oratory used by the counts of Anjou around 1140, and remains of a corner tower from the Roman fortress on the site in the late third century A.D. These architectural fragments were left exposed to view.

THE CATHEDRAL OF ST-MAURICE IS ONLY THE LATest of a succession of churches built on this site. In the fourth century, St. Martin of Tours consecrated one here to St. Maurice and his companions, providing it with a vial of the martyrs' blood.

The aisleless nave of the cathedral,

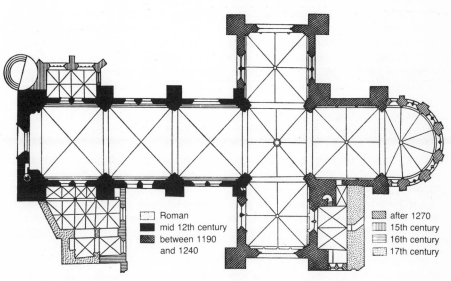

Roman
mid 12th century
between 1190 and 1240
after 1270
15th century
16th century
17th century

Floor plan of St-Maurice.

which numbers only three bays, dates from the mid-twelfth century. Its transept and choir bay were added between 1190 and 1240 by the architect Etienne d'Azé. The choir apse was built after 1270.

The west façade, from the twelfth century, dominates the exterior and serves as a dramatic accent to the city skyline. The approach to the front, the Montée St-Maurice—a flight of steps that descends to the Maine—is most impressive. This is among the most important of Gothic church portals in France. It relates directly to the west portal of the cathedral at Chartres, and presumably dates from 1155 to 1160. Its eight jamb figures are characters from the Old Testament; it is still possible to make out Moses holding the Tablets of the Law, on the far right, and David playing his harp, on the left. These restrained figures have garments with delicate, linear folds, an intricate pattern resulting when one of the women elegantly lifts a corner of her skirt. Angels and four apostles hover above these figures, and in the archivolts are additional angels and representations of the Four Horsemen of the Apocalypse. A Christ in Glory occupies the tympanum along with symbols of the Evangelists. A trumeau column originally divided the doorway in two; but since it stood in the way of ceremonial processions entering the church, it disappeared, along with the lintel and the remaining eight apostles, in the eighteenth century. Some of the portal's details, for example, the head of Christ, were renovated in the nineteenth century.

A gallery containing statues of the military companions of St. Maurice beneath baldachins extends across the façade between the two outer towers. These are copies of the original 1537 figures, and they are attributed to the Angevin sculptors Jean Giffard and Antoine Desmarais.

The central tower above them replaces a wooden bell tower that burned down a short time before 1540, when this stone one was erected.

Huge domelike ribbed vaults resting on deeply projecting piers span the interior of the cathedral. The whole space gives an impression of expansiveness. The windows preserve stained glass from various centuries: those on the left side of the nave date from the twelfth; those in the choir, from the thirteenth; and those in the transept, from the fifteenth. Valuable tapestries from the sixteenth through eighteenth centuries adorn the walls. The treasury, located in the left-hand side chapel off the nave, displays antique fabrics, bishops' croziers, reliquaries, and priceless gold and silver ecclesiastical objects. The chapel across from it, Notre-Dame-de-la-Pitié, was originally a parish church.

Worth exploring outside of the cathedral is the *Maison d'Adam* across from its choir. This is a five-story half-timbered building from the fifteenth century with delightful carvings on the timbers.

Two museums now occupy the elegant Renaissance town houses of former mayors of Angers. The *Hôtel de Pincé* on the Rue Lenepveu was built for Jean de Pincé between 1523 and 1525. It now houses the *Musée Turpin de Crissé*, a collection begun by the local nineteenth-century painter Turpin de Crissé. A fascinating group of painted Greek and Etruscan vases and examples of Egyptian art fill the first two floors of the museum. Ivories, enamels, and ceramics from the medieval and Renaissance periods are exhibited, as are European and Japanese prints. The museum features a small but exceptional collection of Chinese art, a bequest from the comte de Saint-Genys, nephew of Turpin de Crissé.

The cathedral of St-Maurice.

The *Musée des Beaux-Arts* is in the former *Logis Barrault* on the Rue du Musée. This splendid residence was built at the end of the fifteenth century for Olivier Barrault, the treasurer of Brittany and mayor of Angers. In the seventeenth century, the house was converted into a seminary; among its pupils was Talleyrand, future bishop of Autun. Today, the museum comprises a beautiful collection of paintings and decorative arts. From the medieval and Renaissance periods are rare furnishings, sculptures, and exquisite enamels. A group of French primitive paintings is exhibited, as are canvases from the seventeenth century. The museum has an excellent collection of eighteenth-century French paintings, too, with important works by Chardin, Boucher, Watteau, Fragonard, and Nicolas Lancret.

Adjacent to the Logis Barrault is the magnificent ruin of the abbey of *Toussaint*. This Gothic structure with openwork vaulting now provides a dramatic setting for the *Galerie David d'Angers* (a collection that was until recently exhibited in the Musée des Beaux-Arts). David d'Angers (Pierre-Jean David [1788–1856]) was a native son who gained fame as a sculptor through his vast output of portrait statues, busts, reliefs, and medallions. Every time the artist completed a new piece, he presented a copy to the museum; in 1839, a special gallery was set up to display them. David d'Angers's work is important in the development of French sculpture in the first half of the nineteenth century; he led the rejection of classicism in favor of a new concept, realism. With his art, David d'Angers hoped to appeal to the broad mass of the people. Numerous sculptures and hundreds of drawings are exhibited in the abbey. Note the monumental statue of Gutenberg, from 1840, and among the smaller works, the charming *Young Greek Woman*.

The commanding structure near the Logis Barrault is the *Tour St-Aubin*, the bell tower and keep of the former Benedictine abbey of St-Aubin, built from the twelfth to the sixteenth century. The abbey church disappeared around 1800, and the monks' quarters now serve as the Préfecture. The courtyard of the building is closed off by a grille that once stood in the choir of the abbey church at Fontevrault. The porter will show you the richly carved twelfth-century arcades of the former cloister. One of its arches still has remnants of thirteenth-century figural painting—the Adoration of the Magi, the Slaughter of the Innocents—reminding us how splendid medieval decorative architecture must have looked clothed in its original embellishment.

A victim of collapse, in 1828, was the nave of the church of *St-Martin* in the courtyard of the school of St-Maruille (Rue St-Martin). Still surviving are its transept with a capped crossing tower, from the eleventh century; choir, from the eleventh and late thirteenth centuries; and narrow Lady Chapel, on the north side of the choir, from the early thirteenth century. The latter contains especially lovely Angevin vaulting. To visit the church, apply to the *concierge* of the school.

The church of *St-Serge*, also once belonging to an abbey, is rather unimpressive from the outside. Its nave, with flanking tower, dates from the fifteenth century. The side aisles were created much later, in the nineteenth century, when the dividing walls between the side chapels were removed. The transept dates in essence from the eleventh century, although it was reworked in the thirteenth. What makes the church famous is its choir, from around 1200. This is the richest and most mature example of the Angevin style in existence. The church is basically a four-bay hall, with nave and side aisles, ending on the east in a rectangular choir bay of the same width as the nave. Two-bay side choirs open off the aisles, the south one ending in a semicircular apse. The vaults are strengthened with rodlike ribs, and fan out like tightly stretched sails above elegant, slender columns. The entire space appears transparent and weightless. An almost lavish wealth of sculpture, only really appreciated by visitors armed with binoculars, is distributed among the keystones and rib corbels of these vaults; they amount to a great cycle on the theme of the Last Judgment.

Vaulting cycles of this type are seen only in the Angevin style of French architecture in the Early Gothic. St-Serge represents one of the most comprehensive iconographic programs of its kind, and visitors find it easier to make out than similar ones in the churches of St-Martin or Le-Puy-Notre-Dame.

Three of the choir windows (the second and third ones on the left and the second one on the right) still have their original grisaille-painted glass.

THE SECTION OF ANGERS ACROSS THE MAINE IS known as La Doutre (from *d'outre*, "beyond"). It was already built up in the Middle Ages, and it had a ring wall, as did the heart of Angers. Here, too, the walls gave way to broad boulevards during the nineteenth century. Beginning in the sixteenth century, this area came to be inhabited by Anjou's aristocratic families, who in winter moved into town from their country estates. After the Revolution drove them out, the quarter rapidly lost its distinction, although one collection of fine old houses around the Place de la Laiterie remains. A widely visible landmark of La Doutre is the aisleless church of *La Trinité*, from the twelfth century, with a sixteenth-century bell tower by Jean de l'Espine above its crossing.

In the northern part of this quarter stands the *Hôpital St-Jean*, an important example of medieval hospital architecture and one of the oldest structures of its kind in Europe. It was founded in 1174 by the bailiff Etienne de Marchey, who then served as its first administrator, and by Henry II, King of England and Count of Anjou. Its staff was made up of monks.

Medieval hospitals developed from the concept of Christian charity. They were not strictly medical centers, but rather shelters for needy people of all kinds. Although attendants were concerned for the souls of the inmates, the constitution of St-Jean, approved by the pope in 1267, stated that the hospital would be open to people of all religions.

The Salle des Malades, the main building of the complex and the one in which the patients were housed, is a three-aisle, eight-bay hall divided by tall columns from which sinuous ribs sweep upward to form pointed vaults. Forms from religious architecture were used to underscore the building's partially sacred function. From their rows of beds in cubicles along the sides, patients could see the altar set up in the center of the space—a symbol of the omnipresent succor of divine grace.

The fifteenth-century covered arcade in front of the hospital portal replaces a Romanesque portico that also ran around the sides of the building and was linked to a hexagonal lavabo in front. The original portico served as an ambulatory and an open-air lounge.

In the late twelfth century, the monks who staffed the hospital built a chapel next to it for their own use. It could not be en-

Layout of the sculpture in the vaults at St-Serge

1. Pascal lamb
2. Mary
3. St. John the Baptist
4. The crowning of Mary
5. Judgment of Christ
6. Abraham
7. St. John the Evangelist
8. St. Bartholomew
9. St. Simon
10. St. Barnabas
11. Jacob
12. St. Paul
13. St. Andrew
14. Tambourine players
15. St. Philip
16. Archangel Michael
17. St. Peter
18. Christ the King
19. Pascal lamb
20. Apostle
21. Christ as philosopher
22. Apostle
23. Christ with crucifix
24. Symbol of St. Mark the Evangelist
25. Symbol of St. Luke the Evangelist
26. St. Peter
a-b. Three-quarter figures
c-e. Angels
f-i. Angels with crowns
j. Mary betrothed
k. Angel with garland
l. Angel with crucifix
m. Angel with crown of thorns
n. Mary with inscribed band
o. Rich man
p. Poor Lazarus
q. Rich man
r. Poor Lazarus
s. St. John the Evangelist in oil
t. Salvation of St. John
u. Emperor Domitian
v-y. Wise virgins

z-cc. Foolish virgins
dd. Groom with palm branch
ee. Bride
ff. Hunchback
gg. Monk
hh. Annunciation
ii. Meeting
jj. St. Zachary
kk. Shepherd
ll. Harpist
mm. Bagpipe player
nn. Flutist
oo. Lute player
pp. Violinist
qq. Salome
rr. St. John the Baptist in prison
ss. Hunchback
tt-uu. Female heads
vv. St. Christopher
ww. Head of Adam
xx. Head of Eve
yy. Boy's head
zz. Woman's head
a3. Hunchbacked man
b3. Stoning of St. Stephen
c3. Stone thrower
d3. St. Peter at the gates of Heaven
e3. Figure with inscribed band
f3. Angel with book
g3. Singing angel
i3-n3. Heads
o3. Angel
p3-s3. Heads
t3. Head of a king
u3. Head of a queen
v3. Boy's head
w3. Architect or stone mason
x3. Mary
y3. Male half figure
z3. Male head
a4. Woman's head
b4. Male head

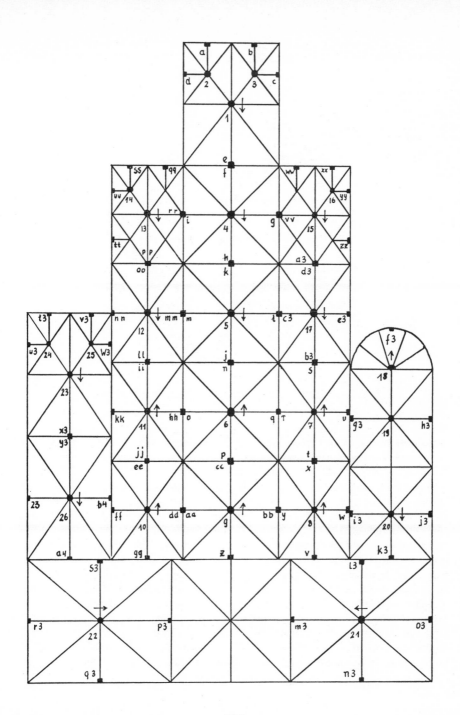

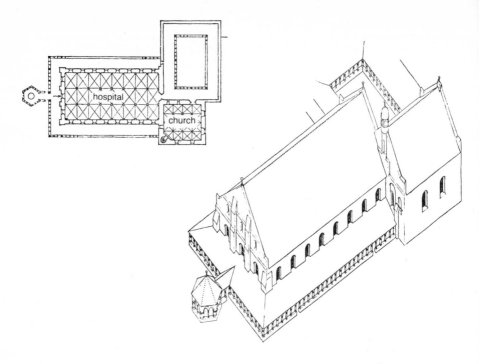

Hôpital St-Jean (reconstruction of the original structure).

tered from the hospital itself, but only from the cloister behind it. Two wings of this Romanesque cloister still stand. The wing opposite the chapel was added by Jean de l'Espine between 1538 and 1549, and the fourth side disappeared with the adjacent convent buildings.

Invalids were still being treated in the hospital until 1865. Today it serves as the Musée Lurçat, which displays a monumental tapestry cycle, Le Chant du Monde, by Jean Lurçat. This work, executed between 1957 and 1966, is a modern Apocalypse in luminous colors against a black background, and was directly inspired by the more famous castle tapestries.

Next to the Salle des Malades is the hos-

pital's dispensary. A small room decorated with fine wood paneling executed in 1612, it is filled with seventeenth-, eighteenth-, and nineteenth-century pots and vessels.

Another part of the hospital complex is a huge *tithe barn*, from the twelfth century, the lower floor of which was carved out of bedrock and used as a wine cellar. The building is now a charming wine museum. It serves to remind us of the major role this beverage has played throughout the history of the "Garden of France."

In around 1100, the abbot Baudri of Bourgueil wrote: "You must come once a year and drink wine with us. We have an abundance of it, and it is soothing to a melancholy heart."

F O O T N O T E S

1. Honoré de Balzac, *Catherine de Médicis*, trans. by K. P. Wormeley (Boston: Roberts Brothers, 1894).

2. Jean de La Fontaine, *A Journey to the Limousin*, Third Letter (1663).

3. Jacques Houlet, *Le Château de Talcy* (Paris: Caisse Nationale des Monuments Historiques, 1966), 73.

4. Quoted in *Merveilles des châteaux du Val de Loire* (Paris, 1964), 29.

5. Honoré de Balzac, *Catherine de Médicis*, trans. by May Tomlinson (Philadelphia: George Barrie and Son, 1897).

6. Quoted in Therésè Imbert, *Chambord* (Paris: Caisse Nationale des Monuments Historiques, 1974), 9.

7. Pierre Gascar, *Chambord* (Lucerne, 1965), 49.

8. Quoted in Bernard Champigneulle, *Loire-Schlösser*, 3d ed. (Munich, 1971), 106.

9. Ibid., 106*ff.*

10. Jacques Androvet Du Cerceau, *La seconde volume des plus excellents bastiments de France* (Paris, 1607), 3.

11. Pierre de Vaissière, *Le Château d'Amboise* (Paris, 1935), 56.

12. Quoted in Marie Luise Gothein, *Geschichte der Gartenkunst*, vol. 2 (Jena, 1926), 3.

13. Quoted in Champigneulle, *op. cit.*, 202*ff.*

14. Ibid., 194*ff.*

15. Gregory of Tours, *History of the Franks*, vol. I (Darmstadt, 1967), 97.

16. François Salet, *La Cathédrale de Tours* (Paris, 1949), 59.

17. Pierre de Cossé, duc de Brissac, *Brissac: Notice historique et descriptive* (Paris, 1957), 17.

18. Adapted from *Merveilles des châteaux, op. cit.*, 175.

19. Pierre Verlet, *La maison du XVIIIᵉ siècle en France* (Paris, 1966), 246. The inventory of Montgeoffroy is published in full on page 260.

20. Quoted in Monique Stucky, *Les tapisseries de l'Apocalypse d'Angers* (Lausanne, 1973), 9.

NOTES

NOTES

NOTES

PRACTICAL
TRAVEL
SUGGESTIONS

This section of the book offers American, Canadian, and British vacationers an overview of all major aspects of traveling in France. In addition to presenting general information about the country, it contains tips about getting to France and getting around in France, about important documents and regulations, and about sources of more detailed information. It also covers local weather, accommodations, entertainment, the addresses and hours of local museums, regional gastronomic specialties, festivals, and so on. Much of this information—addresses and telephone numbers, for example—is notoriously impermanent, so visitors should always try to check local listings upon arrival. Because sudden price changes in France and fluctuations in international exchange rates are inevitable, this guide does not include French prices or their equivalents in dollars or pounds; readers are advised to consult newspapers or banks.

Introduction to France

GETTING TO FRANCE

Air France, Pan Am, TWA, Air Canada, and other airlines provide direct service from the United States and Canada to France. Check with a travel agent for details on schedules, fares, and points of departure and arrival.

People planning to travel to France from the British Isles have many options. Many airlines—British Airways and Air France are only two—connect major cities in both countries. Aer Lingus offers service from Dublin and Cork to Paris and Lourdes.

It is also possible to travel by rail from Britain to France. Most of these services connect with cross-Channel ferries, but through railway carriages between London and Paris also operate overnight. Reservations are advisable, particularly in summer. Contact British Rail or a travel agent for particulars.

Several coach (bus) services offer transportation between major cities throughout Britain and France. Contact a travel agent for details.

Visitors who want to drive to France can use one of many car ferries that connect England and Ireland with France. Reservations on the Sealink services (Dover to Boulogne or Calais, Folkestone to Boulogne or Calais, Newhaven to Dieppe, and Weymouth to Cherbourg) may be made through British Rail (see pages 460–461), but other companies offer car ferries on other routes. The Hovercraft, which crosses the English Channel from Dover to Calais or Boulogne in 30 to 40 minutes, also accommodates cars. There are no customs restrictions on bringing a car into France, assuming one enters as a tourist and for under six months.

GETTING AROUND IN FRANCE

By Air

Air Inter is France's domestic airline, serving thirty major business and holiday centers throughout the country, including Paris (Orly and Charles-de-Gaulle airports), Nice, Marseille, Toulouse, Lyon, Strasbourg, Montpellier, and Nantes. Its central information and reservations number (in Paris) is 1/539-25-25. Information about Air Inter is also available from Air France offices in the United States, Canada, and the United Kingdom. Other domestic airlines include Touraine Air Transport, Air Littoral (serving the South of France, Spain, and Italy), and Compagnie Aérienne du Languedoc. Air France flies key domestic routes as well.

By Rail

The French National Railroads, or SNCF

(Société Nationale des Chemins de Fer Français), offers perhaps the best way to see France. SNCF is a dense network of railways connecting major cities and small towns; it has gained an enviable reputation for speed, safety, punctuality, and passenger comfort. The newest star in this system is the TGV (*train à grande vitesse*, which means simply, "high-speed train"), a train that runs between Paris and Lyon at more than 130 miles per hour and cuts travel time to a mere 2 hours—thereby placing relatively distant parts of France within day-trip distance of the capital.

On most long-distance night trains, a traveler can book either a sleeper or a *couchette* berth in either first or second class. For information about routes, reservations, and up-to-date fares, contact SNCF (in France) or French National Railroads (in the United States, the United Kingdom, and Canada). See page 460 for a listing of French National Railroads offices in these countries.

Passengers must validate their rail tickets (except those bought outside France), using the orange stamping machine, before boarding the train. Failure to do so results in an additional fee.

Americans and Canadians can take advantage of three special packages offered by French National Railroads. The Eurailpass entitles the bearer to unlimited first-class rail travel in sixteen Western European countries, including France, for 15 days, 21 days, or 1, 2, or 3 months. The Eurail Youthpass guarantees unlimited second-class rail travel in these same countries for either 1 or 2 months to anyone under 26 years old. The Frances Vacances pass is issued for 7 days, 15 days, or 1 month of first- or second-class travel. This ticket entitles the holder not only to unlimited travel on all SNCF trains (including the TGV) during the period of validity, but also to:

2, 4, or 7 days of unlimited travel on the Paris Métro, RER, and bus system

a free round-trip rail journey to Paris from Charles-de-Gaulle or Orly airport

a free admission to the Centre National d'Art et de Culture Georges-Pompidou (Centre Beaubourg)

a free one-way trip on the privately owned scenic railroad Chemin de Fer de Provence, which runs between Nice and Digne

a 10 percent discount on SNCF bus excursions

a discount on car rentals through the Budget Train + Auto service

All three passes must be purchased at one of the French National Railroads offices in the United States or Canada; see page 460 for a listing of these addresses.

British travelers should consult a travel agent or the local British Rail booking office for comprehensive packages available to them in France.

By Car

France has about 930,000 miles of roads. This extensive network includes the *autoroutes* (motorways or superhighways, with an A prefix), the *routes nationales* (major national roads, with an N prefix), and the *routes départementales* (relatively minor roads, with a D prefix). The entire system is kept in excellent condition.

In France, as in the United States, Canada, and continental Europe, driving is done on the right-hand side of the road. Foreign visitors may drive in France if they have a valid driver's license from their home country (an international license is not required), valid passport or other identity papers, and an international green insurance card. Insurance is compulsory in France for all overland motor vehicles, including those driven by visitors from abroad. On arrival, if a motorist cannot present an international green insurance card, he or she must take out a temporary *assurance frontière* policy at customs. This policy may be issued for 8, 15, 30 days; it cannot be renewed. Visitors staying longer than 30 days must either contact their insurer at home for a green card or take out a temporary policy with a French firm.

Vehicles used in France are required to have safety belts for the driver and the front-seat passenger, an external driving mirror, spare headlight bulbs, and rear warning lights or a phosphorescent warning signal (triangle) in case of breakdown. Yellow headlights are compulsory on French cars, and dazzling headlights are prohibited. The horn may be used only when absolutely necessary; in Paris and certain other cities, its use is expressly forbidden except in case of imminent danger. Children under 10 years old are not allowed to ride in the front seat of a vehicle.

If an emergency car repair is needed, a motorist can call Touring Secours (telephone 1/531-05-05), set up under the auspices of the Touring Club de France. Towing and emergency repairs are free to drivers who have joined Touring Secours. For further information about Touring Secours or driving in France in general, contact the Touring Club de France, 6-8 Rue Firmin-Gillot, 75737 Paris Cedex 15; telephone 1/532-22-15. The Royal Automobile Club of Great Britain (French headquarters at 8 Place Vendôme, Paris, Ier; telephone 1/260-62-12) is a source of additional information.

In case of accident, the drivers of both cars should find a police officer, who will fill out a report, or *constat*, that can be submitted to insurance companies. If the accident is serious, photographs should be taken, if possible. If the accident involves only one's own car, the report may be filled out by an official (*huissier*) in the nearest community. The Bureau Central Français des Sociétés Assurances contre les Accidents d'Automobiles (118 Rue de Tocqueville, 75017 Paris; telephone 1/766-52-64) should also be notified immediately.

Gasoline (petrol) is sold by the liter. An American gallon is equivalent to 3.78 liters; an imperial gallon, 4.54 liters. Distances are measured in kilometers (1 km = about .62 mile; 1 mile = about 1.61 km).

Speed limits are generally 130 kph (80 mph) on toll *autoroutes*, 110 kph (68 mph) on free *autoroutes* and other major roads, 90 kph (56 mph) on lesser roads, and 60 kph (37 mph) in developed zones. The *autoroutes* have parking and rest areas every 6 to 10 miles and emergency telephones every 11¼ miles.

SNCF offers a service, called Motorail, for drivers going toward any of several major cities. Drivers taking advantage of it are entitled to a berth on the same train that their car travels on. Once the destination is reached, retrieving the car can be done quite quickly. Contact French National Railroads (for addresses, see page 460) for more information.

Car Rental. It is quite easy for travelers from abroad to rent a self-drive car in France. The major agencies—Avis, Budget, Citer, Europcar, Hertz, Inter-Rent, and Mattei—have several offices in France. Car-rental arrangements in France can frequently be made through airlines, travel agents, or local car-rental agencies. For further information about firms in France that offer cars for hire, contact a travel agent or CSNCRA (Chambre Syndicale Nationale du Commerce et de la Réparation Automobile), 6 Rue Léonard-de-Vinci, 75016 Paris; telephone 1/502-19-10.

Renters must be a minimum of 21 years old (sometimes 25) and must be able to show that they have held a valid driver's license for at least one year.

For information about hiring a chauffeur-driven car, contact a travel agent or the Chambre Syndicale Nationale des Entreprises de Remise et de Tourisme, 48 Rue de la Bienfaisance, 75008 Paris; telephone 1/562-06-66.

By Coach (Bus)

Long-distance coach services are operated in France by Europabus and other companies. In addition, many local services and sightseeing tours are available; many of these are run by SCETA (Services de Tourisme SNCF-Europabus), 7 Rue Pablo-Neruda, 92532 Levallois-Perret Cedex; telephone 1/270-56-00, ext. 536. Contact SCETA or a travel agent for more details.

By Water

France has a great network of inland waterways—not only famed rivers such as the Seine, the Loire, and the Rhône, but also canals that connect them—and it is possible to rent a boat equipped with living accommodations to explore these byways or to take an organized inland cruise. For further information, you can contact a travel agent or the Syndicat National des Loueurs de Bateaux de Plaisance, Port de la Bourdonnais, 75007 Paris; telephone 1/555-10-49. This organization can also provide information about berthing yachts along France's beautiful Atlantic and Mediterranean coasts and about renting small craft to sail these waters.

By Bicycle

Thousands of miles of bicycle routes throughout France may be explored by energetic travelers. Fixed itineraries are offered by the following organizations:

La Fédération Française de Cyclotourisme
8 Rue Jean-Marie-Jego
75013 Paris
1/580-30-21

Le Bicyclub de France
8 Place de la Porte-Champerret
75017 Paris
1/766-55-92

Loisirs Accueil Loiret
3 Rue de la Bretonnerie
45000 Orléans
38/62-04-88

Loisirs Accueil Loir-et-Cher
11 Place du Château
41000 Blois
54/78-55-50

In addition, the French Government Tourist Offices (see page 459) and local bureaus (*syndicats d'initiative*) provide lists of suggested itineraries. Bicycles may be rented at more than 200 SNCF stations throughout France, and through other outlets as well.

On Foot

France can be crossed on foot on an excellent system of long-distance footpaths and hiking trails. The Fédération Française de la Randonnée Pédestre, Comité National des Sentiers de Grande Randonnée, 8 Avenue Marceau, 75008 Paris, will send out a list of these routes on request.

DOCUMENTS AND REGULATIONS

Passports

Visitors to France from the United States, the United Kingdom, and Canada are required to hold valid passports. No visa is necessary.

Currency

Visitors may bring an unlimited amount of French or foreign currency into France. Visitors who arrive with more than 5,000 francs (or the equivalent sum in other currency) are advised to fill out a special form (declaration of entry of foreign banknotes into France) that customs will provide on request and countersign. Visitors leaving France may not take out more than 5,000 francs (or the equivalent) unless they present this duly certified declaration.

Duty-Free Goods

In addition to personal clothing, jewelry, and effects such as cameras and sports equipment, visitors who are over 17 years old may bring the following goods into France duty-free (see list).

For information, contact the French Government Tourist Office (addresses on page 459) or the French customs office: Bureau IRP, Direction Générale des Douanes, 8 Rue de la Tour-des-Dames, 75436 Paris Cedex 09; telephone 1/280-67-22.

Item	From United Kingdom/Ireland	From United States/Canada
Alcoholic beverages:		
Table wines	4 liters (3½ quarts)	2 liters (1¾ quarts)
and either		
Spirits with over 22% alcohol content	1½ liters	1 liter
or		
Spirits with 22% alcohol content or less	3 liters	2 liters
Tobacco:		
Cigarettes	300	400
Cigarillos	150	200
Cigars	75	150
or		
Pipe tobacco	14 ounces (400 grams)	17 ounces (500 grams)
Perfumes and toilet water	2½ ounces (37.5 centiliters)	1¾ ounces (25 centiliters)

Prohibited Goods

Narcotics, goods that constitute copyright infringements, gold (other than personal jewelry), and firearms (other than for hunting or target shooting) are forbidden.

Dogs and Cats

Animals less than 3 months old are not allowed into France. A visitor may bring in up to three animals, only one of which may be a puppy. For each animal that comes from a country that has not recorded a case of rabies for at least three years, a certified veterinarian must complete a certificate of origin and health within five days of the animal's departure from home; the certificate confirms that the animal is in good health, that its country of origin has been free of rabies for at least three years, and that the animal has not left that country since birth or for the six months prior to entering France. Otherwise, owners must show a rabies vaccination certificate for each animal, completed by a veterinarian in the animal's home country, stating that it has been vaccinated more than a month but less than a year before entry into France or that it has been revaccinated within the past year.

Owners of all other animals must apply in advance to the Ministère de l'Agriculture, Bureau de la Règlementation Sanitaire aux Frontières, 44-46 Boulevard de Grenelle, 75732 Paris Cedex 15.

Acquisition of Valuables

Special regulations apply to precious metals, jewelry, artworks, and antiques acquired in France. Visitors who cannot prove that they purchased such items from a standard dealer may, on leaving the country, be required to pay a duty equal to 3 to 4 percent of the item's value.

Staying More Than 3 Months

Visitors who stay in France for more than 3 months must obtain a residence permit from the Service des Étrangers, Prefecture de Police, Place Louis-Lépine, Paris, IVᵉ; telephone 1/277-11-00 (open daily except Saturday, Sunday, and holidays, 8:30 A.M. to 5:00 P.M.). A visitor who fails to register at this office after 3 months in the country is subject to a heavy fine.

GENERAL INFORMATION

Money

France's unit of currency is the French *franc*, which is divided into 100 *centimes*. Coins exist in the following denominations: 5c, 10c, 20c, ½F (50c), 1F, 2F, 5F, 10F. There are paper notes for denominations of 10F, 20F, 50F, 100F, and 500F.

Major international credit cards—Access, American Express, Diner's Club, MasterCard, Visa—are honored by many establishments throughout France.

Tipping

Station or airport porters. Usually about 5F, depending on the number of bags.

Taxi drivers. 10 to 15 percent of the fare shown on the meter.

Hotel staff. 10F per piece of luggage to the hotel porter; 10F per day to the chambermaid.

Waiters. In cafés and many restaurants, service is generally included in the bill (*service compris*). If service is not included, tip 15 percent. About 10F should be given to the sommelier.

Coatroom attendants. At least 5F per item; at least 5F for toilet attendants.

Tour guides. About 5F per person in the group.

Public Holidays

By law, France recognizes ten major civil and church holidays, the so-called *jours féries*. These are:

New Year's Day (January 1)

Easter Monday

Ascension Thursday (Sixth Thursday after Easter)

Whit Monday (second Monday after Ascension)

Labor Day (May 1)

Bastille Day (July 14)

Assumption (August 15)

All Saints' Day (November 1)

Armistice Day (November 11)

Christmas (December 25)

On these days, banks and many shops, museums, and restaurants are closed. Check local listings.

Although not a *jour férie*, VE Day (May 8), commemorating the Allied victory in World War II, is also celebrated widely.

Time Zone

France, like most of Western Europe, is 1 hour ahead of Greenwich Mean Time (2 hours ahead in summer). Therefore, for the best part of the year, it is ahead of the following locations by the number of hours indicated:

London, Dublin:	1 hour
Halifax:	5 hours
New York, Montreal, Toronto:	6 hours
Chicago, Houston, Winnipeg:	7 hours
Denver, Calgary:	8 hours
Los Angeles, Vancouver:	9 hours

Banking and Shopping

Banking and business hours vary in different parts of France. In Paris, for example, banks are open Monday through Friday, 9:00 A.M.–4:30 P.M., and they close at 12:00 M. the day before a holiday. In major cities in the South of France, such as Nice and Marseille, many banks are closed between 12:30–1:30 P.M., and in smaller communities, banks are closed 12:00 M.–2:00 P.M.

Store hours also reflect these regional differences. Most Parisian stores and shops are open 9:00 A.M.–6:00 or 7:00 P.M. (many are open Saturday but closed Monday); the fashion boutiques and perfumeries open at 10:00 A.M. and close 12:00 M.–2:00 P.M. In the South of France, department stores and supermarkets do not close for lunch, but smaller shops do—for up to 3 hours (12:00 M.–3:00 P.M.); however, these businesses may open as early as 7:00 or 8:00 A.M. and may close at 7:00 or 8:00 P.M. Food shops remain open on Sunday (during the morning only).

Visitors to France who are at least 15 years old and who stay for less than six months may deduct the value-added tax (VAT) from the price of goods bought in France that are being taken out of the country as personal luggage. The goods must have a certain value to qualify for this deduction. For further information, contact the French Government Tourist Office (addresses on page 459).

Post Offices

Post offices are usually open Monday through Friday, 8:00 A.M.–7:00 P.M., and Saturday, 8:00 A.M. to noon. However, small branches may close for lunch and may have shorter hours. Stamps may also be bought at tobacconists', hotels, cafés, and news agents and from yellow vending machines. Mailboxes (*bôites aux lettres*) are yellow as well.

Telephones

Except in the Paris area, telephone numbers have six digits and a two-digit prefix that is used only when dialing from outside the region. In and around Paris, telephone numbers have seven digits and a single-digit prefix ("1") for the area.

Public telephones accept 50c, 1F, and 5F coins. The ringing tone is high-pitched and periodic; the busy (engaged) tone is deeper and more rapid.

Overseas calls can be dialed direct from France to the United States, the United Kingdom, and Canada, without operator assistance. The prefix for telephoning the United Kingdom is 19-44; for the United States and Canada, 19-1. A zero at the beginning of the *local* dialing code should be ignored.

Voltage

Most electricity in France is run on a 220-volt current (50 cycles AC), although some remote areas may still run on 110 volts. American and Canadian visitors who travel with electric razors, hair dryers, and so on, should also bring along an adapter. (Outlet prongs are shaped differently in France as well.)

Handicapped Travelers

Facilities designed to accommodate the handicapped are becoming increasingly commonplace in France. For information, contact the French Government Tourist Office.

Hitchhiking

Hitchhiking is prohibited on major highways but permitted otherwise.

Sunbathing

Nudity is permissible on many beaches, and toplessness is virtually the norm on many others.

Police

Throughout most of France, the emergency telephone number to reach the police is "17."

USEFUL ADDRESSES

This section contains listings of addresses that may be helpful to Americans, Britons, and Canadians who are planning a vacation in France or who may need assistance or information while there. Although this listing is as up-to-date as possible, readers are reminded that addresses and telephone numbers change regularly.

French Government Tourist Offices

In the U.S.

610 Fifth Avenue
New York, NY 10020
212/757-1125

645 North Michigan Avenue,
Suite 630
Chicago, IL 60611
312/337-6301

World Trade Center, #103
2050 Stemmons Freeway
PO Box 58610
Dallas, TX 75258
214/742-7011

9401 Wilshire Boulevard
Beverly Hills, CA 90212
213/272-2661

360 Post Street
San Francisco, CA 94108
415/986-4161

In Canada

1840 Sherbrooke Avenue West
Montreal, Que. H3H 1E4
514/931-3855

1 Dundas Street West
Suite 2405, Box 8
Toronto, Ont. M5G 1Z3
416/593-4723

In the United Kingdom

178 Piccadilly
London W1V 0A1
01/493-6594

The London office has special departments dealing with Winter Sports and Youth Travel, Yachting and Canal Cruising, and Conferences. Address any inquiry about these specific areas to the appropriate department.

In Paris

Accueil de France
(Paris Tourist Office)
127 Champs-Elysées
75008 Paris
1/723-61-72
(Open daily 9:00 A.M.−10:00 P.M.)

Embassies and Consulates-General

United Kingdom

Embassy
35 Rue du Faubourg-St-Honoré
75383 Paris
(1) 266-91-42

Consulates-General
15 Cours de Verdun
33081 Bordeaux Cedex
(56) 52-28-35, 52-28-36, 52-48-86, 52-48-87

11 Square Dutilleul
59800 Lille
(20) 52-87-90

24 Rue Childebert
69288 Lyon Cedex I
(78) 37-59-67, 42-46-49

24 Avenue du Prado
13006 Marseille
(91) 53-43-32, 37-66-95

The United Kingdom also maintains consulates at Toulouse, Calais, Boulogne-sur-Mer, Dunkirk, Nice, Perpîgnan, Cherbourg, Le Havre, Nantes, and St. Malo-Dinard, and a vice-consulate at Ajaccio (Corsica).

United States

Embassy
2 Avenue Gabriel
75008 Paris
(1) 296-12-02, 261-80-75

Consulates-General
4 Rue Esprit-des-Lois
33000 Bordeaux
(56) 65-95

72 Rue Général-Sarrail
69006 Lyon
(78) 24-68-49

9 Rue Armeny
13006 Marseille
(91) 54-92-00

15 Avenue d'Alsace
67000 Strasbourg
(88) 35-31-04

The United States also maintains a consulate in Nice.

Canada

Embassy
35 Avenue Montaigne
75008 Paris
1/723-0101

Consulates-General
24 Avenue du Prado
13006 Marseille
91/37-19-37

Croix du Mail
Rue Claude-Bonnier
33080 Bordeaux Cedex
56/96-15-61

10 Place du Temple-Neuf
67007 Strasbourg Cedex
88/32-65-96

French National Railroads

French National Railroads maintains the following offices in the United States, the United Kingdom, and Canada.

In the United States

610 Fifth Avenue
New York, NY 10020
212/582-2110

360 Post Street
San Francisco, CA 94102
415/982-1993

9465 Wilshire Boulevard
Beverly Hills, CA 90212
213/274-6934

11 East Adams Street
Chicago, IL 60603
312/427-8691

2121 Ponce de Leon Boulevard
Coral Gables, FL 33134
305/445-8648

In Canada

1500 Stanley Street, Suite 436
Montreal, Que. H3A 1R3
514/288-8255

409 Granville Street, Suite 452
Vancouver, B.C. V6C 1T2
604/688-6707

In the United Kingdom

179 Piccadilly
London W1 0BA
01/493-9731, 32, 33, 34

Britrail Travel International

Britrail Travel International represents British Rail in the United States and Canada. Travelers in these countries who want to make advance bookings on boat-train services between Britain and France, on through trains from London to Paris, or on Sealink car ferries across the English Channel should contact one of the following offices:

630 Third Avenue
New York, NY 10017
212/599-5400

510 West 6th Street
Los Angeles, CA 90014
213/626-0088

333 North Michigan Avenue
Chicago, IL 60601
312/263-1910

Plaza of the Americas
North Tower, Suite 750
LB356
Dallas, TX 75201
214/748-0860

94 Cumberland Street, Suite 601
Toronto, Ont. M5R 1A3
416/929-3333

409 Granville Street
Vancouver, B.C. V6C 1T2
604/683-6896

Reservations for any of these British Rail services may also be made at British Rail booking offices throughout the United Kingdom.

Sports and Leisure

Travelers who intend to observe or participate in sports or leisure activities while in France may obtain information from the following organizations:

Camping

Fédération Française de Camping et de
  Caravaning
78 Rue de Rivoli
75004 Paris
1/272-84-08

Riding

Fédération Equestre Française

164 Rue du Faubourg-St-Honoré
75008 Paris
1/225-11-22

Golf

Fédération Française de Golf
69 Avenue Victor-Hugo
75116 Paris
1/500-62-20

Auto Racing

Automobile Club de France
8 Place de la Concorde
75008 Paris
1/266-43-00

Ice Skating

Fédération Française des Sports de Glace
42 Rue du Louvre
75001 Paris
1/261-51-38

Flying

Aéro-Club de France
6 Rue Galilée
75016 Paris
1/720-93-02

Gliding

Fédération Française de Vol à Voile
29 Rue de Sèvres
75006 Paris
1/544-04-78

Parachuting

Fédération Française de Parachutisme
35 Rue St-Georges
75009 Paris
1/878-45-00

Tennis

La Ligue de Tennis de Paris

74 Rue de Rome
75008 Paris
1/522-22-08

Winter Sports

Association des Maires des Stations
Françaises de Sports d'Hiver
61 Boulevard Haussmann
75008 Paris
1/742-23-32

Basque Pelota

Club de Pelote Basque
8 Rue de la Cavalerie
75015 Paris
1/567-06-34

Mountain Climbing

Club Alpin Français
7 Rue La Boétie
75008 Paris
1/742-36-77

Fishing (permit required)

Conseil Supérieur de la Pêche
10 Rue Péclet
75010 Paris
1/842-10-00

Hunting and Shooting (permit required)

Office National de la Chasse
85-bis Avenue de Wagram
75017 Paris
1/277-81-75

Scuba Diving

Fédération Française d'Etudes et de Sports
   Sous-Marins
24 Quai de Rive-Neuve
13007 Marseille
91/33-99-31

Canoeing

Canoë-Kayak Club de France
47 Quai Ferber
94360 Bry-sur-Marne
1/881-54-26

Sailing

Fédération Française de Yachting à Voile
55 Avenue Kléber
75116 Paris
1/505-68-00

Water Skiing

Fédération Française de Ski Nautique
9 Boulevard Pereire
75017 Paris
1/267-15-66

Surfing

Fédération Française de Surf
Cité Administrative
Avenue Edouard-VII
64200 Biarritz

Wind-surfing

Association Française de Wind-Surf
29 Rue du Général-Delestraint
75016 Paris

Motorboating (license required)

Fédération Française Motonautique
8 Place de la Concorde
75008 Paris
1/073-89-38, 265-34-70

Cave Exploring

Fédération Française de Spéléologie
130 Rue St-Maur
75011 Paris
1/357-56-54

The Loire Valley

PLANNING YOUR VISIT

The many châteaux and rivers of the Loire Valley make this region of of the most distinctive and magical in France. Perhaps the best time to visit is during the spring (average May temperature is 16° C, or 61° F). Thanks to the mild climate, which is moderated by the Gulf Stream, leaves and colorful flowers appear by late March; spring skies tend to be brilliantly clear. Average summer temperatures are 24° C (75°F) in July and 22° C (72°F) in August, and there is often a pleasant breeze from the Atlantic. Summer is also thue peak season here, and the area becomes very crowded, making leisurely touring difficult. Loire autumns are somewhat moody. Morning mists are typical, but they often give way to a fine light. The climate remains mild through October, when the average temperature is 19° C (66°F), and the absence of crowds allows visitors to explore the châteaux unhurriedly. Local residents call the winter *la mauvaise saison* ("the bad season"), but winters in the Loire Valley are actually quite short and by no means harsh. Nonetheless, many of the châteaux curtail their hours or are closed altogether.

Tourist Offices

For further information about the major attractions discussed in this guide or about travel in the Loire Valley, consult:

Tourisme en Loir-et-Cher
11 Place du Château
41000 Blois
54/78-55-50

Tourisme-Accueil-Loiret
3 Rue de la Bretonnerie
45000 Orléans
38/62-04-88

Alternatively, you may write or telephone one of the following *syndicats d'initiative*. Address all correspondence to Office de Tourisme.

Place Kennedy
49000 Angers
41/88-69-93

Place Gare-St-Laud
49000 Angers
41/87-72-50

Pavillon Anne-de-Bretagne
3 Avenue du Dr-Jean-Laigret
41000 Blois
54/74-06-49

14 Place Etienne-Dolet
18000 Bourges
48/24-75-33

Place de la Gare
36000 Châteauroux
54/34-10-74

Place Albert-Ier
45000 Orléans
38/53-05-95

25 Rue Beaurepaire
49400 Saumur
41/51-03-06

Place Maréchal-Leclerc
37042 Tours Cedex
47/05-58-08

Accommodations

The Loire Valley offers visitors a complete range of accommodations, from hostels and inexpensive inns to luxury-class château-hotels, such as Château d'Artigny and Domaine de la Tortinière in Montbazon, Domaine de Beauvois in Luynes, Château de Marçay near Chinon, and Le Prieuré near Saumur. The region's major cities—Orléans, Blois, Tours, Saumur, and Angers—have the greatest selection of hotels, and one of these cities may be used as a base for several nights by travelers taking day trips to sights in the surrounding countryside. (A sample ten-day itinerary based on this plan is included in the following section, "Getting Around the Loire Valley.")

Visitors who prefer to stay outside the major cities still have several options for lodgings. The *logis de France* are simple, well-run, and quite inexpensive country inns that usually rate one or two stars. An annual directory of these inns can be requested from the French Government Tourist Office. Other possibilities are a *gîte rural de France*—a house or a part of a house that can be rented for a weekend, a week, two weeks, or a month, usually in a farm area or small village—or a *gîte chambre d'hôte*, the equivalent of a bed-and-breakfast. Full details are available from La Maison du Tourisme Vert, Fédération Nationale des Gîtes Ruraux de France, 35 Rue Godot-de-Mauroy, 75009 Paris, telephone 1/742-25-43.

Visitors to the Loire Valley may also choose to stay at one of its many campgrounds, caravan sites, or youth hostels. For further information, consult a travel agent, the French Government Tourist Office, or another appropriate source listed in the "Introduction to France."

Dining

Three major factors—the mild climate, the fertile soil, and the numerous rivers—have allied to make the cuisine of the Loire Valley one of the most bountiful and varied in France. *Primeurs*, or early fruits and vegetables, are cultivated here a full two weeks earlier than in the nearby Ile de France, the rivers are rich with freshwater fish, and the forests still attract hunters every autumn, just as they did in the Middle Ages and the Renaissance.

The abundance of game was one of the main reasons kings and aristocrats built châteaux in the Loire Valley, and game is still a key component of the area, especially in Sologne. Solognot specialties include *terrine de lièvre à la Solognote*, a hare or rabbit terrine; *ballotine de faisan au genévrière*, ballotine of pheasant with juniper, served with cooked chestnuts and *chanterelles*; and *perdreaux au verjus*, partridges wrapped in vine leaves and cooked in a casserole with the juice of crushed white grapes.

Fish is another delicacy of the Loire Valley; salmon, trout, carp, pike, perch, and shad are all caught locally. Eels are also a regional favorite, and a distinctive specialty of the area is *matelote d'anguilles au vin de Bourgueil*, eel stewed in a local red wine. Other regional dishes are *andouillettes grillées au vin de Vouvray*, coarse sausages grilled in a local white wine; *coq au vin de Chinon*; *lapin poêlé au vin blanc d'Anjou*, rabbit cooked in a casserole with a semisweet wine; *cul de veau à la façon de grand'mère*, old-fashioned braised veal; and *noisette de porc aux pruneaux*, pork chops with prunes. Strips of pork, cooked for hours in their own fat, are called *rillons* and are perhaps the best-known local dish, along with *rillettes*, a

more diminutive version. Both are widely available in the valley's eating places, especially in and around Tours.

Anjou and Touraine are renowned for their fruits and vegetables. The area produces pears, apples, melons, apricots, peaches, plums, and top-quality grapes that help make the Loire Valley one of France's foremost wine-producing regions. (See the following section, "Wines of the Loire Valley.") The river banks near Saumur are the leading source of mushrooms (*champignons de Paris*) in the country. Asparagus and artichokes are also grown locally, as is sorrel (*oseille*), which is an ingredient in numerous regional dishes.

The area is famous for its dark brown goats (*chèvres*) and, consequently, for its goat cheeses. Desserts are varied; many, such as *tarte aux poires Belle Angevine* (pear tart) make use of the estimable local produce. Simple Solognot desserts include *croquets*, or almond cookies, and *tarte de demoiselles (tarte à l'envers)*, an upside-down apple tart.

Eating places in the Loire Valley range from the most elegant restaurants—for example, those at the Château d'Artigny in Montbazon and the Domaine de Beauvois in Luynes, as well as Le Relais in Bracieux and Barrier in Tours—to simple, unpretentious *charcuteries* and *cafés*. Dishes on the *prix-fixe* menu tend to cost considerably less than dishes *à la carte*.

WINES OF THE LOIRE VALLEY

The Loire Valley is one of the largest and most important wine-producing areas in France, and many of its wines—especially

its whites—are celebrated. In diversity alone, the wines of this region are rarely matched elsewhere.

Toward the mouth of the Loire, near Nantes, a light, very dry, and very popular white wine called Muscadet is made. Upstream in Anjou, the best white wines grow along the Layon River, south of Angers. The vineyards here produce Coteaux du Layon, which are sweet and highly regarded. Two notable *appellations* of this region are Quart de Chaumes and Bonnezeaux, which are sweet, rich dessert wines. The white wines of Anjou are made from the Chenin Blanc grape. Anjou also produces large quantities of rosé wine, which is a favorite in the United States due to its slight sweetness and pleasing color. Brissac is the foremost red wine from this region.

Farther upriver, the region around Saumur primarily produces dry and semisweet still white wines, also from the Chenin Blanc grape. The red wines of Saumur-Champigny, Chinon, and Bourgueil, however, are among the best grown in the Loire Valley.

One of the best and most famous wines of the Loire is made at Vouvray, upstream from Tours. Made from the Chenin Blanc grape, it usually ranges from dry to semisweet; sparkling Vouvray is becoming increasingly popular. Montlouis, a lesser white, is grown directly across the river. Touraine-Azay-le-Rideau (white and rosé) and Touraine-Amboise (red and white) tend to be consumed locally, often with *rillons*, *rillettes*, and the local freshwater fish (see "Dining").

Still farther east, Sancerre produces a fruity and very popular white wine, made from the Sauvignon Blanc grape, that goes well with fish or seafood. Pouilly-Fumé, grown across the Loire, is a more delicate but somewhat similar white that, largely because it is rarer, tends to be far more expensive. Pouilly-Fumé is grown exclusively from the Sauvignon Blanc grape. Wine from the same district but made from the Chasselas grape—with or without Sauvignon Blanc—is called Pouilly-sur-Loire.

Many of the Loire vineyards are open to visitors, and most offer wine tasting. They include:

Cave Mangeant

La Graverie
Rue du Général-de-Gaulle
Chargé
37400 Amboise
47/57-09-75
Open daily, 8:00 A.M.–8:00 P.M.

Cave Touristique de la Dive-Bouteille

Chevrette
37140 Bourgueil
47/97-72-01
Open daily. May–September: 10:00 A.M.–12:30 P.M. and 2:30 P.M.–7:30 P.M. October–November and February–April: 10:00 A.M.–12:30 P.M. and 2:00 P.M.–6:00 P.M. Closed December–January.

Centre Coopératif de Commercialisation des Vins

Le Tivoli
Route de Culan
18370 Châteaumeillant
48/61-33-55
June–August: open daily, 8:30 A.M.–NOON and 2:00 P.M.–6:30 P.M. September–May: open daily, except Saturday, Sunday, and holidays, 8:30 A.M.–NOON and 2:00 P.M.–6:30 P.M.

Cave Manzagol

La Noblaie
Ligré
37500 Chinon
Open daily, except Sunday and holidays, 9:00 A.M.–NOON and 2:00 P.M.–5:00 P.M.

Cave Plouzeau

94 Rue Haute St-Maurice
37500 Chinon
47/93-16-34
Open daily, April–September, except
Monday, Sunday, and holidays, by appointment only.

Cave de la Grande Brosse

Chémery
41700 Contres
54/71-81-03
Open daily.

Cave A. Contoux

5 Chemin des Murs
Seur
41120 Les Montils
54/44-04-58
Open daily, 9:00 A.M.–7:00 P.M.

Cave Coopérative des Producteurs de Vins de Montlouis

2 Route St-Aignan
37270 Montlouis
47/50-80-98
Open daily. July–August: 9:00 A.M.–NOON
and 2:00 P.M.–7:00 P.M. September–December: 8:00 A.M.–NOON and 2:00 P.M.–6:00 P.M.

Caves Montmousseau

71 Rue de Vierzon
41400 Montrichard
54/32-07-04
April 15–May: open daily, 9:00 A.M.–11:30
A.M. and 2:00 P.M.–5:00 P.M. June–September 20: open daily, 9:00 A.M.–11:30 A.M.
and 2:00 P.M.–6:30 P.M. September 21–October: open daily, 9:00 A.M.–11:30 A.M. and
2:00 P.M.–5 P.M. November–April 14: open
daily, except Saturday, Sunday, and holidays, 9:00 A.M.–11:30 A.M. and 2:00 P.M.–
4:30 P.M. Groups by appointment only.

Distillerie "Fraise d'Or"

62 Route de Tours
Chissay-en-Touraine
41400 Montrichard
54/32-32-05
Open daily, April 15–September, 9:00
A.M.–11:30 A.M. and 2:00 P.M.–6:00 P.M.

Covifruit

613 Rue de Pressoir-Tonneau
45160 Olivet
38/63-40-20
Open daily, except Saturday, Sunday, and
holidays, 9:00 A.M.–NOON and 2:00 P.M.–
5:00 P.M.

Caves Brossillon

Domaine de Lusqueneau
Mesland
41150 Onzain
54/79-78-23
Open daily, 8:00 A.M.–NOON and 2:00 P.M.–
6:00 P.M. Groups by appointment.

Cave de l'Union Viticole

Le Carroir
Preuilly
18120 St-Martin-d'Auxigny
48/51-30-78
Open daily, except Sunday and holidays,
9:00 A.M.–NOON and 2:00 P.M.–6:00 P.M.

Caves Gilbert

Les Faucards
Menetou-Salon
18510 St-Martin-d'Auxigny
48/64-80-77
Open daily, 9:30 A.M.–NOON and 1:30 P.M.–
7:00 P.M.

Caves de la Mignonne

Route de Cosne à Bourges
18300 Sancerre
48/54-07-06, 54-00-26, 54-21-68
Open daily, March 15–November 15,
10:00 A.M.–NOON and 2:00 P.M.–5:00 P.M.

Cave Coopérative des Producteurs des Grands Vins de Vouvray

Vallée Coquette
37210 Vouvray
Open daily, except January 1, 8:30 A.M.–
NOON and 2:00 P.M.–6:00 P.M.

Cave Daniel Jarry

La Caillerie
Route de la Vallée Coquette
37210 Vouvray
47/52-78-75
Open daily, 8:00 A.M.–7:00 P.M. Groups by
appointment.

Cave Vigneau-Chevreau

4 Rue du Clos-Baguelin
Chançay
37210 Vouvray
47/52-93-22
Open daily, except Sunday and holidays,
9:00 A.M.–NOON and 2:00 P.M.–7:00 P.M.

Cave des Viticulteurs du Vouvray

Château de Vaudenuits
37210 Vouvray
47/52-60-20
Open daily, April–October, 9:30 A.M.–
NOON and 2:30 P.M.–5:30 P.M.

Travelers interested in visiting a vineyard
should double-check its hours on arrival
in France, or by letter in advance, because
hours may change.

MAJOR CHATEAUX

Every year, the French Government Tourist Office publishes a listing of the visiting hours of the Loire Valley châteaux, churches, abbeys, and museums. Before visiting any of these places, it is advisable to consult the most recent edition of this brochure.

Ainay-le-Vieil

18200 St-Amand-Montrond
48/96-14-39
Thirteenth–fifteenth centuries.
Mid-February–November: open daily,
10:00 A.M.–NOON and 2:00 P.M.–7:00 P.M.
Closed December–mid-February.

Amboise

37400 Amboise
47/57-00-98
Fifteenth–sixteenth centuries.
Open daily. April–October: 9:00 A.M.–
NOON and 2:00 P.M.–6:30 P.M. November–
March: 9:00 A.M.–NOON and 2:00 P.M.–
5:30 P.M.

Angers

49000 Angers
41/87-43-47
July–September: open daily, 9:30 A.M.–
6:30 P.M. Palm Sunday: open 9:30 A.M.–
NOON and 2:00 P.M.–5:30 P.M. Closed
October–June.

Apremont

18150 La Guerche-sur-l'Aubois
48/74-09-62
Thirteenth and nineteenth centuries; features collection of horse-drawn carriages. April 15–September 15: open daily, except Tuesday, 2:00 P.M.–7:00 P.M. Closed September 16–April 14.

Azay-le-Ferron

36290 Mézières-en-Brenne
54/38-20-06, 47/05-68-73
Fifteenth, seventeenth, and eighteenth centuries.
February–March: open Wednesday, Saturday, Sunday, and holidays: 10:00 A.M.–NOON and 2:00 P.M.–4:30 P.M. April–September: open daily, except Tuesday, 10:00 A.M.–NOON and 2:00 P.M.–6:00 P.M. October: Wednesday, Saturday, Sunday, and holidays: 10:00 A.M.–NOON and 2:00 P.M.–5:00 P.M. November–December: open Wednesday (afternoon), Saturday, Sunday, and holidays: 10:00 A.M.–NOON and 2:00 P.M.–5:00 P.M. Closed January, November 11, and December 25.

Azay-le-Rideau

37190 Azay-le-Rideau
47/43-32-04
Sixteenth century.
Open daily. April 15–September: 9:15 A.M.–NOON and 2:00 P.M.–6:30 P.M. October–November 14: 9:15 A.M.–NOON and 2:00 P.M.–5:00 P.M. November 15–April 14: 9:30 A.M.–NOON and 2:00 P.M.–4:45 P.M.

Baugé

49150 Baugé
41/89-18-07
Fifteenth century.
June 15–September 15: open daily, 11:00 A.M.–NOON and 3:00 P.M.–6:00 P.M. Closed September 16–June 14.

Beauregard

Cellettes
41120 Les Montils
54/44-20-05, 1/747-05-41
Sixteenth–seventeenth centuries.
April–June: open daily, 9:30 A.M.–NOON. July–August: open daily, 9:30 A.M.–6:30 P.M. September: open daily, 9:30 A.M.–NOON and 2:00 P.M.–6:30 P.M. October–March: open daily, except Wednesday, 9:30 A.M.–NOON and 2:00 P.M.–5:00 P.M. Closed January–February 5.

Blois

41000 Blois
54/78-06-62, 74-16-06
Thirteenth, fifteenth, and seventeenth centuries; contains museum of fine art.
Open daily. March 15–March 31: 9:00 A.M.–NOON and 2:00 P.M.–6:30 P.M. April: 9:00 A.M.–6:30 P.M. May: 9:00 A.M.–NOON and 2:00 P.M.–6:30 P.M. June–August: 9:00 A.M.–6:30 P.M. September: 9:00 A.M.–NOON and 2:00 P.M.–6:30 P.M. October–March 14: 9:00 A.M.–NOON and 2:00 P.M.–5:00 P.M. Open afternoons only, January 1, November 1, and December 25.

Bouges

36110 Levroux
54/35-88-26
Eighteenth century; features park and collection of horse-drawn carriages.
April–June: open daily, except Tuesday, 10:00 A.M.–NOON and 2:00 P.M.–6:00 P.M. July–September: open daily, 9:00 A.M.–NOON and 2:00 P.M.–6:00 P.M. October: open daily, except Tuesday, 10:00 A.M.–NOON and 2:00 P.M.–6:00 P.M. November–

March: open Wednesday (afternoon only), Saturday, Sunday, and holidays, 10:00 A.M.–NOON and 2:00 P.M.–5:00 P.M.

Bourges

Palais Jacques-Coeur
18000 Bourges
48/24-06-87
Fifteenth century.
Open daily. April–October: 9:00 A.M.–11:15 A.M. and 2:00 P.M.–5:15 P.M. November–March: 10:00 A.M.–11:15 A.M. and 2:00 P.M.–4:15 P.M. Closed January 1, May 1, November 1, December 25.

Brissac

49320 Brissac-Quincé
41/91-23-43
Middle Ages–seventeenth century.
February 7–March 15: open daily, except Tuesday, 9:30 A.M.–11:30 A.M. and 2:15 P.M.–4:15 P.M. March 16–June: open daily, except Tuesday, 9:30 A.M.–11:30 A.M. and 2:15 P.M.–5:15 P.M. July–August: open daily, 9:30 A.M.–11:30 A.M. and 2:15 P.M.–5:45 P.M. September 1–November 15: open daily, except Tuesday, 9:30 A.M.–11:30 A.M. and 2:15 P.M.–5:15 P.M. Closed November 16–February 6.

Chambord

41250 Bracieux
54/46-31-32, 78-19-47
Sixteenth century.
Open daily. April–mid-June: 9:30 A.M.–NOON and 2:00 P.M.–6:00 P.M. Mid-June–August: 9:30 A.M.–NOON and 2:00 P.M.–7:00 P.M. September–October: 9:30 A.M.–NOON and 2:00 P.M.–6:00 P.M. November–March: 9:30 A.M.–NOON and 2:00 P.M.–5:00 P.M. Closed January 1, May 1, November 1, November 11, December 25.

Châteaudun

28200 Châteaudun
37/45-22-70, 36-45-85
Twelfth, fifteenth, and sixteenth centuries.
Open daily. April 15–October: 9:30 A.M.–11:45 A.M. and 2:00 P.M.–6:00 P.M. November–April 14: 10:00 A.M.–11:45 A.M. and 2:00 P.M.–4:00 P.M.

Chaumont-sur-Loire

41150 Onzain
54/78-19-47, 46-98-03
Sixteenth century.
Open daily. April–September: 9:30 A.M.–11:35 A.M. and 1:45 P.M.–5:35 P.M. October–March: 9:45 A.M.–NOON and 2:00 P.M.–4:00 P.M. Closed January 1, May 1, November 1, and December 25.

Chazé-sur-Argos

49114 Chazé-sur-Argos
41/92-13-62
Fifteenth century.
May 15–September 15: open daily, 3:00 P.M.–5:00 P.M. Closed September 16–May 14.

Chenonceau

37150 Bléré
47/29-90-07, 29-93-52
Sixteenth century; features waxworks museum.
Open daily. February 15–28: 9:00 A.M.–5:30 P.M. March 1–15: 9:00 A.M.–6:00 P.M. March 16–September 15: 9:00 A.M.–7:00 P.M. October: 9:00 A.M.–6:00 P.M. November 1–15: 9:00 A.M.–5:00 P.M. November 16–February 14: 9:00 A.M.–NOON and 2:00 P.M.–4:30 P.M.

Cheverny

41700 Contres
54/79-96-29
Seventeenth century.
Open daily. March: 9:00 A.M.–NOON and
2:15 P.M.–5:30 P.M. April–May 15: 9:00
A.M.–NOON and 2:15 P.M.–6:15 P.M. May
16–June 14: 9:00 A.M.–NOON and 2:15 P.M.–
6:30 P.M. June 15–September 15: 9:00 A.M.–
6:30 P.M. September 16–October: 9:00
A.M.–NOON and 2:15 P.M.–6:00 P.M. November–February: 9:30 A.M.–NOON and 2:15
P.M.–5:00 P.M.

Chinon

37500 Chinon
47/93-13-45
Thirteenth and fifteenth centuries.
March 15–May: open daily, 9:00 A.M.–
NOON and 2:00 P.M.–6:00 P.M. June–September: 9:00 A.M.–6:00 P.M. October–March 14:
9:00 A.M.–NOON and 2:00 P.M.–5:00 P.M.
Closed December–January.

Gien

45500 Gien
37/67-24-11
Fifteenth century; features international
hunting museum.
Open daily. April 16–October: 9:15 A.M.–
11:45 A.M. and 2:15 P.M.–6:30 P.M. November–April 15: 9:15 A.M.–11:45 A.M. and 2:15
P.M.–5:30 P.M.

La Bussière

45230 Châtillon-Coligny
38/35-93-35
Sixteenth, seventeenth, and nineteenth
centuries; features aquarium and museum
of fishing.
March 15–November 15: open daily, except Tuesday, 9:00 A.M.–NOON and 2:00
P.M.–6:00 P.M. November 15–March 14:
open Sunday and holidays only, 9:00 A.M.–
NOON and 2:00 P.M.–5:00 P.M.

La Chapelle-sur-Oudon

49500 Segré
41/92-20-04
Eighteenth century.
July–September 15: open daily, except
Tuesday, 3:00 P.M.–6:00 P.M. Closed September 16–June.

Langeais

37130 Langeais
47/96-72-60, 1/329-55-10
Fifteenth century.
March 15–June: open daily, except Monday, 9:00 A.M.–NOON and 2:00 P.M.–6:30 P.M.
July–August: open daily, except Monday
(morning), 9:00 A.M.–6:30 P.M. September
1–15: open daily, except Monday (morning), 9:00 A.M.–NOON and 2:00 P.M.–6:30
P.M. September 16–30: open daily, except
Monday (morning), 9:00 A.M.–NOON and
2:00 P.M.–6:00 P.M. October–November 1:
open daily, except Monday, 9:00 A.M.–
NOON and 2:00 P.M.–5:00 P.M. November 2–
March 14: open daily, except Monday,
9:00 A.M.–NOON and 2:00 P.M.–4:30 P.M.

La Verrerie

Ozion
18700 Aubigny-sur-Nère
48/58-06-91
Fifteenth–sixteenth centuries.
February 15–November 15: open daily,
10:00 A.M.–NOON and 2:00 P.M.–7:00 P.M.
Closed November 16–February 14.

Le Grand Pressigny

37350 Le Grand Pressigny
47/94-90-20
Twelfth, fifteenth, and sixteenth centuries; features museum of prehistory.
March 15–September: open daily, 9:00 A.M.–NOON and 2:00 P.M.–6:00 P.M. October–December and February–March 14: open daily, except Wednesday, 9:00 A.M.–NOON and 2:00 P.M.–5:00 P.M. Closed January.

Loches

37600 Loches
Logis Royal
47/59-01-32
Fifteenth–sixteenth centuries.
Open daily. March 15–May: 9:00 A.M.–NOON and 2:00 P.M.–6:00 P.M. June–September: 9:00 A.M.–6:00 P.M. October–March 14: 9:00 A.M.–NOON and 2:00 P.M.–5:00 P.M. Closed December–January.

Donjon

47/59-07-86
Twelfth and fifteenth centuries.
March 15–May: open daily, 9:30 A.M.–12:30 P.M. and 2:30 P.M.–5:30 P.M. June–September: open daily, 9:30 A.M.–6:30 P.M. October–March 14: open daily, except Wednesday, 9:30 A.M.–12:30 P.M. and 2:30 P.M.–5:30 P.M.

Meillant

18200 St-Amand-Montrond
48/96-16-51
Fifteenth–sixteenth centuries; features collection of automobiles and horse-drawn carriages.
Open daily, 9:00 A.M.–11:45 A.M. and 2:00 P.M.–6:45 P.M.

Montgeoffroy Mazé

49250 Beaufort-en-Vallée
41/80-60-02
Eighteenth century.
Palm Sunday–November 1: open daily, 9:30 A.M.–NOON and 2:00 P.M.–7:00 P.M. Closed November 2–Palm Sunday.

Montreuil-Bellay

49260 Montreuil-Bellay
41/52-33-06
Middle Ages–Renaissance.
April–June: open daily, except Tuesday, 10:00 A.M.–NOON and 2:00 P.M.–6:00 P.M. July–August: open daily, except Tuesday (morning), 10:00 A.M.–NOON and 2:30 P.M.–6:30 P.M. September–October: 10:00 A.M.–NOON and 2:00 P.M.–6:00 P.M. Closed November–March.

Montsoreau

49370 Montsoreau
41/51-70-25
Fifteenth century; features museum.
Open daily. April–September: 9:00 A.M.–NOON and 2:00 P.M.–7:00 P.M. October–March: 9:00 A.M.–NOON and 2:00 P.M.–5:00 P.M.

Nohant

36400 La Châtre
54/31-06-04, 34-97-85
Nineteenth century (house of George Sand).
Open daily. April–October 15: 9:00 A.M.–11:15 A.M. and 2:00 P.M.–5:30 P.M. October 16–March: 10:00 A.M.–11:15 A.M. and 2:00 P.M.–3:30 P.M.

Saché

37190 Azay-le-Rideau
47/28-86-50
Sixteenth and nineteenth centuries; features Balzac museum.
March 15–May: open daily, 9:00 A.M.–NOON and 2:00 P.M.–6:00 P.M. June–September: open daily, 9:00 A.M.–6:00 P.M. October–November and February–March 14: open daily, except Wednesday, 9:00 A.M.–NOON and 2:00 P.M.–5:00 P.M. Closed December–January.

St-Martin-de-la-Place (Boumois)

49160 Longue-Jumelles
41/51-35-50
Middle Ages–Renaissance.
Easter–November 1: open daily, except Tuesday, 10:00 A.M.–NOON and 2:00 P.M.–6:00 P.M. Closed November–Easter.

Saumur

49400 Saumur
41/51-30-46
Middle Ages; features museum.
April–June: open daily, 9:00 A.M.–11:30 A.M. and 2:00 P.M.–6:00 P.M. July–August: open daily, 9:00 A.M.–7:00 P.M. September: open daily, 9:00 A.M.–6:30 P.M. October: open daily, 9:00 A.M.–6:00 P.M. November–March: open daily, except Tuesday, 10:00 A.M.–11:30 A.M. and 2:00 P.M.–5:00 P.M. Closed November 1, December 25, and January 1.

Sully-sur-Loire

45600 Sully-sur-Loire
38/62-04-88
Fourteenth and sixteenth centuries.
Open daily. May–September: 9:00 A.M.–NOON and 2:00 P.M.–6:00 P.M. October–April: 10:00 A.M.–NOON and 2:00 P.M.–5:00 P.M. Closed December–January.

Ussé

Rigny-Ussé
37420 Avoine
47/95-54-05
Fifteenth–seventeenth centuries.
Open daily. March 15–April 22: 9:00 A.M.–NOON and 2:00 P.M.–6:00 P.M. April 23–September: 9:00 A.M.–NOON and 2:00 P.M.–7:00 P.M. October: 10:00 A.M.–NOON and 2:00 P.M.–6:00 P.M. Closed November–March 14.

Valençay

36600 Valençay
54/00-10-66
Sixteenth–seventeenth centuries.
Mid-March–mid-November: open daily, 9:00 A.M.–11:15 A.M. and 2:00 P.M.–6:15 P.M. or until sunset. Closed mid-November–mid-March.

Villandry

37300 Joué-les-Tours
47/50-02-09
Twelfth, sixteenth, and eighteenth centuries; features Renaissance gardens.
Open daily. March 15–May: 9:00 A.M.–6:00 P.M. June–September: 9:00 A.M.–7:00 P.M. October–November 11: 9:00 A.M.–6:00 P.M. Closed November 12–March 14.
Gardens only: open daily, year-round. January–March: 9:00 A.M.–6:00 P.M. April–May: 9:00 A.M.–7:00 P.M. June–September: 8:30 A.M.–8:00 P.M. October–December: 9:00 A.M.–sunset.

MUSEUMS AND COLLECTIONS

Archeology and Prehistory

Argentomagus

St-Marcel
36200 Argenton-sur-Creuse
54/24-12-51, 24-25-12
Gallo-Roman ruins.
Open daily, year-round.

Musée des Fouilles

4 Rue du Prieuré
36200 Argenton-sur-Creuse
54/24-12-51, 24-25-12
May 16–September 15: open daily, 10:00
A.M.–NOON and 2:00 P.M.–6:30 P.M. September 16–May 15: open Sunday and holidays, 2:00 P.M.–6:00 P.M., and by appointment.

Drevant

18200 St-Amand-Montrond
48/96-34-20
Gallo-Roman site.
April 22–November 1: open Saturday, Sunday, and holidays only, by appointment.
Closed November 2–April 21.

Montbouy

45230 Châtillon-Coligny
38/92-52-03
Gallo-Roman amphitheater.
Open daily, year-round.

Musée Archéologique

Prison d'Etape
Rue de Glatigny
45410 Artenay
38/80-40-17, 80-06-95

Open daily, year-round. Open only to groups, by appointment.

Musée Archéologique

Château de Blois
41000 Blois
54/78-06-62, 74-16-06
July–August: open daily, 2:00 P.M.–5:30 P.M.
September–June: open Monday and Wednesday, 9:00 A.M.–NOON and 2:00 P.M.–5:30 P.M.

Musée Lapidaire

Cloître St-Saturnin
Rue Munier
41000 Blois
54/78-06-62, 74-10-06
March 15–October: open daily, except Monday and Tuesday, 10:00 A.M.–NOON and 2:30 P.M.–5:30 P.M. November–March 14: open Wednesday, Saturday, Sunday, and holidays, 10:00 A.M.–NOON and 2:00 P.M.–5:00 P.M.

Musée Bonnevalais

Rue St-Roch
28800 Bonneval
38/73-61-85
Open daily, year-round, by appointment only.

Hôtel Bertrand

2 Descente des Cordeliers
36000 Châteauroux
54/27-26-31
(For hours, see listing under Fine and Decorative Arts.)

Musée du Vieux-Cravant

Mairie
Cravant-les-Coteaux
37500 Chinon
47/93-12-40
Open daily, except Tuesday, 2:30 P.M.–
6:00 P.M.

Musée de la Préhistoire

37350 Le Grand Pressigny
47/94-90-20
(For hours, see *Le Grand Pressigny*, under
Major Châteaux.)

Musée Historique et Archéologique de l'Orléanais

Hôtel Cabu
Place Abbé-Desnoyers
45000 Orléans
38/53-39-22
Open daily, except Tuesday. April–September: 10:00 A.M.–NOON and 2:00 P.M.–
6:00 P.M. October–March: 10:00 A.M.–NOON
and 2:00 P.M.–5:00 P.M.

Musée Municipal

17 Rue de la Couronne
45300 Pithiviers
38/30-10-72
(For hours, see listing under Fine and
Decorative Arts.)

Musée Archéologique M. de Marcheville

Le Carroir Doré
La Chancellerie
14 Rue de la Résistance
41200 Romorantin
54/76-22-06, 76-31-10 (mornings)
Open daily, year-round, by appointment
only.

Musée St-Vic

Cours Manuel
18200 St-Amand-Montrond
48/96-55-20
Open daily, year-round. Tuesday–Saturday, 10:00 A.M.–NOON and 3:00 P.M.–6:00
P.M. Sunday and holidays, 3:00 P.M.–7:00
P.M.

Musée Archéologique de Touraine

25 Rue du Commerce
37000 Tours
47/66-22-32
March 15–September: open daily, 9:00
A.M.–NOON and 2:00 P.M.–6:00 P.M. October–March 14: open daily, except Friday,
9:00 A.M.–NOON and 2:00 P.M.–5:00 P.M.

Musée de Minerve

Place du Musée
37290 Yzeures-sur-Creuse
47/94-55-01
Open daily, 9:00 A.M.–5:30 P.M.

Automobiles and Horse-Drawn Carriages

Musée des Voitures Hippomobiles

La Cave aux Bussards
Bords de Vienne
Route d'Avoine
37500 Chinon
47/61-08-94
April–September: open Saturday, Sunday,
and holidays, 9:00 A.M.–NOON and 2:00
P.M.–6:00 P.M. Groups by appointment,
Monday–Friday. Closed October–March.

Musée Municipal de la Course Automobile

29-31 Faubourg d'Orléans
41200 Romorantin
54/76-07-06
Open daily, except Tuesday. April–September: Monday, 10:00 A.M.–NOON and 2:00 P.M.–5:00 P.M.; Wednesday and Saturday, 10:00 A.M.–NOON and 2:00 P.M.–7:00 P.M.; Thursday and Friday, 10:00 A.M.–NOON and 2:00 P.M.–6:00 P.M.; Sunday and holidays, 2:00 P.M.–7:00 P.M. October–March: Monday, 11:00 A.M.–NOON and 2:00 P.M.–5:00 P.M.; Wednesday and Saturday, 11:00 A.M.–NOON and 2:00 P.M.–7:00 P.M.; Thursday and Friday, 11:00 A.M.–NOON and 2:00 P.M.–6:00 P.M.; Sunday and holidays, 2:00 P.M.–7:00 P.M.

Musée des Voitures Automobiles Anciennes

36600 Valençay
54/00-10-66
January–mid-March: open Saturday, Sunday, and holidays, 9:00 A.M.–NOON and 2:00 P.M.–sunset. Mid-March–mid-November: open daily, 9:00 A.M.–NOON and 2:00 P.M.–7:00 P.M. Closed mid-November–December.

See also listings for *Apremont, Bouges,* and *Meillant,* under Major Châteaux.

Faïence and Porcelain

Ecomusée de la Forêt des Loges

Nibelle
45340 Beaune-la-Rolande
38/33-78-75

May–October: open Sunday and holidays, 3:00 P.M.–6:00 P.M. Groups by appointment, Monday–Saturday. Closed November–April.

Musée de la Faïencerie

Manufacture de Gien
Place de la Victoire
45500 Gien
38/67-00-05
Open daily, by appointment only.

Fine and Decorative Arts

Musée des Beaux-Arts

10 Rue du Musée
49000 Angers
41/88-64-65
Winter: open daily, except Tuesday, 10:00 A.M.–NOON and 2:00 P.M.–4:00 P.M. Summer: open daily, 9:00 A.M.–NOON and 2:00 P.M.–6:00 P.M.

Musée des Tapissiers

Château d'Angers
49000 Angers
Outstanding collection of tapestries.
(For hours, see listing for *Angers,* under Major Châteaux.)

Musée Turpin-de-Crissé

Hôtel Prince
32-bis Rue Lenepveu
49000 Angers
41/88-94-27
Winter: open daily, except Tuesday, 10:00 A.M.–NOON and 2:00 P.M.–4:00 P.M. Summer: open daily, 9:00 A.M.–NOON and 2:00 P.M.–6:00 P.M.

Musée des Beaux-Arts

Château de Blois
41000 Blois
54/78-06-62, 74-16-06
(For hours, see listing for *Blois*, under Major Châteaux.)

Hôtel Lallemant

6 Rue Bourbonnoux
18000 Bourges
48/70-19-32
Open daily, except Monday. April–October 15: 10:00 A.M.–11:30 A.M. and 2:00 P.M.–5:00 P.M. October 16–March: 10:00 A.M.–11:30 A.M. and 2:00 P.M.–4:00 P.M. Closed January 1, May 1, November 1, and December 25.

Hôtel Bertrand

2 Descente des Cordeliers
36000 Châteauroux
54/27-26-31
Also includes archeological and Napoleonic collections and an exhibition on the folklore of Berry.
June–September: open daily, except Monday, 9:00 A.M.–NOON and 2:00 P.M.–6:00 P.M. October–May: open daily, except Monday, 2:00 P.M.–5:00 P.M.

Musée Oscar-Roty

3 Place du Petit Cloître
45150 Jargeau
1/222-24-96
May–October: open Saturday afternoon, Sunday, and holidays, 10:00 A.M.–NOON and 2:00 P.M.–6:00 P.M. Closed November–April.

Musée Municipal

17 Rue de la Couronne
45300 Pithiviers
38/30-10-72

Open daily, except Tuesday, 10:00 A.M.–NOON and 2:00 P.M.–6:00 P.M.

Musée des Arts Décoratifs et Musée du Cheval

Château de Saumur
49400 Saumur
41/51-30-46
(For hours, see listing for *Saumur*, under Major Châteaux.)

Musée des Beaux-Arts

18 Place François-Sicard
37000 Tours
47/05-68-73
April–September: open daily, 9:00 A.M.–NOON and 2:00 P.M.–6:00 P.M. October–March: open daily, except Tuesday, 9:00 A.M.–NOON and 2:00 P.M.–5:00 P.M. Closed January 1, May 1, July 14, November 1 and 11, and December 25.

Musée du Gemmail

7 Rue du Murier
37000 Tours
47/61-01-19
April 15–October 15: open daily, except Monday, 10:00 A.M.–NOON and 2:30 P.M.–6:00 P.M. Closed October 16–April 14.

Folklore, Popular Art, and Local History

Musée de l'Hôtel de Ville

Rue François-Ier
37400 Amboise
47/57-00-98
Open daily, except Saturday, Sunday, and

holidays, 9:00 A.M.–NOON and 2:00 P.M.–
6:00 P.M. By appointment only.

Musée Régional des Arts et Traditions de l'Orléanais

Château Dunois
45190 Beaugency
38/44-55-23
March 15–September: open daily, 9:00
A.M.–NOON and 2:00 P.M.–6:00 P.M. October–March 14: open daily, except Tuesday, 9:00 A.M.–NOON and 2:00 P.M.–4:00 P.M.
(Groups may visit on Tuesday by
appointment.)

Musée du Berry

Hôtel Cujas
4 Rue des Arènes
18000 Bourges
48/70-41-92
Open daily, except Tuesday, 10:00 A.M.–
11:30 A.M. and 2:00 P.M.–5:30 P.M. Closed
January 1, May 1, November 1, and December 25.

Musée de Folklore du Berry

Hôtel Bertrand
2 Descente des Cordeliers
36000 Châteauroux
54/27-26-31
(For hours, see listing under Fine and
Decorative Arts.)

Musée des Arts et Traditions Populaires

Chapelle Ste-Radegonde
37500 Chinon
47/93-17-85
January–April 22 and July–August 15:
open daily, 10:00 A.M.–6:00 P.M., by appointment. Closed April 23–June 30 and
August 16–December 31.

Musée des Arts Populaires et Traditions Paysannes

Château du Plaix
Route de St-Hilaire
81600 Lignières-en-Berry
70/29-77-94
July–mid-September: open Sunday and
holidays, 3:00 P.M.–8:00 P.M. Closed mid-
September–June.

Musée de Sologne

Hôtel de Ville
41200 Romorantin
54/76-07-06
Open daily, except Tuesday. April–September: Monday and Wednesday, 9:30
A.M.–11:30 A.M. and 2:00 P.M.–5:30 P.M.;
Thursday–Saturday, 10:00 A.M.–11:30 A.M.
and 2:00 P.M.–5:30 P.M.; Sunday and holidays, 10:00 A.M.–11:30 A.M. and 2:00 P.M.–
6:00 P.M. October–March: Monday,
Wednesday, Thursday, and Friday, 10:00
A.M.–11:30 A.M. and 2:00 P.M.–5:00 P.M.; Saturday, 10:00 A.M.–11:30 A.M. and 2:00 P.M.–
5:30 P.M.; Sunday and holidays, 11:00 A.M.–
NOON and 2:00 P.M.–5:30 P.M.

Musée St-Vic

Cours Manuel
18200 St-Amand-Montrond
48/96-55-20
(For hours, see listing under Archeology
and Prehistory.)

Musée d'Histoire Locale

Château des Rohan
37800 Ste-Maure-de-Touraine
47/65-66-35
June 15–September 15: open daily, except
Sunday and holidays, 10:00 A.M.–NOON and
3:00 P.M.–6:00 P.M. September 16–June 14:
Open only to groups, by appointment.

Centre Artistique Jean-Baffier

Mairie de Sancoins
18100 Sancoins
48/74-50-81
Open daily, by appointment only.

Musée Municipal d'Histoire et de Traditions Locales

41130 Selles-sur-Cher
54/97-40-19
July–August: open Tuesday and Thursday, 3:00 P.M.–6:00 P.M.; Saturday, Sunday, and holidays, 10:00 A.M.–NOON and 2:30 P.M.–6:30 P.M. September–June: open by appointment only.

Musée Municipal

Cloître de la Trinité
41100 Vendôme
54/77-26-13
Open daily, 9:00 A.M.–NOON and 2:00 P.M.–6:00 P.M.

History

Musée de Cires

Chenonceaux
37150 Bléré
47/29-90-07, 29-93-52
Waxworks museum depicting four centuries of history.
(For hours, see listing for *Chenonceau*, under Major Châteaux.)

Hôtel Bertrand

2 Descente des Cordeliers
36000 Châteauroux
54/27-26-31
(For hours, see listing under Fine and Decorative Arts.)

Musée du Vieux-Chinon

Maison des Etats-Généraux
44 Rue Haute
37500 Chinon
47/93-17-85
Open daily, except Tuesday. June–August: 10:00 A.M.–NOON and 3:00 P.M.–7:00 P.M. September–May: 10:00 A.M.–NOON and 2:00 P.M.–5:00 P.M. Closed January.

Musée Charles-VII

18500 Mehun-sur-Yèvre
48/57-30-25
April 15–June 9: open Monday and Saturday, 2:30 P.M.–6:30 P.M.; open Sunday and holidays, 10:30 A.M.–NOON and 2:30 P.M.–6:30 P.M. June 10–30: open Monday and Wednesday–Saturday, 2:30 P.M.–6:30 P.M.; open Sunday and holidays, 10:30 A.M.–NOON and 2:30 P.M.–6:30 P.M. July–August: open daily, except Tuesday, 10:30 A.M.–NOON and 2:30 P.M.–6:30 P.M. September 1–15: open Monday and Wednesday–Saturday, 2:30 P.M.–6:30 P.M.; open Sunday and holidays, 10:30 A.M.–NOON and 2:30 P.M.–6:30 P.M. September 6–30: open Monday and Saturday, 2:30 P.M.–6:30 P.M.; open Sunday and holidays, 10:30 A.M.–NOON and 2:30 P.M.–6:30 P.M. October: open Sunday and holidays, 2:30 P.M.–5:30 P.M. Closed November–April 14.

Maison de Jeanne d'Arc

Place du Général-de-Gaulle
45000 Orléans
38/53-39-22
Open daily, except Monday. May–October: 10:00 A.M.–NOON and 2:00 P.M.–6:00 P.M. November–April: 2:00 P.M.–6:00 P.M.

Musée de l'Hôtel de Ville

37120 Richelieu
47/58-10-13
July–August: open daily, except Tuesday,
10:00 A.M.–NOON and 2:00 P.M.–6:00 P.M.
September–June: open daily, except Tuesday, Sunday, and holidays, 10:00 A.M.–
NOON and 2:00 P.M.–4:00 P.M.

Historial de la Touraine

Château Royal de Tours
Quai d'Orléans
37000 Tours
47/66-75-92
Open daily. April–May: 10:00 A.M.–6:00
P.M. June–September: 10:00 A.M.–8:00 P.M.
October: 10:00 A.M.–6:00 P.M. November–
December: 2:00 P.M.–6:00 P.M. Closed Janu-
ary–March.

Hunting

Salle des Trophées

Château de Cheverny
41700 Contres
54/79-96-29
(For hours, see listing for *Cheverny*, under
Major Châteaux.)

Musée International de la Chasse

Château de Gien
45500 Gien
38/67-24-11
(For hours, see listing for *Gien*, under Major Châteaux.)

Musée de Vénérie

Château de Montpoupon
Céré-la-Ronde
37460 Montrésor
47/94-23-62
April 1–23: open daily, 2:00 P.M.–6:00 P.M.

April 24–June 14: open Saturday, Sunday,
and holidays, 2:00 P.M.–6:00 P.M. June 15–
September 30: open Monday–Friday,
10:00 A.M.–NOON and 2:00 P.M.–7:00 P.M.;
open Saturday, Sunday, and holidays,
10:00 A.M.–7:00 P.M. October: open Saturday, Sunday, and holidays, 2:00 P.M.–6:00
P.M. Closed November–March.

Literature

Musée Balzac

Château de Saché
37190 Azay-le-Rideau
47/26-86-50
(For hours, see listing for *Saché*, under
Major Châteaux.)

Musée Rabelais

La Devinière
Seuilly
37500 Chinon
47/93-13-45
Rabelais's birthplace.
March 15–September: open daily, 9:00
A.M.–NOON and 2:00 P.M.–6:00 P.M. Octo-
ber–March 14: open daily, except
Wednesday, 9:00 A.M.–NOON and 2:00 P.M.–
5:00 P.M. Closed December–January.

Musée René Descartes et René Boylesve

29 Rue Descartes
37160 Descartes
47/94-91-02
Open daily, except Tuesday, 2:00 P.M.–
6:30 P.M.

Maison de Tante Léonie

4 Rue du Dr-Proust
28120 Illiers-Combray
37/36-21-93
Mementos of Marcel Proust.

Open daily, except Tuesday, 2:15 P.M.–
7:00 P.M.

Musée George Sand et de la Vallée Noire

71 Rue Venose
36400 La Châtre
(For hours, see listing for *Nohant*, under
Major Châteaux.)

Musée Girodet

2 Rue de la Chaussée
45200 Montargis
38/85-28-16
Open daily, except Monday, 9:00 A.M.–
NOON and 1:30 P.M.–5:30 P.M.

Musée Peguy

11 Rue du Tabour
45000 Orléans
38/53-20-23
Open daily, except Sunday and holidays,
1:30 P.M.–6:00 P.M.

Maison de George Sand

Villa Algira
Gargilesse
36190 Orsennes
54/47-84-14
Open daily. April–June: 10:00 A.M.–NOON
and 2:00 P.M.–6:00 P.M. July–September:
9:30 A.M.–12:30 P.M. and 2:30 P.M.–7:00 P.M.
Closed October–March.

Souvenirs d'Alain-Fournier

Ecole
Epineuil-le-Fleuriel
18360 Saulzais-le-Potier
48/56-02-23
Open daily, by appointment, except during school hours.

Military History

Musée des Trois Guerres (1870, 1914, 1940)

Diors
36130 Déols
54/26-02-16, 26-01-84
Open daily, except Tuesday. January: 2:00
P.M.–6:00 P.M. March–December: 9:00 A.M.–
NOON and 2:00 P.M.–6:00 P.M. Closed
February.

Musée de la Bataille de Loigny

(November 2, 1870)

Loigny-la-Bataille
28140 Orgères-en-Beauce
Open daily, except Sunday/holiday morning, 9:00 A.M.–5:00 P.M.

Musée des Equipages Militaires et du Train

Rue du Plat d'Etain
37000 Tours
47/61-44-46
Open year-round, Monday–Friday, 1:30
P.M.–5:00 P.M. Saturday, Sunday, and holidays, open only to groups by appointment.

Natural Science

Museum d'Histoire Naturelle

Rue Messire-Jacques
18000 Bourges
48/70-19-82
Open daily, except Monday and Tuesday,
2:00 P.M.–6:00 P.M.

Collections d'Insectes et de Monnaies Anciennes

Mairie
36210 Chabris
54/40-03-32
July–August: open Sunday and holidays, 3:00 P.M.–5:00 P.M. Closed September–June.

Grotte du Foulon

35 Rue des Fouleries
28200 Châteaudun
37/45-19-60, 45-01-59
Open daily, except Monday. May–September: 10:00 A.M.–NOON and 2:00 P.M.–6:00 P.M. October–April: 2:00 P.M.–6:00 P.M.

Musée d'Ornithologie et d'Antiquités Egyptiennes

3 Rue Toufaire
28200 Châteaudun
37/45-55-36
Open daily, except Tuesday. April–September: 10:00 A.M.–NOON and 2:00 P.M.–6:00 P.M. October–March: 10:00 A.M.–NOON and 2:00 P.M.–5:00 P.M. Closed October 15–November 15.

Musée des Oiseaux

Cour des Moines
Maison pour la Nature de Cambrai
36300 Le Blanc
54/37-19-31
Open only to groups, by appointment.

Caves Pétrifiantes

Savonnières
37300 Joué-les-Tours
47/50-00-09
April–September 15: open daily, 9:00 A.M.–6:30 P.M. September 16–December 23 and March: open daily, except Thursday, 9:00 A.M.–NOON and 2:00 P.M.–6:00 P.M. Closed December 24–February.

Musée de Sciences Naturelles

2 Rue Marcel-Proust
45000 Orléans
38/42-25-58
Open daily, except Saturday. Monday, Tuesday, Thursday, and Friday, 2:00 P.M.–6:00 P.M. Wednesday, Sunday, and holidays, 10:00 A.M.–NOON and 2:00 P.M.–6:00 P.M.

Musée des Faluns Savignéens

Faubourg de la Rue
37340 Savigny-sur-Lathan
47/24-60-19
July–August: open daily, except Thursday, 2:30 P.M.–6:00 P.M. September–June: Saturday, Sunday, and holidays, 2:30 P.M.–6:00 P.M. Closed November 15–March 15.

Wines and Viticulture

Musée de la Cave Touristique

37140 Bourgueil
47/97-72-01
Open daily. April–September: 10:00 A.M.–12:30 P.M. and 2:00 P.M.–7:30 P.M. October–March: 10:00 A.M.–12:30 P.M. and 2:00 P.M.–6:00 P.M. Closed December–January.

Musée de la Tonnellerie

1 Avenue de Patay
45430 Chécy
38/62-72-45
June: open by appointment only. July–September: open Sunday and holidays, 3:00 P.M.–6:00 P.M. Closed October–May.

Musée Animé du Vin et de la Tonnellerie

12 Rue Voltaire
37500 Chinon
47/93-25-63, 93-32-87
Open daily, except Thursday. April–June:
10:00 A.M.–NOON and 2:00 P.M.–6:00 P.M.
July–August: 10:00 A.M.–NOON and 2:00
P.M.–7:00 P.M. September: 10:00 A.M.–NOON
and 2:00 P.M.–6:00 P.M. Closed October–
March.

Souvenirs de l'Agriculture et de la Viticulture Anciennes

Oisly
41700 Contres
54/79-52-69
June 15–September 15: open Tuesday and
Saturday, 2:30 P.M.–6:30 P.M.

Musée des Vins de Touraine

Celliers St-Julien
16 Rue Nationale
37000 Tours
47/61-07-93
Open daily, except Tuesday, 9:00 A.M.–
NOON and 2:00 P.M.–6:00 P.M.

Miscellaneous

Maquettes d'Inventions de Léonard de Vinci

Manoir de Clos-Lucé
37400 Amboise
47/57-62-88
Open daily. June–September 15: 9:00 A.M.–
6:30 P.M. September 16–May: 9:00 A.M.–

11:30 A.M. and 2:00 P.M.–6:30 P.M. Closed
January and December 25.

Musée de la Poste (postal service)

Hôtel de Joyeuse
6 Rue de Joyeuse
37400 Amboise
47/57-00-11
Open daily, except Tuesday. April–September: 9:30 A.M.–NOON and 2:00 P.M.–6:30
P.M. October–March: 10:00 A.M.–NOON and
2:00 P.M.–5:00 P.M. Closed January 1, May
1, Ascension Day, and December 25.

Château des Pêcheurs (fishing)

La Bussière
45230 Châtillon-Coligny
38/35-93-35
(For hours, see listing for La Bussière, under Major Châteaux.)

Musée de Pharmacie St-Roch (pharmacy)

Rue de l'Hospice St-Roch
36100 Issoudun
54/21-01-76
Open daily, except Tuesday. January–
March: Monday and Wednesday, 2:00 P.M.–
6:00 P.M.; Thursday–Sunday and holidays,
2:00 P.M.–7:00 P.M. April–September: 10:00
A.M.–NOON and 2:00 P.M.–7:00 P.M. Closed
October–December.

Fermette Beauceronne Reconstituée et Musée Agricole (agriculture)

Le Grand Bréau
Tivernon
45170 Neuville-aux-Bois
38/39-41-46
Open daily, except Saturday, Sunday, and
holidays, 9:00 A.M.–6:00 P.M.

Musée des Transports (trains)

Rue Carnot
45300 Pithiviers
38/30-50-02
May–October 15: open Sundays and holidays, 2:30 P.M.–6:00 P.M. Closed October 16–April.

Musée des Arts Décoratifs et Musée du Cheval (horses)

Château de Saumur
49400 Saumur
41/51-30-46
(For hours, see listing for *Saumur*, under Major Châteaux.)

GETTING AROUND THE LOIRE VALLEY

By Bus

Coach tours of the major châteaux can be booked from Orléans, Blois, Tours, or Angers. Excursions to the Loire Valley, lasting one to several days, are also available from Paris. For further information, consult a travel agent or SCETA, 7 Rue Pablo-Neruda, 92532 Levallois-Perret Cedex; telephone 1/270-56-00, ext. 536.

By Bicycle

Loisirs Accueil Loiret (3 Rue de la Bretonnerie, 45000 Orléans, telephone 38/62-04-88) not only offers bicycles for hire but also organizes cycling trips. Bicycles may also be rented at certain SNCF stations in the area.

By Rail

Trains run from Paris (Gare d'Austerlitz) to Orléans, Blois, and Tours, and from Paris (Gare Montparnasse) to Angers. Local services connect Tours, Saumur, and Angers. For more detailed information, consult French National Railroads (see "Introduction to France").

By Air

Aerial tours of the Loire châteaux can be booked from the airports at Orléans, Blois-le-Breuil, Tours-St-Symphorien, Saumur, and Angers-Avrille. Travelers may also fly directly to Tours from London's Gatwick Airport via Touraine Air Transport. Consult Air France or a travel agent for particulars.

By Water

The Loire Valley is crisscrossed by rivers and canals. It is possible to rent a boat equipped with living accommodations or to take an organized inland cruise on a boat with or without living accommodations. For information, consult a travel agent, the French Government Tourist Office, or Loisirs Accueil Loiret, 3 Rue de la Bretonnerie, 45000 Orléans, telephone 38/62-04-88.

By Car

The best way to see the Loire Valley is by car, as many of the châteaux and other attractions are not easily accessible by public transportation. The *autoroute* A10 goes directly from Paris to Orléans (about 70 miles) and then to Blois and Tours. The A11 leads through Chartres and Le Mans, where one can turn off for Saumur or Angers. For more information about driving and car rental in France, see the "Introduction to France."

CALENDAR OF FESTIVALS AND MAJOR EVENTS IN THE LOIRE VALLEY

Easter	Celebration in the Benedictine abbey church, St-Benoît-sur-Loire
May 7–8	Joan of Arc Festival, Orléans
Pentecost	Rhododendron Festival, Châteauneuf-sur-Loire
June	*Grand Sacre*, Angers (Sunday after Corpus Christi)
June–July	*Festival d'Anjou*, Angers (theatrical events)
Late June– early July	Touraine Music Festival, Tours International Music Festival, Langeais
July	Friday and Saturday concerts, Sully-sur-Loire
Mid-July	World Folk Festival, Montoire-sur-le-Loir
July 14–15	Traditional Country Market, Loches
Late July	*Carrousel de Saumur* (dressage exhibitions), Saumur
Late July– mid-August	Festival of Classical Music, Palluau
August 4–5	Medieval Market, Chinon
August 16	Feast of St. Roch, St. Satur
Late August	Historical pageant, Ferrières-en-Gatinais
Late August– early September	Summer Festival, International Harp Contest, Gargilesse
Late October– December	International Music Weeks, Orléans
December 24	Midnight Mass, Benedictine abbey church, St. Benoît-sur-Loire

For more specific information, consult the French Government Tourist Office, local publications, or *syndicats d'initiative*.

Son-et-lumière is a form of entertainment that originated along the banks of the Loire in 1952. Literally meaning "sound and light," *son-et-lumière* combines striking sound and lighting effects with spoken narrations or dramatic performances; music is often an important component of these spectacles. They take place in the evening and usually re-create historical events or settings. Several of the Loire châteaux offer *son-et-lumière* presentations, primarily in July–August, but sometimes as early as March or as late as October. These châteaux include Amboise, Azay-le-Rideau, Blois, Chambord, Chenonceau, Cheverny, Chinon and Fougères-sur-Bièvres.

I N D E X

Index of Names

Index of Places

Entries and numbers in boldface indicate the main points of interest and main discussions of the place cited. References to color plates are in italics.

The Publisher has made every effort
to verify that the information in this book
is accurate and up to date.
Readers are invited
to write with more recent information.

The text was set in ITC Garamond by TGA Communications, Inc.
New York.
The book was printed and bound by Novograph, S.A.
Madrid

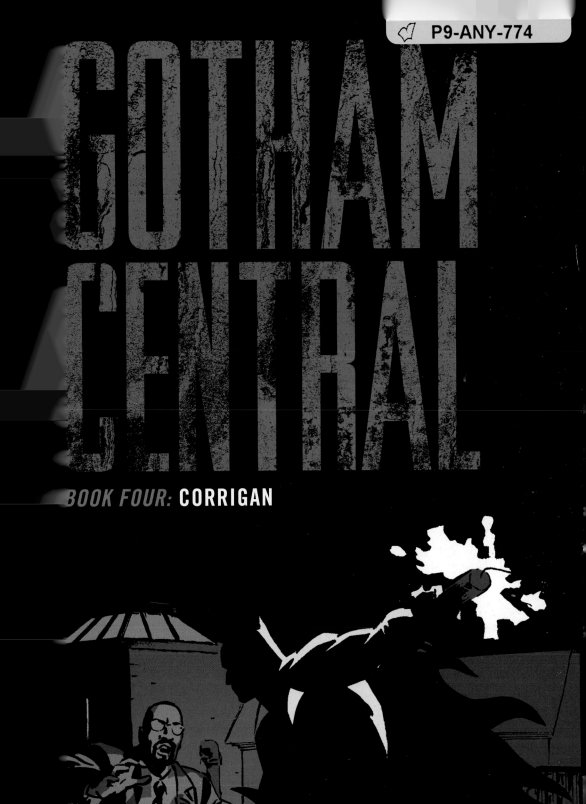

GOTHAM CENTRAL

BOOK FOUR: CORRIGAN

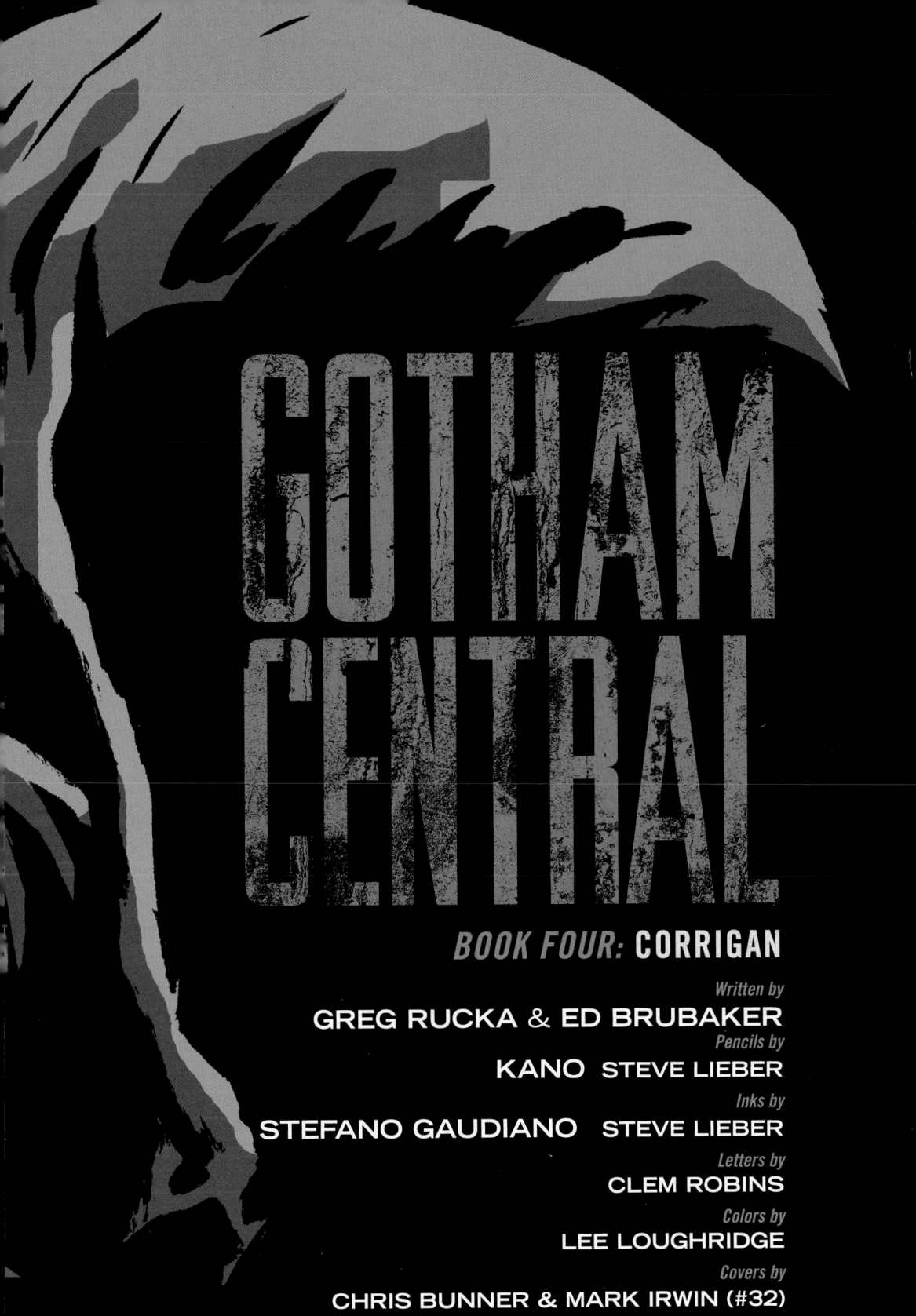

GOTHAM CENTRAL

BOOK FOUR: CORRIGAN

Written by
GREG RUCKA & ED BRUBAKER

Pencils by
KANO   STEVE LIEBER

Inks by
STEFANO GAUDIANO   STEVE LIEBER

Letters by
CLEM ROBINS

Colors by
LEE LOUGHRIDGE

Covers by
CHRIS BUNNER & MARK IRWIN (#32)
SEAN PHILLIPS (#33-35, #37-40)
JOSH MIDDLETON (#36)

DETECTIVE
JOELY BARTLETT
Partner of Vincent
Del Arrazio.

CAPTAIN
MAGGIE SAWYER
First shift commander;
formerly head of Metropolis
Special Crimes Unit.

SGT. VINCENT
DEL ARRAZIO
First shift
second-in-command;
partner of Joely Bartlett.

DETECTIVE
CRISPUS ALLEN
Partner of Renee Montoya.

GOTHAM CITY

POLICE DEPARTMENT
MAJOR CRIMES UNIT

SGT. JACKSON
"SARGE" DAVIES
Second shift
co-second-in-command;
partner of Crowe.

SECOND
SHIFT

DETECTIVE CROWE
Partner of Sarge Davies.

LT. DAVID CORNWELL
Second shift commander.

DETECTIVE
JOSH AZEVEDA
Partner of Trey Hartley.

DETECTIVE
NATE PATTON
Partner of Romy Chandler.

DETECTIVE
TREY HARTLEY
Partner of Josh Azeveda.

DETECTIVE
MARCUS DRIVER
Last MCU officer to be selected

LT. RON PROBSON
Second shift
co-second-in-command.

**DETECTIVE
TOMMY BURKE**
Partner of
Dagmar Procjnow.

**DETECTIVE
ERIC COHEN**
Partner of Andi Kasinsky.

**DETECTIVE
ANDI KASINSKY**
Partner of Eric Cohen.

**DETECTIVE 2ND GRADE
RENEE MONTOYA**
Partner of Crispus Allen.

**DETECTIVE
JOSEPHINE "JOSIE
MAC" MACDONALD**
Has the distinction of being
the first MCU officer selected after
Jim Gordon's retirement.

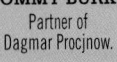

**DETECTIVE
ROMY CHANDLER**
Partner of Nate Patton.

**DETECTIVE
DAGMAR
PROCJNOW**
Partner of Tommy Burke.

POLICE
SUPPORT

NORA FIELDS
City coroner.

STACY
Receptionist;
only person permitted to
operate the Bat-Signal.

**COMMISSIONER
MICHAEL AKINS**
Former commissioner
for Gateway City,
replaced James W. Gordon.

JIM CORRIGAN
GCPD crime scene
investigator.

JAMES W. GORDON
Former Gotham City police
commissioner, and 20-year
veteran of the force. Currently
teaches criminology at
Gotham University.

Cover by Josh Middleton.

GOTHAM CENTRAL BOOK FOUR: CORRIGAN

Library of Congress Cataloging-in-Publication Data

Rucka, Greg.
  Gotham Central. Book four, Corrigan / Greg Rucka, Ed Brubaker, Kano, Steve Lieber.
    p. cm.
  " Originally published in single magazine form in Gotham Central #32-40."
  ISBN 978-1-4012-3194-1
  1. Graphic novels. I. Rucka, Greg. II. Brubaker, Ed. III. Kano. IV. Lieber, Steve. V. Title. VI. Title: Book four, Corrigan
PN6728.G65 R836 2011
741.5'973–dc23
                              2012372680

SUSTAINABLE FORESTRY INITIATIVE

Certified Chain of Custody
20% Certified Forest Content,
80% Certified Sourcing
www.sfiprogram.org
SFI-01042
APPLIES TO TEXT STOCK ONLY

NATURE

Written by
GREG RUCKA

Art by
STEVE LIEBER

Colors by
LEE LOUGHRIDGE

Letters by
CLEM ROBINS

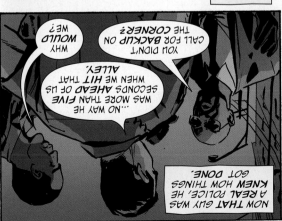

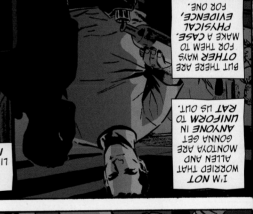

I MEAN, WHEN YOU LIVE IN A WORLD WITH THE JOKER, CAN YOU EVEN SAY WHAT EVIL IS ANYMORE?

DOES ANYONE WHO'S EVER SEEN THE BATMAN--AND I CAN COUNT THE COPS I KNOW WHO HAVE ON ONE HAND--THINK HE'S A GOOD GUY?

I MEAN, C'MON, GROW UP.

THERE'S NO SUCH THING AS GOOD GUYS AND BAD GUYS.

IT'S ALL JUST PEOPLE.

JUST PEOPLE TRYING TO SURVIVE.

AND THAT MEANS THAT SOME OF THEM JUST WON'T.

SO FORGIVE THE HELL OUT OF ME IF I DO WHAT IT TAKES TO MAKE SURE I'M NOT ONE OF THEM.

CUZ AT THE END OF THE DAY, IF IT'S GONNA BE ME OR YOU...

WILCO THREE-TWELVE MOBILE.

BACK IN SERVICE.

...THE SMART MONEY'S GONNA BE ON ME.

19

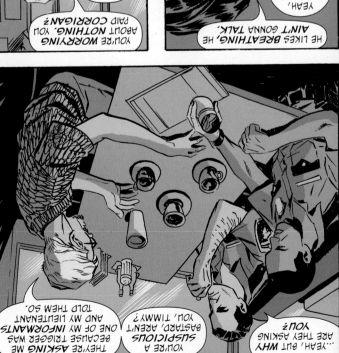

COUPLE OF *BLACK MASK'S* GUYS GOT TAKEN DOWN LAST WEEK SOMETHING *UGLY.*

THE *MAN* HIMSELF IS REACHING OUT, *OFFERING* A *BIG* PAYDAY TO WHOEVER RETURNS THEIR *EFFECTS* TO HIM.

NO QUESTIONS *ASKED,* HE JUST WANTS THE *CONTENTS* OF EVIDENCE BIN #*4678.*

YOU DEALING WITH HIM *DIRECT* ON THIS?

NO, A *CUTOUT,* SOME *CHICK.* BUT THIS IS ON THE *LEVEL,* I'M SURE--

THAT'S NOT *WHY* I'M *ASKING.* SAY WE *CLEAR* THIS *BIN.* YOU MAKING THE *DELIVERY?*

HADN'T *GOT* THAT *FAR.*

WHAT'RE YOU THINKING?

I'M THINKING BLACK MASK IS WHERE THE *NEW* ACTION IS, *ROGER.*

MIGHT BE THE *RIGHT* KIND OF *GUY* TO DO A *FAVOR* FOR, YOU KNOW?

WE DO THIS JOB, YOU LET HIM KNOW WHO WE ARE?

ESTABLISH A *RELATIONSHIP,* SEE WHAT I MEAN?

I GET IT. BUT THAT MEANS I'M *KEEPING* THE FEE.

NO, YOU'LL PAY THE *FEE,* TOO, BECAUSE YOU DON'T HAVE ANYONE *ELSE.*

AND IT'S *TEN GRAND* FOR *EACH* OF US, NOT TOGETHER.

22

BE HAPPY TO.

HEY, DON'T SUPPOSE YOU TWO COULD GIVE ME A HAND WITH THIS STUFF OUT TO THE VAN?

HERE YOU GO.

THANKS.

ALWAYS GOOD TO HAVE SOMETHING LINING YOUR POCKETS.

LOOKS LIKE YOU'LL BE RACKING UP THE O.T.

NO WONDER HE'S SMILING.

"...AND 4678, PLEASE, MARV."

STARTING TO RUN UP A BILL, HERE.

PLUS THE FEE FOR TAKING CARE OF THE STREET RAT. CORRIGAN'S PULLED ME FOR ALMOST TEN GRAND IN TWO DAYS.

"...THAT SHOULD BE THE ATTANASIO SHOOTING..."

DAMN, YOU'RE STILL WORKING THAT ONE?

DRIVER AND MACDONALD WANT TO GO OVER IT AGAIN...

"...BIN 2328, BIN 4409..."

AND I LOVED HER AS A DAUGHTER, AS I LOVE ALL THE ORPHANS WHO LIVE IN THIS PARK UNDER MY CARE.

UNDER MY PROTECTION.

RHKK

UKKK

"...AND SHE LOVED TO READ.

SHE WOULD DUMPSTER-DIVE BEHIND THAT USED BOOK STORE ON PARK FOR ANYTHING SHE COULD SALVAGE.

HER NAME WAS DEE DEE, OFFICERS...

I WOULD.

SOME RUNAWAY GIRL, AND WHO WOULD POSSIBLY MISS HER?

JUST A STREET SLIT, IS THAT WHAT YOU CALLED HER?

DEAD ROBIN

Written by
ED BRUBAKER & GREG RUCKA
Art by
KANO & STEFANO GAUDIANO
Colors by
LEE LOUGHRIDGE
Letters by
CLEM ROBINS

In an effort to regain control over Gotham following a brutal Gang War, Commissioner Akins outlawed masked vigilantes from roaming the city's streets. Officers are ordered to stop Batman and his crew by any means necessary. The Caped Crusader, not wanting to share his risk of retribution, ordered all of his colleagues to leave Gotham. Robin, along with Batgirl, was banished to Bludhaven, where he patrols the alleys looking for crime… or does he?

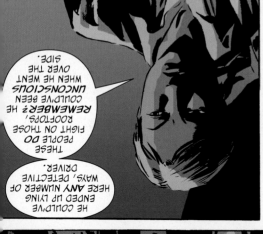

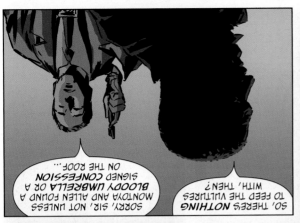

BOREN, GONNA NEED SOME *SHOTS* OVER HERE.

GOT YOU *COVERED*, DETECTIVE.

THIS GOES *STRAIGHT* TO THE *LAB*, AND THEY PROCESS IT *IMMEDIATELY*.

YES, MA'AM.

AND MAKE SURE YOU KEEP IT AWAY FROM *CORRIGAN*...

...I DON'T WANT IT GOING *MISSING* OUT OF *EVIDENCE*.

NO, MA'AM.

BOREN, WHEN YOU'RE *DONE* HERE, WE'RE GONNA NEED SOME *SHOTS* OF THE *LEDGE*.

HOW FAR YOU FIGURE TO THE *ADJACENT* ROOFTOP, RENEE?

MAYBE *TEN* FEET ACROSS? HALF AGAIN THAT *HIGH*?

YEAH, THAT'S HOW IT *LOOKS* TO ME, *TOO*.

THAT SEEM *ANY* HARDER THAN THE KIND OF JUMP ROBIN WOULD *NORMALLY* MAKE?

IF YOU'RE THINKING THIS WAS AN *ACCIDENTAL* DEATH, CRIS, I'M NOT SEEING THE *EVIDENCE* ONE WAY OR THE *OTHER*.

OTHER THAN THAT *BATARANG*, I'M NOT SEEING ANY SIGN OF A *STRUGGLE*, EITHER.

SO HE GOT *DUMPED*. OR *PUSHED*.

HELL, *MAYBE* IT'S *SUICIDE*.

THE KID WORKED FOR *BATMAN* AFTER ALL.

36

GREAT. YOU WANT TO ASK HIM IF ROBIN'S BEEN FEELING *DEPRESSED* RECENTLY?

"HOW'S HE BEEN SLEEPING? ANY SIGNS OF *DRUG USE?* TROUBLE AT *SCHOOL?*"

WE'RE GOING TO HAVE TO TALK TO BATMAN, ONE WAY OR *ANOTHER.*

YOU DON'T *SERIOUSLY* THINK HE'S A *SUSPECT.*

HE'S THE *PRIME* SUSPECT, FAR AS I'M CONCERNED--

THAT'S *CRAP.*

--HE KNEW THE *VICTIM,* KNEW HIM *WELL.* THEY WORKED *TOGETHER.*

FORGET THAT IT'S *MAYBE* ROBIN THE BOY WONDER IN THE ALLEY AND *YOU* TELL ME HOW WE SHOULD PURSUE THIS.

ANY OTHER CASE, WE'D PUT THE *PARTNER* AT THE TOP OF THE LIST OF *SUSPECTS.*

ASSUMING THIS IS MURDER, AND WE DON'T *KNOW* THAT YET.

YEAH, *ASSUMING* IT'S--

OH MY GOD. OH MY GOD, CRIS.

THINK ABOUT IT.

IF THAT *REALLY* IS *ROBIN* AND WE *I.D.* THE *BODY,* EVERYONE'S GONNA *KNOW* WHO HE *WAS.*

OBVIOUSLY.

NO, YOU DON'T *GET* IT. WE PUT ROBIN'S *SECRET IDENTITY* UNDER THE *MICROSCOPE...*

...WE COULD END UP DISCOVERING *BATMAN'S,* AS WELL.

WE DONE UP HERE?

...YEAH...

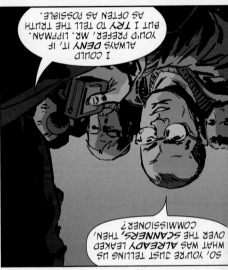

LOOKING AT HIS X-RAYS, YOU CAN SEE HE'S GOT OLD *FRACTURES* IN BOTH ARMS, AND ONE LEG.

WHICH, IF THERE *IS* A REAL ROBIN, IS THE KIND OF THING I'D EXPECT TO SEE, PROBABLY.

SO, I WOULDN'T RULE IT *OUT*...BUT AT THE SAME TIME, THIS *COULD* JUST BE A KID WHO'S INTO SPORTS.

WHICH PROBABLY DOESN'T HELP YOU *AT ALL*, DOES IT?

NOT REALLY, NO.

DID YOU RUN HIS PRINTS?

YOU THINK HE'S GOT A *CRIMINAL RECORD*?

HE'S DENSE TONIGHT, ISN'T HE?

HE HASN'T BEEN GETTING ANY LATELY. IT BOTHERS HIM.

HEY!

SHE'S TALKING ABOUT *CHILD REGISTRATION*, MARCUS. IT'S BECOMING MORE AND MORE COMMON THE PAST FEW YEARS.

LET'S JUST SEE IF OUR LITTLE ROBIN'S PARENTS ARE AMONG THE SCARED PARENTS CONTINGENT...

AND, WHAT DO YOU KNOW...?

OH, YOU HAVE *GOT* TO BE *KIDDING* ME...

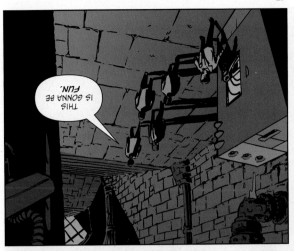

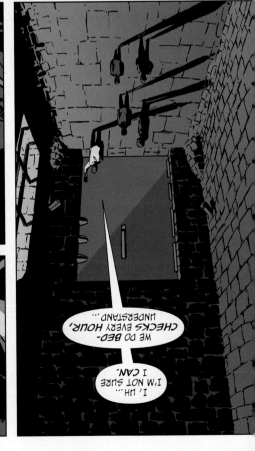

--NO, DON'T WALK AWAY!

RENEE! RENEE!

RENEE!!

I'LL TELL YOU WHAT I TOLD HIM.

DON'T BE ABSURD.

...AND JUST A CHILD, THAT IS A TERRIFYING THOUGHT...

...TELL ME, DETECTIVE PROCTNOW...

...DO YOU HAVE CHILDREN?

...COURSE I DID IT, CRACKED HIS BONES AND SUCKED THE MARROW--

NAH, I, UH... TRIPPED...

--MY TEETH?

ROBIN?

BIRDS INTEREST ME EVEN LESS THAN LITTLE BOYS.

BUT YOU, DETECTIVE...BURKE, IS IT...? YOU LOOK LIKE QUITE A MAN...

WE'RE ALWAYS CHASING BATMAN.

CHASING BATMAN.

EASY, PARTNER!

SON OF A BITCH!

DON'T TELL ME EASY!

WE'RE DOING THIS AGAIN, RENEE! IT'S THE SAME THING, OVER AND OVER!

SON OF A BITCH!

SHUT UP, TOMMY.

WHAT, ASIDE FROM THE FACT THAT TWO-FACE STILL HAS A THING FOR RENEE?

NO, WE LEARNED SOME THINGS.

WASTE OF #$%ING TIME, MAN.

NOW LISTEN, TAKAHATA...I KNOW THIS IS THE PENGUIN'S PLACE, AND HE'S A TOTAL SCUMBAG...BUT LEGALLY, THIS PLACE IS LEGIT.

ICEBERG LOUNGE

SO DON'T GO IN THERE WAVING YOUR GUN AROUND. THIS ISN'T SOME NARCO BUST.

I DID THAT *ONE TIME*, CHANDLER, FOUR *MONTHS* AGO. THINK YOU MIGHT LET IT *DROP* SOMEDAY?

SOMEDAY.

MAYBE.

ANYWAY, I THOUGHT PENGUIN WAS OPERATING OUT OF BLÜDHAVEN THESE DAYS?

HE IS, BUT HE'S STILL GOT THE *ICEBERG*, SO HE'S BACK IN GOTHAM ALL THE TIME. JUST LIKES TO KEEP IT QUIET.

MY SNITCH SAYS HE'S IN TOWN THIS WEEKEND, SO...

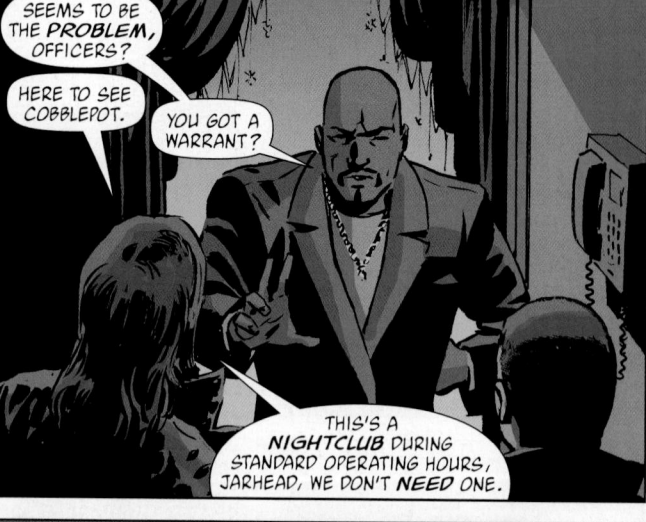

SEEMS TO BE THE *PROBLEM*, OFFICERS?

HERE TO SEE COBBLEPOT.

YOU GOT A WARRANT?

THIS'S A *NIGHTCLUB* DURING STANDARD OPERATING HOURS, JARHEAD, WE DON'T *NEED* ONE.

LEMME CALL AHEAD, ANYWAY.

WHATEVER TURNS YOU ON.

"...WHAT DID YOU JUST DO!?"

ROMY...?

OH MY GOD...

BRAM

FREEZE!

FREEZE!

DON'T YOU MAKE ANOTHER MOVE, YOU FREAK! HANDS OVER YOUR HEAD, NOW!

I DON'T THINK SO.

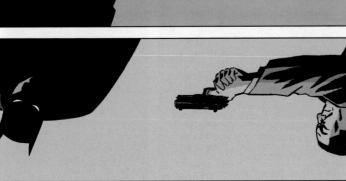

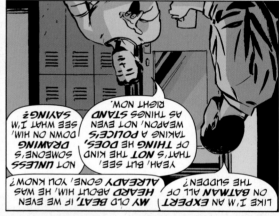

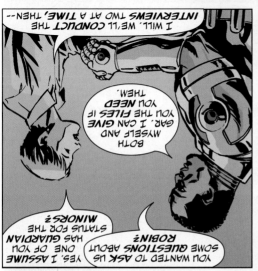

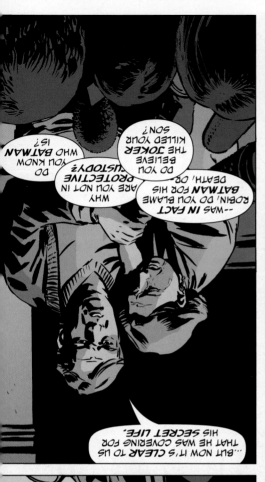

WOW.

YOU SHOULD SEE WONDER WOMAN.

HOLY #$%¢&.

WHERE ARE THE *REST* OF THEM?

SIMON LIPPMAN.

WOULD YOU *JOIN* ME IN MY OFFICE PLEASE, MR. LIPPMAN?

BE MY *PLEASURE* TO, CAPTAIN SAWYER.

IS SHE ACTUALLY *GLOWING* OR IS THAT MY *IMAGINATION?*

SHE'S ACTUALLY *GLOWING.*

MONTOYA, YOU'RE *DROOLING.*

SHOVE IT, SIMON.

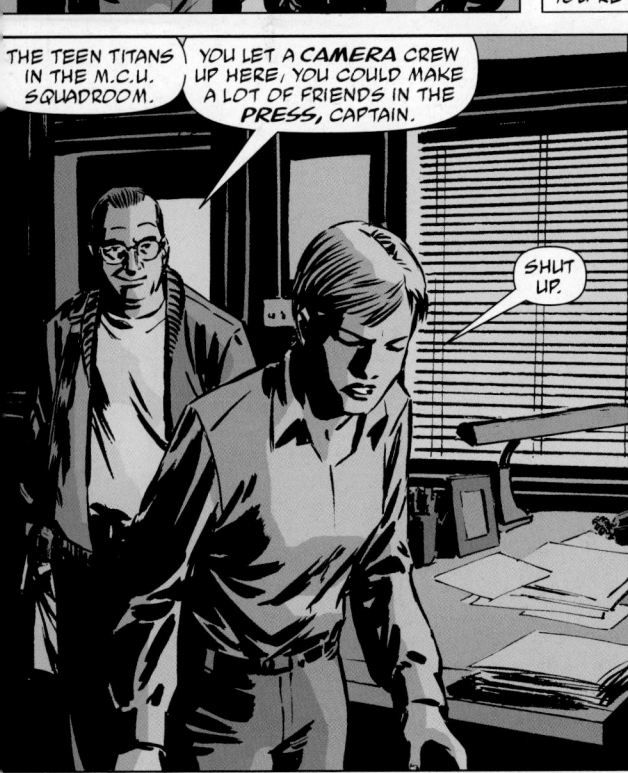

THE TEEN TITANS IN THE M.C.U. SQUADROOM.

YOU LET A *CAMERA* CREW UP HERE, YOU COULD MAKE A LOT OF FRIENDS IN THE *PRESS,* CAPTAIN.

SHUT UP.

WHAT?

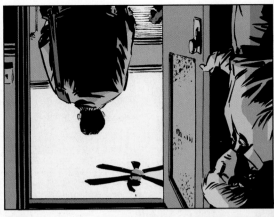

CAN YOU REPEAT THAT?

MAJOR CRIME UNIT...

DEEDEE! DEET

MOM.

THANK YOU!

I'LL SEE WHAT I CAN DO.

"...WE'VE FOUND ANOTHER ONE..."

I NEED SOME DETECTIVES AND THE C.S.U. DOWN HERE...

--SAID THIS IS HARBOR PATROL KELLY-TWELVE.

GOTHAM HARBOR PATROL

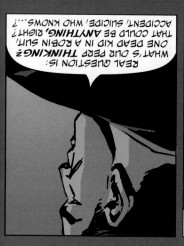

REAL QUESTION IS: WHAT'S OUR PERP *THINKING?* ONE DEAD KID IN A ROBIN SUIT, THAT COULD BE *ANYTHING,* RIGHT? ACCIDENT, SUICIDE, WHO KNOWS...?

"...SO, IT'S REALLY MORE OF A SHOCK THEY DIDN'T FIND HIM *SOONER.*"

NO. HARBOR CAPTAIN SAID HE WAS FLOATING IN A *REGULAR PATROL ROUTE,* WITH NO ANCHOR TO PULL HIM UNDER...

THE FIRST BODY WAS IN *PLAIN SIGHT.* THIS ONE COULD'VE DRIFTED OUT TO SEA.

THIS DOESN'T *FIT,* MARCUS. OUR KILLER JUST SNUFFS THIS KID AND DUMPS HIM OFF A *BRIDGE?*

DEAD ROBIN
PART THREE OF FOUR

DON'T TELL ME THIS ONE *DROWNED?*

NO. PETECHIAL HEMORRHAGES IN BOTH EYES. HE WAS SUFFOCATED SOME-HOW BEFORE HE HIT THE WATER.

--SAY HE'D BEEN IN THE WATER APPROXIMATELY TEN HOURS, GIVE OR TAKE.

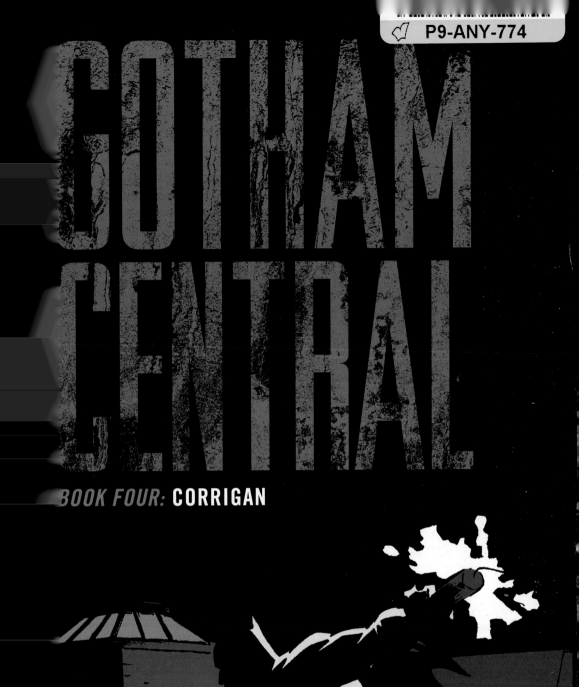

GOTHAM CENTRAL

BOOK FOUR: CORRIGAN

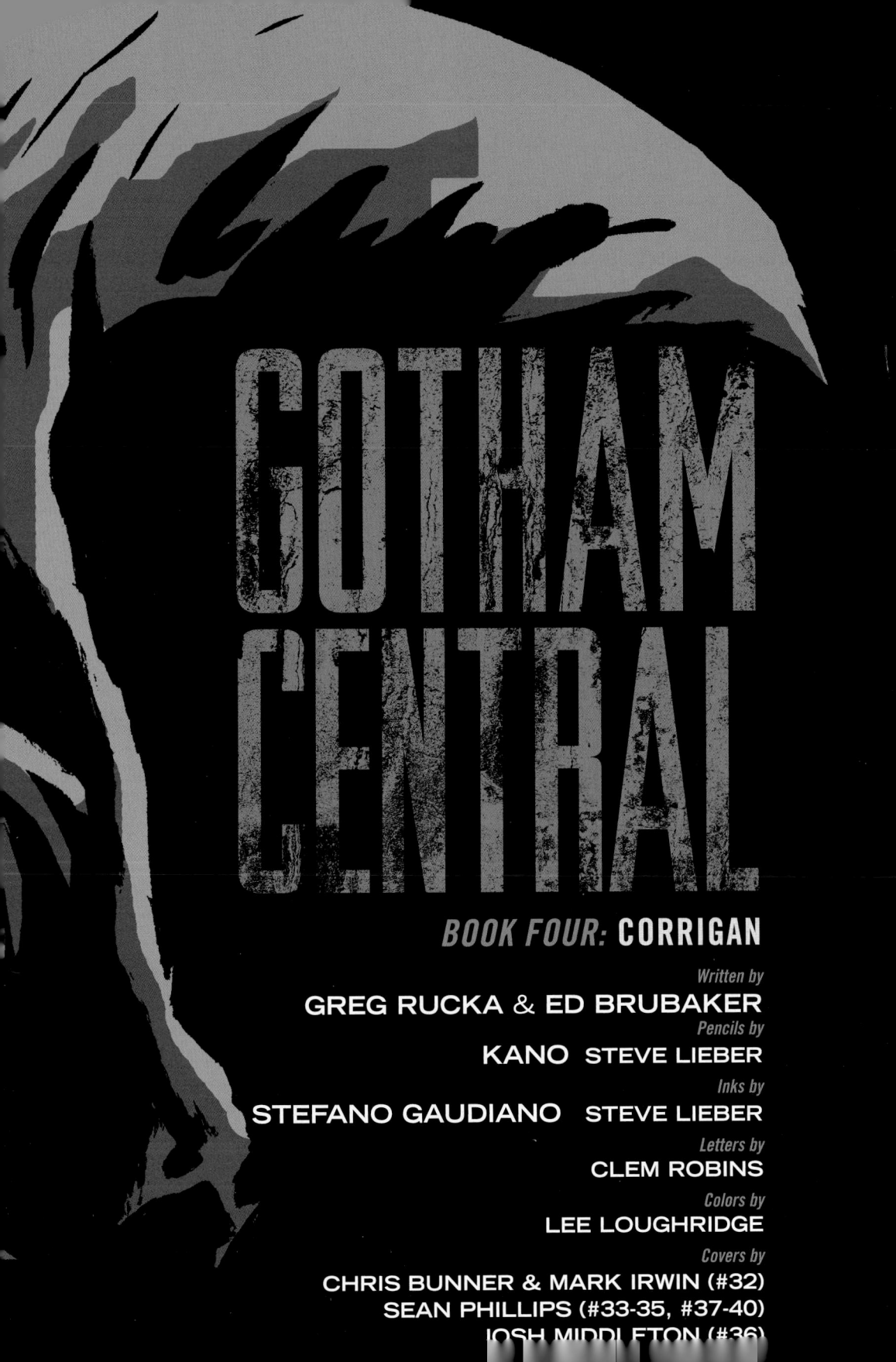

GOTHAM CENTRAL

BOOK FOUR: CORRIGAN

Written by
GREG RUCKA & ED BRUBAKER
Pencils by
KANO   STEVE LIEBER
Inks by
STEFANO GAUDIANO   STEVE LIEBER
Letters by
CLEM ROBINS
Colors by
LEE LOUGHRIDGE
Covers by
CHRIS BUNNER & MARK IRWIN (#32)
SEAN PHILLIPS (#33-35, #37-40)
JOSH MIDDLETON (#36)

FIRST SHIFT

**CAPTAIN
MAGGIE SAWYER**
First shift commander;
formerly head of Metropolis
Special Crimes Unit.

**DETECTIVE
JOELY BARTLETT**
Partner of Vincent
Del Arrazio.

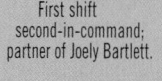

**SGT. VINCENT
DEL ARRAZIO**
First shift
second-in-command;
partner of Joely Bartlett.

**DETECTIVE
CRISPUS ALLEN**
Partner of Renee Montoya.

GOTHAM CITY
POLICE DEPARTMENT
MAJOR CRIMES UNIT

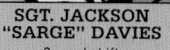

**SECOND
SHIFT**

**SGT. JACKSON
"SARGE" DAVIES**
Second shift
co-second-in-command;
partner of Crowe.

DETECTIVE CROWE
Partner of Sarge Davies.

LT. DAVID CORNWELL
Second shift commander.

**DETECTIVE
JOSH AZEVEDA**
Partner of Trey Hartley.

**DETECTIVE
NATE PATTON**
Partner of Romy Chandler.

**DETECTIVE
TREY HARTLEY**
Partner of Josh Azeveda.

**DETECTIVE
MARCUS DRIVER**
Last MCU officer to be selected
by former Commissioner James
W. Gordon.

LT. RON PROBSON
Second shift
co-second-in-command.

POLICE SUPPORT

COMMISSIONER MICHAEL AKINS
Former commissioner for Gateway City; replaced James W. Gordon.

JIM CORRIGAN
GCPD crime scene investigator.

JAMES W. GORDON
Former Gotham City police commissioner, and 20-year veteran of the force. Currently teaches criminology at Gotham University.

STACY
Receptionist; only person permitted to operate the Bat-Signal.

NORA FIELDS
City coroner.

DETECTIVE TOMY CHANDLER
Partner of Nate Patton.

DETECTIVE JOSEPHINE "JOSIE MAC" MACDONALD
Has the distinction of being the first MCU officer selected after Jim Gordon's retirement.

DETECTIVE DAGMAR PROCJNOW
Partner of Tommy Burke.

DETECTIVE TOMMY BURKE
Partner of Dagmar Procjnow.

DETECTIVE ANDI KASINSKY
Partner of Eric Cohen.

DETECTIVE ERIC COHEN
Partner of Andi Kasinsky.

DETECTIVE 2nd GRADE RENEE MONTOYA
Partner of Crispus Allen.

ANTON KAWASAKI   EDITOR
ROBBIN BROSTERMAN   DESIGN DIRECTOR-BOOKS

BOB HARRAS   SENIOR VP – EDITOR-IN-CHIEF, DC COMICS

DIANE NELSON   PRESIDENT
DAN DIDIO AND JIM LEE   CO-PUBLISHERS
GEOFF JOHNS   CHIEF CREATIVE OFFICER
AMIT DESAI   SENIOR VP – MARKETING & FRANCHISE MANAGEMENT
AMY GENKINS   SENIOR VP – BUSINESS & LEGAL AFFAIRS
NAIRI GARDINER   SENIOR VP – FINANCE
JEFF BOISON   VP – PUBLISHING PLANNING
MARK CHIARELLO   VP – ART DIRECTION & DESIGN
JOHN CUNNINGHAM   VP – MARKETING
TERRI CUNNINGHAM   VP – EDITORIAL ADMINISTRATION
LARRY GANEM   VP – TALENT RELATIONS & SERVICES
ALISON GILL   SENIOR VP – MANUFACTURING & OPERATIONS
HANK KANALZ   SENIOR VP – VERTIGO & INTEGRATED PUBLISHING
JAY KOGAN   VP – BUSINESS & LEGAL AFFAIRS, PUBLISHING
JACK MAHAN   VP – BUSINESS AFFAIRS, TALENT
NICK NAPOLITANO   VP – MANUFACTURING ADMINISTRATION
SUE POHJA   VP – BOOK SALES
FRED RUIZ   VP – MANUFACTURING OPERATIONS
COURTNEY SIMMONS   SENIOR VP – PUBLICITY
BOB WAYNE   SENIOR VP – SALES

Cover by Josh Middleton.

GOTHAM CENTRAL BOOK FOUR: CORRIGAN

DC Comics, 1700 Broadway, New York, NY 10019
A Warner Bros. Entertainment Company
Printed by RR Donnelley, Salem, VA, USA. 4/17/15. Fifth Printing.
ISBN: 978-1-4012-3194-1

Library of Congress Cataloging-in-Publication Data

Rucka, Greg.
Gotham Central. Book four, Corrigan / Greg Rucka, Ed Brubaker, Kano, Steve Lieber.
    p. cm.
" Originally published in single magazine form in Gotham Central #32-40."
ISBN 978-1-4012-3194-1
1. Graphic novels. I. Rucka, Greg. II. Brubaker, Ed. III. Kano. IV. Lieber, Steve. V. Title. VI. Title: Book four, Corrigan
PN6728.G65 R836 2011
741.5'973–dc23
                                2012372680

SUSTAINABLE FORESTRY INITIATIVE

Certified Chain of Custody
20% Certified Forest Content,
80% Certified Sourcing
www.sfiprogram.org
SFI-01042
APPLIES TO TEXT STOCK ONLY

NATURE

Written by
GREG RUCKA

Art by
STEVE LIEBER

Colors by
LEE LOUGHRIDGE

Letters by
CLEM ROBINS

NATURE

THIS ONE, MONTOYA... TALK ABOUT A *PIECE* OF WORK. SHE USED TO PARTNER WITH BULLOCK.

STREET NAME? YEAH, IT'S *TRIGGER.*

BUT THERE'S *NO* WAY HE *DID* THE KID, DETECTIVE...

NOW *THAT* GUY WAS A *REAL* POLICE, HE *KNEW* HOW THINGS GOT *DONE.*

...*NO* WAY HE WAS MORE THAN *FIVE* SECONDS *AHEAD* OF US WHEN WE *HIT* THAT ALLEY.

YOU DIDN'T CALL FOR *BACKUP* ON THE *CORNER?*

WHY *WOULD* WE?

HE'D *NEVER* TURN ON A FELLOW BADGE.

IT WAS JUST A STANDARD *ROUST,* NOT SOMETHING YOU'D *CALL* THE *BAT* ABOUT.

NO OFFENSE.

UH-HUH.

NOT SO WITH *THESE TWO.*

THEY'D *BURN* ME AND ROGER IN AN INSTANT, THEY THOUGHT THEY COULD FIND THE WAY.

ALL RIGHT, THAT *COVERS* IT. THANKS, GUYS.

NO SENSE OF *LOYALTY.*

ROGER AND KENZIE BALANCE THE BOOKS. TRIGGER SKIPPING OUT MEANS WE'RE GONNA HAVE TO MAKE UP THE DIFFERENCE SOMEWHERE ELSE.

IT WON'T BE A PROBLEM, KENZIE. WE'LL FIND US SOMETHING.

LOYALTY, SEE?

IT IS NOW. STANDING SHOULDER-TO-SHOULDER, BROTHER.

ALL BECAUSE TRIGGER DROPPED THIS STREET SLIT? THAT WHAT EVERYONE'S SAYING?

--YEAH, SERIOUSLY, SO INSTEAD OF GETTING POLICE WE CAN WORK WITH, WE GET THE M.C.U. SNIFFING UP OUR LEGS.

TRIGGER AIN'T THE PROBLEM. YOSHIMURA AND FONTANA GOT THEMSELVES HUNG UP ON A CALL OUT IN THE WESTERN--

AWW, YOU'VE GOT TO BE FRIGGING KIDDING ME--

I'D HEARD YOU BOYS HAD A FINE NIGHT OF IT. NEVER FIGURED TRIGGER'D BE THAT DAMN DUMB.

WHAT COMES FROM SAMPLING THE PRODUCT, I SUSPECT...

C'MON OVER HERE, BOY-OS!

HOW ABOUT YOU MAKE YOURSELF USEFUL, KENZIE...

...AND POUR US SOMETHING TO GET THE TASTE OF THIS CITY OUT OF OUR MOUTHS.

...HOME OF THE REAL GOTHAM COP.

AND THAT'S WHY WE HIT FINNIGAN'S AFTER SHIFT. IT'S AN OCEAN OF BLUE, OUR PLACE...

THAT'S WHY ROG AND ME GOT NOTHING TO FEAR FROM THOSE HUMPS IN THE M.C.U. WE UNDERSTAND THE VALUE OF LOYALTY.

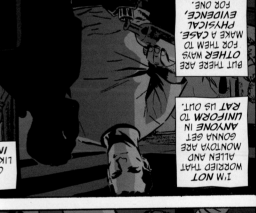

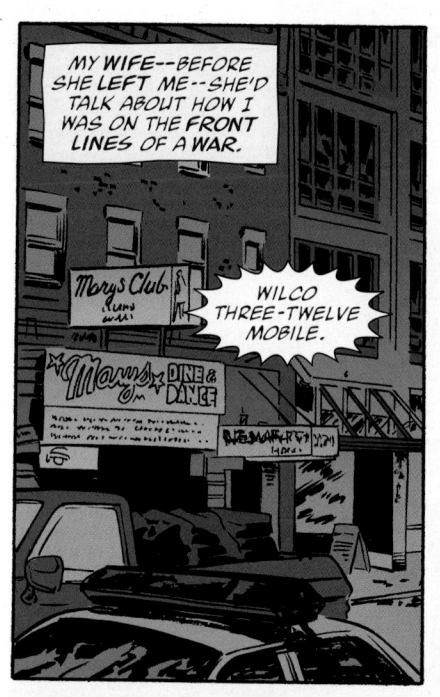

MY *WIFE*--BEFORE SHE *LEFT* ME--SHE'D TALK ABOUT HOW I WAS ON THE *FRONT LINES* OF A WAR.

WILCO THREE-TWELVE MOBILE.

GOOD AND EVIL, SHE'D SAY.

THREE-TWELVE.

WE'RE TEN-SIXTY-THREE.

TEN-FOUR...

YOU'RE FIGHTING FOR *GOOD*, TIMMY, SHE'D SAY.

...CALL WHEN YOU'RE BACK IN SERVICE.

ENJOY YOUR DINNER.

TEN-FOUR, WILCO THREE-TWELVE.

HELLO, LEAH...

SHE WAS AN IDIOT.

402

WE'RE HERE FOR DINNER...

I DON'T FIGHT IN THAT WAR.

SON OF A BITCH.

IF CORRIGAN SCREWED US, I'LL KILL HIM.

KEEP IT COOL.

WHAT THE HELL?

...SAID YOU'D KNOW WHERE TO FIND THIS GUY?

I CAN KEEP AN EYE OPEN, THAT'S THE BEST I CAN PROMISE, DETECTIVE.

OFFICERS.

KINDA OFF THE M.C.U. TRACK, ISN'T THIS, DETECTIVE ALLEN?

IF YOU NEED TO SPEAK TO US, WE'D BE GLAD TO COME DOWN TO CENTRAL.

WE WERE LOOKING FOR DETECTIVE KENZIE, ACTUALLY...

...HOPING HE MIGHT HAVE A LINE ON YOUR MAN, TRIGGER.

HAVEN'T SEEN HIM AROUND, HAVE YOU?

CAN'T SAY WE HAVE.

WELL, LET US KNOW IF YOU DO.

STAY SAFE.

YEAH... YOU, TOO.

THE ONLY RECORD WILL BE MARY'S MEMORY, AND THAT'S NOT DOING TOO WELL VERSUS THE GIN, YOU KNOW WHAT I MEAN?

WHAT'S IN THE REPLACEMENT BAG?

GARBAGE.

I THINK OF IT AS MY WAY OF GIVING BACK TO THE CITY.

SO WHAT NOW?

NOW YOU GUYS GET THE HELL OUT OF HERE.

I WAIT ANOTHER FIVE MINUTES...

...DURING WHICH TIME I LABEL THIS BAG TO MATCH THE OTHER.

...AND THEN I GO BACK DOWN TO DEAR OLD MARY AND TELL HIM I MADE A MISTAKE.

WHILE HE'S PUTTING IT BACK IN ITS BIN, I SNAKE THE DRAW SHEET.

HAVE TO ADMIT, HE MADE IT LOOK GOOD.

STAY OUT OF MY WAY.

BATMAN, WAIT!

WAIT JUST A SECOND, YOU'VE GOT TO ANSWER--

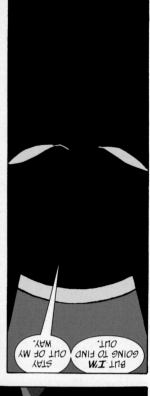

STAY OUT OF MY WAY.

BUT I'M GOING TO FIND OUT.

I DON'T KNOW.

--THEN WHO--

--JESUS--

ROBIN'S IN BLÜDHAVEN.

"...LET'S SEE WHAT JO AND MARCUS GOT, TAKE IT FROM THERE..."

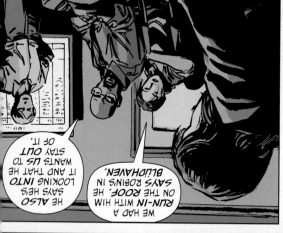

ALLEN AND MONTOYA ARE HEADING OUT TO **ARKHAM** TO QUESTION THE USUAL SUSPECTS. BURKE AND PROCJNOW, YOU GO **WITH** THEM.

AS FOR THE **REST** OF YOU, START **BEATING** THE **BUSHES**, LOOK AT ALL OF ROBIN'S **KNOWN** ENEMIES AND ACQUAINTANCES.

THE **MEDIA'S** ALREADY ALL OVER THIS, KIDS.

WE'RE GONNA NEED TO MOVE **FAST**.

GET TO **WORK**.

YOU OKAY, PARTNER?

C'MON, LET'S GO **BREAK** SOME **ICE**.

LOOKING AT HIS X-RAYS, YOU CAN SEE HE'S GOT OLD *FRACTURES* IN BOTH ARMS, AND ONE LEG.

WHICH, IF THERE *IS* A REAL ROBIN, IS THE KIND OF THING I'D EXPECT TO SEE, PROBABLY.

SO, I WOULDN'T RULE IT *OUT*...BUT AT THE SAME TIME, THIS *COULD* JUST BE A KID WHO'S INTO SPORTS.

WHICH PROBABLY DOESN'T HELP YOU *AT ALL*, DOES IT?

NOT REALLY, NO.

DID YOU RUN HIS PRINTS?

YOU THINK HE'S GOT A *CRIMINAL RECORD?*

HE'S DENSE TONIGHT, ISN'T HE?

HE HASN'T BEEN GETTING ANY LATELY. IT BOTHERS HIM.

HEY!

SHE'S TALKING ABOUT *CHILD REGISTRATION*, MARCUS. IT'S BECOMING MORE AND MORE COMMON THE PAST FEW YEARS.

LET'S JUST SEE IF OUR LITTLE ROBIN'S PARENTS ARE AMONG THE SCARED PARENTS CONTINGENT...

AND, WHAT DO YOU KNOW...?

OH, YOU HAVE *GOT* TO BE *KIDDING* ME...

LOOK, DETECTIVE... ALLEN, RIGHT? WE'VE BEEN HAVING A... HARD NIGHT.

EXPLAIN.

THE INMATES AREN'T THE ONLY ONES GOING TO BE AGITATED, DIRECTOR McKENNA.

ARKHAM'S REVOLVING DOOR DOESN'T GIVE YOU A LOT OF ROOM TO MANEUVER HERE.

ALL IT TAKES IS ONE.

ESCAPES ARE DOWN FORTY-SEVEN PERCENT--

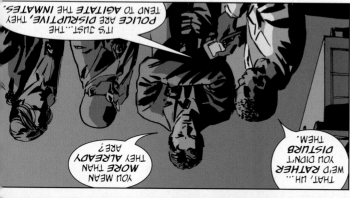

THAT, UH... WE'D RATHER YOU DIDN'T DISTURB THEM.

YOU MEAN MORE THAN THEY ALREADY ARE?

IT'S JUST...THE POLICE ARE DISRUPTIVE. THEY TEND TO AGITATE THE INMATES.

WE'RE GOING TO WANT TO CHECK ON THE INMATES ANYWAY.

DID THE HEAD COUNT AT SHIFT CHANGE, THAT WAS FOUR HOURS AGO.

YOU'RE SURE?

NOPE, ALL PRESENT AND ACCOUNTED FOR.

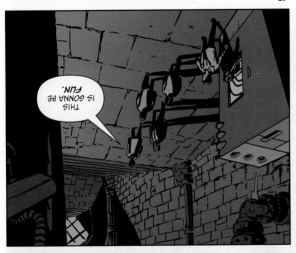

YOU SEE THIS?

EXTRA
Gotham Gazette
IS ROBIN DEAD?

ONLY IN *GOTHAM* WOULD THEY PUT OUT AN *EXTRA* IN THE MIDDLE OF THE GODDAMN NIGHT.

BARS DON'T CLOSE 'TIL *FOUR*, CAPTAIN...EVERY DRUNK IN THE CITY'LL BE READING THIS ON THE SUBWAY HOME.

I KNOW IT.

BUT WHAT I'D *LIKE* TO KNOW IS HOW THE HELL THE GAZETTE GOT A HOLD OF OUR *CRIME SCENE* PHOTO.

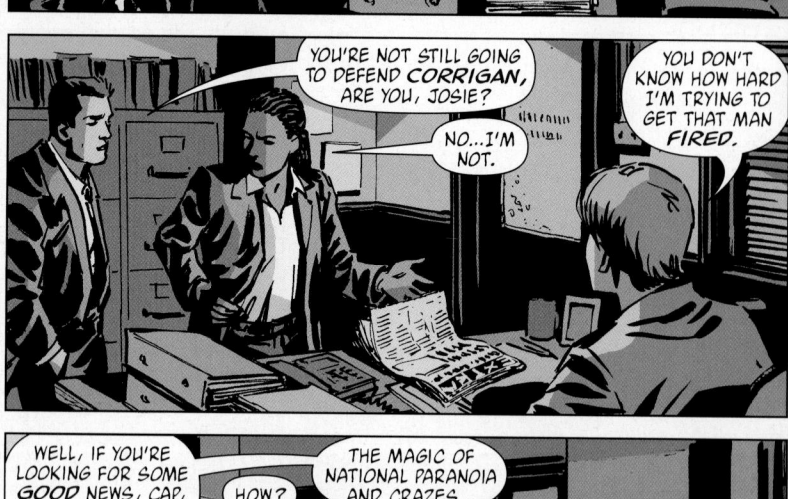

YOU'RE NOT STILL GOING TO DEFEND *CORRIGAN*, ARE YOU, JOSIE?

NO...I'M NOT.

YOU DON'T KNOW HOW HARD I'M TRYING TO GET THAT MAN *FIRED*.

WELL, IF YOU'RE LOOKING FOR SOME *GOOD* NEWS, CAP, WE'VE GOT AN I.D. ON OUR VIC.

HOW?

THE MAGIC OF NATIONAL PARANOIA AND CRAZES...

CHILD REGISTRATION.

YES SIR... TURNS OUT OUR VIC IS ONE *ROGER BAUMBACH*, THE ONLY CHILD OF A FAMILY FROM THE PARK ROW AREA.

BUT ACCORDING TO RECORDS THEY'VE ONLY LIVED IN THE CITY LITTLE OVER A YEAR, SO THERE'S *NO WAY* THIS KID IS THE REAL ROBIN.

NO ONE WANTS THAT TO BE TRUE MORE THAN ME, DETECTIVE, BUT WE *CAN'T* MAKE THAT ASSUMPTION.

AS OUR FRIEND SIMON LIPPMAN SO *ELOQUENTLY* POINTS OUT IN THIS ARTICLE, WE HAVE NO WAY OF KNOWING THAT THERE'S ONLY *ONE* ROBIN TO BEGIN WITH.

WHAT, SO ROBIN'S LIKE *LASSIE?*

WE DON'T KNOW, *THAT'S* WHAT I'M SAYING, AND UNTIL WE DO, YOU NEED TO GO TALK TO THE PARENTS OF THE DECEASED...

AND TOMORROW WE'VE GOT TO GET ROBIN'S *KNOWN ASSOCIATES* IN HERE FOR QUESTIONING.

YOU'RE GOING TO HAUL IN A BUNCH OF TEENAGE *SUPER HEROES?* HOW YOU PLANNING TO PULL THAT ONE OFF, CAPTAIN?

I'VE GOT MY WAYS...

NOW GO WAKE THE BAUMBACHS UP WITH THE BAD NEWS AND SEE WHAT THEY'VE GOT TO SAY.

YES SIR, MA'AM...

LOIS... SORRY TO WAKE YOU. IT'S MAGGIE SAWYER, CALLING FROM GOTHAM.

YEAH, I KNOW, *SORRY...* BUT I NEED A *FAVOR...*

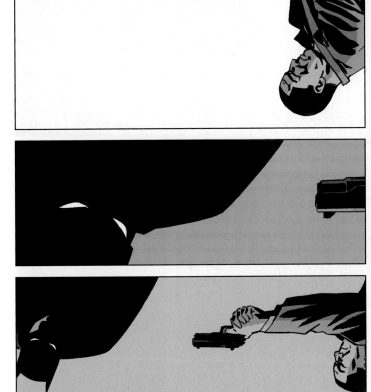

SHE'S YOUR PARTNER, NOOB.

BACK HER UP.

FOUR IN THE MORNING WHEN WE BROKE THE NEWS, THE BAUMBACHS WERE PRETTY RATTLED.

JO AND I ARE HEADING BACK TO TALK TO THEM AGAIN.

LET CRIS AND ME KNOW IF WE CAN HELP.

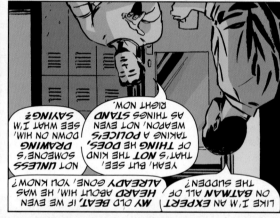

LIKE I'M AN EXPERT ON BATMAN ALL OF THE SUDDEN?

MY OLD BEAT, IF WE EVEN HEARD ABOUT HIM, HE WAS ALREADY GONE, YOU KNOW?

YEAH, BUT SEE, THAT'S NOT THE KIND OF THING HE DOES, TAKING A POLICE'S WEAPON, NOT EVEN AS THINGS STAND RIGHT NOW.

NOT UNLESS SOMEONE'S DRAWING DOWN ON HIM, SEE WHAT I'M SAYING?

HEY, MARCUS, GET ANYTHING FROM ROBIN'S PARENTS?

I DON'T KNOW, BURKE...IT HAPPENED REALLY FAST, ALL RIGHT?

HE TOOK HER WEAPON?

SO FAST NONE OF US EVEN SAW IT.

ONE SECOND ROMY'S STANDING, THE NEXT SHE'S GUSHING BLOOD FROM HER NOSE AND HER HANDS ARE EMPTY.

WHY WOULD HE TAKE HER PIECE?

WHERE THE HELL IS SIMON LIPPMAN?

STACY!

HE WAS AROUND, I DON'T--

YOU FIND THAT SON OF A BITCH AND YOU GET HIM INTO MY OFFICE RIGHT NOW.

HE DOESN'T WORK FOR US, I MEAN, HE'S PROBABLY AT--

NOW, STACY!

CAPTAIN?

YOU SEE THIS? HE DID IT AGAIN! WHERE THE HELL IS HE GETTING THESE FROM?

NONE OF US HAVE TALKED TO HIM, HE CAN'T HAVE LEAKED--

NOT US!

THE C.S.U., HE'S GOT SOMEONE IN THE C.S.U., CORRIGAN OR ONE OF HIS WINGED MONKEYS--

--THEY'RE LEAKING THE CRIME SCENE PHOTOS, THIS IS THE SECOND DAMN ONE!

Sidekick on the sidewalk - Did Batman Teen Adventurer off the ledge?

I'LL KILL HIM, I SWEAR I'LL--

UHMM... CAN I...

...CAN I HELP YOU?

62

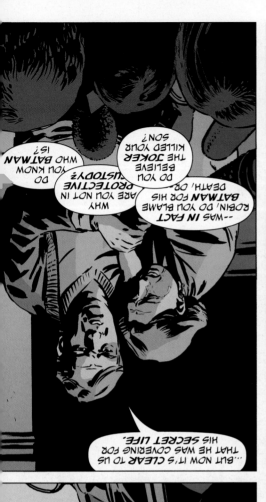

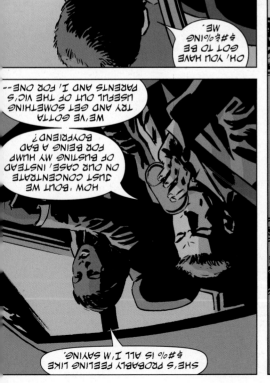

--BUT LAST NIGHT YOU DIDN'T WANT TO TALK, AND THIS MORNING WE FIND YOU HOLDING COURT WITH THE *MEDIA*.

WELL, LAST NIGHT...IT WAS JUST...HOW ARE YOU SUPPOSED TO REACT TO...?

DON'T YOU *DARE* JUDGE US, DETECTIVE. IF WE WANT TO SHARE OUR GRIEF WITH THIS CITY, THAT'S OUR BUSINESS.

LET'S NOT FORGET WHO LOST THEIR ONLY CHILD LAST NIGHT.

I HAVEN'T *FORGOTTEN*, MR. BAUMBACH.

BUT YOU'RE OUT THERE TELLING THE WHOLE WORLD YOUR SON WAS *ROBIN*. DO YOU *REALIZE* THE DANGER THAT COULD PUT YOU IN?

WHAT ARE YOU *TALKING* ABOUT?

TWO WORDS FOR YOU-- *THE JOKER*.

OH...OH *GOD*...

SO, WAIT...YOU *DON'T* THINK THAT ROGER *WAS* ROBIN? THE GAZETTE SAID THERE MAY BE MORE THAN *ONE*, SO WE THOUGHT--

WE DON'T KNOW, HONESTLY, MRS. BAUMBACH, BUT WE'RE LEANING TOWARDS *NOT*.

OH...BUT THEN, WHY WOULD HE BE WEARING THAT *OUTFIT*...?

THAT'S WHAT WE'RE TRYING TO *FIND* OUT.

NOW, IF WE COULD JUST GET SOME *DETAILS* ABOUT ROGER'S *ACTIVITIES*... YOU MENTIONED *GYMNASTICS* CLASSES...

I SEE....

I HAVE BEEN TRYING TO EXPLAIN THAT ROBIN IS ALIVE AND WELL.

AND IF THESE CIVIL SERVICE BUREAUCRATS WOULD ONLY LET US, WE COULD SOLVE THIS CASE FOR THEM.

YOU THINK?

MEN.

"...PERHAPS I CAN BE MORE PERSUASIVE, RAVEN?"

OVER HERE, STARFIRE.

I'M NOT OFFICIALLY WITH THE TITANS AT THE MOMENT, BUT I WAS HOPING I COULD HELP, YOU UNDERSTAND.

UHM...YES...UH....

WHAT?

SHUT UP.

THE TEEN TITANS IN THE M.C.U. SQUADROOM.

YOU LET A CAMERA CREW UP HERE, YOU COULD MAKE A LOT OF FRIENDS IN THE PRESS, CAPTAIN.

SHOVE IT, SIMON.

YOU'RE DROOLING, MONTOYA.

SHE'S ACTUALLY GLOWING.

BE MY PLEASURE TO, CAPTAIN SAWYER.

IS SHE ACTUALLY GLOWING OR IS THAT MY IMAGINATION?

WOULD YOU JOIN ME IN MY OFFICE PLEASE, MR. LIPPMAN?

SIMON LIPPMAN.

WHERE ARE THE REST OF THEM?

HOLY #$%¢.

YOU SHOULD SEE WONDER WOMAN.

WOW.

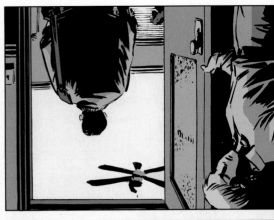

SO YOU JUST **TELL** HER THAT, NO **PROBLEM.**

THAT'S NOT THE **POINT,** DUNNING. SHE **NEVER** SHOULD HAVE ASKED FOR MY SOURCE.

IT'S THE **PRINCIPLE** OF THE THING.

GET **REAL!**

YOU **OKAY,** MAN? YOU LOOK LIKE YOUR **DOG DIED.**

SAWYER JUST BUSTED MY **CHOPS** ABOUT THE **FRONT PAGE** OF THE **GAZETTE.** SHE THINKS THE PHOTOS ARE **MY FAULT.**

WANTED ME TO GIVE UP **MY SOURCE.**

THE PHOTOS **DIDN'T** COME FROM YOU, THOUGH, DID THEY?

I DON'T **KNOW** WHERE THE PHOTOS CAME FROM.

LIPPMAN!

DID THE **BAUMBACHS** HAVE ANY **FURTHER** COMMENT-- --ASK THAT **WONDER GIRL** ANSWER A **FEW** QUESTIONS FOR US?

IS IT **TRUE?** THE **TEEN TITANS** ARE UP **THERE?**

NO **BATMAN,** THOUGH, **HUH?**

THEY **WERE,** ALL OF THEM BUT **SUPERBOY,** THEY JUST LEFT FROM THE **ROOF.**

CAN YOU **SEE THEM? CAN ANYONE--**

DETECTIVES! DETECTIVES!!

--IF IT **WAS** STARFIRE, THEN IT'S THE **OUTSIDERS,** SO LOOK FOR--

"...WITH NO SIGNS OF **SUPERBOY,** ISN'T YOUR STATEMENT A LITTLE **DISINGENUOUS?**

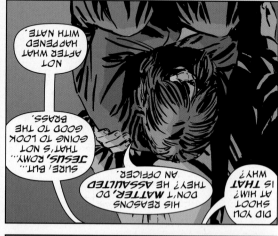

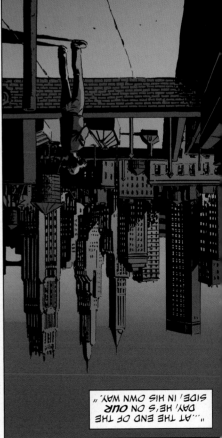

ME, TOO, REALLY.

I REALLY MISS THE OLD DAYS.

BATMAN *TOOK* HER WEAPON?

"...*SHOT* HIM?"

YEAH, BUT... WELL, I THINK SHE KINDA...UM...SHE MIGHT'VE...

OF COURSE I KNOW HIS NAME.

YOU *KNOW* HIS NAME?

DETECTIVE NATE PATTON.

"WAIT..."

YOU KNOW, IN THAT WHOLE *JOKER* THING AT THE TOY STORE?

SHE'S GOING TO GET IN A *LOT* OF TROUBLE, AND SHE'S REALLY REALLY *NICE*, AND, UM, KINDA JUST BEEN, SINCE SHE'S *MAD* AT BATMAN, HER PARTNER GOT KILLED...

CAN YOU GET DETECTIVE CHANDLER'S GUN BACK FROM HIM?

CAN YOU DO ME A FAVOR, THEN?

I CAN TRY. WHAT?

"...WE'VE FOUND ANOTHER ONE..."

GOTHAM HARBOR PATROL

I NEED SOME DETECTIVES AND THE C.S.U. DOWN HERE...

--SAID THIS IS HARBOR PATROL KELLY-TWELVE.

REAL QUESTION IS: WHAT'S OUR PERP THINKING? ONE DEAD KID IN A ROBIN SUIT, THAT COULD BE ANYTHING, RIGHT? ACCIDENT, SUICIDE, WHO KNOWS...?

...SO, IT'S REALLY MORE OF A SHOCK THEY DIDN'T FIND HIM SOONER.

NO, HARBOR CAPTAIN SAID HE WAS FLOATING IN A REGULAR PATROL ROUTE, WITH NO ANCHOR TO PULL HIM UNDER...

THE FIRST BODY WAS IN PLAIN SIGHT. THIS ONE COULD'VE DRIFTED OUT TO SEA.

THIS DOESN'T FIT. MARCUS, OUR KILLER JUST SNUFFS THIS KID AND DUMPS HIM OFF A BRIDGE?

DEAD ROBIN
PART THREE OF FOUR

NO, PETECHIAL HEMORRHAGES IN BOTH EYES. HE WAS SUFFOCATED SOME- HOW BEFORE HE HIT THE WATER.

DON'T TELL ME THIS ONE DROWNED?

--SAY HE'D BEEN IN THE WATER APPROXIMATELY TEN HOURS, GIVE OR TAKE.

BUT TWO KIDS, **BOTH** IN THESE EXPENSIVE OUTFITS...BOTH KILLED WITHIN **A DAY** OF EACH OTHER?

HEY, REINER, ANY SIGN OF SEXUAL ASSAULT ON THIS ONE?

SORRY TO DISAPPOINT, DETECTIVE.

SEE, THAT'S JUST... WEIRD.

YOU'D BE **MORE COMFORTABLE** IF OUR PERP WAS MOLESTING THE VICS?

HELL YES...AT LEAST **THAT** I'VE SEEN.

THIS IS JUST... **NUTS.**

IS IT JUST ME, OR DOES THAT KID LOOK FAMILIAR?

WELL, WE **DID** JUST HAVE ONE OF THESE **YESTERDAY,** REMEMBER?

HA HA...

NO, SERIOUSLY... I'VE SEEN THIS KID BEFORE SOME-WHERE.

AH, #¢¢%IN' HELL...

LOOKS LIKE SOMEONE ALREADY ALERTED THE FRIGGING MEDIA ON US.

CHRIST, CAPTAIN SAWYER'S GONNA BE **THRILLED...**

MOTHER*%$¢!

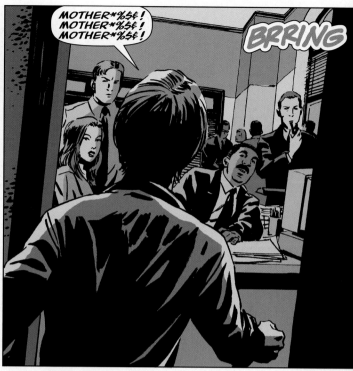

MOTHER*%$¢!
MOTHER*%$¢!
MOTHER*%$¢!

BRRING

BRRING BRRING

CAPTAIN! THE **PHONES** WON'T **STOP** RINGING!

I'VE GOT **KLEX** HERE, THEY WANT TO KNOW IF WE CAN **CONFIRM** A **SECOND** DEAD ROBIN --

NO *%$#ING COMMENT!

EVERY-ONE GOT THAT?

YES, MA'AM.

YES, CAPTAIN.

GOT IT.

YES'M.

84

FREEDOM OF THE PRESS IS A BASIC RIGHT, A *TENET* ON WHICH OUR NATION IS *BUILT FREEDOM OF THE PRESS IS A BASIC RIGHT* --

MIKE!

MAGGIE, IF YOU'RE *ABOUT* TO TELL ME WE'VE CAUGHT A *SECOND* ONE...

HELL YEAH! ROBIN NUMBER *TWO* JUST *BOBBED* TO THE SURFACE OF THE *SPRANG RIVER!*

BUT *DON'T* FEEL *BAD* IF YOU'RE MISSING THE DETAILS, COMMISSIONER...

...IT'LL BE *ON* THE *NEWS* AT *ELEVEN.*

HOW'D THE *PRESS* GET IT SO *QUICK?*

TWO DOZEN WAYS AT LEAST, YOU *KNOW* THAT.

THERE'RE ANY *NUMBER* OF PEOPLE IN THIS *DEPARTMENT* WHO'D BE HAPPY TO *LEAK* INFORMATION FOR *CASH* OR JUST TO $£#% WITH US.

THAT *SAID,* I'M *PERSONALLY* BLAMING SIMON LIPPMAN.

I'LL CALL *EDWARDS* IN MEDIA, GET *ANOTHER* PRESS CONFERENCE SCHEDULED *IMMEDIATELY.*

YOU'LL HAVE TO *JOIN* ME FOR IT.

I'LL TRY TO KEEP MY *LUNCH* DOWN.

COMMISSIONER! COMMISSIONER!

--CONFIRM YOU RECEIVED A CALL FROM THE *RIDDLER* CLAIMING RESPONSIBILITY?

--IDENTITY OF *BOTH* ROBINS AND THEIR *CONNECTION* TO THE BATMAN--

--THAT YOU IN *FACT* HAVE *NO* LEADS AND *NOTHING* TO GO ON?

--RUMORS THAT *STARFIRE* WAS STRIP-SEARCHED PRIOR TO--

ALL RIGHT, LET'S SEE IF WE CAN ACT LIKE *HUMAN BEINGS* AND NOT A PACK OF *FRENZIED HYENAS,* SHALL WE?

A LITTLE OVER AN *HOUR* AGO A *SECOND* YOUNG MAN *DRESSED* IN *IDENTICAL* FASHION AND *COSTUME* AS THE *FIRST* WAS PULLED FROM THE SPRANG...

...M.C.U. DETECTIVES ARE *STILL* PROCESSING THE *SCENE,* AND ARE *TREATING* THIS AS A *RELATED* HOMICIDE.

WE EXPECT INITIAL *AUTOPSY* RESULTS WITHIN THE NEXT TWO HOURS, AT WHICH TIME WE'LL BE ISSUING A *SECOND* STATEMENT.

I'LL TAKE *THREE* QUESTIONS, SO *MAKE* THEM GOOD.

WHY HAVEN'T THE *POLICE* BROUGHT *BATMAN* IN FOR *QUESTIONING?*

WHO SAYS WE *HAVEN'T?*

NEXT QUESTION...

FAASH

I SEE WHAT YOU MEAN, JOSIE...HE *DOES* LOOK SOMEWHAT FAMILIAR.

HE LOOKS JUST LIKE THE *OTHER* KID.

NO...THERE'S SOMETHING ABOUT HIS EYEBROWS...

DUDE, IT'S YOUR *BREATH*.

WHAT THE #¢¢% DID YOU JUST SAY TO ME?

NOT YOU, *HIM*. THAT'S THE KID FROM THE *MIGHTY MINTS* ADS LAST YEAR, REMEMBER?

DUDE, IT'S YOUR BREATH!

...BUT NOTHING MORE ON THE *SECOND* BODY?

--HEY! HEY, THAT'S WHY I'M ASKING *YOU*, DAMMIT!

GO TO *HELL.*

DUNNING!

HEY, SIMON.

GIVE ME THE *BULLET,* WHAT'D I MISS?

IT WAS WHAT YOU'D *EXPECT,* MAN, NOTHING *NEW.*

AKINS *CONFIRMS* THAT A *SECOND* BOY WAS *PULLED* FROM THE RIVER, SAYS HE WAS *DRESSED* LIKE *ROBIN.*

THEY I.D. THE *KID* YET?

IF THEY *HAVE,* THEY WOULDN'T *SAY.*

LOOKS LIKE ONE OF THE *BAT'S* FREAKS IS AT *WORK* HERE, DRESSING UP *KIDS* AND *OFFING* THEM.

THAT IGNORES THE *MULTIPLE* ROBIN THEORY.

WHAT?

YOU LOOK AT THE *HISTORIES,* DUNNING, THERE'VE BEEN *DIFFERENT* KIDS INSIDE THAT *SUIT,* IT'S *OBVIOUS.*

HELL, APPARENTLY THERE WAS A *GIRL WONDER* A COUPLE MONTHS *BACK.*

YOU THINK THESE KIDS ARE THE *REAL* THING?

I'M SAYING IT'S *POSSIBLE*.

THING IS, THERE'S *NO* KNOWN *HISTORY* OF *MULTIPLE* ROBINS BEING ACTIVE AT THE *SAME* TIME.

C'MON, *TELL* ME. THEY SAY *ANYTHING* ELSE?

THEY HAVE ANY *SUSPECTS*, AT LEAST?

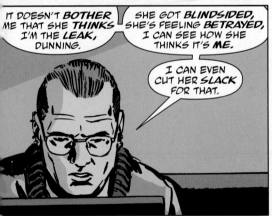

NOTHING, MAN. THEY'RE *STONEWALLED*, YOU CAN TELL.

SAWYER MUST *REALLY* WANT YOUR *HEAD* IN A *SACK* TO HAVE YOU EJECTED FROM THE *CONFERENCE* LIKE THAT.

YEAH, YOU *DON'T* WANT TO PISS HER *OFF*.

WHY DON'T YOU *JUST* TELL HER THE *PHOTOS* WEREN'T YOUR *FAULT*?

I ALREADY TOLD YOU, IT'S THE *PRINCIPLE*.

IT DOESN'T *BOTHER* ME THAT SHE *THINKS* I'M THE *LEAK*, DUNNING.

SHE GOT *BLINDSIDED*, SHE'S FEELING *BETRAYED*, I CAN SEE HOW SHE THINKS IT'S *ME*.

I CAN EVEN CUT HER *SLACK* FOR THAT.

BUT SHE *EXPECTED* ME TO GIVE UP A *SOURCE*.

SHE SHOULD *KNOW* ME BETTER THAN THAT BY *NOW*, Y'KNOW?

YOU'RE *OLD SCHOOL*, LIPPMAN, YOU KNOW THAT?

NO SCHOOL LIKE THE OLD SCHOOL, MAN.

HAVE A *NIGHT*, DUNNING.

YOU WANT ME TO *LET* YOU GUYS *INSIDE?*

I'VE GOT *KEYS* FOR JUST ABOUT *EVERY* OFFICE IN THE *BUILDING.*

IT'S ALL RIGHT, WE'VE GOT THE *OWNER* COMING DOWN.

YOU'RE SURE?

WE'RE *SURE.*

YEAH, *SUPPOSE* YOU'D NEED A *WARRANT* OR SOMETHING LIKE THAT, HUH?

WELL, YOU *NEED* ANYTHING, I'LL BE *DOWN* IN THE *LOBBY.*

SHINING EYES

THANKS, MISTER GERARD.

DING

YOU LOOK *BEAT.*

I AM BEAT.

WHAT'S GOING ON *BETWEEN* YOU AND *CORRIGAN?*

I BEG YOUR *PARDON?*

NOT LIKE *THAT.*

THEN LIKE *WHAT?*

I *NEVER* ASKED YOU HOW YOU *CLEARED* ME FOR THE *LAMONICA* SHOOT--

DING

I'M *SORRY*, I'M *SORRY*, I GOT HERE AS *SOON* AS I *COULD*--

--YOU'RE THE *POLICE*, YOU'RE THE *DETECTIVES* WHO CALLED ABOUT *SCOTT BENJAMIN?*

MISTER *SWACK?*

RIGHT, YES, FELIX SWACK.

DETECTIVE *ALLEN*, THIS IS DETECTIVE *MONTOYA*.

YOU *REPPED* SCOTT BENJAMIN FOR THE MIGHTY MINTS CAMPAIGN?

THAT AND HALF A DOZEN *OTHER* JOBS...

...*NONE* AS *BIG* AS THE *M.M.* ACCOUNT, OF COURSE.

VERY TALENTED KID, SCOTT. GREAT *CHARISMA*, WONDERFUL *STAGE* PRESENCE...

...COMPLETE *MASTERY* OF HIS INSTRUMENT, EVEN AT *FIFTEEN*.

INSTRUMENT?

HIS *BODY*, THE ACTOR'S *TOOL*. SCOTT WAS *PROBABLY* THE MOST *TALENTED* ADOLESCENT WE *REPPED*.

Mighty Mints

DUDE, YOUR BREATH!

Mighty Mints

ARE *MOST* OF YOUR *CLIENTS* ADOLESCENTS?

ROUGHLY *HALF*, I'D SAY.

ROGER BAUMBACH?

YOU KNOW *ROGER?*

MISTER SWACK, ROGER BAUMBACH WAS *MURDERED* NIGHT BEFORE *LAST.*

JESUS CHRIST.

WE'RE GOING TO NEED A *LIST* OF *ALL* YOUR *MALE* CLIENTS BETWEEN THE AGES OF THIRTEEN AND EIGHTEEN.

WE'RE GOING TO NEED THEIR *EMPLOYMENT* RECORDS, ALL *JOBS* OR *AUDITIONS* FOR THE LAST *SIX* MONTHS.

JESUS CHRIST.

THEY'RE JUST... THEY'RE JUST *KIDS*, DETECTIVE.

WE *REALLY* NEED THOSE *RECORDS*, MISTER SWACK.

THEY'RE... THEY'RE *THIS* WAY...

NO, DETECTIVE DRIVER AND JOSIE ARE WITH THE VICTIMS' **PARENTS**, RENEE, BUT THAT'S GOOD NEWS. LET ME TRANSFER YOU TO THE CAPTAIN... HOLD...

MAJOR CRIMES, HOW MAY I DIRECT YOUR CALL?

BRRNGG

STACY?

YES...?

YOU KNOW WHO THIS IS. MEET ME ON THE ROOF.

93

HI...

HI...SORRY TO SURPRISE YOU LIKE THAT.

THAT'S ALL RIGHT...

I GOT IT BACK FOR YOU.

BACK...?

DETECTIVE CHANDLER'S WEAPON.

OH, RIGHT, THAT. I'M SORRY...IT'S BEEN A WEIRD WEEK.

YEAH, FOR ME TOO.

I CAN ONLY *IMAGINE*...

WELL, THANKS *SO MUCH*. THIS WILL SAVE ROMY A LOT OF TROUBLE.

DON'T WORRY ABOUT IT...BUT...

...HE SAID TO TELL HER *NOT* TO SHOOT HIM AGAIN.

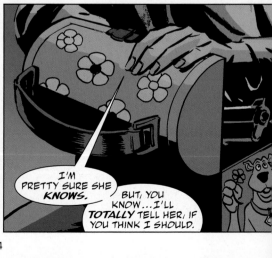

I'M PRETTY SURE SHE *KNOWS*.

BUT, YOU KNOW...I'LL *TOTALLY* TELL HER, IF YOU THINK I SHOULD.

IT'S REALLY YOUR CALL. HE *DID* BREAK HER NOSE, RIGHT?

SO...

HAS THERE BEEN ANY PROGRESS IN THE INVESTIGATION? I HEARD THE SECOND VICTIM WAS ALREADY IDENTIFIED?

YEAH, I'LL JUST LET HER FIGURE IT OUT HERSELF, MAYBE...

YOU DID? WE JUST FOUND OUT ABOUT AN HOUR AGO...

OH, RIGHT... *BATMAN.*

SORRY.

WELL, SO, YEAH...THE SECOND VICTIM IS AN ACTOR, SCOTT BENJAMIN, AND IT TURNS OUT HE AND THE FIRST VICTIM WERE BOTH REPRESENTED BY THE SAME TALENT AGENCY...

...*SHINING EYES* OR SOMETHING LIKE THAT.

SO THEY'RE GOING OVER THE REST OF THE CLIENT LIST FOR BOYS THIRTEEN TO EIGHTEEN. HOPING TO FIND OUT MORE.

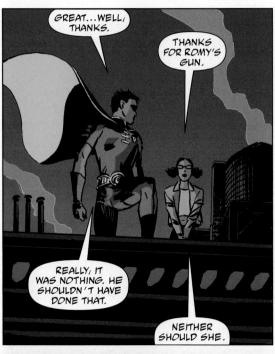

GREAT...WELL, THANKS.

THANKS FOR ROMY'S GUN.

REALLY, IT WAS NOTHING. HE SHOULDN'T HAVE DONE THAT.

NEITHER SHOULD SHE.

SEE YA LATER.

BYE.

HMM... THAT'S WHAT I THOUGHT.

--CONNECTING ROGER BAUMBACH AND SCOTT BENJAMIN *THROUGH* THE SHINING EYES *TALENT* AGENCY.

THERE ARE SOME *TWO HUNDRED AND EIGHT* MALES BETWEEN THIRTEEN AND EIGHTEEN SHINING EYES CURRENTLY REPRESENTS.

WE'RE GOING TO HAVE TO *CHECK* THEM *ALL*, AND *PRONTO.*

WE LOOKING AT THIS FELIX SWACK AS A *SUSPECT?*

NAME LIKE *SWACK*, WE DAMN WELL *BETTER.*

TOMMY, *SHUT UP.*

NOT AT THE MOMENT.

THERE ARE STACKS OF RÉSUMÉS, HEAD SHOTS AND CONTACT INFO.

THEY *HAVEN'T* BEEN *SORTED*, SO IF YOU'VE GOT AN *OBVIOUS* NO-GO, HERE...

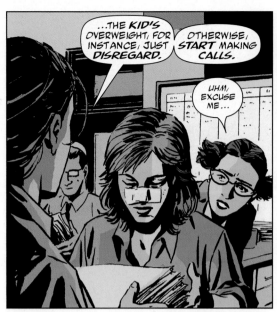

--THIS CAN'T BE HAPPENING...

I *KNOW*, MRS. BENJAMIN... WE'LL HAVE A PATROL CAR TAKE YOU TO IDENTIFY THE BODY, JUST TO BE SURE.

BUT WE *HAVE* MATCHED SCOTT'S HEAD SHOT WITH OUR VICTIM. I'M SORRY.

OH, OH GOD...

IS YOUR *HUSBAND* HERE, MRS. BENJAMIN?

MY HUSBAND... NO...GARY MOVED TO CHICAGO AFTER THE DIVORCE...

OH, GOD, I HAVE TO CALL HIM...I HAVE TO TELL HIM.

I'M SORRY TO HAVE TO ASK YOU THESE QUESTIONS RIGHT NOW, MA'AM, BUT TIME IS OF THE ESSENCE HERE.

DO YOU KNOW OF ANY REASON WHY SCOTT WOULD BE WEARING A ROBIN COSTUME?

WHAT? NO... OF COURSE NOT.

WAS HE FRIENDS WITH *ROGER BAUMBACH?* DID THEY KNOW EACH OTHER?

NO, I DON'T KNOW...OH, GOD...SCOTT...WHO WOULD DO THIS?

WE'RE TRYING TO FIND THAT OUT, MRS. BENJAMIN.

WOULD YOU MIND IF WE SEARCHED SCOTT'S ROOM?

FINE, FINE... DO WHATEVER YOU WANT...

99

...MONTOYA, YES, RENEE MONTOYA...

...NO, I'D LIKE TO SPEAK WITH HIM IN PERSON...

...IF YOU COULD HAVE HIM CALL ME...

...NO, MA'AM, JORDAN'S NOT IN TROUBLE...

...I SWEAR--

--SON OF A BITCH!

UH, CRIS?

IT'S NOT THE SAME!

IT'S NOT THE SAME DAMN PHOTO!

THE FRONT PAGE PHOTO, RENEE...

...IT WAS TAKEN BEFORE WE GOT THERE, BEFORE WE STARTED WORKING THE CRIME SCENE...

...IT WAS TAKEN BY THE SON OF A BITCH WHO KILLED HIM...

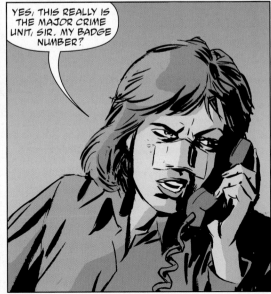

DOWN!

JESUS CHR--

GET DOWN ON THE GROUND!

NOW!

DEAD ROBIN

CONCLUSION

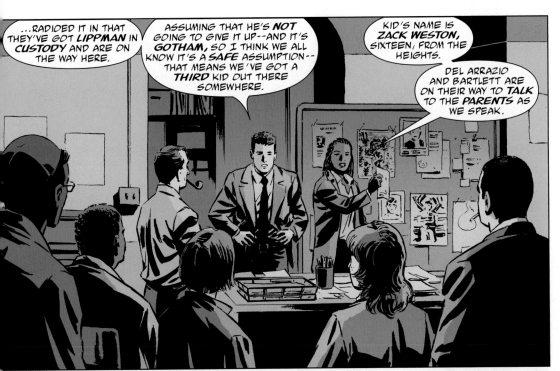

...RADIOED IT IN THAT THEY'VE GOT *LIPPMAN* IN *CUSTODY* AND ARE ON THE WAY HERE.

ASSUMING THAT HE'S *NOT* GOING TO GIVE IT UP--AND IT'S *GOTHAM*, SO I THINK WE ALL KNOW IT'S A *SAFE* ASSUMPTION-- THAT MEANS WE'VE GOT A *THIRD* KID OUT THERE SOMEWHERE.

KID'S NAME IS *ZACK WESTON*, SIXTEEN, FROM THE HEIGHTS.

DEL ARRAZIO AND *BARTLETT* ARE ON THEIR WAY TO *TALK* TO THE *PARENTS* AS WE SPEAK.

ZACK'S PARENTS *REPORTED* HIM *MISSING* YESTERDAY, WHICH PUTS THE *CLOCK* AT ROUGHLY *FIFTY HOURS* SINCE HE WAS *LAST SEEN*.

ASSUMING HE'S *STILL* ALIVE, WE NEED TO *FIND* HIM.

ASSUMING HE *ISN'T*...

...WE NEED TO FIND THE *BODY*.

UNLESS MISTER *LIPPMAN* DECIDES HE WANTS TO *SAVE* US THE *TROUBLE*.

THIS IS ALL A *MISTAKE*.

NO, THE *MISTAKE* WAS *TRUSTING* YOU IN THE *FIRST* PLACE...

...BUT WE'RE **AIMING** TO **CORRECT** THAT ONE.

DAMMIT, MAGGIE! I **DIDN'T** SCREW YOU GUYS!

AND I **SURE** AS **HELL** HAVEN'T **KILLED** ANYONE!

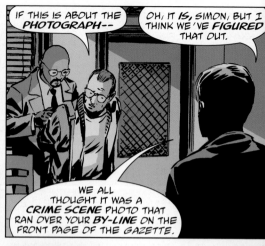

IF THIS IS ABOUT THE **PHOTOGRAPH**--

OH, IT **IS**, SIMON, BUT I THINK WE'VE **FIGURED** THAT OUT.

WE ALL THOUGHT IT WAS A **CRIME SCENE** PHOTO THAT RAN OVER YOUR **BY-LINE** ON THE FRONT PAGE OF THE GAZETTE.

FIGURED YOU'D **BOUGHT** IT OFF OF **CORRIGAN**, THAT EITHER **HE** OR ONE OF HIS BUNKIES WAS YOUR **SOURCE**.

BUT THEY **WEREN'T**, WERE THEY? BECAUSE THE GAZETTE'S PHOTO **WASN'T** OUR PHOTO AT ALL...

...IT WAS A **DIFFERENT** ONE ALTOGETHER, TAKEN **BEFORE** WE EVEN **ARRIVED**...

...TAKEN BY **SOMEONE** WHO WAS ON THE **ROOF** AT THE **TIME** OF THE MURDER.

AND YOU THINK IT WAS **ME**?

I THINK IT'S A **HELL** OF A PHOTO TO **RUN** OVER YOUR **BY-LINE**, SIMON.

AND YOU'VE **ALWAYS** HAD A **NOSE** FOR A **GOOD** STORY.

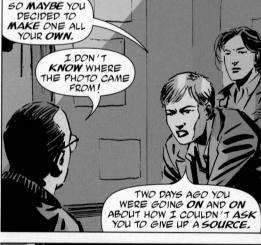

SO **MAYBE** YOU DECIDED TO **MAKE** ONE ALL YOUR **OWN**.

I DON'T **KNOW** WHERE THE PHOTO CAME FROM!

TWO DAYS AGO YOU WERE GOING **ON** AND **ON** ABOUT HOW I COULDN'T **ASK** YOU TO GIVE UP A **SOURCE**.

WHICH STORY IS IT, SIMON?

BOTH. I *DIDN'T*--I *DON'T*--KNOW WHO TOOK THE PICTURE...

...AND YOU *DIDN'T* HAVE THE *RIGHT* TO ASK ME TO GIVE UP A *SOURCE!*

WHAT'S YOUR *CONNECTION* WITH SCOTT BENJAMIN, SIMON?

WHAT? WAIT, *THAT'S* THE *SECOND* VICTIM? *NONE!* WHY THE *HELL* WOULD YOU *EVEN* ASK ME *THAT?*

KID HAD ONE OF *YOUR* BUSINESS CARDS. WHY WOULD A SIXTEEN-YEAR-OLD HAVE ONE OF *YOUR* CARDS?

Gotham Gazette

HALF THIS *DEPARTMENT* HAS MY *CARD,* CRIS!

IT *CONNECTS* YOU TO HIM.

I'M THINKING IT'S *JEALOUSY.*

MOLINA MADE *HAY* OUT OF THAT WHOLE *JOKER* CLUSTER-%¢*#¢ LAST CHRISTMAS; MAYBE YOU WERE LOOKING TO MAKE SOME YOURSELF?

YOU DECIDED TO *MAKE* NEWS INSTEAD OF *COVERING* IT; GET A *BIG* STORY ALL YOUR *OWN.*

JINGLE HELL

C'MON, YOU GUYS *KNOW* ME.

YOU *KNOW* ME!

NO--

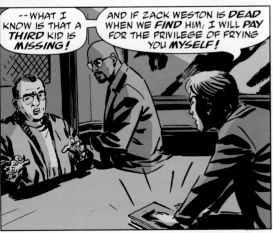

--WHAT I KNOW IS THAT A *THIRD* KID IS *MISSING!*

AND IF ZACK WESTON IS *DEAD* WHEN WE *FIND* HIM, I WILL *PAY* FOR THE PRIVILEGE OF FRYING YOU *MYSELF!*

COME *CLEAN,* SIMON. *HELP* YOURSELF.

WHERE'S THE *KID?*

HEY, UH... ROMY?

ON THE PHONE, STACY.

YEAH, BUT I'VE GOT--

EXCUSE ME?

YES?

WHO ARE THE DETECTIVES IN CHARGE OF THE DEAD ROBINS CASE?

THAT WOULD BE DETECTIVES DRIVER AND MACDONALD. I'M SORRY, AREN'T YOU *PRESS*?

YEAH, JUST *FREELANCE,* BUT...I NEED TO TALK TO DRIVER AND MACDONALD.

I'M AFRAID THAT'S NOT GOING TO BE *POSSIBLE.* YOU'RE NOT SUPPOSED TO BE *UP HERE,* EVEN.

HOW DID YOU GET PAST THE DESK SERGEANT?

JUST WALKED PAST HIM LIKE I KNEW WHAT I WAS DOING, NO ONE SAID A THING.

AMAZING... AND THEY *WONDER* ABOUT THE CRIME RATE...

WELL, LOOK, YOU'RE GONNA HAVE TO LEAVE, BECAUSE WE DON'T ALLOW--

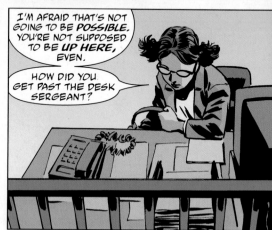

I NEED TO SEE THEM ABOUT *THIS.*

EADMONTE ACADEMY GOTHAM

Zack Weston

CHARY WESTON NO. 7699-9085-08   NOT VALID FOR USE OFF CAMPUS

Zack Weston

110

JOSIE, CAN YOU AND MARCUS COME **HERE?**

JUST A SEC, STACY.

UH, MAYBE **NOW?**

STACY? WHAT'S GOING ON?

I UNDERSTAND YOU'VE TAKEN **SIMON LIPPMAN** INTO CUSTODY?

I'M SORRY. WHO ARE **YOU?**

STACE, WHO **IS** THIS?

HE'S GOT--

YOU'VE GOT THE WRONG MAN, DETECTIVE.

MOTHER$#%--

--YOU THE GOD'S HONEST **TRUTH** HERE, MAGGIE.

--IS THE **KID,** YOU SONNUVVABICH! WHERE **IS** HE?!

...WHAT THE **HELL?**

WHAT'D YOU DO WITH THE KID, YOU SICK--

DETECTIVES!

WHAT THE **HELL** IS GOING ON HERE?

SON OF A BITCH JUST WALKED IN WITH ZACK WESTON'S **SCHOOL I.D. CARD.**

WE'VE GOT THE **WRONG** GUY IN THE **BOX,** CAPTAIN.

WHAT?

IT'S **THIS** HUMP.

WHAT?

IS SIMON **IN THERE?** IN THE BOX?

YES, HE IS... WHO **ARE** YOU?

I'M **NOBODY.** JUST LIKE YOU.

BUT I'M A FRIEND OF SIMON'S. AND I'D LIKE TO TALK TO HIM.

GIVE HIM AN **EXCLUSIVE** FOR ALL HIS TROUBLE.

I DON'T LIKE THIS ONE BIT.

THAT'S WHY YOU'RE **SECOND SHIFT,** DETECTIVE.

I COULD **NOT** TELL.

HEY, I **GOT** THE GUY.

-- ANY CHANCE YOU COULD LEAVE US ALONE?

I'M **SURE** YOU'LL BE **RECORDING** THIS, ANYWAY.

'FRAID NOT, MR. DUNNING. CONSIDER US **BODYGUARDS...**WHAT YOU JUST PUT YOUR **FRIEND** HERE THROUGH, YOU MAY **NEED** ONE.

I'M SURE THAT'S NOT... TRUE?

SIMON?

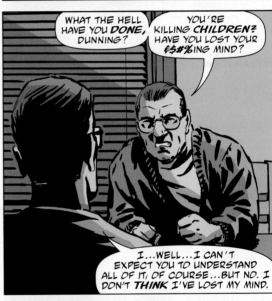

WHAT THE HELL HAVE YOU **DONE,** DUNNING?

YOU'RE KILLING **CHILDREN?** HAVE YOU LOST YOUR £$#%ING MIND?

I...WELL...I CAN'T EXPECT YOU TO UNDERSTAND ALL OF IT, OF COURSE...BUT NO. I DON'T **THINK** I'VE LOST MY MIND.

THEN **WHY?**

IT'S KIND OF COMPLICATED--

WHY SET ME UP? WE WERE **FRIENDS,** JACK.

WE STILL ARE. I **CAME DOWN** AS SOON AS I **HEARD** THEY ARRESTED YOU.

I JUST WANTED TO BE SURE YOU'D BE HERE...FOR THE STORY.

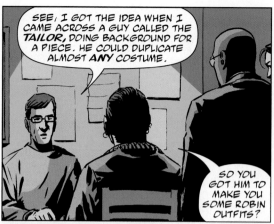

SEE, I GOT THE IDEA WHEN I CAME ACROSS A GUY CALLED THE *TAILOR*, DOING BACKGROUND FOR A PIECE. HE COULD DUPLICATE ALMOST *ANY* COSTUME.

SO YOU GOT HIM TO MAKE YOU SOME ROBIN OUTFITS?

NO. HE HAD SOME FROM *BEFORE. JOKER* ORDERED A FEW HE NEVER PICKED UP OR SOMETHING.

ANYWAY, THAT'S ALL *SIDEBAR* STUFF, HUMAN INTEREST, MAYBE...THE POINT IS, IT GAVE ME AN *ENTRY POINT*, YOU KNOW?

ENTRY POINT TO *WHAT?*

THE WORLD.

YOU'RE *IN* THE WORLD, DUNNING.

NO...*THIS* ISN'T THE WORLD. NOT THE ONE YOU AND I LIVE IN, SIMON...THIS *ISN'T* THE *WORLD.*

LOOK, HOW ABOUT YOU TWO FINISH THIS ILLUMINATING LITTLE CHAT AFTER YOU TELL US WHERE *ZACK WESTON* IS... ASSUMING HE'S STILL *ALIVE?*

ZACK SHOULD BE *FINE* FOR ANOTHER FEW HOURS. BUT I CAN'T TELL *YOU* WHERE HE IS.

CAN YOU TELL *SIMON*, THEN?

NO, NOT *HIM*, EITHER... YOU STILL DON'T UNDERSTAND WHY I'M *HERE*, DO YOU? I CAN'T TELL ANYONE BUT THE BATMAN.

THIS IS MY ENTRY POINT. THIS IS HOW I ENTER *THEIR* WORLD.

C'MON, CAPTAIN, WE **KNOW** HOW THIS **ENDS**...

WAIT, MARCUS.

I JUST--

NO GODDAMN WAY!

LOWER YOUR **VOICE** AND **CLOSE** THE **DOOR**.

YOU **CANNOT** SERIOUSLY **CONSIDER** THIS, CAPTAIN!

TELL ME THIS IS **NOT** AN **OPTION**, HERE!

WHY THE HELL **NOT?**

WE **DO** THIS, WE **GIVE** DUNNING WHAT HE **WANTS**, MARCUS! WE END UP **VALIDATING** HIS **CRIME!**

THAT HAPPENS AND IT'LL BE **LET'S MAKE A DEAL** EVERY TIME WE RUN AN **INTERROGATION!**

WHICH WOULD **BOTHER** ME **MORE** IF THERE WASN'T A **KID'S** LIFE AT **STAKE**.

LET US **RUN** AT HIM **AGAIN**--

THERE **ISN'T** TIME, CRIS.

YOU **HEARD** DUNNING. HE'S GIVING ZACK WESTON A FEW HOURS TO **LIVE**, ON THE **OUTSIDE**.

COULD BE HE'S **BLUFFING**, CAPTAIN?

YOU **REALLY** WANT TO **TAKE** THAT **CHANCE?**

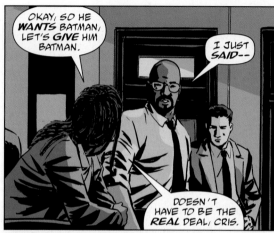

OKAY, SO HE **WANTS** BATMAN, LET'S **GIVE** HIM BATMAN.

I JUST **SAID**--

DOESN'T HAVE TO BE THE **REAL** DEAL, CRIS.

WHAT, YOU **FIGURE** I SHOULD JUST **SHOOT** OVER TO THIS **TAILOR'S** PLACE, GET MYSELF A **BATMAN** COSTUME?

DRESS UP AND TRY TO MAKE DUNNING **WET** HIMSELF?

YEAH, ON **SECOND** THOUGHT IT'S PROBABLY **NOT** SUCH A **GOOD** IDEA...

...ROMY MIGHT **TRY** TO **BUST A CAP** IN YOUR ASS.

YEAH, WELL, HE'D HAVE TO GIVE HER **WEAPON** BACK, **FIRST.**

WHAT WAS **THAT?**

OH, HELL.

NICE ONE, RENEE.

DID **I HEAR** THAT **RIGHT?** DID DETECTIVE CHANDLER TAKE A **SHOT** AT BATMAN?

DID BATMAN **TAKE** HER DUTY WEAPON?

IT'S **NOT** WHAT YOU **THINK,** CAPTAIN--

YOU HAVE **NO** IDEA **WHAT** I THINK, DETECTIVE DRIVER!

JESUS CHRIST, SHE'S A **POLICE!** SHE DOESN'T GO **SHOOTING** AT PEOPLE BECAUSE SHE DOESN'T **LIKE** THEM!

HE BROKE HER NOSE, **DIDN'T** HE?

117

MICHAEL AKINS
Commissioner
of Police

YOU HAVE **GOT** TO BE **KIDDING** ME.

WE NEED TO PUT THE **SIGNAL** BACK UP, COMMISSIONER.

NO, SERIOUSLY, YOU HAVE **GOT** TO BE **KIDDING** ME, RIGHT?

THIS IS SOME **JOKE**, TRYING TO **LIGHTEN** THE MOOD BECAUSE OF ALL THE **CRAP** WE'VE BEEN GETTING FROM THE **PRESS**, RIGHT?

I THINK THERE'S A **SPARE** IN **STORAGE**.

TELL **STACY** TO MEET ME ON THE **ROOF**.

YES, SIR.

IT WOULD'VE BEEN A **GOOD** JOKE, THOUGH, YOU HAVE TO **ADMIT**.

YES, SIR.

I CAN **FIRE** YOU, YOU **KNOW** THAT, RIGHT, MAGGIE?

SO WHAT'S THIS, LIKE, THE **BACKUP** BAT-SIGNAL?

SOMETHING LIKE THAT. DEPARTMENT GOT IT AS A **GIFT** FROM KORD INDUSTRIES A FEW YEARS BACK, BUT WE HAD TO DECOMMISSION IT NOT LONG AFTER I GOT HERE.

CITY COUNCIL SAID IT WAS AN **INAPPROPRIATE** GIFT, SO WE WENT BACK TO THE OLD ONE.

POLITICS.

ABSOLUTELY.

PRETTY CONVENIENT THAT THIS ONE IS SO EASY TO SET UP.

YES. A LASER SIGNAL VISIBLE FOR 25 MILES IN ALL DIRECTIONS **IS** PREFERABLE TO PAINTING A BAT ON A FLASH-LIGHT, I SUPPOSE.

OKAY, THEN YOU JUST...

I THINK...OH, **THERE** IT IS.

THAT'S **IT?**

PRETTY MUCH.

I LIKE THE OTHER ONE BETTER.

WHAT DO **YOU** THINK, JOSIE? I --

JESUS!

THAT WAS QUICK. DID YOU ACTUALLY **WAIT** FOR THE SIGNAL, OR DO YOU HAVE **LISTENING DEVICES** IN MY OFFICE?

IS THERE A **REASON** YOU LIT THAT?

YOU THINK I'D **WASTE** MY RESOURCES ON YOU IF THERE WASN'T A **DAMN GOOD** REASON?

OKAY, ENOUGH. YOU TWO CAN FIGHT IT OUT LATER.

BUT RIGHT NOW, THERE'S A KID'S LIFE AT STAKE, REMEMBER? THAT'S WHY WE'RE HERE.

SIMON LIPPMAN ISN'T THE KILLER.

WE **KNOW** THAT. WE'VE GOT THE **REAL** PERP DOWNSTAIRS, AND THE THIRD VIC IS STILL BREATHING FOR NOW. BUT HE WON'T SAY **WHERE** HE IS...

YES, HE'LL ONLY GIVE **THAT** PIECE OF INFORMATION TO **YOU.**

KILL THE LIGHTS IN THE SQUAD ROOM... **AND** THE BOX.

121

...I SAW HIM, HE SPOKE TO ME...

SURE.

YOU'RE *BLOCKING* MY *OFFICE,* SIMON.

I KNOW.

IF YOU'RE LOOKING FOR AN *APOLOGY*...

I KNOW YOU BETTER THAN *THAT,* EVEN IF *YOU* DON'T KNOW *ME.*

I WILL TAKE A *COMMENT,* HOWEVER. SOMETHING ABOUT *BATMAN'S* INVOLVEMENT.

ON THE RECORD.

AKINS WILL *KILL* ME.

THEN WE'LL BE ABOUT *SQUARE.*

"HIS *HELP* WAS *INSTRUMENTAL* IN THE *ARREST,*" M.C.U. CAPTAIN SAWYER SAID.

"AS WAS THE ASSISTANCE OF CERTAIN JOURNALISTS FROM THE LOCAL MEDIA."

HOW'S *THAT?*

PROBABLY *WON'T* USE THE LAST PART.

GET SOME *SLEEP,* MAGGIE.

YOU LOOK *BEAT.*

--CORRECT, ZACK WESTON WAS RETURNED TO HIS FAMILY SAFELY. HE WAS BEING HELD IN A SUBBASEMENT IN THE EAST END.

COMMISSIONER, WE UNDERSTAND THAT SIMON LIPPMAN FROM THE GAZETTE WAS TAKEN INTO CUSTODY EARLIER. WAS MR. LIPPMAN A SUSPECT?

NO, MR. LIPPMAN WAS A SUBJECT, NOT A SUSPECT. AND AS I'M SURE YOU'LL READ, HE WAS INSTRUMENTAL IN AIDING THE G.C.P.D. IN THIS INVESTIGATION...

LOOK AT THAT MAN...DEFLECTS THE QUESTION LIKE A CONSUMMATE POLITICIAN AND COVERS OUR ASSES AT THE SAME TIME.

HE REALLY SHOULD RUN FOR MAYOR.

HE PROBABLY **WILL**, SARGE.

--SAY TO REPORTS OF THE **BAT-SIGNAL** BEING SIGHTED EARLIER TONIGHT, COMMISSIONER?

NO COMMENT?

NO COMMENT.

NO COMMENT. NEXT?

--IS DETECTIVE CHANDLER?

HAVE NOT SEEN HER, CAP. TRY THE BREAK ROOM YET?

DETECTIVE ROMY CHANDLER. JUST THE WOMAN I WAS LOOKING FOR.

OH, UH... WHAT'S UP, CAPTAIN?

I BETTER GET BACK TO MY DESK...

AM I TO UNDERSTAND THAT **IN ADDITION** TO YOUR APPARENT **SHOOTING** OF BATMAN...

...THAT YOU **ALSO** LOST YOUR SERVICE WEAPON?

...THAT'S NOT...

SORRY TO **INTERRUPT**, CAPTAIN, BUT I THINK THERE'S BEEN A **MISUNDERSTANDING.**

I JUST **PICKED UP** ROMY'S PIECE FROM REPAIR. HER SIGHTS WERE **WAY OFF.**

YEAH... THAT'S WHY MY **WARNING SHOT** ACCIDENTALLY HIT.

IS THAT THE STORY YOU'RE STICKING WITH?

IF YOU'LL BUY IT.

NEVER HAPPEN AGAIN, CAPTAIN. SCOUT'S HONOR.

SEE THAT IT DOESN'T. YOU'RE A GOOD DETECTIVE, ROMY. WE'D HATE TO LOSE YOU.

STACY GOT IT FROM ROBIN.

I KNOW.

DAMN.

WHAT *IS* IT WITH THIS CITY...?

IT'S A LOVE/HATE THING, ROMY...

THERE'S A LOT HERE TO LOVE...THAT YOU WON'T FIND IN ANY OTHER CITY IN THE WORLD...

...BUT THERE'S JUST AS MUCH THAT'LL KILL YOU, EITHER IN AN INSTANT OR SLOWLY...DAY BY DAY...

ROBIN KILLER CONFESSES

BUT WHAT ARE YOU GONNA DO? *QUIT?* LEAVE?

NO...THIS IS MY *CITY.*

I COULD SOONER LEAVE *YOU.*

HEY!

AND THAT'S *NOT* GOING TO HAPPEN, MARCUS...

LET'S GO HOME.

126

THE END

SUNDAY BLOODY SUNDAY

Written by
GREG RUCKA
Art by
STEVE LIEBER
Colors by
LEE LOUGHRIDGE
Letters by
CLEM ROBINS

The cosmic cataclysm known as the Infinite Crisis is wreaking havoc
all across the Galaxy. As an-all-too powerful madman is molding the laws
of nature and physics like clay, the properties of magic are also changing,
and all of the wielders of magic are losing control of their powers. The most
powerful of all the supernatural guardians is the Spectre — the living spirit
of vengeance. The Spectre relies on a human host for moral guidance, but
has been without one for too long. Whoever he chooses as his next host will
become the arbiter of morality for all humankind.

THEY SAY THE **WORLD** IS COMING TO AN **END.**

WOULDN'T BE THE **FIRST** TIME.

FACT IS, IT HAPPENS MORE OFTEN THAN MOST PEOPLE CARE TO **ADMIT.**

HELL, **SOME** SCIENTISTS CLAIM THE EARTH HAS HAD ITS TICKET **PUNCHED** A HALF-DOZEN TIMES IN THE LAST FOUR **BILLION** YEARS.

GOTHAM, GA- KILLER BODY!

AND THAT'S **NOT** COUNTING WHAT HAPPENED TO THE **DINOSAURS.**

CURRENT THINKING IN **PHYSICS** IS THAT **UNIVERSES**--PLURAL--ARE **BEGINNING** AND **ENDING** ALL THE TIME.

THAT **OURS** IS JUST A **BLIP** IN THE **COSMIC** SCHEME, THAT'S **ALL.**

EXTINCTION **HAPPENS** ON SOME SCALE **EVERY** MOMENT. MURDER OR EVOLUTION OR DIVINE ACT, **PICK** YOUR **POISON.**

SOME MORE **NATURAL** THAN **OTHERS.**

THERE'S AN **OLD** MURDER POLICE JOKE.

WELL?

HOMICIDE. WE WORK FOR **GOD.**

IT'S **DEAD.**

I DON'T THINK ABOUT GOD THAT MUCH ANYMORE.

AFTER YOU'VE SEEN A **GOOD** COP FROZEN **SOLID** BY MISTER FREEZE AND THEN **SHATTERED** LIKE A PORCELAIN **DOLL**, YOUR **FAITH** TAKES A **BEATING**.

...DISPATCH AND A **TOW TRUCK**, AND SOONER RATHER THAN LATER, OKAY?

TEN-FOUR.

SEE ENOUGH ACTS LIKE **THAT**, IT'S **EASIER** NOT TO THINK ABOUT GOD'S **MERCY** AND HIS **DIVINE WILL** TOO MUCH.

GONNA BE **HALF** AN HOUR, AT THE **LEAST**.

BUSY NIGHT?

OR ELSE YOU FIND YOURSELF ASKING **QUESTIONS** THAT HAVE **NO** ANSWER.

THAT'S THE **THING**. THERE'S **NOTHING** HAPPENING, THE WHOLE DAMN **CITY** IS **DEAD**.

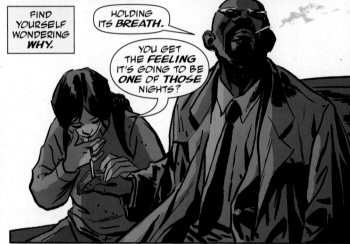

FIND YOURSELF WONDERING **WHY**.

HOLDING ITS **BREATH**.

YOU GET THE **FEELING** IT'S GOING TO BE **ONE OF THOSE** NIGHTS?

SO I **TRY** NOT TO **THINK** ABOUT IT TOO MUCH. IT'S LIKE THAT LINE IN THE PLAY, MEDEA.

HELL YEAH.

"WE MUSTN'T **THINK** TOO MUCH. PEOPLE GO **MAD** IF THEY **THINK** TOO MUCH."

MY WIFE, DORE, SHE DOESN'T **UNDERSTAND** WHY I WON'T GO TO CHURCH ANYMORE.

...NO, THE **UNMARKED** BROKE DOWN, SO RENEE AND I ARE OUT OF THE SQUAD ROOM UNTIL WE CAN GET A **LIFT** BACK...

...I WILL...YES, I'LL TELL HER...KISS THE **BOYS** FOR ME...

YOU, TOO, BABY.

IT'S ONE OF THE **FEW** THINGS WE ACTUALLY **FIGHT** ABOUT. SHE THINKS IT GIVES OUR **SONS** THE **WRONG** IMPRESSION.

SO I DID SOME **DIGGING** ON THE **CORRIGAN** THING --

SHE TELLS ME THAT'S **NOT** THE POINT.

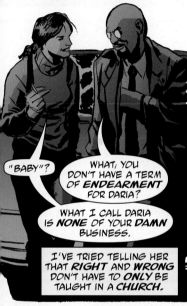

"BABY"?

WHAT, YOU DON'T HAVE A TERM OF **ENDEARMENT** FOR DARIA?

WHAT I CALL DARIA IS **NONE** OF YOUR **DAMN** BUSINESS.

I'VE TRIED TELLING HER THAT **RIGHT** AND **WRONG** DON'T HAVE TO **ONLY** BE TAUGHT IN A **CHURCH**.

DAMMIT, CRIS, **NOT** AGAIN --

YES, **AGAIN**. THERE'S A **STORY** GOING AROUND, RENEE, ABOUT YOU AND CORRIGAN AT FINNIGAN'S BAR...

IT **ENDS** THERE, BECAUSE THE ONLY THING I CAN SAY TO HER MY WIFE DOESN'T **WANT** TO HEAR.

...THAT YOU **TOOK** HIM OUT BACK AND **BEAT** THE LIVING **HELL** OUT OF HIM.

I DON'T BELIEVE IN GOD ANYMORE.

IS THAT HOW YOU GOT THE **MISSING** BULLET, THE **ONE** THAT **CLEARED** ME?

CRIS --

I WANT AN **ANSWER**, PARTNER.

YOU **OWE** ME AN **ANSWER**.

131

RENEE MONTOYA'S BEEN MY *PARTNER* FOR *YEARS* NOW.

CORRIGAN *SOLD* IT; I HAD TO FIND OUT WHO TO, AND HE *WASN'T* TALKING.

I *DID* WHAT I *HAD* TO, CRIS.

IN MANY WAYS, SHE KNOWS ME *BETTER* THAN MY OWN *WIFE*.

GOD *DAMMIT*, RENEE! WHAT THE HELL WERE YOU *THINKING*?

WE'RE *NOT* GOING TO *HAVE* THIS --

IN MANY WAYS, I KNOW *HER* BETTER THAN HER LOVER, DARIA.

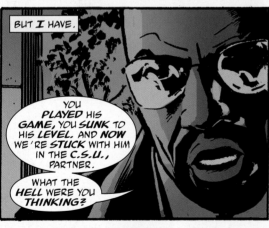

I DON'T KNOW IF DARIA'S *SEEN* IT.

NO, WE *ARE* GOING TO HAVE THIS CONVERSATION!

GET *OFF* OF ME!

I *KNOW* FOR A *FACT* THAT CAPTAIN SAWYER *HASN'T*.

ARE YOU *OUT* OF YOUR *MIND*, RENEE?

BY *BEATING* CORRIGAN DOWN, YOU *KILLED* ANY CHANCE OF *US* OR I.A.D. *EVER* MAKING A *CASE* AGAINST THAT *ROTTEN* SON OF A BITCH.

BUT *I* HAVE.

YOU *PLAYED* HIS *GAME*, YOU *SUNK* TO HIS *LEVEL*. AND *NOW* WE'RE *STUCK* WITH HIM IN THE C.S.U., PARTNER.

WHAT THE *HELL* WERE YOU *THINKING*?

SHE'S IN *TROUBLE*.

I WAS THINKING THAT *PROTECTING* YOU WAS MORE IMPORTANT THAN *NAILING* HIM, CRIS.

THAT'S WHAT I WAS THINKING.

=SKSHHS=-- ANY *AVAILABLE* UNIT!

IT *STARTED* AFTER THE THING WITH *TWO-FACE*.

TEN-THREE! TEN-THREE, CATHEDRAL SQUARE!

MULTIPLE FREAKS, WE'VE GOT--

SHE'S BEEN GETTING **MORE** AND **MORE** RECKLESS EVER SINCE.

KRAK KRAK KRAK KRAK

EEEEEEE

"GOD OH MY GOD IT'S RIDDLER IT'S--"

ANGRIER AND ANGRIER.

DAMMIT DAMMIT DAMMIT DAMMIT!

EEEEEEEEEE

WHERE SHE **USED** TO **HATE** THE **VIOLENCE** OF THE JOB...

PULL OVER!

PULL IT OVER!

...**NOW** SHE ALMOST **RUNS** INTO ITS **EMBRACE**.

M.C.U.! WE'RE **TAKING** YOUR **RIDE**!

THE **HELL**?

GOTHAM

AND I'M **SCARED** FOR HER.

OUT OF THE **WAY**, BARBIE!

HEY!

SCARED FOR WHERE IT MAY **LEAD** HER.

WE'LL HAVE **DISPATCH** SEND A **PICKUP** FOR YOU!

THERE'S *RELIEF* IN BEING ON THE *MOVE* AGAIN, AT LEAST.

ALL UNITS, RESPOND CATHEDRAL SQUARE, TEN-THIRTY-THREE.

CHARLIE TANGO FOUR, MOBILE, RESPONDING...

NO ONE WANTS TO BE *SITTING* ON THEIR *HANDS* WHEN THE *APOCALYPSE* COMES, AFTER ALL.

...BE ADVISED CHARLIE TANG FOUR NOW THREE-TWO BAKER.

BETTER TO AT LEAST *FEEL* LIKE WE'RE DOING SOMETHING.

ALL UNITS, SUSPECTS *IDENTIFIED* AS THE RIDDLER, THE SCAVENGER, MURMUR, THE BODY DOUBLES, RED PANZER AND THE FISHERMAN...

WE'RE NOT *DONE*, BY THE *WAY*.

THE *IRONY* THAT WE'RE HEADING TO *CATHEDRAL SQUARE* HASN'T *ESCAPED* ME, EITHER.

...OTHERS MAY BE *PRESENT*, PROCEED WITH *CAUTION*. E.S.U. IS RESPONDING.

THIS THING WITH *CORRIGAN* IS --

WOULD YOU *SHUT UP* ABOUT *CORRIGAN*, ALREADY?

YES, HE'S *CORRUPT* AND YES, HE'S *STILL* ON THE *FORCE*, BUT THEN AGAIN SO ARE *YOU!*

AND THAT'S A *FAIR TRADE* IN MY...

THE *EDGE* IN HER *VOICE* VANISHES.

...BOOK UH... CRIS...?

I RAISE MY *EYES*...

...AND SEE THE IMPOSSIBLE...

SUNDAY BLOODY SUNDAY

...TELL ME YOU'RE SEEING THAT?

THE SKY BEGINS TO RAIN FIRE.

AH!

MOTHER%#$#!

METAL *TEARS* AS SOMETHING *CRUSHES* THE ENGINE BLOCK.

THE WINDSHIELD *EXPLODES* INWARDS, SHOWERING ME WITH *SAFETY* GLASS.

I TUMBLE OUT OF THE *CAR* AND INTO *AIR* THAT *STINKS* OF *SULFUR* AND BURNING *FLESH.*

MY SIGHT *CATCHES* ON ONE *WORD* AND A *FACE...*

...AND I *FREEZE* FOR A *MOMENT,* STARING INTO THE *EYES* OF A *SIN.*

SCREAMS AND EXPLOSIONS ECHO THROUGHOUT THE SQUARE.

RENEE'S SAYING *SOMETHING,* BUT I CAN'T *HEAR* HER.

OF ALL THE THINGS THAT SHOULD BE *FRIGHTENING* ME AT *THIS* MOMENT AND *AREN'T*...

IS THAT...?

CAPTAIN MARVEL.

...THIS ONE *DOES*.

AND THEN HE *SPEAKS*, AND I DON'T *UNDERSTAND* WHAT HE'S SAYING.

THE ROCK OF ETERNITY... THE *ROCK*....HE... DID IT...

...THE *SPECTRE*...

...HE *KILLED* HIM...

AND NOW I AM *TRULY* AFRAID.

...HE *KILLED* THE *WIZARD*...

137

THE **THINGS** I'VE SEEN, SO **MANY** THINGS...

WHAT... WHAT **IS** THAT...?

...**BATMAN** IN THE **NIGHT** SKY AND THE **JOKER** IN THE **BOX** AND **MURDER** A THOUSAND TIMES OVER...

...BUT **NOTHING** LIKE THIS, NOTHING **EVER** LIKE THIS...

THE **SPECTRE**, THE **AGENT** OF DIVINE **VENGEANCE**.

BUT HE'S GONE **MAD**, HE'S **UNRAVELING** ALL **MAGICK**--

HNH!

RENEE MAKES A **NOISE**, IT'S THE **SOUND** I IMAGINE A **SHARK** WOULD MAKE WHEN IT SMELLS **BLOOD** IN THE **WATER**--

PARTNER?

BASTARDS BASTARDS--

--AND SUDDENLY IT'S AS IF **ALL** THAT **ANGER** SHE'S BEEN CARRYING CAN NO **LONGER** BE CONTAINED.

RENEE!

--BASTARDS DO **THIS** TO ME TO THE **CHILD** THEY **THINK** I DON'T **KNOW**--

--WHAT THEY **THINK** THEY'RE SAYING BEHIND MY BACK WHAT ALL OF YOU **THINK** YOU SAY YOU BASTARDS--

I'VE GOT **JUST** LONG ENOUGH TO SEE THE **IRONY** IN BEING KILLED BY MY **BEST FRIEND**...

--I'LL **KILL** YOU, I'LL £*%#ING SON OF A--

...AND THEN CAPTAIN MARVEL MAYBE SAVES **BOTH** OUR LIVES, JUST LIKE THAT.

--HANDS OFF OF ME YOU **NAIVE** DO-GOODING--

LEAVE HER ALONE.

NOW.

SOMETHING... **LEAVES** HER BODY...

UNNH!

...THE **FURY** OF THE **DEVIL** HIMSELF.

THEN CAPTAIN MARVEL IS **TALKING** TO ME LIKE I **UNDERSTAND** WHAT'S GOING ON.

CAN YOU TAKE **CARE** OF HER?

THE **POSSESSION** WAS ONLY **TEMPORARY**, BUT SHE'LL NEED A FEW **MINUTES** TO REGAIN HER **STRENGTH**.

POSSESSION?

WITH THE ROCK OF ETERNITY **SHATTERED**, THE **SEVEN DEADLY SINS** ARE **FREE** UPON GOTHAM, OFFICER.

AND I CANNOT **STAY** TO HELP **FIGHT** THEM.

BUT YOU'RE--

THE WIZARD IS DEAD, I DON'T EXPECT YOU TO UNDERSTAND.

BUT MY FAMILY... MY FAMILY MAY BE IN GREAT DANGER, I MUST GO TO THEM.

MY STOMACH SHRINKS, THE FEAR RACING UP MY SPINE.

I'M SORRY.

IF HE'S WORRIED ABOUT HIS FAMILY SURVIVING THIS NIGHT...

...THEN WHAT HOPE DOES MINE HAVE?

I'VE GOT TO GET TO THEM.

CRIS?

EASY, PARTNER.

I'VE GOT TO GET TO THEM NOW.

I'M SORRY, I'M SO SORRY, I DIDN'T—I DIDN'T MEAN IT...

WHAT I SAID... I DIDN'T MEAN...

DON'T WORRY ABOUT IT RIGHT NOW...

...WE'VE GOT TO GET MOVING.

I'VE GOT TWO **HUNDRED** BLOCKS TO **COVER** FROM HERE TO **HOME**.

TWO HUNDRED **BLOCKS** THROUGH A GOTHAM THAT HAS ONCE **AGAIN** GONE **MAD**.

TWO HUNDRED **BLOCKS** WITH MY **PARTNER** ON MY ARM AND SEVEN DEADLY SINS HAVING A **FIELD** DAY...

...JUST TAKE IT **ONE** STEP AT A **TIME, CRIS**...

THE **WIND** THAT'S BEEN **HOWLING** FOR THE LAST THREE MINUTES WHIPS **TEAR GAS** INTO MY **FACE**.

:KAFF KAFF:

:KOFF:

JUST THE **BAREST** TOUCH AND IT'S **ENOUGH** TO START THE **WATERWORKS** FLOWING.

THAT'S THE **LEAST** OF OUR **PROBLEMS**.

I **RECOGNIZE** HIM FROM SOME **PERP BOOK** OF **FREAKS** FROM YEARS AGO...

...THE **FISHERMAN**, I THINK HE'S **CALLED**, ONE OF **AQUAMAN'S ROGUES**...

DROP BAIT.

...AND IN **ANY** OTHER CIRCUMSTANCE, I'D BE **LAUGHING** AT THE SIGHT OF **HIM**.

I GO FOR MY GUN.

HE'S FASTER.

WHY ARE THEY ALWAYS FASTER?

NYAA

THE GUN KICKS IN MY HAND.

I MISS.

THIS ISN'T CATCH AND RELEASE.

I DON'T GET A SECOND SHOT.

HNHH

PAIN SPIRALS UP MY ARM.

ANOTHER &*$%ING COP, HUH?

BETWEEN THE **TEAR GAS** AND HIS **GRIP**, MY **LUNGS** HAVE **NOTHING**.

I £%6*ING HATE **COPS**.

KRAK

THE **EDGES** OF THE **WORLD** TURN TO **WHITE**. I HEAR THE **ROAR** OF THE **OCEAN** IN MY **EARS**.

I'M BEING **SUFFOCATED** BY A **LUNATIC** CALLED THE **FISHERMAN**.

I THINK OF MY **FAMILY**, AND THAT THIS IS A **STUPID** GODDAMN WAY TO **LEAVE** THEM.

HUH?

KRAKKRAKKRAK

WHAZZIT?

IT TAKES A **SECOND** FOR ME TO **RECOGNIZE** DETECTIVES MARCUS DRIVER AND JOSIE MACDONALD.

IT TAKES *ANOTHER* BEFORE I CAN SPEAK.

CRIS? YOU *OKAY?*

RENEE... RENEE'S BEEN *HURT.*

DOESN'T LOOK *TOO* BAD.

'M FINE.

WE GOT TO GET HER *OFF* THE *STREET*, MARCUS.

HERE, HOLD *STILL.*

LISTEN, MARCUS, CAN YOU AND *JO* TAKE CARE OF HER, GET HER *HOME?*

ARE YOU *KIDDING* ME? HAVE YOU *LOOKED* AROUND YOU, CRIS?

WORLD IS COMING TO AN *END*, IT'S *HATS* AND *BATS* TIME FOR THE *G.C.P.D.*, ALL *COPS* ON THE *STREET.*

I'VE GOT TO GET TO MY *FAMILY*, MAN. AND RENEE NEEDS *HELP.*

THIS'LL *HURT.*

SONOFABITCH

YOU'RE GONNA NEED THIS *STITCHED* UP.

I'VE GOT TO GET TO MY *FAMILY.* CAN YOU AT *LEAST* GET RENEE TO AN *AMBO?*

THERE *ARE* NO AMBULANCES, CRIS. THERE'S *NOTHING*...

...I'M SORRY, MAN, BUT YOU GUYS ARE *ON* YOUR *OWN*...

I TRY **NOT** TO **BLAME** HIM, BECAUSE I KNOW HE'S RIGHT.

I SHOULD BE STANDING **BESIDE** THEM, HOLDING THE **LINE**.

BUT I'M **NOT**, AND I **DO** BLAME HIM.

NO CROSSING

DRIVER, JOSIE...THEY **DON'T** HAVE **FAMILIES** WAITING FOR THEM.

I TRY MY **PHONE**, DESPERATE TO HEAR DORE'S VOICE, OR THE **BOYS**...

--CIRCUITS ARE **BUSY**, PLEASE TRY YOUR CALL **AGAIN**...

IT TELLS ME WHAT I **EXPECTED**, BUT **NOT** WHAT I'D **HOPED**.

WITH **ALL** THE **LOOTING** GOING ON, I DON'T **SEE** THEM UNTIL THEY'RE IN FRONT OF US.

WHERE YOU GOING, **BOY?**

GOTHAM IS **BURNING**, BUT IT SEEMS THERE'S **ALWAYS** TIME FOR A LITTLE OLD-FASHIONED **RACISM**.

YOUR **GIRLFRIEND** DOESN'T **LOOK** SO GOOD, SPOOKY.

WHY DON'T YOU **LEAVE** HER WITH **US?** WE'LL TAKE **CARE** OF HER.

I THINK ABOUT WHAT **MARVEL** SAID, ABOUT SEVEN DEADLY SINS LET LOOSE IN THE **WORLD**...

...AND I WONDER HOW **MUCH** OF THIS IS **THEIR** DOING...

WALK **AWAY.** NOW.

LOOK AT **THAT**, THE **MONKEY'S** GOT A BADGE...

THAT'S **RIGHT,** HE'S A **COP**...

...AND HOW **MUCH** IS **ALL** OURS.

...WHICH MEANS HE'S GOT A **GUN**...

F&*%$.

...TOO...

NOT SO **TOUGH** WITHOUT **HEAT**...

I DON'T WANT TO **DIE** LIKE THIS.

...ARE YOU, BOY?

I HAVE TO GET **HOME**.

AAHGGG!!

BLAMM

CRIS.

HELP ME UP.

HNN NHHNN HNH!

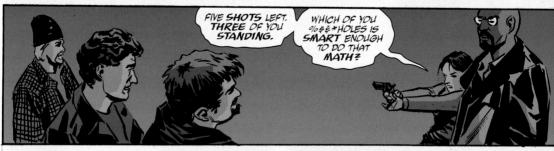

FIVE **SHOTS** LEFT. **THREE** OF YOU STANDING.

WHICH OF YOU %¢&*HOLES IS **SMART** ENOUGH TO DO THAT **MATH**?

YEAH, THAT'S WHAT I THOUGHT.

I'M GETTING YOU **HOME**, RENEE.

NO...

xenon

...THERE...

I **POUND** ON THE **DOOR** HOPING THAT **EVERYONE** HASN'T GONE **HOME**.

DARIA! **DARIA HERNANDEZ**!

IT'S DETECTIVE ALLEN!

THEY **HAVEN'T**.

RENEE!

IT'S THE **FIRST** PIECE OF **LUCK** WE'VE **CAUGHT** THE WHOLE **NIGHT**.

WHAT **HAPPENED**?

HEY, BABY. WHAT'S THE **SPECIAL**?

THE CITY'S GONE **MAD**, THAT'S WHAT'S **HAPPENED**, DEE!

ARE YOU **GOOD** HERE?

WE'VE GOT **FOOD** FOR AT LEAST A **WEEK** AND **WINE** FOR AT LEAST A **MONTH**.

AND LEO THERE IS DAMN **QUICK** WITH HIS **EIGHT-INCH HOLLOW EDGE KERSHAW**.

GOOD, OKAY, THEN I'M GOING TO LEAVE YOU GUYS **HERE**, ALL RIGHT?

YOU'RE HEADED **HOME**?

YEAH.

THANK YOU. FOR TAKING **CARE** OF HER.

SHE'S MY **PARTNER**, DEE.

SHE HAS NO IDEA HOW **LUCKY** SHE IS TO **HAVE** YOU.

OR TO HAVE **YOU**.

TAKE MY **CAR**, IT'S IN THE **LOT** AROUND **BACK**.

GIVE DORE AND THE BOYS MY LOVE.

BY THE TIME I'VE GONE **FOUR BLOCKS,** I'VE **ALREADY** COUNTED **SEVENTY-NINE** FELONIES.

I THINK ABOUT **STOPPING,** ABOUT DOING MY **JOB.**

THEN I THINK THAT I HAVE **NO** WEAPON, **NO** RADIO, AND **NO** HOPE OF **BACKUP.**

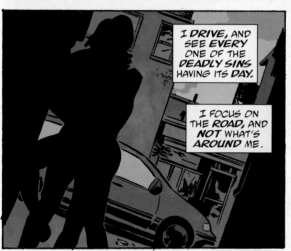

I **DRIVE,** AND SEE **EVERY** ONE OF THE **DEADLY SINS** HAVING ITS **DAY.**

I FOCUS ON THE **ROAD,** AND **NOT** WHAT'S **AROUND** ME.

NORTH OF NINETY-SECOND, GOTHAM TURNS TO A **GHOST TOWN.**

I TAKE IT UP TO **NINETY** AND **RUN** EVERY LIGHT.

I'M **STILL** NOT GOING **FAST** ENOUGH.

I JUST WANT TO GET HOME.

Equal Rights Are Not Special Rights

I JUST WANT TO GET HOME...

...DOZENS KILLED, THE **MAYOR** IS APPEALING TO THE GOVERNOR FOR **HELP...**

DAD!

I GOT HOME AS **SOON** AS I COULD.

OH, CRIS...

...I WAS **PRAYING** YOU WERE ALL RIGHT.

CRISPUS, YOUR **ARM**.

IT'S **NOTHING**, DON'T **WORRY**--

WHAT'S GOING ON, DAD? WHAT'S **HAPPENING**?

I DON'T **KNOW**, JAKE. **CRAZY** THINGS.

THE GUY ON THE **TV** SAID THE **WORLD** WAS **ENDING**...

...HE SAID IT WAS THE **END** OF THE **WORLD**.

WHAT ARE WE **SUPPOSED** TO DO?

THE EN

CORRIGAN II

Written by
GREG RUCKA
Art by
KANO & STEFANO GAUDIANO
Colors by
LEE LOUGHRIDGE
Letters by
CLEM ROBINS

In a Police Department with a well earned reputation for being one of the most corrupt, Crime Scene Technician Jim Corrigan has mastered the art of payoffs, extortion and exploitation. While investigating Corrigan, Inspector Manuel "Manny" Esperanza of the Internal Affairs Division learned of a scheme to frame M.C.U. Detective Crispus Allen. Manny informed Allen's partner, Renee Montoya, of the plot. Montoya used excessive force to get the information she needed from Corrigan, which cleared Allen, but her actions spared Corrigan from further investigation into his illicit affairs. He is essentially untouchable. Allen knew nothing of Montoya's actions or their repercussions, until now...

Officer
TIMOTHY
MUNROE
(Western)

Officer
ROGER
CARLO
(Western)

JAMES "Jimmy"
CORRIGAN
CSU-Head Tech

Inspector
MANNY
ESPERANZA
- IAD

Detective
WILLIAM
KENZIE
- Narcotics

The Gotham City Police Department employs over 35,000 officers, with several thousands more retained in support roles. Since its founding, it has been a department renowned for corruption in a city infamous for crime. From the rookie on the street to the Chief of Patrol working out of Central, almost every officer, every administrator, every detective, is in some manner, in some way, guilty of corruption — either actively abusing their power and authority, or passively reaping its rewards.

With the notable exception of the detectives of the Major Crimes Unit, being "on the take" in the G.C.P.D. is the rule, not the exception.

JAMES CORRIGAN is the lead Crime Scene Technician assigned to the Western Division Headquarters. Working out of the Western, he has exploited his position to make himself the king of his domain, leading a cadre of officers and detectives who follow his example of graft, extortion, and abuse.

INSPECTOR MANUEL "MANNY" ESPERANZA of the Internal Affairs Division had been pursuing Corrigan, until M.C.U. DETECTIVE CRISPUS ALLEN found himself in danger of losing his badge. Esperanza pointed Allen's partner, RENEE MONTOYA at Corrigan. Montoya beat Corrigan until he provided her with the evidence that would save Allen's career.

As a result of both Montoya's and Esperanza's actions, Corrigan has become essentially untouchable, and spared from further investigation into his illegal activities.

Detective Allen has only recently learned of what his partner did to save his badge, and the trade-off does not sit well with him…

CORRIGAN II

PART ONE

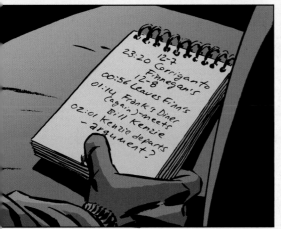

12-7
23.20 Corriganto
        Finnegan's
12-8
00:56 Leaves Finn's
01:14 Frank's Diner
        (again) meets
        Bill Kenzie
02:01 Kenzie departs
    - argument?

LATE NIGHT?

THIS FROM THE GUY WHO LOOKS LIKE HE GOT MAYBE AN *HOUR'S* SLEEP?

THAT'S AN HOUR MORE THAN *YOU*, FROM THE LOOKS OF IT, AND AT LEAST I MANAGED A *CHANGE* OF CLOTHES.

DORE SAYS THAT *DARIA* CALLED *AGAIN* LAST NIGHT, LOOKING FOR YOU.

DORE SAYS? *NOT* YOU?

I WAS *OUT*.

YOU WERE OUT AT *MIDNIGHT*?

SO WERE *YOU*, APPARENTLY...

...DIFFERENCE IS, I'M NOT MAKING A REGULAR *THING* OF IT, AND DORE *KNEW* I WAS GOING TO BE *LATE*.

SO NOW I'M WONDERING WHY *YOUR* GIRLFRIEND IS CALLING *MY* WIFE AT *MIDNIGHT* LOOKING FOR YOU.

AND *I'M* WONDERING WHY *YOU* WEREN'T AT *HOME* TO TAKE THAT CALL, BUT YOU *DON'T* HEAR *ME* ASKING, DO YOU?

ALL RIGHT, COME HERE.

CRIS, GET YOUR *HAND*--

COME. *HERE.*

...PUBLICIST CLAIMS HE IS **NOT** THE **FATHER**...

OOOH, I SMELL A **PATERNITY** SUIT.

SHUT UP, TOMMY.

...CLAIMING HE IS STILL HAPPILY MARRIED TO THE STAR OF FALLING DOWN IS FUNNY, IONA SHAUGHNESSY...

CURIOUSER AND CURIOUSER.

DON'T EVEN **THINK** ABOUT IT.

CRIS, I'VE GOT **WORK** TO--

SHUT **UP** AND **LISTEN.**

HEY, DON'T **TALK** TO ME LIKE **THAT!**

OR **WHAT,** YOU'RE GONNA **HIT** ME? THAT'S YOUR **NEW** THING, **RIGHT?**

A LITTLE **VIOLENCE** TO **EASE** YOUR PAIN, WHATEVER IT IS?

YOU ARE **SO** OFF-BASE HERE, PARTNER--

AM I?

YOU **MISSED A** SPOT.

PARTNER.

CHRIST.

YOU'RE COMING **APART,** RENEE.

AND I DON'T WANT TO **WATCH** IT ANYMORE.

I'M **FINE.**

YOU'RE **NOT!** DAMMIT, I'M YOUR **PARTNER,** YOU THINK I HAVEN'T **SEEN** IT?

YOU USED TO BE A **GOOD** POLICE, RENEE. YOU USED TO BE THE KIND OF POLICE **GORDON** WAS **PROUD** OF.

I AM A GOOD POLICE.

THEN **EXPLAIN** THIS TO ME, BECAUSE I **DON'T** GET IT!

EXPLAIN TO ME WHY YOU USED YOUR **FISTS** ON A **BASTARD** LIKE CORRIGAN INSTEAD OF YOUR **BRAINS!**

EXPLAIN TO ME WHY DOCTOR ALCHEMY NEEDED TO BE **HOSPITALIZED** AFTER YOU GOT **DONE** WITH HIM!

AND **EXPLAIN** TO ME WHY YOU'RE **CRUISING** FOR **FIGHTS** AT NIGHT INSTEAD OF BEING **HOME** WITH SOMEONE WHO **LOVES** YOU.

IT'S **GOT** TO **STOP,** RENEE.

OR ELSE YOU'RE FINDING YOURSELF A **NEW** PARTNER.

...POCKET TEST ON IT, BUT IT SURE AS HELL *LOOKS* PURE...

...ANYONE SEEN KENZIE?

LONG.

...DOWN TO THE WESTERN FOR *QUESTIONING*...

HEY, CORRIGAN.

YOU GOT HERE *FAST*.

YOU KNOW ME, *WHEREVER* THERE'S *CRIME*...

...I'LL BE *THERE*.

YOU *DROPPED* THIS AT *FINNIGAN'S* LAST NIGHT.

YOU'D *THINK* I'D BE *MORE* CAREFUL WITH MY *MONEY*.

THANKS FOR *HOLDING* THIS FOR ME, JIMMY.

YEAH, WELL, THANKS FOR THE *TIP*.

KENZIE IN THERE?

IN THE *BEDROOM*, THAT'S WHERE THE *MAJOR* OPERATION WAS.

RIGHT.

GIVE MULCAHEY MY *BEST*, WOULD YOU?

SURE THING.

159

160

CRIS.

HMM?

CRIS.

I'M SORRY, OKAY?

YEAH, THERE'S SINCERITY JUST DRIPPING FROM THAT APOLOGY.

CUT ME A LITTLE SLACK, WE'RE IN THE MIDDLE OF THE GODDAMN SQUADROOM!

THAT'S A GOOD EXCUSE. TELL ME ANOTHER.

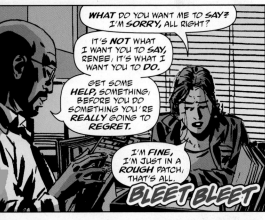

WHAT DO YOU WANT ME TO SAY? I'M SORRY, ALL RIGHT?

IT'S NOT WHAT I WANT YOU TO SAY, RENEE; IT'S WHAT I WANT YOU TO DO.

GET SOME HELP, SOMETHING, BEFORE YOU DO SOMETHING YOU'RE REALLY GOING TO REGRET.

I'M FINE, I'M JUST IN A ROUGH PATCH, THAT'S ALL.

BLEET BLEET

SURE. AND I'M THE SCARECROW.

BLEET

BLEET

M.C.U., ALLEN...

...I CAN DO IT NOW, JUST TELL ME WHERE...

...NO, NOT THERE...

...THAT'LL WORK. GIVE ME TWENTY MINUTES.

I'VE GOT TO GO OUT.

WHO WAS THAT?

I'LL BE BACK IN AN HOUR OR SO.

I'LL COME WITH YOU.

NO.

I'M YOUR PARTNER--

IT'S ONE OF MY C.I.'S, HE GETS TWITCHY IF ANYONE SHOWS UP BESIDES ME, OKAY?

I KNOW ALL YOUR CONFIDENTIAL INFORMANTS, CRIS.

THIS ONE'S NEW, I HAVEN'T REGISTERED HIM YET.

I'LL BE BACK IN AN HOUR.

Corrigan
Finnigan's 10:30
FINNIGAN'S BAR

CORRIGAN.

162

...THEN *DOWN* FOR THE *HEARING* AT *TWO*.

INTERNAL AFFAIRS DIVISION

I'LL CALL AND LET THEM KNOW.

THANKS, LIZ.

ESPERANZA!

DETECTIVE MONTOYA, WHAT BRINGS YOU TO I.A.D.?

EXPLAIN THIS!

WHERE'D YOU *GET* IT?

YOU KNOW *DAMN WELL* WHERE I *GOT* IT!

NO, THAT'S WHY I'M *ASKING*.

BUT IF YOU WANT TO ACCUSE ME OF *ANYTHING*, PLEASE, FEEL FREE TO JOIN ME IN MY *OFFICE*.

M. ESPERANZA INSPECTOR

YOU'VE GOT MY *PARTNER* WORKING ON *CORRIGAN!*

I DON'T HAVE *ANYONE* WORKING ON *CORRIGAN*, DETECTIVE MONTOYA, AND I THINK YOU *KNOW* WHY.

OR HAVE YOU *FORGOTTEN* THE LITTLE *TWO-STEP* YOU AND HE *DANCED* OUTSIDE OF *FINNIGAN'S* LAST FALL?

WAIT...

...ARE YOU *SAYING* THAT DETECTIVE ALLEN IS *INVESTIGATING* JAMES CORRIGAN?

YOU EXPECT ME TO **BELIEVE** YOU DIDN'T **KNOW** ABOUT THIS, INSPECTOR?

USE YOUR GODDAMN **HEAD.**

ANYTHING COMING OUT OF **THIS** OFFICE IN REGARD TO CORRIGAN IS **TAINTED** BECAUSE OF WHAT **WE** DID TO GET ALLEN OUT OF THE **JACKPOT** ON THE **LAMONICA** SHOOTING.

CORRIGAN **KNOWS** THAT.

AND **APPARENTLY** YOUR **PARTNER** DOES, **TOO.**

HE'S DOING THIS ON HIS **OWN?** ARE YOU TELLING ME THAT CRIS IS GOING AFTER CORRIGAN ON HIS **OWN?**

I'M NOT TELLING YOU **ANYTHING.**

BECAUSE IF I **DID** TELL YOU ANYTHING, IT WOULD MEAN I HAD **KNOWLEDGE** OF DETECTIVE ALLEN'S BUSINESS.

AND AS I **ALREADY** SAID, ANY **INVESTIGATION** OF JIM CORRIGAN'S **ILLEGAL** ACTIVITIES COMING FROM THIS **OFFICE** IS **TAINTED.**

JESUS CHRIST. HE'S TRYING TO **MAKE** IT **RIGHT.**

YOU **WEREN'T** HERE, DETECTIVE.

I **NEVER** SAW THAT **FOLDER** YOU'RE CARRYING, I DON'T EVEN **KNOW** IT **EXISTS...**

...AND IF YOU **WANT** YOUR PARTNER TO TAKE CORRIGAN **DOWN, NEITHER** DO **YOU,** UNDERSTAND?

M. ESPERANZA
INSPECTOR

YOU'RE AS **TAINTED** IN THIS AS I AM.

--TO HELL, LELAND! THIS IS THE **THIRD** TIME WE'VE BEEN CALLED **DOWN** HERE!

SHOW SOME **PITY**, OFFICER LONG. ALL THE **SHELTERS** ARE FULL-UP BECAUSE OF THE **SNOW**...

Tell me off for $2.00

...WE'RE JUST **LOOKING** TO STAY **WARM**.

DO IT SOMEPLACE ELSE.

LIZ AND I HAVE TO COME DOWN HERE **AGAIN**, ALL OF **YOU** ARE GOING IN FOR **TRESPASSING**...

...AND **THIS** TIME THE **OWNER** SAYS HE'LL **PRESS** CHARGES.

'LEAST WE'D BE **WARM**.

I AM SO SICK OF THE **STINK** OF **PISS** OFF THESE GUYS.

I **KNOW** THEY'RE **HOMELESS**, BUT FOR CHRIST'S SAKE, USE A DAMN **BATHROOM** ALREADY!

IS **THAT** KENZIE?

WHAT, THE **NARC**?

THINK **SO**.

WAIT **HERE**.

STEVE!

JUST **WAIT**, DAMMIT!

165

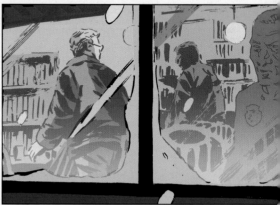

KENZIE, YOU SON OF A BITCH.

...AND *THAT,* MY *FRIENDS,* BALANCES THE *BOOKS* NICELY.

ROURKE, YOU STILL LEANING ON ED KARL?

I *CAN* BE. YOU NEED SOMETHING PASSED ALONG?

YEAH, ABOUT *TEN* KEYS OF UNCUT *HEROIN.* TELL HIM I'LL BE IN *TOUCH* ABOUT THE *PRICE.*

JIMMY!

OFFICER LONG.

AND THE *LOVELY* OFFICER MULCAHEY.

HEY, BABY.

JIMMY, WE'VE GOT A *PROBLEM.*

THERE'S *NO* PROBLEM CAN'T BE *SOLVED,* STEVE, *RELAX.*

IT'S *KENZIE,* JIMMY.

HE'S *RATTING* YOU *OUT,* MAN...

...I SAW HIM *TALKING* TO THAT *M.C.U.* DETECTIVE, *ALLEN.*

WHEN WAS THIS?

NOT HALF AN HOUR AGO.

DAMMIT.

OKAY, OKAY...

...STEVE, I WANT YOU AND LIZ TO *DO* SOMETHING FOR ME...

167

RENEE! C'MON, YOU **KNOW** WHY I COULDN'T **TELL** YOU WHAT I WAS **DOING.** SAME REASON I CAN'T TELL ESPERANZA.

IS THAT WHAT THAT **CALL** WAS? THAT **WHY** YOU DIDN'T WANT ME **ALONG?**

I **CAN'T** TALK ABOUT THIS WITH **YOU!** YOU **CAN'T** BE ANYWHERE **NEAR** THIS INVESTIGATION.

I'M YOUR GODDAMN **PARTNER,** CRIS! I'M YOUR **BACKUP,** YOU DON'T **DO** THIS AND **NOT** TELL ME!

WHERE JIM CORRIGAN'S CONCERNED, **YEAH, I DO.**

I'M TAKING HIM **DOWN,** RENEE, AND I'M GONNA DO IT SO IT **STICKS.**

NO DISMISSALS, NO **DISAPPEARING** EVIDENCE, NO TECHNICALITIES, NO DEALS...

...I'M GOING TO **NAIL** THE BASTARD, AND IF **YOU'RE** INVOLVED, THEN YOU **JEOPARDIZE** THAT.

JUST TELL ME YOU'RE NOT DOING THIS **ALONE!** TELL ME THAT YOU'VE GOT SAWYER **COVERING** YOUR **BACK,** SOMETHING LIKE THAT.

HOW THE HELL DO I DO **THAT?** THE **WHOLE** DAMN **DEPARTMENT** IS CORRUPT, RENEE!

I TELL **ANYBODY,** HOW LONG YOU THINK BEFORE ONE OF HIS **BUNKIES** FINDS OUT AND TIPS HIM TO ME, HUH?

YOU CAN **TRUST** THE CAPTAIN, YOU **KNOW** YOU CAN.

SOON AS I HAVE **ENOUGH** TO GET A **WARRANT,** I'LL BRING SAWYER **IN,** ALL RIGHT?

BUT **NOT** YET.

WHEN?

SOON.

ALL GOES WELL, **REAL** SOON.

HNH!

GET UP!

STAND UP **STRAIGHT**, RAT.

I **DIDN'T**...

DON'T **LIE**, BILL.

THAT'S JUST GOING TO MAKE THINGS **HARDER** ON YOU, YOU **LIE** TO ME.

I **NEED** TO KNOW WHAT YOU TOLD ALLEN, BILL...

I SAID...

GNN

...GET UP!

...**EVERYTHING** YOU TOLD ALLEN.

JESUS CHRIST, JIMMY...

...**DON'T** DO THIS, MAN, YOU **DON'T** HAVE TO **DO** THIS...

YOU TWO ARE GOING TO WANT TO STEP **BACK**...

...THERE'S BOUND TO BE SOME **SPLATTER**...

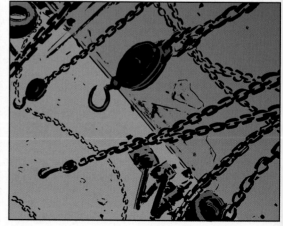

HON? CAN YOU TAKE THE *BOYS* TO *SCHOOL* TOMORROW?

I'M SUPPOSED TO BE AT THE CLEARY STREET SITE FIRST THING IN THE MORNING TO GO OVER THE *BLUE-PRINTS* WITH THE *FOREMAN.*

ALL RIGHT.

...SHE DID LAST NIGHT...

CHRIST, NOT *AGAIN...*

OH, CRIS...*TELL* ME YOU'RE NOT GOING OUT AGAIN.

THIS SHOULD BE THE *LAST TIME,* DORE.

NO *FIGHTS* TONIGHT, OKAY, HON?

NO PROMISES, JILL.

DON'T WAIT UP.

RIGHT, WHY SHOULD *BOTH* OF US LOSE OUT ON *SLEEP?*

KENZIE?

RENEE?

HERE.

SO YOU DO REMEMBER WHERE YOU *LIVE*, I'M *SURPRISED*.

WHERE THE *HELL* WERE YOU LAST NIGHT?

I *DESERVE* AN EXPLANATION--

I'M SORRY, DEE.

MOTHER*¢#$.

I'M SO SORRY...

RENEE!

172

KRAK

JUST... JUST GIVE ME THE GUN, RENEE...

I DON'T KNOW WHAT'S WRONG WITH ME...

BLAMBLAM

HNGH!

...OH GOD, DEE...

CORRIGAN.

WHERE'S CORRIGAN?

CORRIGAN II PART TWO

...RESULTS OF THE CANVASS TO THE **CAPTAIN** WHEN SHE GETS BACK.

YEAH, PROBABLY BROKE IT TO HER FIRST SO SHE COULD COME **WITH** TO BREAK IT TO ALLEN'S **WIFE.**

SHE'S WITH **MONTOYA?**

CHRIST, HE HAD **KIDS,** DIDN'T HE? HE HAD --

YEAH, **TWO.** BOTH BOYS.

SARGE! SARGE!

YEAH, DAG?

I WANT YOU AND CROWE TO START PULLING ALLEN'S OLD CASES, CROSS-REF, SEE IF THERE'S ANYONE HE PUT INSIDE WHO'S **OUT.**

ON IT.

HE WAS WEARING HIS **VEST,** THAT'S THE THING, AND IT DIDN'T DO HIM A DAMN BIT OF **GOOD.**

WHAT PUNCHES THROUGH **KEVLAR** LIKE IT'S NOT EVEN **THERE?**

BULLOCK WAS AROUND, HE'D BE ABLE TO TELL YOU. NOT A THING THAT GUY DIDN'T KNOW ABOUT **GUNS.**

GONNA BE A COUPLE HOURS BEFORE WE GET A PRELIM ON THE **BALLISTICS,** THAT'S IF WE'RE **LUCKY...**

...I'D LIKE TO START NARROWING DOWN THE WEAPON **BEFORE** THEN.

VINCENT? YOU GOT ANYONE AT THE **F.B.I.** WHO COULD MAYBE HELP WITH THAT?

YEAH, MY **EX-WIFE.** I'LL GIVE HER A CALL --

CORRIGAN.

RENEE...

CORRIGAN DID IT.

CRIS WAS TRYING TO TAKE HIM DOWN...

...THERE'S A FILE...

...CRIS HAD A FILE HE'D PUT TOGETHER...

...IT'S NOT HERE...

RENEE, MAYBE YOU SHOULD...

...IT'S NOT HERE, IT WAS RIGHT HERE--

--WHERE THE F&%$ IS IT--

--WHERE THE F$%$ IS IT?!!

RENEE!

184

WHY DON'T YOU SIT DOWN?

NO...

...NO, I NEED TO GET *OUT* THERE, I NEED TO *HELP*...

JUST TAKE A COUPLE MINUTES, OKAY, RENEE?

CATCH YOUR *BREATH.*

I...I CAN'T *FEEL* ANYTHING, MARCUS...

...JUST...JUST THIS *ANGER*, THAT'S ALL THERE *IS*, AND...AND I DON'T KNOW WHAT TO *DO*, I DON'T KNOW WHAT I *SHOULD* DO...

...IT'S LIKE... IT'S LIKE...

...LIKE EVERYTHING'S WRAPPED IN GRAY WOOL.

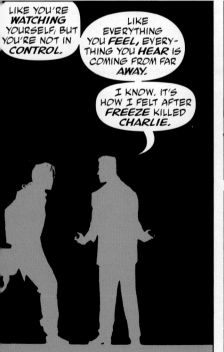

LIKE YOU'RE *WATCHING* YOURSELF, BUT YOU'RE NOT IN *CONTROL.*

LIKE EVERYTHING YOU *FEEL*, EVERYTHING YOU *HEAR* IS COMING FROM FAR *AWAY.*

I KNOW. IT'S HOW I FELT AFTER *FREEZE* KILLED *CHARLIE.*

WHEN DOES IT *END?*

WHEN IT'S *OVER.*

LOUGHRIDGE!

HOW YOU *DOING*, CORRIGAN?

NOT TOO BAD, CLEM.

SO WHAT CAN I *DO* FOR YOU, JIMMY?

JUST MAKING SURE WE'VE GOT OUR *STORIES* STRAIGHT.

MMMM WE BETTER GO *OVER* IT AGAIN...

...THANKS FOR THE *LOAN.*

IT HAD QUITE A *KICK* TO IT.

YEAH, IT FIRES A BIG ROUND...

...MADE TO PUNCH THROUGH *BODY ARMOR*, OR SO I'M *TOLD.*

TECHNICALLY, IT'S A *RIFLE* ROUND, AND NOT A PISTOL ROUND AT *ALL*...

...AND SINCE WE BOTH KNOW YOU HAVE A *THING* FOR *BIG GUNS*...

EVER SINCE I WAS A LITTLE *GIRL* MMMM...

186

--THOSE NOTES, YOU **KNOW** MONTOYA'S RIGHT! LET'S PUT HIM IN THE BOX AND GIVE HIM A SHAKE!

I'M NOT PUTTING CORRIGAN IN THE BOX UNTIL I KNOW WE CAN PUT A **FORK** IN HIM, TOMMY!

YOU FIND ME THE WEAPON, **THEN** WE'LL TALK!

DOCTOR FIELDS.

HEY, NORA.

DETECTIVES.

EXCELLENT TIMING, WE JUST **FINISHED.**

YOU'VE GOT PRELIMINARY FINDINGS FOR US?

I WAS JUST ABOUT TO TYPE UP MY **NOTES**--

HEY, **ASS%$¢#**--

--HOW 'BOUT A LITTLE **RESPECT** FOR THE **DEAD** HERE, **HUH?**

I'M SORRY, I--

COVER HIM UP!

I MEAN, JESUS **CHRIST.**

WHY DON'T WE TALK IN MY **OFFICE?**

I JUST FINISHED THE **AUTOPSIES**, DETECTIVE BURKE. THERE'S **NO** NEED TO SPEAK THAT WAY TO MY STAFF.

THAT'S ONE OF **US** ON THE TABLE THERE, **DAMMIT**.

WHAT CAN YOU **TELL** US, NORA?

OFFICER LONG DIED FROM A MASSIVE HEMORRHAGE OF THE LEFT HEMITHORAX, BROUGHT ABOUT BY TWO **GUNSHOT WOUNDS** TO THE CHEST.

WE RECOVERED BOTH ROUNDS, AND HAVE SENT THEM TO **BALLISTICS**...

...PRESUMABLY THEY'LL MATCH WITH DETECTIVE ALLEN'S **DUTY WEAPON**.

WHAT ABOUT **CRIS**?

DETECTIVE ALLEN WAS SHOT FIVE TIMES IN THE BACK, EACH OF THE ROUNDS TRAVERSING THE THORAX AND PRESENTING CORRESPONDING **EXIT WOUNDS**.

ADDITIONALLY, I FOUND **KEVLAR** FRAGMENTS ALONG THE WOUND TRACKS THROUGHOUT THE THORAX.

GIVEN **THAT,** AND THE **SIZE** OF THE TRAUMA, I'D SAY YOU SHOULD BE LOOKING FOR A **RIFLE**.

WE RECOVERED ROUNDS AT THE SCENE, BALLISTICS IS TRYING TO **IDENTIFY** THEM.

DA-DA, DA-DAAA

DRIVER AND MACDONALD NOTED **POWDER STIPPLING** ALONG THE BACK OF CRIS' JACKET. THAT'S INDICATIVE OF A **PISTOL**.

BURKE.

I CAN'T SPEAK FOR WHAT MARCUS SAW, DETECTIVE PROCJNOW, BUT DETECTIVE ALLEN'S WOUNDS ARE CONSISTENT WITH ROUNDS FROM A RIFLE, **NOT** A PISTOL.

YEAH, GO **AHEAD**, VINCENT...

HOW'S **DETECTIVE MONTOYA** HOLDING UP?

ABOUT AS BADLY AS CAN BE **EXPECTED**...

OUTSTANDING! OKAY, RUN A **CHECK**--

...SHE HAD A PURE **DISASSOCIATIVE MOMENT** IN THE SQUAD ROOM ABOUT AN HOUR AGO, WASN'T PRETTY.

--YOU **ALREADY DID?**

NOTHING ABOUT THIS WORK IS PRETTY.

THEN **BRING HIM IN**, WE'LL BE **RIGHT THERE!**

DEL ARRAZIO THINKS HE'S **I.D.**ED THE WEAPON, SOME KIND OF MODIFIED **GLOCK**.

FIRES A ROUND CALLED THE **.224 BOZ.** IT PUNCHES THROUGH **BODY ARMOR** LIKE IT'S NOT EVEN **THERE**.

THAT FITS, THE **.224** IS A **RIFLE** ROUND.

RIGHT, BUT **THIS** FIRES FROM A **PISTOL**.

THING IS, IT'S **ONLY** AVAILABLE TO **LAW ENFORCEMENT**, AND GUESS WHAT THE G.C.P.D. E.S.U. HAS **SIX** OF IN **INVENTORY?**

WHO'S THE **RANGEMASTER** FOR THE E.S.U.? **LOUGHRIDGE?**

DRIVER AND MACDONALD ARE BRINGING HIM IN FOR QUESTIONING RIGHT NOW.

LET'S **ROAST** THE BASTARD.

--WHY WE COULDN'T DO THIS DOWN AT THE RANGE.

YOU BRING ME IN *HERE,* YOU'RE MAKING ME FEEL LIKE I'VE DONE SOMETHING *WRONG,* GUYS.

HAVE YOU DONE SOMETHING WRONG, SERGEANT LOUGHRIDGE?

DON'T PLAY ME LIKE THAT, DRIVER. I'M ON THE *JOB,* JUST LIKE *YOU* GUYS.

YOU GOT A *QUESTION* FOR ME, JUST *ASK* IT.

HOW MANY *G-TWO-TWO-FOUR* SEMI-AUTOS YOU GOT IN E.S.U. INVENTORY, SARGE?

SIX, *ALL* OF THEM *ACCOUNTED* FOR.

YOU SIGN ANY OF THEM *OUT* IN THE LAST DAY OR SO?

NO.

GNNNT! WRONG ANSWER!

AND BEFORE YOU *THINK* OF STICKING TO YOUR LAME-ASS *LIES,* SARGE...

...ALLOW ME TO INFORM YOU THAT WE THINK ONE OF YOUR TWO-TWO-FOURS WAS USED IN A *CAPITAL CRIME.*

WHICH MAKES YOU AN *ACCESSORY,* AND FIRST IN LINE FOR THE *ELECTRIC CHAIR.*

CARE TO TRY *AGAIN?*

CALM *DOWN,* MAN!

I SAID I DIDN'T *SIGN* ANY OF THEM *OUT...*

...BUT *MAYBE* I LET SOMEONE *BORROW* ONE AS A *FAVOR...*

YOU RAN AT HIM WITHOUT *US?*

COOL YOUR *JETS,* DAG, WE *GOT* WHAT YOU NEED.

SERGEANT LOUGHRIDGE COPS TO THE FACT THAT HE *RENTS OUT* SOME OF THE ARSENAL ON THE *SIDE.*

SEEMS THAT CORRIGAN QUOTE RENTED UNQUOTE ONE OF THE TWO-TWO-FOURS YESTERDAY AFTERNOON TO GO *SHOOTING* WITH HIS GIRLFRIEND, RETURNED IT THIS *MORNING.*

SON OF A *BITCH.* HE SAY WHICH *ONE?*

YEAH, BUT I'M THINKING WE SHOULD RUN THEM *ALL* TO BALLISTICS, JUST TO BE ON THE SAFE SIDE.

GETS BETTER. THE GIRLFRIEND, *MULCAHEY?* SHE WAS OFFICER LONG'S *PARTNER...*

RENEE. WE'RE GOING TO *GET* HIM, DON'T WORRY.

WE'LL *FIND* THE WEAPON. WE'RE GOING TO *NAIL* CORRIGAN.

191

--GET WARRANTS FROM THE **D.A.** FOR THE GUNS **RIGHT NOW.**

IN THE **MEANTIME,** I WANT BOTH **CORRIGAN** AND **MULCAHEY** IN FOR QUESTIONING.

HE'LL HAVE **COACHED** HER ON THE **ALIBI,** CAPTAIN--

IT'S A SET-UP.

HOW DO YOU FIGURE?

LOUGHRIDGE GAVE CORRIGAN UP BECAUSE THAT'S WHAT CORRIGAN **WANTED** HIM TO DO.

YOU THINK MAYBE YOU'RE A LITTLE **BLIND** ON THIS ONE, RENEE?

WE'LL **FIND** THE **GUN,** RENEE, GOD AS MY **WITNESS.**

LOUGHRIDGE ALREADY PUT IT IN CORRIGAN'S **HANDS,** ALL WE HAVE TO DO IS PROVE IT'S THE **SAME** WEAPON THAT KILLED **CRIS...**

...AS SOON AS WE FIND THE GUN, **CLEM** DOWN IN **BALLISTICS** CAN **MATCH** IT WITH THE ROUNDS RECOVERED AT THE **SCENE.**

WE'RE GOING TO **GET** HIM, **TRUST** ME.

FIND THAT GUN.

AND BRING **CORRIGAN** AND **MULCAHEY** IN FOR **QUESTIONING.**

193

UH...IS THERE A **PROBLEM**, DETECTIVE DRIVER?

EXERCISING A **WARRANT**, STEFANO. WHERE ARE THE G-TWO-TWO-FOURS--

OVER HERE.

ALL **RIGHT**, I'M **COMING**, DAMMIT--

BZZZT BZZZT

JIMMY.

YEAH, I **KNOW**.

COME TO **MOMMA**.

--STOP LEANING ON THE **BUZZER**...

OFFICER MULCAHEY?

I'M **DETECTIVE BARTLETT**, THIS IS SERGEANT **DEL ARRAZIO**. WE WERE HOPING YOU'D **ACCOMPANY** US BACK TO **CENTRAL**...

...TO HELP US ANSWER A FEW **QUESTIONS**. YOU DON'T MIND COMING WITH US, **DO** YOU, JIMMY?

IT'D BE MY **PLEASURE**, DETECTIVE **BURKE**...

...ANYTHING TO **HELP**...

DETECTIVE?

DETECTIVE... I, UH...

...I BROUGHT YOU A CUP OF COFFEE.

BLACK, HOW YOU LIKE IT.

THANKS, STACY.

I'LL UH... I'LL BE AT MY DESK...

RENEE?

DORE.

THIS IS THE WORST DAMN DAY OF MY LIFE, RENEE.

TELL ME ABOUT IT.

AH, DAMMIT... ...THOUGHT I WAS FINISHED CRYING FOR NOW.

NO, IT'S OKAY.

C'MON, WE'LL TALK IN THE BREAK ROOM.

DARIA SAID YOU'VE BEEN HERE ALL DAY.

THAT YOU CAME STRAIGHT HERE WHEN YOU GOT...WHEN YOU GOT THE *NEWS.*

YEAH.

THE BOYS AND I WERE HOPING TO *SEE* YOU.

I *KNOW,* I'M SORRY.

HOW...HOW ARE *JAKE* AND *MAL* DOING?

IT HASN'T REALLY *SUNK IN* YET.

I WAS GOING TO TAKE THEM TO MY *SISTER'S* IN *DETROIT,* BUT *DARIA* OFFERED TO STAY WITH THEM.

I'LL COME OVER *TONIGHT,* IF YOU WANT.

WE'D *LIKE* THAT.

WHY DIDN'T YOU COME WITH CAPTAIN SAWYER TO BREAK THE *NEWS,* RENEE?

WE...WE REALLY *NEEDED* YOU.

I WANTED TO. I *COULDN'T.*

I'M SO *ANGRY,* DORE...AND I DIDN'T WANT TO BRING THAT INTO YOUR *GRIEF.*

IT'S *YOUR* GRIEF, TOO.

IT'S NOT THE *SAME.*

196

THEY'RE BRINGING THE GUY *IN*, DORE.

YOU'VE GOT A *SUSPECT*?

HE'S NOT A SUSPECT. HE *DID* IT.

AND I'M *TERRIFIED* HE'S GOING TO *WALK*.

CRIS *LOVED* BEING A COP. EVEN *HERE*, IN *GOTHAM*, WITH ALL OF THE *CORRUPTION*, WITH ALL OF THE *EVIL*, HE LOVED IT.

BECAUSE EVEN HERE, IN GOTHAM, HE *BELIEVED* IN IT.

HE BELIEVED IN WHAT *YOU* DID, IN WHAT *HE* DID...

"...AND *I* DO, *TOO,* RENEE...

"...RIGHT NOW, I *HAVE* TO...

"...WHAT *CHOICE* DO I HAVE? BECAUSE IF I *DON'T*...

"...OH, LORD, IF I *DON'T,* RENEE...

"...THEN MY HUSBAND HAS DIED FOR *NOTHING...*"

CORRIGAN II

PART THREE

SORRY TO HEAR ABOUT YOUR PARTNER.

YEAH. YEAH, IT PRETTY MUCH *SUCKS.*

YOU AND LONG HAD BEEN *PARTNERED* FOR, WHAT, THREE YEARS?

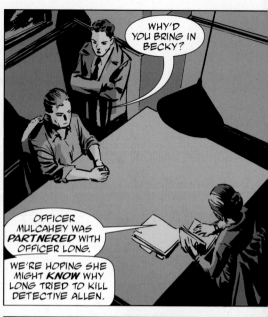

WHY'D YOU BRING IN BECKY?

OFFICER MULCAHEY WAS *PARTNERED* WITH OFFICER LONG.

WE'RE HOPING SHE MIGHT *KNOW* WHY LONG TRIED TO KILL DETECTIVE ALLEN.

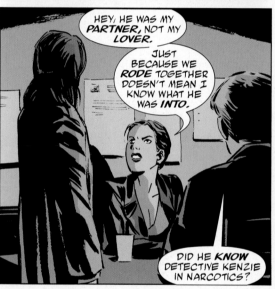

HEY, HE WAS MY *PARTNER,* NOT MY *LOVER.*

JUST BECAUSE WE *RODE* TOGETHER DOESN'T MEAN I KNOW WHAT HE WAS *INTO.*

DID HE *KNOW* DETECTIVE KENZIE IN NARCOTICS?

YOU THINK LONG KILLED KENZIE, THEN TRIED TO KILL ALLEN?

DON'T YOU?

C'MON, DETECTIVE PROCJNOW, MY JOB IS TO *COLLECT* THE EVIDENCE, *NOT* TO *INTERPRET* IT.

NO, I WAS OUT WITH *JIMMY,* AS I'M SURE YOU ALREADY *KNOW,* DETECTIVE DEL ARRAZIO.

DOING WHAT?

WE WENT *SHOOTING.*

NO, NOT AT THE RANGE, WE WENT OUT TO BRENTWOOD.

TO THE WOODS.

DID ANYONE *SEE* YOU?

WE WENT OUT TO THE WOODS SO WE WOULDN'T **DISTURB** ANYONE, DETECTIVE, OF COURSE NOBODY SAW US.

WHY NOT GO SHOOTING ON THE **RANGE**? YOU'VE GOT **ACCESS**.

WE WANTED **PRIVACY**, DETECTIVE. NOTHING WRONG WITH THAT, IS THERE?

YOU SURE YOU WANT TO WATCH THIS, RENEE?

I'M SURE, CAPTAIN.

THING IS, JIMMY, THAT MAKES OFFICER MULCAHEY YOUR **ALIBI**.

ALIBI? FOR **WHAT**?

HOW MUCH DID YOU PAY BILL KENZIE TO **UNDERCOUNT** THE DOPE HIS NARCOTICS SQUAD **CONFISCATED**?

WHAT?

HE TOLD DETECTIVE ALLEN YOU'D PAID HIM OVER **SIXTY GRAND** IN THE LAST THREE YEARS.

SIXTY GRAND... THAT'S...THAT'S A **LOT** OF **MONEY**, JIMMY.

WHICH MEANS YOU WERE PULLING IN A LOT **MORE** THAN THAT...

GO GET HIM, DAGMAR.

I DON'T KNOW ANYTHING ABOUT THAT.

I ALREADY TOLD YOU, JIMMY AND I WENT SHOOTING.

ALL RIGHT, LET'S TALK ABOUT THAT, THEN.

WHAT'S UP WITH THAT? WHY WEREN'T YOU AT THE RANGE?

WE WANTED PRIVACY.

WHAT CAN I TELL YOU, SARGE? GUNS GET ME HOT.

YOU AND ME BOTH.

JUST GOT A TITANIUM SLIDE P99 FOR MY COLLECTION, YOU WOULDN'T BELIEVE HOW SWEET THIS PISTOL IS.

YOU GET THAT IN NINE?

S&W FORTY, WITH THE LAW-ENFORCEMENT MAGAZINES.

OH, DAMN, THAT'S SWEET.

YOU GOTTA GO WITH THE FORTY, I JUST GOT AN HK P2000 IN FORTY.

WHAT ABOUT TWO-TWO-FOUR?

THAT'S A RIFLE ROUND, SARGE, NOT A PISTOL ROUND.

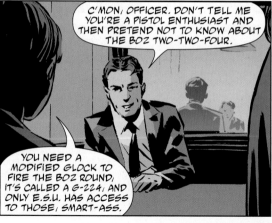

C'MON, OFFICER. DON'T TELL ME YOU'RE A PISTOL ENTHUSIAST AND THEN PRETEND NOT TO KNOW ABOUT THE BOZ TWO-TWO-FOUR.

YOU NEED A MODIFIED GLOCK TO FIRE THE BOZ ROUND, IT'S CALLED A G-224, AND ONLY E.S.U. HAS ACCESS TO THOSE, SMART-ASS.

THEN WHAT WAS CORRIGAN DOING WITH ONE LAST NIGHT?

--HIM TWO HUNDRED BUCKS TO **LOAN** ME ONE, THAT'S ALL! THERE ARE SIX OF THEM, JUST SITTING IN INVENTORY!

I BROUGHT IT BACK THIS MORNING, NO HARM, NO FOUL!

SO YOU'RE ADMITTING YOU TOOK ONE OF THE G-22A's FROM E.S.U. INVENTORY?

YOU TOOK A GUN MADE TO BLOW THROUGH BODY ARMOR FROM E.S.U. INVENTORY YESTERDAY, THAT'S WHAT YOU'RE SAYING?

BECKY WANTED TO TAKE ONE SHOOTING, THAT'S --

INTERESTING. WE'VE GOT **THREE** BODIES...

...KENZIE, WHO WASN'T WEARING BODY ARMOR...

...AND BESIDES, THE BULLET THROUGH HIS HEAD CAME FROM THE GUN WE FOUND ON OFFICER LONG...

...AND NO VEST ON OFFICER LONG HIMSELF, OR ELSE ALLEN'S SHOTS WOULDN'T HAVE **KILLED** HIM...

CAPTAIN?

...BUT HERE'S DETECTIVE ALLEN, **WEARING** HIS KEVLAR...

WE'VE GOT A PROBLEM WITH THE BALLISTICS REPORT.

...AND YOU JUST PUT THE GUN THAT **KILLED** HIM IN **YOUR** HAND.

PROVE IT.

WHAT THE HELL'S HAPPENED?

ROBINS ₺₺#*ED US, THAT'S WHAT ₺*%$ING HAPPENED!

EXPLAIN.

WE BROUGHT ALL SIX OF THE G-224s IN FOR TESTING, *INCLUDING* THE MURDER WEAPON, SWEAR TO GOD.

ROBINS SAYS *NONE* OF THE GUNS MATCH, HE SAYS THE ROUNDS THAT KILLED CRIS CAME FROM A ₺*%#ING *RIFLE*...

...A *BUSHMASTER .223,* LIKE THE *BELTWAY SNIPERS* USED, AND *NOT* FROM A G-224.

SON OF A BITCH.

HE THINKS MAYBE THE ROUNDS ARE *HANDLOADS,* CUSTOM MADE, TO GO WITH THE RIFLE THAT SHOT CRIS.

HE'S *LYING!* I HAD THE DAMN PISTOL IN MY *HAND,* CAPTAIN!

YOU HAD IT? WHAT DO YOU *MEAN,* YOU HAD IT?

I JUST...I *KNOW* HE'S LYING, CAPTAIN.

CORRIGAN BOUGHT HIM OFF, *SOMETHING,* HE'S *LYING.*

SO WE CAN PUT THE GUN IN CORRIGAN'S HAND, BUT WE *CAN'T* PROVE IT'S THE WEAPON THAT KILLED *CRIS.*

SON OF A BITCH...

...HE *PLAYED* US...

--GETTING TOO *CLOSE*? WAS ALLEN FINALLY GOING TO TAKE YOU *DOWN,* YOU CORRUPT LITTLE MOTHER&$*(#+!?

PEOPLE HAVE BEEN ACCUSING ME OF THINGS FOR *YEARS,* DETECTIVE BURKE.

LIKE I SAID BEFORE...

...*PROVE* IT.

DETECTIVES.

A MOMENT, PLEASE.

GET OUT OF HERE.

I'M SORRY?

YOU HEARD ME.

YOU KNOW WHERE TO FIND ME IF YOU WANT TO TRY AGAIN.

THIS ISN'T OVER. DON'T JUST STAND AROUND LICKING YOUR WOUNDS, GET OUT THERE AND MAKE THE DAMN CASE.

MACDONALD'S SO SURE WE HAVE THE MURDER WEAPON, TAKE IT TO THE BUREAU FOR FURTHER TESTING.

IF CORRIGAN BOUGHT ROBINS AND LOUGHRIDGE OFF, FIND THE MONEY.

THIS ISN'T OVER.

SURE IT IS.

WHAT WAS THAT?

C'MON, THE WHOLE CASE RESTED ON THE WEAPON AND THE BUREAU WON'T BE ABLE TO MAKE THE MATCH.

THERE'S NO WAY ROBINS DIDN'T DO A BARREL SWAP ON THE GUN, SOMETHING TO &%*& THAT UP.

SO WE JUST GIVE UP, THAT'S IT? LET THAT COP-KILLING *&#%SUCKER WALK?

C'MON, SARGE, YOU KNOW THAT'S NOT WHAT I MEANT.

HEY.

THEN YOU TELL ME WHAT YOU DID MEAN, MARCUS, BECAUSE IT SOUNDS LIKE YOU DON'T CARE IF CRIS' NAME STAYS IN THE RED!

HEY, IT'S NOT MY FAULT YOU COULDN'T GET MULCAHEY TO ROLL OVER ON HER BOYFRIEND--

HEY!

ANYBODY SEEN RENEE?

BEG YOUR PARDON.

...FOR THE FUNERAL, THAT'LL BE THURSDAY...

...HIS BROTHER IN DETROIT GETS IN LATER TONIGHT, GRACE AND I'LL PICK HIM UP...

...COFFEE? SWEET AND LIGHT, RIGHT?

...MAKE AN ARREST...

...AT ST. AGNES', I THINK, BUT I'M NOT SURE...

YOU TRY THE BUTTER COOKIES? THESE ARE OUTSTANDING.

UNCLE GARY? YOU AND AUNT GRACE STAYING TONIGHT?

YEAH, WE'RE STAYING, MAL. LONG AS YOU AND YOUR MOM NEED US.

YEAH, I CAN HEAR YOUR ARTERIES HARDENING FROM HERE.

MRS. ALLEN? I THOUGHT YOU MIGHT LIKE A PLATE.

IT'S VIOLET, DEAR. THANK YOU.

HEY, RENEE! WHAT'S THE GOOD WORD?

CORRIGAN WALKED.

MAKE SURE JAKE AND MAL *EAT* SOMETHING, *WOULD* YOU, THERESE?

SURE, MRS. ALLEN.

RENEE! I DIDN'T SEE YOU COME *IN.*

JUST *GOT* HERE.

ARE YOU *HUNGRY?*

DARIA'S BEEN COOKING *COMFORT FOOD* ALL *DAY,* WE'VE GOT LAMB STEW AND MAC AND CHEESE, JUST ABOUT ANYTHING YOU COULD *WANT.*

I'M FINE, THANKS, DORE.

HOW DID IT GO WITH THE *SUSPECTS* THEY BROUGHT IN? WITH *CORRIGAN* AND THAT *WOMAN?*

WE'RE *MAKING PROGRESS.*

THESE THINGS TAKE *TIME.*

I JUST WANTED TO CHECK IN WITH YOU, THAT'S ALL.

I'M GONNA *GO,* THERE'S SOME STUFF I NEED TO *DO.*

YOU'RE *SURE* YOU WON'T *STAY* FOR A BIT?

I CAN'T.   I'M *SORRY.*

RENEE?

RENEE, *WAIT!*

YOU'RE NOT GOING BACK TO *CENTRAL,* ARE YOU?

IT DOESN'T *MATTER* WHERE I'M GOING.

IT *DOES* TO *ME!*

I'LL COME *WITH* YOU. WE CAN GO *HOME.*

NO, YOU SHOULD STAY HERE. DORE NEEDS YOU HERE.

DORE NEEDS *YOU* HERE, *TOO.*

I CAN'T STAY.

YOU SHOULDN'T BE ALONE.

PLEASE, BABY, DON'T SHUT ME OUT. LET ME *HELP* YOU.

I'M *PAST* HELP, DEE.

AND THE BEST THING YOU CAN DO NOW IS TO STAY *AWAY* FROM ME.

214

WHAT ARE YOU *DOING* OUT HERE, JAKE?

NOTHING.

YOUR MOM *KNOW* YOU'RE SMOKING?

NO.

MY DAD'S NEVER COMING *HOME*, RENEE.

HE'S *NEVER* COMING HOME.

I KNOW.

I KEEP ASKING MYSELF THE SAME THING, RENEE.

AND I *HATE* MYSELF FOR ASKING IT, BUT I KEEP ASKING IT *ANYWAY*, I CAN'T *HELP* IT.

WHY WASN'T IT *YOU?*

I KEEP ASKING *MYSELF* THAT ONE, *TOO.*

YOU WANT ME TO CALL YOU A *CAB*, HON?

S'ALLRIGHT.

KEEP THE CHANGE.

CORRIGAN.

CORRIGAN!

YOU MOTHER-#5%¢!

217

...I'M BEGGING YOU...

...PLEASE DON'T KILL ME...

...GONNA HAVE THE FUNERAL?

TOMORROW AFTERNOON.

COMMISSIONER AKINS SAYS IT'S FULL-DRESS...

RENEE...

DETECTIVE, WHAT'RE *YOU* DOING HERE?

YOU SHOULD BE AT *HOME*...

...YOU NEED SOME *TIME*--

MORE THAN YOU KNOW.

I CAN'T *DO* IT ANYMORE, CAPTAIN.

GREG RUCKA

is the author of several novels, including *Finder, Keeper, Smoker, Shooting at Midnight, Critical Space,* and *Patriot Acts* (all of which feature the bodyguard character Atticus Kodiak), plus *Private Wars* and *A Gentleman's Game* (featuring the *Queen & Country* character Tara Chace), *A Fistful of Rain* and more.

In comics, he has written some of the most well known characters in the world, on titles such as ACTION COMICS, DETECTIVE COMICS, BATMAN, WONDER WOMAN, *Wolverine,* and *Elektra.* Other work includes titles such as 52 (with Geoff Johns, Grant Morrison and Mark Waid), GOTHAM CENTRAL and *Daredevil* (with Ed Brubaker), CHECKMATE, and FINAL CRISIS: REVELATIONS. His BATWOMAN: ELEGY book (with J.H. Williams III) has made it to numerous "Best of" lists of 2010, including *Publishers Weekly.*

His creator-owned comics include the award-winning *Queen & Country* and *Whiteout* (which became a major motion picture starring Kate Beckinsale).

ED BRUBAKER

is a one-time cartoonist whose early work in comics includes *Pajama Chronicles, Purgatory USA,* and *Lowlife.* He soon began predominantly writing comics, garnering attention for stories such as the Eisner Award-nominated "An Accidental Death," *The Fall,* and SCENE OF THE CRIME.

Brubaker began alternating his writing projects between DC's mainstream comics line, their mature-readers imprint Vertigo, and their WildStorm imprint. Some projects included BATMAN, DEADENDERS, SANDMAN PRESENTS: DEAD BOY DETECTIVES, CATWOMAN, SLEEPER, THE AUTHORITY, and GOTHAM CENTRAL (with Greg Rucka).

He has also written for Marvel Comics, including *Secret Avengers* and *Captain America* for their superhero line, and *Criminal* and *Incognito* for their Icon imprint.

KANO

is a Spanish comic book artist who broke into the comics industry in 1998 as the artist on Virtex for Oktomica Comics. He soon moved on to work for DC Comics, where he had a lengthy run on ACTION COMICS starring Superman. He also illustrated stories in the series H-E-R-O and GOTHAM CENTRAL. For Marvel, he has worked on titles such as *The Immortal Iron Fist, Beta Ray Bill: Godhunter* and *Marvel Zombies 5.*

STEFANO GAUDIANO

was born in Milan, Italy, and moved to the U.S. in the early '80s. Soon after, Gaudiano became a comic-book artist and published the Eisner Award-nominated limited series *Kafka* (with Steven T. Seagle) while still in college. His art has since been featured in *Dark Horse Presents,* SANDMAN MYSTERY THEATRE, CATWOMAN, BATMAN: FAMILY, *Daredevil, The Pulse, Captain Marvel,* and many more books.

STEVE LIEBER

is best known for his work on Oni Press' *Whiteout* (which became a major motion picture) and its Eisner Award-winning sequel *Whiteout: Melt.* He has also illustrated runs on DC's DETECTIVE COMICS and HAWKMAN, as well as *Conan the Usurper, Grendel Tales: The Devil's Apprentice, Civil War: Frontline, Thunderbolts: Desperate Measures,* and much more. Lieber is also the co-author (with Nat Gertler) of *The Complete Idiot's Guide to Creating a Graphic Novel.*